S0-BCK-624

"Excellent . . . a distinguished public service."
Peter F. Drucker

"The authenticity of PARACHUTE is what makes it stand out over what could be called the glut of job-hunting books coming out today."
Journal of College Placement

"Everyone agrees that the giant title in the field is Richard N. Bolles's WHAT COLOR IS YOUR PARACHUTE?, which first appeared in 1972 and has been updated annually ever since. [Five] million copies have been sold, and it has been on the *New York Times* best-seller list for four years."
The New York Times

"One of the most useful manuals for job-hunters and career changers. Written with humor and humanity . . ."
*Washington Opportunities
for Women*

"In a domain positively viscous with lame books, this perennial best-seller has no serious competition. It is updated *annually* (that's impressive), it is cheery for a reader who probably could use some cheer, it has sound, detailed advice for an all-important task that is well-served with a bit of skill. (Suggested by everybody.)"
Stewart Brand
The Next Whole Earth Catalog,
Second Edition

"One of the finest contributions to the literature of life/work planning, this book is written in a light tone, which serves to hold the reader's interest while showing that job hunting, self-assessment, and career planning need not be dull, arduous, awesome tasks. Other literature suggests that successful life-style planning requires a large investment of time and effort, but Bolles shows the reader a way to do it that is enticing . . ."
Harvard Business Review

"*What Color Is Your Parachute?* is probably the finest contribution written to date on the joint theme of career planning/job hunting . . . Bolles must have read every other book on the subject — his footnotes are extensive and there is a lengthy bibliography. But the content is such that little further reading will be necessary . . . Bolles' prescription is a lot of work. But the rewards are worth the effort."
*The Business Graduate
(Journal of the Business Graduates
Association in Great Britain)*

This is an annual. That is to say,
it is substantially revised each year, the
new edition appearing each November.
Those wishing to submit additions,
corrections, or suggestions for the
1996 edition should submit them prior
to February 1, 1995, using the form
provided in the back of this book.
(Forms reaching us after that date will,
unfortunately, have to wait for the
1997 edition.)

What Color Is Your Parachute?

Other Books by Richard N. Bolles

The Three Boxes of Life,
  And How To Get Out of Them

Where Do I Go From Here With My Life?
  (co-authored with John C. Crystal)

1995 Edition

What Color Is Your Parachute?

A Practical Manual
for
Job-Hunters
& Career-Changers

by

Richard Nelson Bolles

Ten Speed Press

PUBLISHER'S NOTE

This publication is designed to provide accurate and authoritative information in regard to the subject matter covered. It is sold with the understanding that the publisher is not engaged in rendering professional career services. If expert assistance is required, the service of the appropriate professional should be sought.

The drawings on pages 106, 172, 174–175, 180, 183, 286–287, 334, 337, and 357 are by Steven M. Johnson, author of *What The World Needs Now*.

Copyright © 1995, 1994, 1993, 1992, 1991, 1990, 1989, 1988, 1987, 1986, 1985, 1984, 1983, 1982, 1981, 1980, 1979, 1978, 1977, 1976, 1975, 1972, 1970 by Richard Nelson Bolles.

All rights reserved. Without limiting the rights under copyright reserved above, no part of this publication may be reproduced, stored in or introduced into a retrieval system, or transmitted, in any form or by any means (electronic, mechanical, photocopying, recording, or otherwise), without the prior written permission of both the copyright owner and the above publisher of this book, except for brief reviews.

Library of Congress Catalog Card No. 84-649334
ISBN 0-89815-633-5, paper
ISBN 0-89815-632-7, cloth
Published by Ten Speed Press, P.O. Box 7123, Berkeley, California 94707

© Copyright 1981. United Feature Syndicate, Inc. Used by permission.

Type set by Haru Composition and Hannah Associates, San Francisco, California
Consolidated Printers, Inc., Berkeley, California
Printed in the United States of America

Contents

This is dedicated to the one I love
(my wife, Carol)

Preface

Twenty-five years ago the first edition of this book began with these words: "*'Give me a fish, and I will eat for today; teach me to fish, and I will eat for the rest of my life.' (Ancient Proverb) This book is an attempt to teach you how to fish, with respect to the most difficult task any of us faces in life: the job-hunt (whether it be a hunt for a career, or for a way to 'do your own thing,' or just for bread, to make ends meet). This book is an attempt to, in other words, empower you, so that no matter how many times you have to go about the job-hunt during your life, you will know how to do it.*"

That, as I said, was twenty-five years ago -- 1970 to be exact. This 1995 edition marks, therefore, *Parachute's* silver anniversary, as you may have noted from the front cover.

Looking back, I sometimes yearn for those earlier years. For one thing, *Parachute* was a thin little book, then. I liked its thinness, *a lot*. But alas, the times have gotten more complicated as the years have unfolded. Readers have written regularly, asking for more commentary or assistance with this topic or that. Hence, the book has grown thicker, as job-hunting has grown more complicated. The body of the book (not counting Appendices) was 110 pages originally; the body of the book (not counting Appendices) is 377 pages, now. That's a sign of the times.

The good news is: you are not expected to read it all. You do not need to read Chapter 7 if you are not interested in moving. You do not need to read Chapter 6, if you are not interested in new ways to work. Etc.

I began, twenty-five years ago, with several assumptions:

(1) *A well-researched book, based on successful job-hunters' experience, should be able to help many of my friends who were floundering in their job-hunt, and had asked me for advice and help.*

(2) *But, some wouldn't be able to use the book.* (No book can reach all people.)

(3) *Some of those* would *be able to use some other book* (hence the importance of a bibliography in the back of *Parachute*) *while the*

rest would not be helped by any book, but only by a career counselor (hence the importance of a section on choosing a counselor, in the back of *Parachute*).

These assumptions have been validated; and yet, it's been amazing and humbling to see, over twenty-five years, that so many people *have* been able to use a book -- this book -- not just to job-hunt, but literally to change their life.

A friend of mine who is also an author, Roger Parker, has suggested that a really appropriate celebration of this silver anniversary of *Parachute* would be to issue a book of letters from people who have used *Parachute* successfully. So, herewith, a request: if you are an old reader of Parachute, and you have such a success story, why not send it to me, and we'll see if there is any interest in such a book of stories. What kind of story am I interested in? Well, like this one that a reader, Eileen Beal, just sent me. I have edited it slightly, as I do most letters, for brevity's sake:

"Back in 1984 I was a restless teacher. I'd won awards, written curriculum used throughout the public schools in my area, etc. -- but I didn't feel good about what I was doing. On a whim I picked up that year's What Color Is Your Parachute? and I sat down and read it. Then I decided to do your Quick Job-Hunting Map there, bought a set of colored markers, and sat down for two days to honestly answer the questions there. When I was done, I taped all the 'petals of the flower' diagram together, and it looked like a rainbow. My diagram showed me many things I already knew: I was good with words; I was thorough; I was organized; I was a born teacher.

"My diagram showed me why I loved teaching: I was sharing information; I was entertaining people (I'm a ham); I liked growing with new information; I liked helping others grow and change and become "better" (for lack of a better term).

"But the diagram also showed me why I hated teaching: I'm a perfectionist; I'm a loner; I like doing things my way; I hate bureaucracy; I hated working with people who hated kids.

"As you can imagine, I was a little shocked to realize that I hated what I loved doing. Fortunately, Parachute also showed me where I could use my love of words and my teaching skills . . . in writing. In the next year I wrote a dozen articles, and sold two of them for real money to

education publications. The year after that, I quit my job and jumped -- untutored and untrained -- into writing. I got a degree at 'experience university' and have been making my living as a freelance feature writer ever since. I love writing and doing interviews. What other kind of job pays you to learn! I write, belatedly, to thank you."

Great story! Just the kind I'm looking for. Two or three paragraphs, step by step -- what you did, what you learned. Okay?

I have discovered our readers like to read what other readers have written, so three or four times in these twenty-five years I have shared some of that mail. Other readers seem to derive encouragement and hope from such letters shared. It's kind of like a cheering section at your own Olympics, comprised of previous Olympic winners. So, here are some edited excerpts from the cheering section, this year, for you who are just starting:

"I wanted to express the gratitude I have for your book. Quite simply, it has done wonders in helping me retarget my career objectives. For several years I investigated careers by looking at the want ads; however, by using the methods described in your book I found employment in an area for which I have a keen interest. Consequently, I have obtained the highest marks for two years straight, and have received several awards for my contribution."

"Just a deep 'thank you' for a book that took me out of 10 yrs. of job unhappiness into the discovery of my 'mission' -- teaching writing to disadvantaged students. I have been walking on air for the past four years, thanks to you. I run a writing center at a multicultural university, and I teach self-discovery workshops at homeless shelters. Your book taught me how to learn about what mattered most to me, and -- invaluably -- taught me to interview for information. I urge all my students to read you."

"I read Parachute during a time when I was very depressed because I had run out of ideas for how to look for a job. You and your book gave me a framework for a plan. Having that plan gave me something important to do every day, and made a meaningful difference in my frame of mind. Thank you very very much."

"I would just like to say what a great fan of your book I am, it has helped me enormously. I have recommended it to a large number of my family, friends and colleagues."

"Parachute has proved to be one of the most influential books in my life. Back in 1980, it taught me that my own uniqueness is a gift, and that it is to be nurtured and celebrated, rather than criticized and reformed into what other people want. Though I thought at that time I should leave the military, I found ways (using all the exercises in Parachute) to do what my heart ached to do *within that structure.* Eventually I worked into a job where I counseled drug- and alcohol-addicted and obese sailors (not an easy job to get, since I was not a medical person), enjoyed it, and made a real contribution to the Navy's efforts in this area, until my retirement. Now I am living in Naples, Italy, with my Navy wife, and have been hired by a university to teach a seminar on Career Transitions. I am *really* excited. Part of my 'flower' diagram in Parachute was to someday teach career counseling in a university or college setting without my having a Ph.D., and I did it!"

"This is a quick note of thanks from a grateful reader. Your book is a wonderful resource -- it is inspiring, encouraging and is full of useful tools. I found that it provided me with a much-needed 'Plan of Action' at a critical time, for me, of re-evaluating my career. I also enjoyed your section on 'How to Find Your Mission in Life.' Thanks for your great contribution."

"I cannot express to you how much I truly appreciate all the advice, strategies, and exercises in *Parachute.* Your book was especially helpful to me in that I was considering moving out of state to find a job, so Chapter 7 was very useful. After four months of job-hunting, I found a job in my chosen career! Thank you again for writing such a wonderful book."

"Your book has helped me immensely. After over a month of my own hopeless job-hunt, I got your book and it gave me hope. Since then I've recovered from a desperate situation and moved on. New Job in a New Field. Life is in session again, for me, and I feel at the top of my class."

"I was recently laid off from my job, and then, ten days after I was let go, 'The Great Quake' of January 17, 1994 hit -- just a few miles to the north. This did not leave me feeling very optimistic. I picked up your book the other day, an impulse purchase, and having just finished chapter 5 (on 'Depression') I had to stop and write to send you a big hug. Your sincere and sage advice brought tears to my eyes. Thank you so much for recognizing and putting into words what so many are going through, and offering such sound advice. I bought your book expecting to find 'a Practical Manual.' What I have found is *a caring guide,* and suddenly I don't feel so all alone."

"I would just like to thank you for writing such a wonderful book. Your book cuts to the heart of the matter -- you don't sugarcoat the facts. You just state the best possible way to find a job. I have had a great deal of luck with your book, and have told all my friends about it. I just wish I had found it sooner."

"Your books have changed my life."

In the twenty-five years this book has been in print (revised annually), over five million people have bought it, and in the period October, 1993–May, 1994, it was one of the top 100 best-selling books in the U.S. -- as it has been for much of its history.

Twenty-five years ago, this was a book strictly for U.S. readers; now, *Parachute's* regular readers are in *the U.S., Canada, England, Australia, New Zealand, The Philippines, Thailand, Japan, Hong Kong, China, India, Russia, Bulgaria, Estonia, Latvia, The Slovak Republic, Poland, Germany, Switzerland, France, The Netherlands, Belgium, Spain, Italy, Saudi Arabia, Israel, South Africa, Puerto Rico, Brazil, and Mexico.* In some of these countries as many as 15,000 copies are in use, and I have heard from readers in every one of these countries -- most of whom use the English language (U.S.) edition that you hold in your hands, though *Parachute* does exist in seven other languages, as well -- of which the Italian and Polish translations are the most recent, and also the best.

Many readers from other countries have asked, of course, for their own national edition of *Parachute,* that would list *regional* resources and statistics rather than just those of the U.S.

I love this idea, but unhappily it is a task equivalent to cleaning the Aegean stables. You would not believe how quickly, even in the U.S., our statistics get out of date, our resources go out of print. Keeping the book up to date, just for the U.S., is a full-time, year-round occupation. I myself spend *weeks* each year just entering the *changes* we accidentally stumble across. I spend *months*, each year, further revising, updating and rewriting the book, in order to keep it current and helpful. *(I also do all the research, all the typing, and most of the design and paste-up of the individual pages -- under Bev Anderson's inspired direction -- but that's another story.)*

The work of commissioning someone in every other country to do this work is so daunting, that we have only tried it once, in the case of one other country, and the work fell far short of its goal. Many important resources were missed, some career counselors who were crooks got inadvertently included. So, we gave it up.

But, since this English language edition is perforce an international book, I have tried to talk about U.S. statistics and resources as *indicative,* or *instructive* or *typical* -- with a heightened consciousness that these are being read in other countries than the U.S. As for resources, you can order many of the books and other tools listed throughout *Parachute* from the catalogs that you will find on pages 406*f,* or directly from the publisher, whose address I have therefore included. And in the counseling section I have tried to indicate *principles* for choosing a decent career counselor in *any* country, and the ways in which you hunt up *names.*

And now, in closing this preface, my annual litany of heartfelt thanks. In order that this book could be written in the first place, endless travel and interviewing was conducted originally around the whole U.S. covering some 65,000 miles. Then, and since, I want to extend:

• My thanks to the over two thousand readers who write me each year, to tell me how the book affected, changed, or uplifted their life, and what they have learned from it. I regret that I can no longer answer these letters. I labor by choice without a secretary, and at the age of 67, now, I do enjoy *'having a life'* with my family -- which answering all my mail once precluded. Yet, I still read *every one* of the letters I receive, and deeply appreciate them. No man could possibly ask for more loving, appreciative, and helpful readers -- not in a million years.

• My thanks to those creative souls, who first pointed out to me what was wrong with this country's whole job-hunting and career-changing *system,* and gave me documentary evidence of the same -- in particular Dick Lathrop, Sidney Fine, the late Bob Wegmann, Daniel Porot, Tom and Ellie Jackson, Howard Figler, Arthur Miller, Bernard Haldane, Nathan Azrin, Carol Christen, John Holland, Peter Drucker, and -- above all -- the late John Crystal, who gave me the framework, now preserved in Chapters 9, 10, and 11 in this book, of *What, Where, and How.* God bless you, John, in your heavenly rest.

• My thanks to Phil Wood, my publisher, and owner of Ten Speed Press, for his unfailing support in my work over these last twenty-five years. He has been a great friend to me.

• My thanks to Bev Anderson, who has done the layout of this book *(and all my other written works)* year after year, since 1972. I love working with her; she is such a delight. I hope for twenty-five more years.

• My thanks to Haru Watanabe for the great care he gives to the type-setting each year; he is a meticulous workman, and it is always a pleasure working with him; we go back *years.*

• My thanks to Jackie Wan over at Ten Speed who has proof-read this book so many times during the past twenty-five years that she could probably recite it from memory. Unbelievably *thorough,* she is however not to blame if any typos still remain.

• My thanks to Mariah Bear, my 'fact-checker' over at Ten Speed, for the truly superlative job she has done of keeping this book up to date this year.

• My thanks to George Young, Senior Editor at Ten Speed, and all the folks over at Fifth Street Design -- Hal, Brent, Jerry, and Torri -- who each year help this book and its cover to get done and get done right.

• My thanks to my dear ninety-two-year-old aunt, Sister Esther Mary, of the Community of the Transfiguration (Episcopal) in Glendale, Ohio, who has taught me from my youth up.

• My thanks -- above all others -- to my dear wife, Carol, for her wit, wisdom, encouragement and love over the years. As my four grown children, Stephen, Mark, Gary, and Sharon, and my 18-year-old stepdaughter, Serena, will attest, she is a *wonderful* woman. I am so grateful to be her husband.

• Finally, no litany of thanks would be complete without my acknowledging The Great Lord God, Father of our Lord Jesus Christ, and source of all grace and wisdom, Who has enabled me to help so many people of different tongues and nations and faiths. I am grateful beyond measure for such a life, and such a privilege.

A Grammar Footnote

I want to explain three points of grammar, in this book: pronouns, commas, and italics. My unorthodox use of them invariably offends unemployed English teachers so much that they write me to apply for a job as my editor.

To save us unnecessary correspondence, let me explain. Throughout this book, I often use the apparently plural pronoun "they," "them," or "their" with singular verbs or antecedents -- such as, "You must approach *someone* for a job and tell *them* what you can do." This sounds strange and even *wrong* to those who know English well. To be sure, we all know that there is another pronoun -- "you" -- that may be either singular or plural, but few of us realize that the pronoun "they," "them," or "their" was also once treated as both plural and singular in the English language. The latter usage changed, at a time in English history when agreement in *number* became more important than agreement as to sexual *gender*. Today, however, our priorities are shifting once again. Now, the distinguishing of sexual *gender* is considered by many to be more important than agreement in *number*.

The common artifices used for this new priority, such as "s/he," or "he/she," are tortuous and inelegant. Hence, Casey Miller and Kate Swift, in their classic *The Handbook of Nonsexist Writing*, argue that it is time to bring back the earlier usage of "they," "them," and "their" as both singular and plural -- just as "you" is/are. They further argue that this return to the earlier historical usage has already become quite common out on the street -- witness a typical sign by the ocean which reads "*Anyone* using this beach after 5 p.m. does so at *their* own risk." I have followed Casey and Kate's wise recommendation.

As for my commas, they are deliberately used according to my own rules -- rather than according to the rules of historic grammar (which I did learn -- I hastily add, to reassure my old Harvard English teachers, who despaired of me then and now). My own rules about commas are: write conversationally, and put in a comma wherever I would normally stop for a breath, were I speaking the same line.

The same conversational rule applies to my use of *italics*. I use *italics* wherever, were I speaking the sentence, I would put *emphasis* on that word or phrase. Rarely, I also use italics where there is a digression of thought, and I want to maintain the main thought and flow of the sentence. I write as I speak.

A reader of this book said it all (and I'd like to think it's true): "You don't *read* this book, it just talks *with* you."

Fairy Godmother,
where were you
when I needed you?
Cinderella

CHAPTER ONE

A Job-Hunting
We Will Go

Okay, this is it.
You've been wondering what it would be like,
To have to go *out there* and do the job-hunt,
And now: that moment has arrived.

You've graduated, or been laid off,
Or gotten real tired of the same old thing,
Anyhow, one way or another,
The moment of truth has arrived.
You've got to ... have to ... must
Go out, and look for a job out there,
Out there in *the job-market*,
Which all your experienced friends speak of
In hushed tones, as though it were
A battlefield, littered with the
Bodies of the unemployed,
Who tried and failed
Before you.

You've heard of course
All the horror stories:
Of workers who loyally gave
Their best
To the same company for 35 years,
And then
Were unceremoniously dumped
On the street, like disposable
Cartons.
Who lost their identity
As well as their job,
And now they wander, lost.
You've heard of graduates
With shiny MBA degrees
Who cannot find
However hard they look
The simplest kind of work
That matches
What they studied for,
And paid for, all this time.

You've heard of friends who
    Studied all the occupational trends
        And then went back to school
            To learn the *hot* trade of the moment, but
            Could find no work in that *hot* trade
          When they went out to look,
           And two years later are still
              Unemployed, disillusioned, and angry
            At false prophets and false prophecies.
            "Where is the job that goes with my degree?"
           They ask. But there is no reply.
           You've heard:
            Of former full-time workers who
           Are now only able to find work
           As temporaries, week by week,
            Of former college profs with two degrees
           Working now at the local deli;
           Of union workers who did strike
           As unions always have,
         Only to find, this time out,
        Something new:
           Their jobs were not waiting for them, anymore.
        They struck, but they struck out.
      And now they wander, lost.
     Such sad and tragic stories
    Are in the papers, every day;
   And so, we know,
  What lies in wait,
  What lies in store
 For us.
 At least we fear we do,
Now that it is *our* turn.

So, what do we do
When our job-hunting time has come?
We procrastinate,
That's what we do.
 We're *busy winding things up*, we say.
 Or, just waiting until we *feel a little less*

'Burnt-out,' and more 'up' for the task
Ahead, we say; though actually, if the truth were known,
We're hoping for a miracle,
You know the one I mean:
A rescuer, an earthly savior,
To solve this problem for us.
We don't care, now *who* it is:
Our old employer,
The government, the union,
A relative or friend,
Anyone in fact who rides
A white horse.
We'd like them to rescue us,
To find a job *for* us.
That's their business, after all,
That's what the world owes us:
A job.
It came with our college degree,
Or our high school diploma,
Or with our citizenship
In this nation,
Or with our birth certificate.
A job was guaranteed,
Or so we thought.
It shouldn't be up to us
To have to go hunting for it;
But, in this 'unfairest of all imagined worlds,'
It *is*.

It's up to *us*,
O woeful truth!
And so we go out, eventually,
Pounding the pavements,
Knocking on door after door,
Getting rejected
At place after place,
Getting discouraged,
Getting depressed --
How pathetic, this is,

How crushing to
Our self-esteem - -
Perusing want ads,
Making the rounds
Of the agencies that we know,
Making up a glorious resume
By ourselves or with some help.
How it sparkles, how it shines,
How quickly it will get us
A job.
And so, we send it out
By the hundreds,
Then sit by the phone
Waiting for that inevitable
Unavoidable, *sure as death and taxes*,
Call, or letter,
From some bright-eyed employer-type
Who, seeing our glorious resume,
Will cry out to the world:
"This is just the person we've been looking for!"
Except for one small detail:
That call
Rarely ever comes,
It's only in our fantasy,
It's only in our dreams,
And we are left to wait
And wait
And wait
While the world goes out of its way,
It seems,
To tell us how little
It values us.
Sixteen weeks - -
That's the median time
That unemployment lasts,
These days.
And it, of course,
Goes *up* from there:
Nineteen weeks,

A half-year or more
Is not unusual.

So at length we turn
To our other strategy:
We'll have to change careers,
Figure out something else
We can do.
So we ask our friends for advice --
And this is what they say:
"Why, Jean or Joe, I've always thought you would make a great teacher."
"Oh, teacher? Well, who do you know
In the academic world?"
And, armed with that name,
We go a-calling
And sitting
And cooling
Our heels in the waiting room
Of the office la Dean,
Until, at last, we are ushered in,
"And what can I do for you, Mr. or Ms.??"
Says the Owl to the Pussycat.
We tell them, of course, that we're job-hunting now,
"And one of my friends thought that you ..." Oh wow!
Look at that face change, are we in the soup!
As we wait for the heave-ho, the ol' Alley-oop!
"You feel I'm over-qualified? I see.
Two hundred applications, you say, already in hand
For five vacancies? I see.
No, of course I understand."

Our friends next suggest
The employment agencies.
So down we go.
Down, down, down to those agencies.
The ante-room, and all those hopeful, haunted faces.
Our first bout
With *The Dreaded Application Form.*

"Previous jobs held.
        List in reverse chronological order."
          We answer all the questions, then we sit
            And wait.
                The interviewer, at last, calls us in;
                  She (or he) of the over-cheerful countenance,
                  Who we know will give us good advice.
                  "Let's see, Mr. or Ms.,
                      What kind of a job are you looking for?"
                  "Well," say we,
                  "What do you think that I could do?"
                  She studies, again, our application form;
                  "It seems to me," she says, *"that with your background*
                  -- It is a bit unusual --
                  You might do very well in sales."
                  "Oh sales," say we, "Yes, sales," says she, *"in fact*
                  I think I could place you almost immediately.
                  We'll be in touch. Is this your phone?
                  I'll call you tomorrow night, at home."
          We nod, and shake her hand, oh dear
        That is the last time we ever hear
      From her.

      We seek out our friends' advice once more
      "What kind of a job are you looking for?"
        Say they; and we respond,
      "Well, you know me best,
      I mean, with all the kinds of things I've done --"
    You know; this and that, here and there,
  Over all the years.
What else I could do, perplexes me,
But I was thinking -- you're so much wiser than I --
That you would know, what career this might be;
I'll try 'most anything,"
  Our friends look at us
  And see themselves
    Three years hence,
    We are *the future mirror* to them,
        They are so wrapped in their own thoughts

Of impending panic and flight,
That they have no helpful suggestions
For us,
At least not on that night.
So we are left on our own
To make our own
Best guess
At a new career.
We study the papers
The little boxes called 'want ads,'
To see if any ideas are *there*.
But we are dumbfounded at the sight
Of all the misery that is hidden in
Those little boxes. Misery in jobs that are built
As little boxes to contain the larger spirits of men
And women.

And so it goes,
And so we go,
And ever we are thinking:
The job-hunt seems the loneliest task in the world.
Is it this difficult for other job-hunters
Or career-changers?

Well, friend, the answer is *YES*.

Are other people this discouraged, and desperate
And frustrated, and so low in self-esteem after
A spell of job-hunting?

The answer, again -- unhappily -- is

YES.

YES.

YES.

We're Don Quixote, with lance in our hand;
Our windmill, the job-hunt. Out there, a great land,
The wind blows, we tremble, we feel a great fright--
There's not an employer, at all, in our sight.

I've tried to be content
With my lot in life.
But, boy, I hate all this soot,
And seeing my sisters get out,
While I stay here, cleaning the hearth.
Come on, now, where
Is that glass slipper
You promised?

Cinderella

CHAPTER TWO

Rejection Shock

Chapter 2

U.S. Statistics[1]

2 out of every 14 workers are basically unemployed[2] *(by common definition, not the government's)*, 6 out of the 14 are employed but worried about losing their job, and 6 out of every 14 workers are employed and not worried about losing their job. And among the 12 who are employed, 1 is voluntarily changing careers, no matter how tough the economy.

The job-hunt.

Ah, the job-hunt.

What a ludicrous episode in our lives!

All of our lives if there's one thing we hate it's rejection. Most of us, most of the time, want to avoid rejection, like the plague. We want to be accepted, sometimes at any price.

We'll often reshape ourselves, be who our family or peers want us to be, just in order to avoid rejection.

We die to avoid rejection when we are very small, in our family.

We don't want to be rejected in school, by our class or friends or the gang we run with.

We don't want to be rejected by the girl or boy that we are sweet on, in high school.

We don't want to be rejected by our college teachers, if we go there.

We don't want to be rejected by the person we fall in love with, and hope to marry.

Avoiding rejection is the story of our life.

And throughout that life, we'll do anything to avoid being rejected, and I mean *anything*. We'll even play the game of rejecting others before they have a chance to reject us. The history of human dating is littered with such games.

Thus we spend our life practicing how to avoid being rejected.

And then we have to go job-hunting.

Whoops!

It all goes out the window.

What we have spent our life trying to avoid, we here embrace. Job-hunting is *nothing but* a process of rejection, until the very end.

As we go *out there*, as we send resumes, write, call, and visit one prospective employer after another, this is what we run into:

NO NO NO NO NO NO NO NO NO NO NO NO NO NO NO

NO NO NO NO NO NO NO NO NO NO NO NO NO NO NO

NO NO NO NO NO NO NO NO NO NO NO NO NO NO NO

NO NO NO NO NO NO NO NO NO NO NO NO NO NO YES.[3]

And we submit ourselves to this rejection process not once, but eight times in our lifetime, on average.

The thing which would astound a visitor from Mars, given how much we hate rejection, is not the frequency of our job-hunts, but that we often *choose* to go job-hunting, rather than waiting until we are compelled to.

How many of us choose to do it? Well, in a survey conducted recently in the U.S. it was found that 39 million, or 33% of all workers, had thought seriously about chucking their jobs in a given year, and 16 million of them, or 14% of all workers, actually did, during the following two years.[4]

----

1. These figures were put together from various government sources, such as The Bureau of Labor Statistics. They are for the U.S., and are for the month of February, 1992. However, I believe this overview is pretty generally true of most of the industrialized nations -- at a minimum -- and will remain true so long as the vast restructuring of the world's workplace continues for the next few years.

2. This adds up to 14.3%. *Harpers* Magazine, in its March 1992 issue, thinks the figure should be 12.7% for that period; but we're not disagreeing by much. The U.S. government's unemployment figures, which are much lower, get criticized with regularity in the media. In addition to the *Harpers* article, there is also "Why Jobless Figures Can Be Bunk," a front page article in the *San Francisco Chronicle*, 4/3/92; and "America's Undercounted Unemployed," from the *New York Times*, summarized in Manpower Argus, March 1992.

3. This is my friend Tom Jackson's description of the typical job-hunt, in his famous book, *Guerrilla Tactics in the Job Market*.

4. The survey was published in 1991.

REASONS FOR CHANGING CAREERS

We may be sick and tired of our job. We get bored,
fed up, and hungry for something challenging,
exciting, and risky, that demands more of us.

Our job may have gone
through profound changes
we do not like, so that it is
no longer our dream job,
if ever it once was. Jobs can
alter profoundly in a day
and a night. Our much-
beloved supervisor moves
on, leaving us working for
a jerk. Or we are given
additional responsibilities,
without any raise in
salary. Or we are promoted
into an administrative
position which uses none
of the skills we like to
use. Or, our workplace comes
under stringent budget cuts.
Or our funding is lost.
Whatever. The job which
was a perfect match for us
just a couple of years ago,
is now 'the job from hell.'
And we want out.

We may find ourselves asking the question: "Is
this *really* what I want to do for the rest of my life?"
And if the answer is "No," then eventually we
may screw up the courage to take the leap.

We may be stressed, burnt out, exhausted, and
hungry for something peaceful, calm, and secure,
that demands less of us.

We may want to change careers for deeper reasons.
Most of us are engaged in a life-long search for,
and journey toward, *meaning* -- through all the
varying jobs or careers that we may hold in our
life. We may want a career that has more meaning.

Many of us believe ourselves to be both body and
spirit. When we are very young, the body pre-
occupies us. Work is largely a matter of how we
can find bread to eat, and clothes to wear, and
how we can put a roof over our head. But as we
move through the various stages of our life, and
get older, concern for our spirit moves to the
forefront of our consciousness. And we begin to
hunger for work which will honor our spirit's
values. For example, if we have been working too
hard (which 97% of the workforce has), we
want to figure out how we can have more time
'to smell the flowers.'

We may increasingly want to find the work we
feel we were *born* to do, what we speak of as *our
vocation,* or calling. We may hunger for work
which is the deepest fulfillment of our being,
reflecting who we most truly are.

It may look as though we're going to be laid
off or fired, and we decide to leap before we're
pushed.

If a career-change looks appetizing, it does not matter what the state of the job-market is. If your internal time clock has struck midnight, then *that is that.*

If we volunteer to go through this process of rejection, called the job-hunt, it is because the goal, at the end, seems worth all the rejection we will have to go through, in order to reach it.

NOBODY'S JOB IS SAFE ANYMORE

Many times, of course, we don't volunteer to go through the job-hunt. It is thrust upon us, sometimes when we least expect it -- and least want to go through it. And this is happening to us increasingly, in the world's workplace.

The reason for this increase is that throughout the world, the workplace is being reshaped -- as a profound kind of *workquake* is taking place beneath its surface. We are seeing throughout the world, in these days, a major and profound restructuring of the whole way in which business is done.

We all know this.

We have seen this restructuring attended by waves of unannounced and unexpected layoffs, as companies, organizations, corporations, the armed forces, defense work, and government programs *downsize.*

We have seen the increasing disappearance of well-paying jobs.

We have seen an increase in the number of hours that present full-time employees have to work, as employers prefer to use employees who already are being paid *benefits,* rather than hire new workers to whom such benefits would have to be given.

We have seen more and more of the unemployed forced to take part-time jobs, or work as 'temporaries,' through Temporary Employment Agencies.

We have seen the unemployed find new jobs where their paycheck is smaller, sometimes *much* smaller, than they were formerly accustomed to -- forcing an attendant drop in their standard of living.

We have seen more and more workers anxious about their jobs. And with good reason.

What this all adds up to, is that nobody's job is safe anymore.

Your job can disappear in a moment, in the twinkling of an eye.[5] One day you'll have the job; the next day you won't. There may be some warning; or there may be none. You may get a decent, even handsome severance pay; or you may get nothing. Your boss may continue to be friendly toward you; or may treat you as though he or she never knew you.

You may understand why this happened to you; or you may not understand at all. If you are let go because your employer went out of business, you may be philosophical about it. But if you are caught in a 'downsizing' or 'restructuring' you will likely find it much more difficult to be so understanding -- particularly if you have worked there *for years*. 'Monday-morning quarterbacking' will be epidemic among the employees being let go.[6]

Welcome to *The World Of Work*.

Most of us don't understand the nature of that world until we bump our head or stub our toe on that nature. High school or college doesn't prepare us for it. Only out there in the hard school of life do we begin to slowly and painstakingly piece this information together, usually completing the task by the time we're 65.

Earlier than that, all of this may come as a complete shock. Rejection shock. If you've been fired, laid-off, or 'made redundant' you will probably be hurt, dejected, angry and aghast.[7]

And especially so, if you had worked at that place for quite a number of years, given them your loyalty and your best, expected to get their loyalty in return -- but they let you go, anyway.

You are suffering from 'Rejection Shock.' And you are suffering from it because *(among other things)* you didn't expect to be treated this way. In fact, you didn't think *The World of Work* even functioned in this manner.

But it does.

If you study the world of work long enough -- not as you would like it to be, but as it is -- you will eventually realize there are 12 'rules' in *The World Of Work* about Hiring and Firing -- some of them a kind of *Bill of Rights* for the employer, some of them a kind of *Bill of Rights* for you. Here they are.

THE TWELVE RULES ABOUT HIRING AND FIRING

1 Nobody owes you a job.

4 Your employers may lay you off, or fire you, anytime they want to. They may do this because they have run out of money, and can't afford you anymore. They may do this because they have to decrease the size of their business, or are going out of business. They may do this because they find your skills do not match the work that they need to have done. Or they may do this because they have a personality conflict with you.

6 Your employers may fire you, or lay you off, without any warning or much notice at all to you, dumping you unceremoniously out on the street.

8 If you are fired, your former employer may do everything in the world to help you find other employment, or may do nothing.

10 As you look back, you may feel that your employers treated you very well, in accordance with their stated values -- or you may feel that your employers treated you very badly, in total contradiction of their stated values.

11 If *you* were the only one who was fired or let go, the other employees may promise they will fight to save your job, but you need to be prepared for the fact that when the chips are down, they may actually do nothing to help you. You will feel very alone.

2 You have to fight to get a job.
     ("Fight" means "persevere," "use ingenuity," "compete.")

3 You have to fight to keep a job.
Loyalty, years of service, or personal
friendship with the boss, do not
in any way guarantee you a
job at that place for the rest of
your life.

5 You may quit anytime you want to.

7 You may quit without any warning
or much notice at all to your
employer, leaving them high and
dry.

9 If you quit, you may do everything
you can to help your employer find
a suitable replacement, or you may
do nothing.

12 Nonetheless, you remain a rare and unique individual,
no matter how the world of work treats you.
Your worth is not defined simply by your work, but
by your spirit, your heart, and your compassion
toward others.

Reprinted by permission; Tribune Media Services. Not to be reproduced without permission of Tribune Media Services.

HOW TO PREPARE
TO DEAL WITH REJECTION

Given that we spend all of our life trying to avoid rejection, how can we stand this kind of rejection that we meet when we lose our job, or have to go job-hunting?

The key is preparation. Preparation begins above all else with your *philosophy of life*. It is immensely useful when you're going through a time where you feel rejected, to sit down and listen to a recording of some famous symphony -- say Tchaikovsky's Fifth. The second movement is particularly instructive. As you listen to it, and think about what it is that makes it so interesting, you

---

5. In the U.S., larger organizations now have to give a certain amount of warning about their planned layoffs or 'downsizing,' but smaller organizations don't.

6. Most of the time when a 'downsizing' is announced, it is precisely that: an attempt to decrease the cost of the labor force there, so as to increase profitability. Typically, if a 'downsizing' eliminates 200 well-paying jobs, the employer saves ten million dollars *a year*. Sometimes however, this measure permits the employer to also include in the 'downsizing' a number of employees regarded as undesirable, thus 'killing two birds with one stone.'

7. I've been fired twice, myself, once when I was 22, and once when I was 41 years old. In the world of work today, you get fired for 'screwing up' on the job, of course, but you also get fired (or laid off) even when you're doing an excellent job. Sometimes you get fired because there's bad chemistry between you and your boss or supervisor. In the latter case, should your next employer ask *why* you were fired, it is sufficient to say, "Usually, I get along well with everyone, but in this particular case the boss and I just didn't get along with each other. Difficult to say why." *You don't need to say any more than that. You shouldn't say any more than that.* Bosses often regard any boss as a brother or sister.

will be struck by the fact that there are two major themes or melodies in that movement, not just one. The horn melody, with which the movement opens, is somber; the second melody, picked up by the strings, and the clarinet, is soaring and joyous. Throughout the remainder of the movement these two themes keep alternating. They keep reappearing and interacting with one another, with ever brightening intensity. Two themes; not just one.

What makes the music so interesting, of course, is that it mirrors our *life*. Our life, too, has not one theme but two major themes alternating throughout. We may describe these two themes in various ways. We may say:

Life is sometimes somber; life is sometimes joyous.
Life is sometimes difficult; life is sometimes easy.
Life is sometimes tawdry; life is sometimes beautiful.
Life is sometimes worse; life is sometimes better.
Life finds us sometimes struggling; life finds us
      sometimes well off.
Life is sometimes sickness; life is sometimes health.
Life is sometimes depressing; life is sometimes elating.
Life is sometimes sorrow; life is sometimes happiness.
Life is sometimes death; life is sometimes resurrection.
Life sometimes casts us down; life sometimes exalts us.
Life is sometimes a battle; life is sometimes glorious.

To have a *philosophy of life* is to know this about life. And to know not to expect to find life always easy, or always happy. Nor, on the other hand, to expect to find it always difficult, and always a struggle. For most of us, the two themes alternate, in music and in life, both on this earth and beyond.

Thus, you need not feel your life has suddenly taken a permanent turn for the worse when you lose your job, or are fired, when you are out pounding the pavements, and not finding anyone who wants you. Such a difficult time in life is *one* of the themes of life, and therefore in that sense *natural* and *inevitable*.

You've been laid off? The horns are sounding the somber theme, in the movement of life. You're going through a difficult job-hunt with lots of NOs? The horns, again.

But the most helpful thing to know about all of this is that it is not the permanent theme for the rest of your life. Your life has two themes, not one. This difficult somber time will yield eventually to the lilting voice of strings, to the contrasting theme of joy and happiness, all in due time. You need to know this, and thus put this period of your life in some perspective.

This is how you begin, in dealing with rejection shock.

WHO WILL RESCUE YOU?

The other step, in dealing with rejection shock is to decide to take firm control of your own job-hunt. You're going to have to do this again, you know. There are eight job-hunts, typically, in a worker's lifetime. Might as well learn, now, how to do it on your own, and how to do it well. It will serve you in good stead for the rest of your life.

Says one job-hunter: *"As a mid-level executive, I've lost my job two times in less than ten years, and used* Parachute *both times to help me through the re-employment process. This book helped me through the roughest months of my life."* Twice in less than ten years is not remarkable. Jobs last an average of 4.2 years, in the U.S. -- and probably a similar length in other countries.[8]

Many of us, when we are unemployed, act as though this were the only time we were ever going to have to go job-hunting. And so, we wait to be rescued.

Many of us have sat at home for months, waiting for God to prove that He loves us, by causing a job to just *walk in the door.* It does happen. But not often enough for you to ever count on it.

Settle it in your head, from the outset:

No one else on earth cares as much about what happens to you during your job-hunt as you do. No one else is willing to lavish as much time on it, as you will. No one else will be as persistent as you will. No one else will have so exact a picture of what kind of job or new career you are looking for, as you will.

You only need to be taught *how* to go about the job-hunt or career-change, since the job-methods we learn about *on the streets,* are often about as reliable as what we pick up *on the streets* about sex.

---

8. Of course a particular job you have may last longer than that -- especially as you grow older.

So, fasten your seat-belts, as we are about to go on a journey --
learning the least effective methods of job-hunting (where our
rejection is most guaranteed) to the most effective methods of
job-hunting and career-change. In Chapters 9–11 we will tell you
about the creative method of job-hunting, that has the greatest
success rate, and puts us through the least rejection.

But our goal throughout this book is to empower you, during
this one experience in your life, so that you will know hereafter
how to do this on your own.

Who's going to have to go about the job-hunt?

You are.

Who's in control of that job-hunt?

You are.

You may do it with support from others.

You may do it with coaching from others.

You may do it with God's help.

But, in the end, the one who will rescue you, is

YOU . . . YOU . . . YOU.

I saw, of course, the cliff,
I saw the turbulent ocean blue;
But everyone else was going that way,
So I thought that I would, too.

Larry Lemming

CHAPTER THREE

The Least Effective
Job-Hunting Methods:
Resumes, Agencies
and Ads

Chapter 3

"I don't have a parachute of any color."

© 1988 by Sidney Harris.

OUR NEANDERTHAL JOB-HUNTING SYSTEM

Well, since you have decided to take over the management of your own job-hunt, you need to decide how you are going to proceed.

Your normal temptation will be to do what everyone tells you to do: send out your resume to as many places as you can, visit private and public employment agencies, and peruse all the want ads.

That's the traditional way of going about the job-hunt. Everyone says so. Even so-called personnel experts will tell you so.

"Resumes, agencies, and ads -- there's the key!" With that kind of advice floating around, no wonder over eight million people are out of work, in the U.S. alone. And a like number in Europe, and elsewhere.

No, no, no, my friend. Before you draft one resume, visit one agency, or look at even one want ad, you must look at what we know today about this beast called *The Job-Hunt.* Unlike our ancestors who had to strike out blindly, we live in the scientific age, which studies *everything.* Consequently, job-hunting has been studied up and down, and sideways, and ten ways to Sunday.

What we now know is that there are at least twenty methods of job-hunting. Furthermore, we know which are the five most effective of these twenty, and which are the five most ineffective methods.

Let's begin by taking a look at the five most *ineffective* ways of going about the job-hunt. Studies have shown these to be:

1. Using Computer Bank listings or **'registers'** (this doesn't lead to a job for 96 out of every 100 job-hunters who try it).

2. Answering local newspaper **ads** (this doesn't lead to a job for between 76 to 95 out of every 100 job-hunters who try it -- *depending on the level sought; the higher the level, the less effective).*

3. Going to private **employment agencies** (this doesn't lead to a job for 76 to 95 out of every 100 job-hunters who try it -- *again, depending on the level sought).*

4. Answering ads in professional or trade **journals** within your field (this doesn't lead to a job for about 93 out of every 100 job-hunters who try it).

5. Mailing out **resumes** by the bushel (this doesn't lead to a job for 92 out of every 100 job-hunters who try it).

Notice anything? The methods of job-hunting that we are instinctively drawn to -- resumes, agencies, and ads -- are all on this list of the Five Most Ineffective Ways of Going About Your Job-Hunt.

Oops.

Well, let's take a closer look at each of them in turn, resumes, agencies, and ads. Maybe we can see why they work so poorly.

OUR FAVORITE WAY OF AVOIDING REJECTION:

RÉ-SU-MÉ rez-e-ma n [F. *résumé* fr. pp. of *résumer* to resume, summarize] SUMMARY *specif:* a short account of one's career and qualifications prepared typically by an applicant for a position.   *Webster's*

Resumes have a lousy track record. A study of employers done a number of years ago discovered that there was one job offer tendered and accepted, for every 1470 resumes that employers received, from job-hunters. Would you take a plane flight if you knew that only one out of every 1470 planes ever made it to its destination?

The few for whom resumes work talk a lot about it; the vast majority for whom resumes don't work, usually keep quiet about it. Hence, the widespread impression that 'this is a method which works for almost everyone.'

If you believe resumes generally *work,* and you send out loads of resumes, and you don't even get a nibble, you're going to think that something is wrong with *you.* Hence, plummeting self-esteem, thence depression, emotional paralysis, and worse symptoms *often* follow. This has happened to tens of thousands of job-hunters. It has even happened to me. Don't let it happen to you. You have to get back to point #1, above: resumes have a lousy track record. If you don't get even a nibble, that doesn't mean that anything's wrong with you. Something's desperately wrong with resumes . . . as a job-hunting technique.

Those employers who like resumes like them because they enable employers to screen you out *fast* without ever 'wasting their time' on an interview. *Most* employers, or their subordinates, can *screen you out* in approximately thirty seconds, if your resume is sitting in a stack of, say, fifty, on their desk. And if it's in a stack of several hundred, the employer picks up speed and -- we know by actual count -- can screen you out in as little as eight seconds. So, in eight to thirty seconds, *you're gone.* And, with it, any chance for a job there.

RESUMES

In spite of the evidence, almost everyone -- including career counselors and job-hunting books -- will advise you to send out your resume *(or 'curriculum vitae,' c.v. for short)* to a lot of employers, and in answer to a lot of ads for job vacancies. Many people love the *idea* of a resume, no matter how ineffective it is. Never was love more blind. Only 1 in 1470 gets through, remember.

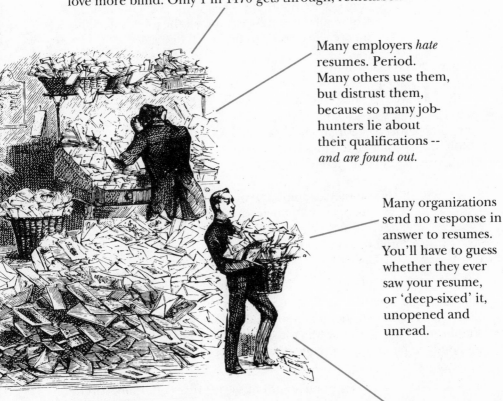

Many employers *hate* resumes. Period. Many others use them, but distrust them, because so many job-hunters lie about their qualifications -- *and are found out.*

Many organizations send no response in answer to resumes. You'll have to guess whether they ever saw your resume, or 'deep-sixed' it, unopened and unread.

Job-hunters will always love resumes, in spite of all the above, because job-hunters *hate* rejection. With resumes, your name gets out there, and though it usually doesn't lead to a job, at least you're not standing there in front of a would-be employer, staring into his or her face while you hear the bad news. With resumes, it's rejection all right. But it doesn't feel so . . . *personal.* Resumes are a nice way to kid ourselves, so that we *feel* we are doing something about our job-hunt, even if -- so far as effectively finding a job is concerned -- we are actually doing next to nothing.

EMPLOYMENT AGENCIES

The second job-hunting strategy that we instinctively turn to, in our Neanderthal job-hunting system, is agencies.

Agencies seem like a wonderful idea, when you are unemployed. My goodness, there's actually some-one out there who can link employers looking for jobs with very-qualified me. We all like to think that somewhere out there is just such a switchboard, where all the employers and all the job-hunters, in an area, can come to find each other.

Unhappily, no place in this country has even a clue as to where all the jobs are. The best that any place can offer you is a kind of sampling, a sort of smorgasbord, if you will, of some of the jobs that are available, out there.

So, if you want a sampling, you will naturally want to visit an agency. Agencies are of several types: federal/state; private; and those retained by employers. Let's look at them in turn, beginning with The Federal/State Employment Service.

The local State employment office in your town or city is actually part of a nationwide Federal network, called "The United States Employment Service," or USES for short. USES has seen its staff and budget, nationwide, greatly reduced in recent years.

About one-tenth of these offices offer job-search workshops, from time to time -- depending on the demand, and whether or not a counselor is avail-able who knows how to teach such a workshop. Beyond that, they have listings of some of the jobs available in your geographical area -- usually ones that employers have already tried to fill in every other way they can.

According to one study, USES placed only 13.7% of those who sought a job there. This means of course that they failed to find a job for 86.3% of the job-hunters who went there to find a job.

Because it is part of a nationwide network, your local USES or Job Service office should have access to the Interstate Job Bank listings, which will tell you about job opportunities in other states or cities that may be of interest to you. The normal number of these listings runs around 6,000 at any one time; 98% of the USES offices have these listings on microfiche, and 20% of the offices also have a computer hookup. The listings are typically two weeks old before you see them, but many of them are for 'constant hires,' so that may not matter.

Another study claimed that approximately 30% of those who search the job listings at USES find a job thereby. But (according to yet another study) 57% of those who find jobs at USES are not working at that job just 30 days later. (Many of the jobs USES finds are only temporary, of course.) This reduces the 30% claimed by the first study, to just 17%, after one month, which is pretty close to the 13.7% cited above.

If you go to your State employment office's job listings, be realistic about your chances of finding a job thereby. Your chances are 13 out of a 100. Don't put all your job-hunting eggs in this one basket.

PRIVATE EMPLOYMENT AGENCIES

Employment agencies are either for long-term work, or for temporary work. The latter are called 'temporary agencies.'

Some agencies list all kinds of jobs. Most specialize. Typical specialties, among long-term as well as temporary agencies: accountants, office services, data processing, legal, insurance, sales/marketing, underwriting, industrial (assemblers, drivers, mechanics), construction, engineering, management/executives, financial, data processing, nannies (for young and old), and health care/dental/medical, *among others.* You can find them listed in the Yellow Pages of your local phone book, under such headings as *Employment Agencies; Employment Service–Government, Company, Fraternal, etc.; and Employment–Temporary.* If they specialize, their listing or their ads will usually indicate what their specialties are.

If you go to an agency where you, not the employer, are going to have to pay the fee, you should know that the application form that you fill out is a legal contract. If the contract states that you give them *exclusive* handling, and then you go out and find a job independently of them, you may still have to pay *them* a fee. Beware. Fees vary from state to state. Ask what it is, and if there's a limit. In some states, for example, a fee cannot exceed 60% of one month's salary, i.e., a $15,000-a-year job will cost you $750, payable (usually) in weekly installments of 10% (e.g., $75 on a $750 total). Sometimes in the U.S., such fees are tax deductible, but not if your new job represents a career-change.

Experts allege that the average placement rate for employment agencies is only 5% *of those who walk in the door.* That means a 95% failure rate, right? *Tilt.* Incidentally, you should know that some agencies play games with their figures, so they can *claim* a high placement rate. They boast something like: "95% of all our clients find jobs through our agency." The trick is in whom they consider to be clients. They don't mean all those who come through that door. No, no, no. They make this game work, by accepting as 'clients' only a small percentage of those who walk in the door. And who might these be? You guessed it. The job-hunters that the agency thinks will be easiest to place. *Cute.* Of course they can place 95% of *them!*

Most often, the fees are paid by employers, but sometimes it is the job-hunter who pays. Be sure to ask which is the case. *Naturally,* you want agencies that make no charge to the job-hunter, if you can find them.

While agencies claim to represent employer and job-hunter equally, when push comes to shove (like, when the job listing they have doesn't quite match you) their loyalty will lie with those who pay the bills (which in most cases is the employer), and those who represent repeat business (again, employers). This means that some agencies may try to talk you into taking a job that doesn't fit you at all, just so they can get the employer's business (and fee).

Agencies' usefulness to *career-changers* is very limited. Agency business is primarily a volume business, requiring rapid turnover of clientele, little time given to the individual job-hunter, with their primary focus on the most-marketable job-hunters, especially those on whom they can make a handsome fee. *Career-changers,* who have no previous track record in a particular industry or job, represent huge problems for agencies, which most of the time they are not willing to waste time on.

AGENCIES RETAINED BY EMPLOYERS

One of the things that job-hunters rarely understand is the fact that employers are as baffled by our country's Neanderthal job-hunting 'system' as we are, and **don't know how to find decent employees, any more than job-hunters know how to find decent employers.** Therefore, they have certain agencies which they pay to find employees for them. Naturally, such agencies know about vacancies. They're being paid to fill them!

They are commonly referred to as headhunters, body snatchers, flesh peddlers, or talent scouts.

They are historically referred to as executive search firms, executive recruiters, executive recruitment consultants, executive development specialists, management consultants, recruiters. (In the old days, these firms searched only for executives, hence their now-outdated title.)

It's a hazy category. For one thing, yesterday's employment agencies today often prefer to lump themselves into this category. That is because employment agencies typically have to operate under more stringent state or federal regulations, than executive search firms do. Their only account-ability is that they have to find the exact person with the exact history and exact experience that they are being paid to find!!!

The mission these firms have been given by employers is to hire away from other firms or employers, workers who are already employed, and rising -- executives, salespeople, technicians, data-processing people, or whatever. You will notice it says nothing about their wanting to hire the unemployed.

They are not, therefore, helpful to most job-hunters. But if you research the firms very thoroughly, and find one that deals with your field or specialty, it's always worth sending them your resume -- just in case. Don't count on anything happening, though. You're essentially praying for lightning to strike.[1]

Is there any place out there, set up by employers where employer and job-hunter can meet face-to-face? Well, there are job-fairs in various places around the country, held at various times of the year. Ask your local chamber of commerce if they know of any. These are often remarkably unproductive, but some job-hunters have struck pay-dirt by going to them.

On some college campuses, recruiters from various companies show up to interview seniors (and sometimes others) for jobs they have vacant. But it's a very dicey process, and you should by no means count on it. Most often it leads absolutely nowhere.

1. There are places that will sell you lists of executive search firms. For example:

Directory of Executive Recruiters, published by Consultant News, Templeton Rd., Fitzwilliam, NH 03447. Published yearly. Lists several hundred firms and the industries served.

Directory of Personnel Consultants by Specialization (Industry Grouping). Published by the National Association of Personnel Consultants, Round House Square, 3133 Mt. Vernon Ave., Alexandria, VA 22305. 1-703-684-0180.

If you want to know more about executive search, there is: John Lucht, *Rites of Passage at $100,000+,* rev. ed. Henry Holt and Co., 115 W. 18th, New York, NY 10011. 800-247-3912. Review by one of our readers: "This book describes in depth the methods of headhunters, what to expect and how to deal with them on an on-going basis. Highly recommended for anyone in middle-management or above. . . ."

WANT ADS IN NEWSPAPERS

The third job-hunting strategy that we instinctively turn to, in our Neanderthal job-hunting system -- after resumes and agencies -- is want ads.

Want ads are found in your local newspaper -- in the classified section, and/or in the business section, sports section, education section, or Sunday edition. Also, for management or financial job-hunters, ads are to be found in the *Wall Street Journal* (especially Tuesday's and Wednesday's editions).

Some phrases are designed to lure you in, while concealing what the job is really about. Beware! Examples:

"Energetic self-starter wanted" (= You'll be working on commission)

"Good organizational skills" (= You'll be handling the filing)

"Make an investment in your future" (= This is a franchise or pyramid scheme)

"Much client contact" (= You handle the phone, or make 'cold calls' on clients)

"Planning and coordinating" (= You book the boss's travel arrangements)

"Opportunity of a lifetime" (= Nowhere else will you find such a low salary and so much work)

"Management training position" or "Varied, interesting travel" (= You'll be a salesperson with a wide territory)

Within 48–96 hours after an ad appears (the third day is usually the peak), an employer will typically receive from 20 to 1000 or more resumes, and will proceed to systematically *screen out* 95 to 98 out of every 100.

Many classified ads include the employers' phone number, because they want to see if they can *screen you out* over the telephone, without ever having to take the time to see you in person. This is always to your disadvantage. Therefore, most experts say, don't say anything over the phone, except that you want to set up an appointment. One way to avoid being drawn into conversation, designed to screen you out over the phone, is simply to say: "I'm sorry I can't talk now; I'm at work."

A study conducted in two "typical" cities -- one large, one small -- revealed, and I quote, that "85% of the employers in San Francisco, and 75% in Salt Lake City, did not hire any employees through want ads" during a typical year. Yes, that said *any* employees, *during the whole year.*[2] In other words, if you use ads, they only give you access to (at most) 25% of the employers in that city, during the entire year.

   As if all of this weren't bad enough, your job-hunting career with ads is further compromised by the fact that some of the ads you see are fakes.

Some employers run fake ads to test the loyalty of their employees (the ad lists only a box number to write to).[3]

Some employment agencies run fake ads, usually listing jobs that have already been filled, in order to draw you in (the old 'bait and switch' process).

Some swindlers run fake ads, pretending they are employers, so that they can get your money (the clue is: the ad gives you a 900 number to call) or get your Social Security number and the number of your driver's license (don't ever give these out over the phone, in response to an ad). With these two numbers alone, from you, they can often take you to the cleaners with some of the con games they've invented.

---

2. Olympus Research Corporation, A Study to Test the Feasibility of Determining Whether Classified Ads in Daily Newspapers Are an Accurate Reflection of Local Labor Markets and of Significance to Employers and Job Seekers. 1973. Now out of print.

3. I am citing an actual case here, as my example.

- For Non-profit Organizations Doing Public or Community Service: ACCESS, Networking in the Public Interest, 50 Beacon St., 4th Floor, Boston, MA 02108. 1-617-720-5627. Fax No.: 1-617-720-1318. Listings of job opportunities in the nonprofit sector, ranging from entry level to Executive Director positions, are disseminated through three publications: (1) *Community Jobs: The National Employment Newspaper For The Nonprofit Sector;* (2) *Community Jobs/ New York, New Jersey,* a bi-monthly publication; (3) *Community Jobs/D.C.,* again a bi-monthly publication. ACCESS also provides career development services specifically geared toward the non-profit job seeker. Write or call for details, if you are interested.

- For Teachers: *The NESC Jobs Newsletters* are published by the National Education Service Center, P.O. Box 1279, Dept. PB, Riverton, WY 82501. 1-307-856-0170. Between March and August, this weekly series of newsletters lists about 58,000 job openings annually. Each week's edition contains only new listings, none repeated. The newsletters are published year 'round, with fewer listings in the months August to March. You select one or more of fourteen different job categories, and receive listings of jobs in those categories only.

- For The Blind: Job Opportunities for the Blind, 1800 Johnson St., Baltimore, MD 21230. 1-410-659-9314, or 1-800-638-7518. Exists to inform blind applicants about positions that are open with public and private employers throughout the country. Maintains a computerized listing. Also, they have cassette instructions on everything for the blind job-seeker. Operated by the National Federation of the Blind in partnership with the U.S. Department of Labor.

- For Jobs Outdoors: Environmental Opportunities, Box 788, Walpole, NH 03608, publishes a monthly listing of environmental jobs and internships, with the same name (Environmental Opportunities). Each issue contains sixty to one hundred full-time positions in a variety of disciplines. 1-603-756-4553.

- For Jobs in Horticulture: Jobs in Horticulture, a semi-monthly guide to career opportunities. 154E Chapel Avenue, Carlisle, PA 17013. 1-800-428-2474. Also: Florapersonnel, Inc., 2180 West State Road 434, Suite 6152, Longwood, FL 32779-5013. 407-682-5151.

WANT ADS NOT IN NEWSPAPERS

• For Jobs Overseas: *International Employment Hotline,* a monthly
newsletter which lists international employment opportunities.
International Employment Hotline, Cantrell Corp., Box 3030,
Oakton, VA 22124.

• For Government Jobs: *Federal Career Opportunities,* published biweekly by Federal Research Service, Inc., 243 Church St. NW, Vienna, VA 22183. 1-703-281-0200. Each issue is 64 pages, and lists 3,200+ currently available federal jobs, in both the U.S. and overseas.

• For Jobs in Criminal Justice: The *NELS Monthly Bulletin,* National Employment Listing Service, Criminal Justice Center, Sam Houston State Univ., Huntsville, TX 77341. 1-409-294-1692. A nonprofit service providing information on current job opportunities in the criminal justice and social services fields.

• For Jobs in The Christian Church: Intercristo is a national
Christian organization that lists over 18,000 jobs, covering hundreds of vocational categories within over 1,000 Christian service
organizations in the U.S. or overseas. Their service is called
Christian Placement Network. *(Jeff Trautman, Executive Director.)*
In 1992, 12,500 people used the Christian Placement Network;
one out of every twenty-five job-hunters who used this service
found a job thereby. (That, of course, means twenty-four out of
twenty-five didn't.) Our readers feel that many of these listings
are in very conservative church settings, but if that (and the odds)
don't bother you, you can contact them at 19303 Fremont Ave.
N., Seattle, WA 98133, (phone number: 1-800-426-1342, or 1-206-
546-7330), and ask to be listed with them for three months (cost:
$41.50). *More general* information about Christians in the world
of work (again, from a conservative point of view) is to be found
in the *Strategic Careers Project Forum,* published bi-monthly by
Inter-Varsity Christian Fellowship of the U.S.A., Box 7895,
Madison WI 53707-7895.

And, incidentally, a weekly compilation of newspaper ads is to be found in The Wall Street Journal's *National Business Employment Weekly,* culled from its four regional editions. Available on some newsstands, or order from: 420 Lexington Ave., New York, NY 10170, 1-212-808-6792. Each issue is $3.95. The major problem with all such compilations: how old the listings may be by the time you receive them, and how likely it is that an employer will wait for you to send in your response many days, or even weeks, later, when typically for most ads -- as we saw -- an *avalanche* of responses comes in, as it is, within 96 hours.

Now, despite all these warnings, I'm sure you'll be tempted to try to answer some ads -- at least the ones you *think* are not fakes. In that case, here are some tips (but, *puh-leeze* don't get your hopes up!).

ANSWERING ADS

• Keep your answer brief. All you're trying to do, in answering the ad, is to be invited in for an interview. Period.

• Whether you get hired or not is the task of the interview, not the task of the answer you first send in.

• In answering, just quote the specifications that the ad asked for; nothing else. Then list what qualifications you have that exactly match each of those qualifications. That's the end of your answer.

• List your qualifications as a series of points, with maybe a 'bullet' (as it is called) in front of each -- as appears on this card.

• If there's a specification you don't meet (like, "experienced with motor boats"), you may wish at least to say something like "interested in motor boats." That is, if it's true.

• If there's anything else you're dying to tell them, save it for the interview. All they're looking for, among the answers they receive to their ad, is "who meets our specifications." They'll go on from there, with those that get invited in for an interview.

• Mail it in. Don't expect much. Remember, only 2 out 100 survive.

HOW TO ANSWER
SALARY REQUESTS IN ADS

• If the ad requests, or even demands, that you state your salary requirements, beware. Employers often use this to screen out job-hunters who would otherwise qualify.

• Therefore, experts will give you contradictory advice here. Some say: ignore the request, don't even mention it. This leaves the employer free to think that maybe you just overlooked it.

• Other experts say: employers are not so easily fooled. Make some comment, at least, like: "I have enjoyed my career, because each new position has been increasingly challenging. I have been promoted regularly, with increasing authority, and commensurate increases in my salary."

• Still other experts say: Answer the request. But meet it head-on with a range, rather than a single salary figure. State a range, they say, of at least three to ten thousand dollar variation -- e.g., $15–20,000 -- and then add the words "depending on the nature and scope of my responsibilities," or words to that effect.

• The overarching rule is: if the ad doesn't mention salary, don't you either, in your response to that ad.

CHECKING YOUR RESPONSE BEFORE YOU MAIL IT

• You must make certain that the spelling in your letter (and resume if you include it) is absolutely errorless. Show it to at least two members of your family, or friends, or workmates, whom you know to be excellent spellers.

• If a spelling error is found, redo the entire letter. (White-Out is a no-no.)

• Check to make sure that the final sentence in your letter speaks about the next step, and that it leaves the control in your hands, not theirs. Not "I hope to hear from you," but "I look forward to hearing from you, and will call you next week to be sure you received this letter -- the mails being what they are."

• Be sure to include your phone number, in case that's the way the employer prefers to contact you.

• Consider sending your response by Federal Express; until everyone is doing this (and they're not, yet) your response will stand out in the mind of the employer, or receptionist.

Some experts counsel other strategies -- *such as,* putting "Personal and Confidential" on your envelope; *and/or* mailing your letters so as to *arrive* in mid-week (that's Tuesday, Wednesday, or Thursday); *and/or* following up with a phone call seven days later – at either the beginning of the employer's workday, or near the end of it. The trouble is, some employers are weary of these strategies *(especially, putting "Personal and Confidential" on an envelope containing a resume)* and just grow irritated with people who use it. You don't want an employer irritated with you.

There is another strange strategy which often *does* work, however, and it goes like this. Read your local newspaper every day, and make note of ads which you would like to respond to, except that you don't have all the credentials, qualifications or experience that the ad calls for. You may send your response in, anyway. But, because it falls short, it will usually be ignored.

Naturally, in time, the ad will stop running, so watch during succeeding weeks to see if that ad *starts running again.* It usually won't, because the employer found the person they were looking for. But if it *does* start running again, that's usually a sign that the employer couldn't find a person with the qualifications he or she was looking for. Now you have a chance to bargain.

Here's how one job-hunter reported her success with this strategy: *"The particular ad I answered the first time it ran required at least an associate degree, which I did not have. What I did have was almost ten years' experience in that particular field. When the ad reappeared a month later I sent a letter saying they obviously had not found what they were looking for in the way of a degree, so why not give me a chance; they already had my resume. Well, it worked. I got the interview, I made them an offer that was $6,000 less than they were going to pay a degreed person, but still a $6,000 increase for me, over my prior position. I got the job. Needless to say, everyone was happy. I have recommended this same procedure to three of my friends, and it worked for two out of three of them, also."*

The places where ads congregate, have many different names: classified ads, help wanted, positions available, postings, vacancies, *online* services, registers, and clearinghouses. The average

job-hunter is particularly attracted to the idea of *clearinghouses* which promise to match your resume with various job openings. This idea is even more alluring if it is to be found on a computer.

Small problem, with all registers or clearinghouses, including computer-based ones: they normally attract many more job-hunters (often called *'candidates'*) than they do employers. Typically, a register or clearinghouse will have 9,000 job-hunters registered with them, but only about 100 employer-vacancies per month.

Job-Hunting & The Electronic Highway

In the U.S. out of the 25 million households which have personal computers, there are 4 million households which have attached a modem to their computer, and thus have access to what are called *'online services,'* such as CompuServe, America Online, Prodigy, GEnie Information Exchange, Delphi, eWorld, and The WELL, as well as thousands -- 45,000 at the moment[4] -- of local 'Bulletin Board Services (BBSs).'[5]

Worldwide, it is estimated that at least 25 million computers are *online* to some part of the Internet, the so-called 'information super-highway' we have all been hearing so much about -- which is actually a worldwide linking up of over 32,400 computer networks and online services, in 135 countries and territories.[6]

So, the question is? Of what use are *online services* (a.k.a 'cyberspace') when you are job-hunting?

The answer is that there are five uses of *online services* which suggest themselves when you are job-hunting or planning to change careers.

#1. They are a place to post your **resume**;

#2. They are a place for you to search for **vacancies**, listed by employers;

#3. They are a place to get some job-hunting help or **career counseling**;

#4. They are a place to find out **information** about companies or organizations;

#5. They are a place to make **contacts**, who may help you find information, or may help you get in for an interview, at a particular place.

Let's talk about these five uses, in turn.

#1. *Your resume online.* A resume is a resume is a resume. As we have seen, it is not a very useful job-hunting tool, and it doesn't get any better just because it's online. But belief in magic never ceases, and people think that because it's on a computer, it somehow *works better.* Hey, for a resume to work *online* some employer has got to go there and read it. And there are about 75 million employers in the U.S. alone who are *not* flocking to online services when they're looking for someone.[7] So your beautiful resume is just *sitting there.* But you probably don't believe a word I'm saying, and you've always wanted your resume to be in someone's computer, so you're bound and determined to try it anyway. Ok, you can look in the index of most online services, or type the word 'career' or 'jobs' or 'resumes' when you get online, and see where it takes you. With a little experimentation, you'll discover *where* to post your resume. My estimate of the effectiveness of this use of online, in getting a job: 3%.[8]

#2. *Finding vacancies online, posted by employers.* We are back to the same problem: *how many* employers go online, when they're looking for employees? The answer is: not a lot. But there are *some,* particularly in matters related to computers and data processing. How do you find where vacancies are listed online? Fortunately a nice fellow named Harold Lemon has put together a list of such places, which he tries to keep up to date and is constantly expanding; you can download it from the *Online Opportunities* bulletin board.[9] His kind efforts aside, the major problem of job-postings *online* is that there is not yet any common language used by employers and job-hunters to describe what they're looking for -- except in the case of computer-related or highly technical jobs. My estimate of the effectiveness of this use of online, in getting a job: 5%.

#3. *Getting job-hunting help or career counseling online.* This kind of service is in its infancy, but some providers such as America Online, and eWorld are moving to provide online career-counseling services. Having roamed a number of such places online, I must report that, as you might guess, some of the career advice you will find online is really helpful, but a lot of it is absolutely awful -- in about the same ratio, as you'll find *out there* in the world; the fact that it's online doesn't magically make it better. *Caveat emptor!* My estimate of the effectiveness of this use of online, in getting a job: 6%.

#4. *Finding information about companies online.* If you are adept at using online services, there are all kinds of business reference books online, that you can turn to. Problem: some of them cost *up to* $100 an hour in extra charges, so check the charges *carefully* before signing on. Usefulness? Well, it all depends. If it's a small company you're researching, I think you're likely to strike out. If it's a larger company, I think online research *can* prove very helpful *if you know what you're doing.* In such a case, my estimate of the effectiveness of this use of online, in getting a job: 13%.

#5. *Making contacts.* Here is where the computer really comes into its own for the job-hunter. Finally. The number of contacts you can make online, through what are called forums, 'chat-rooms,' discussion boards and 'newsgroups' devoted to your field of interest, is mind-boggling. Any faraway place that interests you, you'll likely find a contact online. Any question you need an answer to, you'll likely find someone online who knows the answer. Any organization where you need to know how to meet 'the-person-who-has-the-power-to-hire,' you'll likely find someone on line who knows somebody who . . . You can search the membership directories of some commercial online services (for example, America Online and GEnie), using keywords, to turn up the contacts you are looking for, then drop them an electronic note or e-mail. My estimate of the effectiveness of this use of online, in getting a job: 40%.

In conclusion, as I said, there are 75 million employers out there, in the U.S. alone, who are *not* flocking to *online* when it is time for them to hire. In the world at large, the number increases astronomically. So, until employers *love* hunting for employees *online* as much as job-hunters do, the Achilles heel of online resumes and ads will continue to be what it has been for every computerized 'job-bank' since 1970: too many job-hunters, not enough employers.

Add to this, the fact that there are crooks and con artists out there who have discovered *online,* and are peddling their wares to the unwary[10] -- and your online job-hunting self will sometimes feel like Little Red Riding Hood trying to make her way through the woods toward grandmother's house.[11]

---

4. Statistics are from the *Information & Interactive Services Report* newsletter, reported in *U.S.A Today,* 10/7/93.

5. You can find directories of online services in almost any bookstore, not only in the U.S. but in other major countries. For example, Don Rittner's *The Whole Earth Online Almanac: Info from A to Z.* 1993. Brady Publishing, a Division of Prentice Hall Computer Publishing, 15 Columbus Circle, New York, NY 10023, which has the phone numbers, as well as descriptions of each *online service's* or *bulletin board's* general contents. If you have not yet 'gone online,' as the phrase has it, all you need is a computer, a modem, some software for using the modem (it comes with most modems), some book to guide you, plus your credit card. Don't forget your credit card. Please. And be forewarned that 'going online' is addictive for some people, and for such addicts the costs of 'going online' can mount up quickly into telephone/online service bills that easily total over $100 a month, if you're not careful. However, if you only do two hours a month *online,* the charges will typically be between $7–20 a month.

6. Statistics are from *The New York Times* 6/19/94. If you are curious about the Internet, there are *a million* books about it in any large U.S. bookstore. Example: Harley Hahn's and Rick Stout's *The Internet Yellow Pages.* 1994. Osborne McGraw-Hill, 2600 Tenth St., Berkeley, CA 94710, contains a listing of some places on the Internet where you can search for ads or post your resume. (These places are listed in the alphabetical table of contents under Jobs.) You do, however, have to know how to get online with the Internet. If you don't know how, but you're dying to try, then I recommend you canvass all your friends (online and in your address book) to see if there is an experienced Internet-user among them, who can teach you how to link up. If you are a first time user, you will want to remember that someone compared going online with the Internet as roughly analogous to navigating a muddy road on a pogo-stick, with all the signs in a language you don't understand. *(Peter H. Lewis, in The New York Times,* 12/12/93) It can be a daunting task, and you don't lose any points if you try it several times and then decide to give up.

7. An article entitled "The Drawbacks for Big Companies" in *The New York Times* 6/19/94 explains why. It comes down to 'viruses,' security fears, cost, and difficulty of mastering.

Wild Life, by John Kovalic, © 1989 Shetland Productions. Reprinted with permission.

8. These odds improve significantly if it is a job concerned with computers or data processing. Railroad workers go down to the railroad yard to seek for work; data people go down to the computer to seek for work.

9. *Online Opportunities'* phone number is 1-610-873-7170. Log on with your real name, choose the (A)pplicant Menu, then (F)iles/programs, then (2)Other files/programs. At the prompt, download either JOBINFO.ZIP or JOBINFO.DOC. If you'd prefer, Harold will be glad to send you a copy through the mail. It's called "Harry's Job Search BBS & Internet Hot List." The address is: Harold Lemon, 3241 San Carlos Way, Union City, CA 94587, and you need to send him a check for $3 to cover his costs, plus a self-addressed stamped (75 cents postage in the U.S.) business envelope.

10. It's called 'cybercrime.' *San Francisco Chronicle*, 7/1/94.

11. For further reading, see your local bookstore. Books of interest include: Joyce Lain Kennedy's *Electronic Resume Revolution* (written with Thomas J. Morrow). 1994. And the companion volume by the same authors, *Electronic Job Search Revolution*. Both published by John Wiley & Sons, Inc., 605 Third Avenue, New York, N.Y. 10158. For the computer-addicted, there are also such books as Lynn Walford's *Make Money with Your PC!*, 1994, Ten Speed Press, Box 7123, Berkeley CA 94707.

PLAN B

Well, Mr. or Ms. Job-Hunter, that just about covers the favorite job-hunting system of this country: resumes, agencies, and ads.

They all belong on the *honor roll* of the five most ineffective job-hunting methods there are.

But, you may have been born under a lucky star. So, if you send out those bushels of resumes, or visit those dozens of agencies, or scour those thousands of ads, and then find that it all pays off for you, great! *Congratulations on your new job!*

Throw away the rest of this book *(until the next time).*

But if all that hard work doesn't pay off, and you crash and burn, then perhaps you will be ready to take a look at the five most effective methods of job-hunting.

So, it is to that subject, that we now turn.

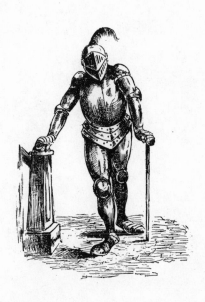

52

Well, yes, you do have
great big teeth; but, never mind
that. You were great to at
least grant me this interview.
                Little Red Riding Hood

CHAPTER FOUR

More Effective Ways of Job-Hunting

Chapter 4

THE MYTHOLOGY: 'THERE ARE NO JOBS'

Before we look at the most effective job-hunting methods on this planet, let us notice something curious, from the previous chapter.

When we rest our job-hunt solely on resumes, agencies, and ads, but these methods don't work for us, you would expect we would then say, "Well, obviously *these methods* don't work." But that is not what we say.

What we say is: "There are no jobs out there."

Our unspoken logic runs something like this: "I can't find any jobs using these methods; therefore, there must not be any jobs."

Wrong!

To see how silly this logic is, let us suppose you moved to a big city, and found a really nice apartment, but you decided you didn't want (or need) a telephone. And now let us suppose that someone over on the other side of that city is asked if you exist. They've never heard of you, so their first response is, "I dunno."

Being resourceful, however, they go and look in the telephone book; they assume that *anyone* who lives in the big city *must* have a telephone. But when they look, there is no mention of you. They call information to ask if you have an unlisted number. Nope. So in this city, they conclude: you don't exist.

Now, you know what's wrong with their conclusion. You do exist! And, in that city! But you can see from this simple illustration that if someone can't find you through *normal* channels, it *does not mean* that you don't exist. It only means that he or she can't find you using those channels.

So it is with you and jobs, during hard times or easy. The fact that you can't find any jobs you want through resumes, agencies, and ads *doesn't* mean that the jobs don't exist.

It only means you can't find them using *those methods.* To be reassured that there really are jobs out there, let us look at some evidence. All of this evidence is taken from one country, the U.S., but similar *patterns* seem to exist in much of the rest of the world.

THE JOBS ARE OUT THERE

Evidence #1: A Survey. In the U.S., there have been nine Recessions since World War II, occurring as regularly as clockwork, every few years. During one of them, the National Federation of Independent Business conducted a survey to discover how many vacancies there were among small businesses. They discovered there were one and a half million, right during that Recession. And that was just for *small* businesses, never mind *large* businesses.

That's why job experts will tell you that even during the hardest of times there are two million vacancies out there, at any given moment. Probably more.

Evidence #2: Logic. It's not hard to understand why the vacancies number two million. Even during the worst of economic times, say during the U.S.'s Great Depression of the '30s, the unemployment figure was 37% at its worst, which means 63% of all workers at that time still had jobs.

Were such a time to return (and in the early '90s, we almost thought it did), 82 million workers would still have their jobs.

Among them, vacancies would inevitably develop. Workers would still get fed up and quit, never mind how hard the times, and need to be replaced. Workers would still get fired for incompetence, and need to be replaced. Workers would still get disabled on the job, and for some time need to be replaced. Workers would still die before reaching their sixties, and need to be replaced. Workers would still retire, and need to be replaced. It's easy to see why two million vacancies would still exist. That would be a vacancy rate of just 2.43% among the active workers, in such a time. In actuality, vacancies -- due to moving, promotion, retirement, and death -- occur at a higher rate than that.

Evidence #3: Government Statistics. I'm speaking of the U.S. government here, although statistics from other countries probably are similar. Anyway, for the last three years, the U.S. government has published each month an unemployment count of at least 8,200,000 people. That's the *monthly* figure. If that's the case, what's the *yearly* figure, you may ask. The answer, at least in 1991, turned out to be 20,000,000. That is, one out of every five workers in the U.S. was out of work, at some time during the year.[1]

Okay, you do the arithmetic: 20,000,000 were unemployed, not by their own choice, sometime during the year. By the beginning of the following year, 'only' 8,200,000 unemployed were still left. On the dark side, that's still a *depressingly* large number. But, on the bright side, it means that:

11,800,000 of the unemployed found jobs, *during the year.*

That works out to almost a million job vacancies found and filled *each month,* just for the unemployed -- never mind workers who changed jobs while still employed.[2]

---

1. In 1991 the Conference Board reported that this was the correct figure. The government claimed it was lower -- 17% -- though during a previous Hard Time, the government came up with the 20% figure also. One poll put the 1991 figure even higher: a Time/CNN poll put it at 23% ("23% of American workers were unemployed, not by their own choice, at some time in 1991," Time, January 13, 1992). Incidentally, in the U.S. the yearly count has been taken over a number of years, and in good times or bad it seems to always work out that one out of every five workers is unemployed *sometime* in any given year.

These three evidences, cited above, explain why experts say "Of course, there are job vacancies out there -- even during the hardest of times."

So when you can't find a job, 9 times out of 10 it means you're using the wrong methods to look for them.

THE FIVE MOST EFFECTIVE JOB-HUNTING METHODS

Okay, let's cut to the chase. What *should* you do, to find a job? Well, the most effective job-hunting methods turn out to be:

> 1. **The** so-called **creative job-hunting approach** -- figuring out your best skills, and favorite knowledges, and then researching any employer that interests you, before approaching that organization and arranging, through your contacts, to see the person there who has the power to hire you for the position you are interested in. This method, faithfully followed, leads to a job for 86 out of every 100 job-hunters who try it.[3]

---

2. Each month, on the first Friday of the month, the U.S. government reports the *net* gain in jobs the previous month. It is arrived at, by taking the total number of jobs one month, and subtracting the total number of jobs for the next month. Why this figure is in sharp contrast to the figure I have reported above is easily illustrated. Suppose in a given month 1,300,000 jobs were lost or eliminated, but in that same month some 1,250,000 vacancies got filled. That means 1,250,000 job-hunters found a job that month. However, the government will subtract 1,300,000 from 1,250,000 and report that the *net* figure for that month was 50,000 jobs lost, implying that *no* job-hunters found a job that month -- or, to be more blunt, that "there are no jobs out there."

3. Nathan Azrin's 'job-club' concept -- see page 404 -- has a somewhat different approach, but the same success rate.

2. **Applying directly to an employer, factory, or office in person**, without first having done the homework I just described (this leads to a job for 47 out of every 100 job-hunters who try it).

3. **Asking friends for job-leads** (this leads to a job for 34 out of every 100 job-hunters who try it).

4. **Asking relatives for job-leads** (this leads to a job for about 27 out of every 100 job-hunters who try it).

5. **Using the placement office at the school or college that you once attended** (this leads to a job for 21 out of every 100 job-hunters who try it).

Among these five, one method's effectiveness-rate stands out like a sore thumb, and that of course is *the creative job-hunting approach*. Its effectiveness-rate of 86% is *astronomically high,* when compared with all other job-hunting methods. Since it is *by far* the most effective method of job-hunting -- or career-changing -- the major part of this book (beginning with Chapter 9) is devoted to explaining this method.

Be forewarned: it requires hard work, as most good things do. If you're not willing to do that work, then you should pursue the other four methods listed above.

TRAVELS WITH FARLEY by Phil Frank © 1982 Field Enterprises, Inc. Courtesy of Field Newspaper Syndicate

THE SECOND MOST EFFECTIVE JOB-HUNTING METHOD

The second Most Effective Job-Hunting Method is where you pick out any employer that interests you, from the Yellow Pages or wherever, and then you go directly to their building, face-to-face rather than sending a resume or cover letter. Even if you haven't done any homework, on yourself or on them, even if you don't know anyone there, except the Personnel Department, this job-hunting method still works almost half the time, *if pursued faithfully over a number of weeks or months.* It works, in any case, far better than resumes, agencies, or ads do.

But it does require you to go there physically. If you don't go there physically, then you may be following some other method, but you are not following this one. Hence, all bets are off.

If the companies or organizations that interest you, are far-away, going face-to-face is of course more difficult. But there are still ways to do this. See page 147 and Chapter 12, for details about using your vacation and your personal contacts in that faraway city.

If you have any control over it, as you will with small companies, you *always* want to see the boss, rather than some go-between. You will also want to try to avoid the personnel department *(or human resources department)* if you can. 85% of all organizations don't have a personnel department, anyway; so this is often an unnecessary warning.

Anyway, as I said, going face-to-face with employers leads to a job for 47 out of every 100 people who try it.

But what if it doesn't? There are, of course, places where it is absolutely *impossible* to get in to see 'the boss,' i.e., the one who has the power to hire you. He or she is surrounded by a castle, with a moat, and eight large over-sized hungry alligators in the moat. You of course will hurl yourself against its ramparts a half-dozen times, anyway, furious that you can't get in to see that person. But, could I ask you a question: "*Why* do you want to work for *a place like that?*"

I mean, never mind that you're taking this *very personally.* Rejection, rejection, rejection, flashes on and off in your brain. But, haven't they *(by these actions)* told you something about themselves that is important information for you to have? And having gained that information, isn't it time for you to reassess *whether you really want to work at a place like that?*

THE THIRD AND FOURTH
MOST EFFECTIVE
JOB-HUNTING METHODS

The third Most Effective Job-Hunting Method, is where you ask every **friend** you have (and I mean *every* friend) about any vacancies they may know of. The fourth most effective method is like unto it, except that you ask every **relative** you have, about any vacancies they may know of. In job-hunting jargon, these are called *your contacts.*

Why are these methods so effective? Because it takes about seventy eyes and ears to find a job. You only have two eyes, and two ears, at most. So, if you tell *everyone* you know or meet that you are job-hunting, and that you would appreciate their keeping their eyes and ears open, and letting you know if they hear of anything, you acquire those seventy eyes and ears.

But there is a catch. For your friends, relatives, and family to be truly helpful to you, you must tell them *exactly* what you are looking for.

It is *not* sufficient to tell your friends, relatives, and working acquaintances, "Hey, I'm looking for a job. Let me know if you hear of *anything.*" What does "anything" mean? Are you willing to take a job as a dishwasher in a local restaurant? Are you willing to work off a garbage truck? Are you willing to be a typist in a typing pool? Are you willing to sweep chimneys? All of these are honorable jobs for people who can do them with a sense of integrity and pride in their work. But do you really mean *anything*?

If you would enlist your friends, relatives, and working acquaintances to help you with your job-hunt, you've got to give them better information than *anything*. You've got to spell out

specifically what kinds of work you're looking for, and what kinds of skills you like to use. Figure out whether you're best with People, or Things, or Information. It makes a difference. A big difference. Get as specific as you can (*"I'm good with my hands,"* or *"I like to help organize events and carry out planning to the last detail."*) You must know which are your best and most enjoyable skills.[4]

And, incidentally, since you never know *when* you may bump into a contact -- someone who could lead you to a job -- don't get *real sloppy* in your appearance while you are out of work. Be comparatively neat, clean, and nicely dressed whenever you go out into the world -- even if it's just downtown, or out to the mall, or grocery shopping. You don't want any *contact* thinking, because of your sloppy dress, that you are 'on the skids.' No, oh no you don't.

---

4. If you don't know how to describe in detail what you do best, then please see Chapter 9. Read it. Do it.

THE FIFTH MOST EFFECTIVE
JOB-HUNTING METHOD

Finally, the fifth Most Effective Job-Hunting Method is like the previous two, except that you approach the Placement Office or Career Planning Office of the high school or college you once attended, to see if they have any job-listings.

Some job-hunters never think of going back to the college, community college, or high school that they once attended, to

visit the placement/career-planning office there. Perhaps they don't even know it has one. Yet most of the 3,280 institutions of higher education in this country do, however informally.[5] So do many high schools, these days -- if they weren't hit by budget-cuts.

---

5. A directory listing many of these offices is published, and is available for perusal in most Placement Offices. It is called the *Directory of Career Planning and Placement Offices,* and is published by the College Placement Council, Inc., 62 Highland Ave., Bethlehem, PA 18017, 1-215-868-1421.

In the placement or career-planning office there, look for bulletin board notices of jobs, vacancies, and even more importantly, look for lists of graduates who live in your geographical area, since they may serve as contacts for you.

If you don't see that information, ask for it.

If you aren't near your school geographically, write to the Alumni office.

OTHER RECIPES
FOR SUCCESS

> The major difference between successful and unsuccessful job-hunters is not some factor out there (such as a tight job-market), but the way they go about their job-hunt.

We would all be better at job-hunting if we studied successful job-hunters.

You know that, already, in other pursuits. If you play tennis, and you want to learn how to improve your game, you would go talk to *good* tennis players, to learn how they do it. If you run, and want to improve your running, you would go talk to *good* runners, and learn how they do it. If you paint, and want to learn how to paint better, you would go study under *master* painters, to see how they do it.

It is the same with job-hunting. If you are job-hunting, and you want to learn how to do it better, you go talk to *successful* job-hunters, people who *were* out of work, and since then have found a job they really love, and learn what *they* did. Over the past twenty-five years, I have studied thousands and thousands of successful job-hunters around the world to learn *what* distinguished them from unsuccessful job-hunters.

My learnings are summarized in the remainder of this chapter.

Some of these points will sound remarkably simple, elementary, and obvious to you. "Well, any fool would know *that!*" you will say. Unhappily, as my studies of job-hunters have revealed, any fool *doesn't* know these things. You'd be amazed at how many job-hunters think they have done *everything* they can, to find a job, when in fact they've ignored most of these points.

That's why I have spelled out even the *simplest* of them in some detail.

Copyright, 1985. Universal Press Syndicate. Reprinted with permission. All rights reserved.

An old saying has it, "It is not that great ideas have been tried, and found inadequate; it is that they have been prejudged as inadequate, and never even tried." If you prejudge these ideas, without even trying them, then you shouldn't wonder that you are having trouble finding a job.

Incidentally, these ideas do not *guarantee* you a job. Life can never be so mechanized. There is always so much, in this life, that depends on luck and chance and serendipity.

But if faithfully followed, these ideas should dramatically *improve* your chances of finding a job, as so many successful job-hunters have discovered, before you.

YOU WILL IMPROVE YOUR
JOB-HUNTING SUCCESS IF YOU
ALWAYS HAVE A 'PLAN B'

The single greatest thing I have learned from studying successful job-hunters (and career-changers) for twenty-five years, is that the *essence* of successful job-hunting is *having alternatives*. Alternative ways of describing what you do. Alternative avenues of job-hunting. Alternative *leads* to jobs. Alternative 'target' organizations that you're going after. Alternative ways of approaching employers. The problem with unsuccessful job-hunters is that often they pursue a plan that has no alternatives. You must not follow in their footsteps, if you want your job-hunt to be successful.

● *Alternatives:* You must not expect that you will necessarily be able to find exactly the same kind of work that you did in the past. Those kind of jobs may be *gone*. So, you need to take the job-label off yourself *("I am an auto-worker," etc.)* and define yourself instead as *"I am a person who . . ."* Define some other line (or lines) of work that you could do, can do, and would enjoy doing. You may be able to describe this right off the top of your head; perhaps something you've done in your spare time *(like: make dresses, repair sailboats, etc.)* However, if you can't think of anything off the top of your head (or the tip of your tongue), then run do not walk to Chapters 9 and 10. Read *and do* the exercises there, thoroughly.

● *Alternatives:* Define more than one *target* employer that you are aiming at. Restricting your efforts to just one organization, and being determined that you'll get hired (or hired back) there, or nothing, is job-hunting *death*. Never, never 'put all your eggs in one basket.' That organization, that office, that group, that church, that factory, that government agency, that volunteer organization may be *the ideal place* where you would like to work. But no matter how appetizing your *first choice* looks to you, no matter how much it makes your mouth water at the thought of working there, *you are committing job-hunting suicide* if you don't have some alternative targets. I mean, maybe you'll get that dream-come-true. But -- *big question* -- what are your plans if you don't? You've *got* to have other plans **now** -- not when that first target runs out of gas, three months from now. You must have other targets. I recommend five, at least.

● *Alternatives:* Look at all the different places where your expertise might be needed. Suppose you love to teach. What kinds of organizations have such jobs? You might answer, *"just schools,"* -- and finding that schools have no openings in your geographical area, you might say, *"Well, I can't find a job doing that."* But no, my friend, the answer is not *'just schools.'* There are countless other *kinds* of organizations and agencies out there which have a teaching arm, and therefore employ teachers. For example, corporate training and educational departments, workshop sponsors, foundations, private research firms, educational consultants, teachers' associations, professional and trade societies, military bases, state and local councils on higher education, fire and police training academies, and so on, and so forth.

● *Alternatives:* Have more than one *form* of work in mind. There is, of course the old 9-to-5 job. But you may not be able to find *that.* Be ready to look at: *a series* of part-time jobs. Or at: becoming an independent contractor, where you take on one project after another, from different companies. Be ready to look at working through a so-called *temporary agency.* Always have alternatives.

By permission of Johnny Hart and Creators Syndicate, Inc.

YOU WILL IMPROVE YOUR JOB-HUNTING SUCCESS IF YOU SPEND MORE HOURS PER WEEK ON YOUR JOB-HUNT

Two-thirds of all job-hunters spend 5 hours or less on their job-hunt each week, according to the U.S. Census Bureau.[6] When that survey was first published, I found it depressing. I also found it totally congruent with what I'd learned from talking to *unsuccessful* job-hunters, for many years.

My advice -- based on successful job-hunters' experience -- is: spend 35 hours a week, at least, on your job-hunt. This should cut down, dramatically, the number of weeks it takes you to find work.

To illustrate, let us imagine that a woman job-hunter's search takes 30 weeks, before she finds a job. If she spent only five hours a week on it, that means it took her 150 hours of job-hunting, to land that job. Now let us suppose that same job-hunter were to be hurled back in time, and she was able to start her job-hunt all over again; but this time she increased the number of hours devoted to her job-hunt, to 35 hours per week. Other things being equal, her 150 hour job-hunt would then take only 4 weeks, or so, instead of 30.[7]

6. Published in "Job Search Assistance Programs: Implications for the School," authored by the late Robert G. Wegmann, and first appearing in *Phi Delta Kappan*, December 1979, pp. 271ff.

7. Of course, there are some factors beyond a job-hunter's control, such as how long it takes an interviewing-committee to schedule the next round of interviews at the place that interests you (you will often be invited back two or three times before they make up their mind about you). Nonetheless, the main point of our example still remains.

YOU WILL IMPROVE YOUR
JOB-HUNTING SUCCESS
IF YOU GO AFTER
SMALL COMPANIES

Job-hunters often concentrate their job-hunt on large, well-known organizations, and when they can't find a job thereby, they assume that no one is hiring.

There is a natural tendency to make large organizations 'the *measure of all things*' going on in the job-market. If the newspapers are filled with the news of companies like Sears, General Motors, and others laying off thousands of workers, most job-hunters *assume* things are bad everywhere. This is a very common, and very costly, mistake.

But the fact is, small companies -- with 100 or less employees -- have been creating two out of every three new positions since 1970. In the U.S., for example, during the 1980s, while the Fortune 500 companies were *cutting* 3.7 million jobs from their payrolls, smaller companies *created* 19 million new jobs.[8]

So, if you would improve your job-hunting success, you need to concentrate on every small firm in your field that is within commuting distance, and has one hundred or less employees. Personally, I would begin with firms that have twenty or less employees.

You would do well to pay particular attention to those small companies which are expanding. They may be *relatively* small now, but they are on their way to *bigger*. One thinks of the example of companies like Apple Computer which started out in a garage, or ASK Group, of Mountain View, California, which started out in a spare bedroom.

It is true that small firms tend to have fewer benefits, such as health care, but on the other hand, they are easier to approach, the boss there is easier to get in to see, there are no forbidding personnel or human resource departments to screen you out, *and* they have the jobs.

---

8. *The San Francisco Chronicle,* 2/1/93.

9. A survey cited by the late Robert G. Wegmann in "Job Search Assistance: A Review," in the *Journal of Employment Counseling,* December 1979, p. 212.

YOU WILL IMPROVE YOUR
JOB-HUNTING SUCCESS
IF YOU SEE MORE
EMPLOYERS EACH WEEK

In the U.S. and elsewhere, the average job-hunter only visits six employers a month. That adds up to little more than one employer *per week.*[9]

That's one reason the job-hunt takes so long. Say you were an average job-hunter, and it took you *thirty* weeks to find a job, that means you would find a job after visiting just 42 employers.

But were you to contact two employers per day, each weekday, that would add up to 42 employers, and perhaps a job, in just a little over *four* weeks!

Therefore, you should determine to see at least two employers per weekday, one in the morning and one in the afternoon, at a minimum. And you should determine to do this for as many months as your job-hunt may last. For thus you may greatly shorten your job-hunt.

When you approach employers, don't be put off by rejection, if they have nothing to offer you. Nor must you start thinking you have some job-hunting handicap that will cause you never to find a job.

Remember, no matter what kind of handicap you have (real or imagined), there are two kinds of employers out there:

• those who won't hire you because of your inexperience, age, race, physical or mental handicap, or because you are over-qualified; *and*

• those who *will* hire you, despite your inexperience, age, race, physical or mental handicap, or being overqualified, so long as you can do the job.

During your job-hunt, you are *not* to be dismayed by the former kind of employer, no matter how many of them you meet. Be polite, ask them if they know of anyone else who might be hiring. Keep going until you find the second kind of employer.

And when you meet *them,* be prepared, always, to tell them what makes you different from nineteen other people who can do the same thing that you do. *(If you need help in doing this, see Chapter 9.)*

YOU WILL IMPROVE YOUR JOB-HUNTING SUCCESS IF YOU USE AS MANY JOB-HUNTING METHODS AS YOU CAN

A study of successful blue-collar job-hunters in West Virginia was made a number of years ago by A. Harvey Belitsky and Harold L. Sheppard.[10] Their finding? They discovered that the greater the number of job-hunting methods a blue-collar job-hunter used, the greater his or her success at finding a job.

There are, as I mentioned earlier, some twenty such job-hunting methods -- or avenues. Most of them are obvious, but let's tick them off anyway: the *creative job-hunting* method described in Chapters 9–11; applying directly to an employer; asking friends about jobs where they work; asking friends about jobs elsewhere; asking relatives about jobs where they work; asking relatives about jobs elsewhere; using your school's placement service; asking a professor or old teacher for job-leads; going to a union hiring hall (if you belong to a union); contacting agencies retained by employers *(executive search firms);* using the Federal/state employment service; going to private employment agencies; contacting trade associations in your field; answering local newspaper ads; answering non-local newspaper ads; answering ads in professional or trade journals; placing ads yourself; taking civil service tests; mailing out resumes by the bushel; and using computer listings or registers.

The average job-hunter uses less than two *(1.6, to be exact)* of these methods, during his or her entire job-hunt. But, as Sheppard and Belitsky found out, the more *you* use, the more likely you are to find a job.

So, you know what you must do.

---

10. The study was published under the title *The Job Hunt: Job-Seeking Behavior of Unemployed Workers in a Local Economy* (now out of print). A summary of it was published by The W.E. Upjohn Institute for Employment Research, 300 South Westnedge Ave., Kalamazoo MI 49007, called *Promoting Jobfinding Success for the Unemployed.* Originally, I did much of my own research on job-hunting when this Institute kindly gave me an office at their Washington D.C. offices. They have since moved entirely to Kalamazoo.

YOU WILL IMPROVE YOUR
JOB-HUNTING SUCCESS IF YOU
FIND OR CREATE A SUPPORT
GROUP FOR YOURSELF

People who job-hunt by themselves often get discouraged --
and this dramatically affects their job-hunting success, as we will
see in the next section. The job-hunt *can be* one of the loneliest
experiences in the world. But it need not be. *Please,* don't set out
to face the job-hunt all by yourself. Find a partner, or a larger
group if you can (commonly called *support groups*). Here are the
candidates you can choose from:

a. Job-hunting groups that already exist in your city or town,
such as "Forty Plus" clubs, "Experience Unlimited" groups, job-
hunt classes at your local Federal/state employment offices, or
at the local Chamber of Commerce, or at your local college or
community college, or at your local Adult Education center, or
at your local church, synagogue, or place of worship.[11] The
likelihood that such help is available in your community increases dramatically for you if you are from certain groups held
to be disadvantaged, such as low income, or welfare recipients,
or youth, or displaced workers, etc. Ask around.

b. A job-hunting group that doesn't currently exist, but that
you could help form with other unemployed people -- at your
local church, synagogue or religious centre. (Often your priest,
minister, rabbi, or leader can put you in touch with such
people.) Some enterprising job-hunters, unable to locate any
group, have formed their own by running an ad in the local
newspaper, near the "help wanted" listings. *"Am currently job-
hunting, would like to meet weekly with other job-hunters for mutual
support and encouragement."*

c. Your mate or partner, grandparent, brother or sister, or
best friend. A loving 'taskmaster' is what you need. Someone
who will make a regular weekly appointment to meet with you,
check you out on what you've done that week, and be very stern

---

11. A sample listing of these kinds of places is to be found in the *National Business
Employment Weekly*, on its pages called "Calendar of Career Events." It's available on
some newsstands, or you can order an issue directly from: National Business Employment Weekly, 420 Lexington Ave., New York, NY 10170, 1-212-808-6792 or 1-800-JOB-
HUNT.

with you if you've done little or nothing since you last met. You want understanding, sympathy, and discipline. If your mate, brother or sister, or best friend, can offer you all of these, run -- do not walk -- to enlist them immediately.

d. A local career counselor. I grant you that career counselors aren't usually thought of as 'a support group.' But many of them do have group sessions; and even by themselves they can be of inestimable support. If you can afford their services, and none of the above suggestions have worked, this is a good fall-back strategy. Before choosing such a counselor, however, *please* read Appendix A, in the back of this book, thoroughly. That Appendix also tells you how to locate such counselors.

YOU WILL IMPROVE YOUR
JOB-HUNTING SUCCESS
IF YOU PREPARE FOR
A LONG JOB-HUNT

One job-hunter out of every three gives up too soon. That is to say, one out of every three becomes an unsuccessful job-hunter *simply because* they abandon their search.

And if you ask them why, they say, "I didn't think it was going to be this hard; I didn't think it was going to take this long."

It's important for you to know that in the U.S. and many other countries, the job-hunt typically lasts from eight to twenty-three weeks, or longer. It depends, of course, on what kind of job you are looking for, where you are living, how old you are, how high you are aiming, and what the state is of the local economy.

But you must be mentally prepared (and financially prepared) for your job-hunt to last a lot longer than you think it will.

What 'does in' so many job-hunters is some *unspoken* mental quota in our head. It goes something like this: *I expect I'll be able to find a job after about 30 phone calls, 15 calls in person, and three interviews.* We go about our job-hunt, fill or exceed those quotas, and then give up. Without a job.

At least one out of every three of us does.

So, don't let this happen to you.

Keep going until you find a job. Don't give up.

Remember that gentle, loving, stubborn **persistence** is the name of the game.

Persistent means being willing to go back to places that interested you, at least a couple of times in the following months, to see if by any chance their 'no vacancy' situation has changed.

How long will it take? Well, this was one man's experience, which is fairly typical:

> *107 places identified in his chosen geographical area*
> *   as "interesting"*
> *126 phone calls placed to them*
> * 45 interviews conducted in person*

Another job-hunter, a woman in New Zealand, cited this experience:

> *"I have been job-hunting for the past twelve months. I'm now writing to tell you of my great success in finding a full-time job after my 205th job application. The job is a fulfillment of my lifetime ambition. I start this week and will be earning $20,384 a year."*

Of course, sometimes lightning strikes. Here's another job-hunter's experience:

> *"After reading Parachute, and completing the homework, I wrote ONE letter to ONE corporation resulting in ONE fabulous job. From logo design to licensing to lesson plans, I was able to help a corporation establish its own on-site child care center. Amazing things happen when mind, heart, and soul are focused on the right task."*

The job-hunt is completely unpredictable, as to its length. *The secret* of success is to be mentally prepared, before you start, for *whatever* it takes.

The latest self-help book for pessimists.

© Bradford Veley, 1989.

WHAT IF NOTHING WORKS?

Following the strategies in this chapter, which we have learned from *successful* job-hunters, you should dramatically improve your chance of finding a job.[12] Good luck, and if you find one, congratulations. You do not need to read the rest of this book -- *until the next time.*

But if you faithfully try everything listed in this chapter, and *none of it works* for you, what then? Well, there is a life-preserver still available to you: flee to Chapters 9, and 10, read them, and painstakingly do the exercises there (it will take you no more than a good weekend, if you keep at it). In those chapters I describe the *creative job-hunting process,* that I mentioned at the beginning of this chapter.

The chapters are in the career-changing section of this book. But they are not solely for career-changers. They are for you if you have tried *everything,* but nothing seems to be working. That job-hunting method has an 86% success rate.

Don't abandon hope, my friend.

---

12. If you want more job-hunting strategies, I refer you to *The Complete Job and Career Handbook: 101 Ways to Get From Here to There,* by S. Norman Feingold and Marilyn N. Feingold. Garrett Park Press, P.O. Box 190B, Garrett Park, MD 20896. 1993. This $15 book lists many other strategies for you to explore, should your job-hunt reach a dead end. Chapter titles include: "Infrequently Used/Non-traditional Job and Career Search Techniques," "Check List of 177 Ways to Help Get A Job and Advance Your Career," etc. Very helpful, and detailed. Dr. Feingold is a pioneer in the career counseling field, and he and Marilyn really know their stuff.

I decided not to wait a long time,
To wait for the mercies of God;
I simply took a broom in my hand,
And started sweeping.

> A Russian Jew, an aeronautical
> engineer, upon immigrating
> to Israel.

CHAPTER FIVE

If It Looks Like It's Going To Be 'A Long Haul': How To Avoid Getting Depressed

Chapter 5

©Copyright 1969 King Features Syndicate, Inc., World rights reserved.
Used by special permission.

U.S. Statistics

At least one out of every five workers in America is unemployed at *some* time during the year. And it can last quite a spell. During the 1990s thus far, at any given moment:

35 out of every 100 unemployed persons have been out of work less than five weeks, thus far;

28 out of every 100 have been out of work between five and fourteen weeks, thus far;

13 out of every 100 have been out of work between fifteen and twenty-six weeks, thus far;

24 out of every 100 have been out of work twenty-seven weeks or longer; and/or have stopped looking altogether.[1]

---

1. Statistics based, in part, on the February 1992 issue of the *Monthly Labor Review*, published by the U.S. Department of Labor, Bureau of Labor Statistics; and, in part, on the figures for discouraged workers for that same time period; and, in part, on a paper by the late Bob Wegmann, entitled, "How Long Does Unemployment Last?"

If you are out of work, there is obviously a chance that you could be in the 35% who find work within five weeks; in which case, the concerns raised in this chapter can be, for the most part, ignored.

But, the odds are twice as great -- 65% -- that your job-hunt will take longer, maybe *much* longer. So, it could be "a long haul" before you find work. Therefore, we need to talk.

IF THERE'S JUST NO MONEY
ON YOUR TABLE

Why people get depressed when unemployed is no great mystery. They have no money. Typically, during Hard Times, over 30% of all adults -- working or not -- describe their financial situation as "shaky." An even higher percentage of unemployed people would thus describe their situation. Many have been living from paycheck to paycheck.

So, the first thing you're going to have to do, when unemployed, is figure out how to survive financially. There are a number of books to help you do this, available in your local bookstore or library.[2]

---

2. Linda Bowman, *Free Food . . . & More.* Probus Publishing Company, 1925 N. Clybourn Ave., Chicago, IL 60614, 1-800-PROBUS-1. 1991.

Ellen Kunes, *Living Well or Even Better On Less.* Perigee Books, Putnam Publishing Company, 200 Madison Ave., New York, NY 10016. 1991.

Charles Long, *How To Survive Without A Salary.* Firefly Books, Box 838, Ellicott Sta., Buffalo, NY 14205.

Voluntary Simplicity: Toward A Way of Life That is Outwardly Simple, Inwardly Rich, by Duane Elgin. Quill Press, William Morrow, 1359 Avenue of the Americas, New York NY 10019. 1993 (revised edition).

For senior citizens, there are special books dealing with savings on transportation, hotel costs, and car rentals, such as: *Unbelievably Good Deals & Great Adventures That You Absolutely Can't Get Unless You're Over 50,* by Joan Rattner Heilman. Contemporary Books, 2 Prudential Plaza, Suite 1200, Chicago IL 60601. Revised regularly.

There are other books, out there, that may also be helpful to you, such as: *Your Money or Your Life: Transforming Your Relationship with Money and Achieving Financial Independence,* by Joe Dominguez and Vicki Robin. Viking Penguin, 375 Hudson St., New York NY 10014. 1992.

Albert Ellis and Patricia A. Hunter, *Why Am I Always Broke? How to Be Sure About Money.* Carol Publishing Group, 120 Enterprise Ave., Secaucus, NJ 07094. 1991.

UNEMPLOYMENT AS
A DEPRESSING TIME

There are three additional reasons why we find unemployment such a depressing time in our life:

(1) It is the end of an era. For months, years, maybe decades, we were used to thinking of ourselves in terms of *that job* at *that place*. It gave our life its coherence, it gave us our daily routine, it gave us our identity. "Who are you?" "*Oh, I'm a foreman at the General Motors plant down the road.*" But when we are laid-off or fired, that era comes to an end. What do we say now? "Who are you?" "*Well, I don't really know, anymore.*" That's depressing.

(2) It goes on too long. Most of us are good at doing difficult things, as long as we only have to do it for a short time. We can walk (quickly) through an area with a bad stench. We can put up with a three-day cold. We can stand to miss one meal. We can hold our breath for thirty seconds. We can run a hundred-yard dash. We can endure a bad relationship, as long as it doesn't last more than one week. But we don't like it when things go on too long. That starts to get us down.

This of course is our situation when we are unemployed. A period of unemployment that lasts only two weeks -- hey, *no problem!* But if it drags on and on and on, we get weary just thinking about it. "Enough, already," we cry. Yet, there is no end in sight. That's depressing.

(3) It makes us feel powerless. We like it when we can make a difference. In our household. In our neighborhood. In our community. At our workplace. We do something, something happens or changes, as a result. That makes us feel good. But we don't like it when we face the opposite situation. This is why unemployment is often about as welcome as a rattlesnake at a picnic. When we're out of a job, we try this. Sometimes it works like a charm. But other times, nothing happens. We try that. Nothing happens. We are still out of work. We still can't find a job. We still are unemployed. It goes on and on, and *nothing* we do seems to make any difference. We begin to feel absolutely powerless. That's depressing. *Very* depressing.

THE MEANING OF 'DEPRESSION'

The word 'depressing' or 'depression' is used, of course, in two different emotional senses: one by the unemployed, and the other by psychiatrists or therapists.

The latter mean by it, an emotional illness of uncertain origin and cure. If we are the victims of *this* kind of depression, it usually antedates our period of unemployment, and is something we have wrestled with for years. It may have a virulency like unto pneumonia, or be as low-grade as a cold. When it is as virulent as pneumonia, the emotional illness of depression is a burden that threatens to crush the soul, and many brave souls have endured this 'dark night of the soul' for years, with astounding courage -- though there are now medicines and treatments that can often hold it completely, or mostly, at bay. Anyone who is unemployed, and is feeling so depressed as to be suicidal, needs to get to a psychiatrist, therapist, or doctor, immediately, for help. *This is a medical emergency.*

Depression can be much milder, and in that form it is like a series of 'blue Mondays,' or it may be a gentle perpetual tinge of sadness that does not keep us from our feasts, but 'is just enough to appear as a death's-head at all our feasts.'[3]

In whatever form, it is estimated by experts that some 10 million Americans experience depression sometime during the year.[4] And sometimes the unemployed are among them.

---

3. The phrase is William Law's, who used it to describe token religion.

4. A patient's guide to Depression is available from Depression, P.O. Box 8547, Silver Spring, MD 20907, free. You may also call 1-800-358-9295, to ask for it. For further reading, I refer you to: *The Good News About Depression: New Medical Cures & Treatments That Can Work for You*, by Mark S. Gold, M.D. 1988. Bantam Books, 1540 Broadway, New York, NY 10036. There is also: *Depression, the Mood Disease*, by Francis Mark Mondimore, M.D., rev. ed. 1993. Available from the Johns Hopkins University Press, 2715 N. Charles St.,, Baltimore, MD 21218, 1-800-537-5487. Let me repeat that depression is not a character failure, but often has a physical basis, in one's body chemistry (e.g., the brain does not produce enough seratonin, etc.). If you cannot move yourself out of the depression by exercise, and activity, then you ought to get yourself to an experienced M.D. or therapist.

de•pres•sion \di-Ëpresh-fln\ n (1): a state of feeling sad : DEJECTION (2): a psychoneurotic or psychotic disorder marked esp. by sadness, inactivity, difficulty in thinking and concentration, a significant increase or decrease in appetite and time spent sleeping, feelings of dejection and hopelessness, and sometimes suicidal tendencies (3): a reduction in activity, amount, quality, or force (4): a lowering of vitality or functional activity (5): a period of low general economic activity marked esp. by rising levels of unemployment.

Webster's

© Copyright 1980, United Feature Syndicate, Inc. Used by special permission.

So much for the medical approach to depression. Now, when we are unemployed and we say, *"I feel depressed,"* we usually mean it in a somewhat different sense than doctors and psychiatrists do. It is not a medical diagnosis on our part; it is, rather, a metaphor, crying out for translation. When we are unemployed and say, "I'm depressed," we mean: *'I've got the blues.'* We mean: *'I feel sad.'* We mean: *'I'm not my usual self.'* We mean: *'I feel down, because it's hard to stay upbeat or optimistic in this situation.'* We mean: *"I'm depressed."* This feeling of being *depressed* is our emotional response to *that situation*. Once we have found a job, it lifts, and we start feeling happy and upbeat once again. So the question is, when your job-hunt is draggin', how do you avoid feeling blue, or feeling down?

HOW TO AVOID FEELING DEPRESSED WHEN UNEMPLOYMENT DRAGS ON AND ON

Anyone who has a facile or glib answer to this problem, should be avoided like the plague. There is no universal guaranteed-to-work formula, believe me. Every person in this world is unique, and what works for one person, doesn't work for another. Especially, when we are dealing with the emotions.

But after talking to thousands of job-hunters, I do think there are five approaches you can take, that seem to banish, or at least lift, feelings of being depressed, for *most* job-hunters.

Those five approaches deal, in turn, with the: (1) physical; (2) emotional; (3) mental; (4) spiritual; and, finally, (5) activity -- during your time of unemployment. And they are not a kind of smorgasbord, from which you choose the one or two that you like best; you need to do all five, because *each* of the five *contributes* toward the feelings of depression. In this sense, depression is like a river, fed by these five tributaries.

THE PHYSICAL REALM

> Problem: you will likely feel depressed if you are short on your sleep, or your body is otherwise run-down.

Let me repeat: you will almost always feel depressed if you are short on your sleep.

The world never looks bright or happy to people who are *very short of sleep.*

The world never looks bright or happy to people who are *feeling depressed.*

It is therefore easy to confuse the two feeling-states. What you may imagine is depression may in fact be simply the feelings that come from sleep-deprivation. So, please don't take this matter lightly. It has been amazing to me, in the past, to see very-depressed job-hunters turn into happier, more upbeat people, just by catching up on their sleep. Turn off the TV by 10 o'clock, and *go to bed!* It may be difficult to do at first, but in time you'll like the new schedule. And, you'll feel better -- sometimes *much* better.

If you are trying to take this seriously, but are having trouble sleeping, the remedies are pretty well-known by now, but -- with my rich skills at overkill -- let me spell them out, anyway:

5 RULES FOR DEALING WITH SLEEP PROBLEMS

1. Try to keep regular hours, going to bed at the same time every night.

2. Go to bed before midnight, preferably by 11 p.m.

3. Avoid things that might keep you awake, such as caffeine, from dinner to bedtime. Reduce drinking to one drink, or none at all.

4. Use the bed only for sleeping or love-making.

5. If you lie awake for more than 30 minutes, get up and read, or meditate, until you get sleepy.

In addition to the sleep thing, there are other things that need to be done to keep yourself physically fit while unemployed.[5] When I was myself out of work I found it important to:

• get out in sunlight as much as possible, or sit under bright lights in your apartment or house, especially during the winter *(it is a well-known fact that many people get particularly depressed during winter, because they need light, and especially sunlight; the affliction is called S.A.D.);*

---

5. Of course, these principles make sense equally when one has found a job.

• get regular exercise, involving a daily walk;

• drink plenty of water each day *(I try for at least eight glasses of water a day -- this seems silly, but it is often very important);*

• eat balanced meals, with plenty of fiber *(don't pig-out just on junk food in front of the telly; if ever you've thought about cutting down on fats [meats, dairy products], sugar, baked goods, and caffeine, now is an excellent time to do it);*

• eliminate sugar as much as possible from the diet;[6]

• take supplementary vitamins daily *(no matter how often doctors and nutritionists may tell you that you already get plenty, just from your daily food);*

• and all that other stuff that our mothers always told us to do.

Physical also means *physical space* around you, in your home or apartment -- which is important because it often mirrors how we feel about ourselves. If our physical environment looks like a disaster area, that in itself can make us depressed. If you've always vowed you wanted to learn to live neater, here is a simple way: each time you handle a *thing,* take it all the way to its destination; don't put it down, thinking that you will deal with it later. Do it now.

e.g., when you take clothes off, either put them in the clothes basket or hang them back up; don't just drop them on the floor.

e.g., when you finish eating, put the dishes where they are to be washed, and put the food back in the refrigerator.

e.g., if you get a screwdriver out, to fix a screw that's dropped out of something, when you're done, take the screwdriver all the way back to the tool chest or wherever its final destination is. Etc., etc., etc.

When things are put away in a timely fashion, neatness will start to appear in your physical environment; it will help lift your spirits immensely. Of course, if you were already keeping your place as neat as a pin, you will ignore this whole thing, and forget I ever mentioned a word, won't you?

---

6. The sugar/depression connection is a matter that has been well-established, and were I feeling depressed the first thing I would eliminate from my diet would be sugar. See *Sugar Blues,* by William Dufty. Warner Books, Inc., 1271 Avenue of the Americas, New York, NY 10020. 1993. Available in bookstores, health-food stores, and your local library.

THE EMOTIONS

Problem: after you are 'let go,' you will likely feel depressed
if you are still carrying around a lot of anger, expressed or
suppressed, about *what they did to you.*

Our instinctive first reaction to the fact that we were laid-off,
fired, terminated, summarily dismissed, or made redundant --
especially *after all these years* -- is usually anger. Sometimes fierce,
hot anger. Sometimes just a kind of dull, cold disillusionment
about the workplace and how it treats people.

Need I mention that we would probably drop our anger
quickly if it were relatively easy to find another job, doing basically the same thing at the same level of responsibility and at the
same salary in the same town. But, given our Neanderthal job-
hunting system, it is not. It is not easy to find such jobs even
when they exist. Hence, much of the blame for our anger should
lie at the door of this so-called job-hunting *'system'* -- which leaves
us feeling devalued and discarded by our society for weeks,
months, and sometimes years. Our anger is justified and understandable, in the beginning.

But if it keeps on and on, then that's another story. And if
our anger is directed not against the job-hunting system in this
country, but against our ex-employers, that's the beginning of
trouble. I see this often, as people who have been let go discuss
the place where they used to work: *'I'll never forgive them. They've
ruined the rest of my life.'*

Of course, the only way our former employers can actually
ruin the rest of our lives is if *we* help them out, by holding on to
our anger forever. This *will* wreck the rest of our lives. I have
seen it happen many many times in the lives of the unemployed.

We forget an ancient truth: that when anger becomes a burning fire within us, that fire gradually consumes not its object,
but its host. Certainly it doesn't achieve its desired effect upon
the objects of our anger. They are sleeping soundly, while it is
we who are lying awake at night. No, anger consumes its host
not its object, and it does this by giving birth within us to
irritability, withdrawal, loneliness, broken relationships, divorce
(often), and sometimes (rarely) suicide.

During this process, the anger very commonly segues into depression. It has struck me forcibly over the years that these two emotions often seem to be reverse sides of the same coin. It is as though *anger/depression* were an energy, which at first is directed outward toward others, but then like a boomerang eventually turns back against the self. This *feels* like depression, but it is born of the anger.

So, if you feel depressed as unemployment stretches on, it is helpful to consider the possibility that anger that may lie beneath that depression. Sometimes that anger is immediate and recent, as derived from being 'let go,' etc. Other times, this immediate anger triggers slumbering anger from the past, sometimes the far past, as in our childhood.[7]

In either case, dealing with that anger often takes away the depressed feelings. People who have successfully done this, cite the following steps:

5 RULES FOR DEALING WITH ANGER

1. Your basic need is to face forward, toward the future, not backward, toward the past. You only have enough energy for one or the other, not both. Staying rooted in your anger keeps you rooted facing toward the past.

2. The way to get out of your anger is to face it, openly and honestly. Talk it out, with a good friend, or write a letter to yourself about it; but do not act it out in real life. Do not write to, or threaten, the objects of your anger. That way lies trouble of major dimensions.

3. If this doesn't help you let go of your anger, seek out a good family therapist, whom friends recommend.

---

7. For help with *this,* see Wayne Muller's *Legacy of the Heart: The Spiritual Advantages of a Painful Childhood.* 1992. Fireside, Simon & Schuster, Order Dept., 200 Old Tappan Road, Old Tappan, NJ 07675.

88

4. If you have a lot of angry energy, so that you feel you'd like to punch someone, punch a pillow instead. A big pillow. Or a mattress. Get the angry energy out of your system, harmlessly. Daily, if necessary.

5. If you are a woman or man of faith, hand the anger over to God, and ask That Higher Power to help you set your face toward the future.

THE MENTAL

Problem: you will likely feel depressed if you view this experience of being laid-off, and having to spend a long time finding a new job, as essentially a random, senseless and meaningless event in your life.

Let us begin here with a riddle:

This is a glass containing fruit-juice. Is it half-empty, or is it half-full?

Most people have heard this riddle, but that doesn't mean it is well-understood. On its surface it seems to say that there are different ways of looking at a situation.

But that is not its major point. Its major point is that you *can change* how you view it. You can go from viewing it as *half-empty* to viewing it as *half-full*.

There is a habit of mind that is deadly, which is to spend much of our time each day, every day, brooding about what is *wrong*. What is wrong with people, what is wrong with our life, what is wrong with our situation, what is wrong with anything and everything. In our conversation with friends or family, we

focus our attention on what we didn't like about the conversation . . . or *them*. In a movie or play, we focus on what we
didn't like about it. When we travel, we focus on what we didn't
like about each place we visited. This habit of mind focusses
always on other people's failings, on what is not the way we want
it to be, on what is (from our point of view) missing. It calls
every glass, and every situation, *half-empty* -- focussing on what is
lost, or never was. On the other hand, *half-full* focusses on what
you have, on what still is, and is good. The first habit of mind
leads to complaint and bitterness; the second habit of mind
leads to gratitude and joy. If you would avoid getting depressed,
it is *crucial* to look at how you think, and what you focus your
attention on, all day long. It is crucial to avoid the deadly habit
of mind alluded to, above. As Baltasar Gracián put it,[8] "Get used
to the failings of your friends, family, and acquaintances. . . ."

Depression arises, in part, from a sense of powerlessness.
However, as the riddle reminds us, we *always* have power -- the
power to change how we view a situation, and thus to alter that
situation. Let me give an example.

At a medical symposium which I attended many years ago, a
doctor was reviewing the puzzle of healing. Two patients, he
said, of the same age and with the same medical history, would
undergo the same operation. Yet, one would heal rapidly, while
the other's healing was long delayed. Doctors had no idea why
this was so. They set up a study at a major New York hospital, to
see if they could identify what factors explained this difference.[9]
Using a computer, they decided to compare *everything* about the
patients who healed quickly, with those same factors -- or to be
more exact, the *absence* of those same factors -- in the patients
who healed slowly. And so they began to ask the computer their
questions.

Were those who healed quickly characterized by *optimism*,
while those who healed slowly were not? No, said the computer;
that wasn't the answer.

8. Baltasar Gracián, *The Art of Worldly Wisdom: A Pocket Oracle*. Doubleday/Currency, Publishers. 1992. Baltasar was a Spanish writer who lived in the 1600s.

9. I have, in the intervening years, tried to go back and identify that study, but have been basically unsuccessful in this search. I am left only with a clear memory of *the findings*, as they were reported by that doctor at the symposium.

Were those who healed quickly characterized by *some kind of religious faith,* while those who healed slowly were not? No, said the computer; that wasn't the answer.

And so it went.

What the answer finally turned out to be was this: those who healed quickly felt there was some meaning to every event that happened to them in their lives, even if they did not understand what that meaning was, at the present time; while those who healed slowly felt that most events which happened to them had no meaning; they were merely random or senseless. Hence, if both patients were being operated on for cancer, the one who viewed the cancer as having some meaning in the larger scheme of things, for their life, healed quickly; while the one who viewed the cancer as a senseless and meaningless interruption in their life, healed slowly. *Everything depended on how they viewed the situation.*

Surely you see how this applies to such events as being terminated. Being fired or terminated is rarely the outrageous, meaningless event that it at first seems to be. It may begin that way; but it does not end that way. You have the power to shape it, by how you choose to view it.

The last time I was fired, the firing occurred shortly before noon, and at 3 o'clock that same afternoon I had an appointment with my dentist, to have some drilling done. *'What a wonderful day this is turning out to be!'* I thought, with rich irony. Anyway, he was a wise man, on in years, and when I told him of my plight, he said some words I have never forgotten: "Someday," he said, "you will say this was the best thing that ever happened to you. I don't expect you to believe a word I am saying now, but wait and see. I have seen this happen in so many people's lives, that I know it will come true for you." Strangely enough, he turned out to be absolutely right. And he helped shape how I viewed that event. I now say, that firing was indeed the best thing that ever happened to me, for it caused me to rethink my whole life and what I wanted to contribute to the world. Thus, it proved to be a great blessing, as light was born out of the darkness of unemployment.

I now believe that every event in our lives has meaning, or can be given meaning, even though we don't always know what that meaning is, at the time. If this is how *you* view your life --

including the experience of being laid-off -- then that depression which arises from a sense of meaninglessness will not afflict you.

Spelling out more specifically what this means, we can state it in terms of our usual five rules (in this case, affirmations):[10]

5 RULES FOR DEALING WITH MEANINGLESSNESS

1. Your life is like a tapestry, being woven by God and history on an enchanted loom. Every bobble of the shuttle has meaning, every thread is important.

2. As a thread in that tapestry every event in your life has some meaning and purpose, for the larger pattern, even if you cannot see what this is, at the moment.

3. You will discover that meaning more quickly if you direct what thoughts you focus your mind on, during your time of unemployment.

4. To aid this, make a list of all the things you enjoy about your life, even while unemployed – the simple pleasures: working with your hands, breathing fresh air, enjoying beautiful music, etc.

5. When you are having any dark times, sit down and write out stories. Stories about your life past, when you were most enjoying yourself. Write down what meaning you now see in those stories. This will increase your confidence that there is meaning in your present story, now unfolding.

---

10. The reference to the *loom*, which follows, comes by analogy to Sir Charles Sherrington's description of the brain: *"It is as if the Milky Way entered upon some cosmic dance. Swiftly the brain becomes an enchanted loom where millions of flashing shuttles weave a dissolving pattern, always a meaningful pattern though never an abiding one; a shifting harmony of subpatterns."*

To rule #4, above, we might add: conversation, cuddling, drives in the country, exercise, praying, helping others, singing, sitting in front of a fireplace, thinking, etc.

Ah, yes, *thinking.* Unemployment is a wonderful time for *thinking.* You've got time to think, contemplate, look at your life, decide on maybe some new directions, etc. In other words, it can be for you a time of philosophical or spiritual renewal.

If you need help there are useful books you can take out of your library, or procure at your bookstore.[11]

THE SPIRITUAL

> Problem: you will likely feel depressed if you believe in God, but feel that He[12] has somehow deserted you in this crisis.

There are about 6% of my readers who would probably prefer I omitted all mention of the spiritual, in a book on job-hunting. I am sensitive to those feelings, but if we are going to discuss depression, there is no way to omit it. According to Gallup Polls conducted since 1960, about 94% of the population in this country believe in *some* concept of God.[13] When they find themselves summarily dismissed from a job that they may have held for *years,* many find their faith in God a bulwark of strength that helps them through this very difficult period, daily.

Others, however, are often plunged into a depressing crisis of faith. The common form of the questioning, when it comes, is:

---

11. Especially helpful is Barbara Ann Kipfer's *14,000 things to be happy about.* Workman Publishing Company, 708 Broadway, New York, NY 10003. 1990.

12. I know there are those, in our time, who do not like the male pronoun applied to God. I am very sensitive to sexist language, but here we are in a different realm. *All* language about God is metaphor, anyway, and because I grew up on the Old Testament (and the New), I myself prefer *this* metaphor, grounded as it is in some 4,000 years of usage. You can always alter it, in your mind, as you read, if you wish.

13. Reported in George Gallup's *The People's Religion: American Faith in the 90s.* Macmillan & Co. 1989. In addition to reporting that 94% of us believe in God, the Gallup polls also discovered that 90% of us pray, 88% of us believe God loves us, and 33% of us report we have had a life-changing religious experience; and these figures have remained pretty unvarying during the last thirty years of opinion polls conducted by the Gallup Organization.

How could God let this happen to me, if He truly loved me? Many of the unemployed decide from this that there must be no God, or at least not One who cares what happens to them. They conclude then that they must face the future resolutely alone, relying on their own strength, and their own strength alone, to carry them through their period of unemployment.

Needless to say, this period is often far more difficult than they had supposed it would be, and their resolution to bear it all by themselves often flounders. They may find their own strength inadequate for the task. They are left feeling very alone. Natu-

rally, a feeling of despair, or depression follows, like the night the day.

What are we to say to all this? What is the remedy when our depression has -- even in part -- a spiritual origin? The remedy, apart from discarding our faith, is obviously that we need to put some energy into rethinking that faith on a higher level.

I said earlier that 94% of the people claim they have *some* concept of God. But what unemployment, or any crisis, often reveals is how poor and inadequate that concept is. It is inadequate because it holds God responsible for *everything*, and makes no allowance for the free will and freedom of choice that He has given to His creatures. The wonder is not that it breaks

down under the pain of unemployment, but that it didn't break down sooner.

Well, then, to what higher concept might we press? Let's try this: imagine that you have, in your dining room, a fine wooden chair, which one day has its back broken off completely -- I mean, into *smithereens* -- by someone in the house. You run down the street, to call a carpenter who lives nearby. He comes and examines the chair. He pronounces the back *unrepairable*. "But," he says, "I think I could make a fine wooden stool out of the remainder of the chair, for you." And so he spends much time, shaping, polishing and sanding it, and fashioning out of the former chair a fine stool, more resplendent than anything you have ever dreamed. He inlays it with gold, and soon it is the treasure of your house.

Let me underline a couple of key points in this parable. First of all, the carpenter did not break the chair. Someone else did that. But the carpenter came quickly, and with all his art and powers, to see if he could not only repair it, but make of it something even finer than it had been before. And, he labored mightily, to that end.

And so, a higher concept of God holds that God does not create our unemployment or any of the calamities in our life -- *that* responsibility belongs to our fellow human beings. *They* are the ones who create our calamities. *But,* God -- like the carpenter -- comes quickly, with all His art and powers, to see if He can not only repair our life, but make of it something even finer than it had been before: not a physical thing, like the stool inlaid with gold, but a work on the spiritual level that corresponds to the stool, in splendor. And He labors mightily, within our mind and heart and spirit, toward that end.

If unemployment pushes us thus to rethink our faith, we should not only find our depression lifting, but also our self-esteem. Here are some helpful rules -- worth pasting up on your bathroom mirror:

5 RULES FOR DEALING WITH A SENSE OF ABANDONMENT

1. The 94% of us who believe in God usually need a larger conception of God, as we face each new crisis in our life. If you've got an old faith hanging in the closet of your mind, now would be a good time to take it out and dust it off.

2. Hold high the truth that God does not save us from hard times. Hard times come to believer and non-believer, alike.

3. On the other hand, God does not cause us to go into hard times (our fellow human beings do that).

4. But God is always in the middle of those times with us because He has promised to be with us, in all times.

His role is that of Sustainer, Strengthener and Rescuer. You should seek that Sustaining, that Strength, daily, even hourly, in prayer, especially when you start feeling that you just can't go on.

5. If you can't feel God's presence during hard times, that does not mean anything. Feelings many times fail to correspond to reality. We can be in a fog, as we say, that obscures our vision. Do not give such feelings more weight than they deserve.

To feel abandoned -- by God or man or woman -- while you are unemployed is *extremely* depressing. Everything you can do to avoid that feeling of being abandoned, will help you greatly in 'chasing away the blues.' You start with your faith in God, you continue on with the people around you: family, relatives, friends and acquaintances. If these last leave you feeling rather alone and unsupported, you should heed the advice in Chapter 4 about seeking, or forming, a support group with others who are unemployed.[14]

ACTIVITY

> Problem: you will likely feel depressed if you only have one goal for your time of unemployment.

Back in the days when you were working, suppose you decided to take a quick vacation with your spouse, or partner, or friend. You weren't quite sure what you wanted the vacation to accomplish for you. You thought that maybe you wanted to get a good rest, and not do a lick of work while you were at your vacation hideaway. On the other hand, you thought that maybe you wanted to catch up on some stuff at work that has been dogging you for weeks. You weren't sure. So, you took the work along, but determined you wouldn't feel guilty if you came back with it absolutely untouched.

Now that was going to be a rewarding vacation for you, as you knew even before you set out. Why? Because you had two alternative goals for the vacation, and *one* of them was bound to be achieved. *Either* you were going to get a good rest, *or* you were going to get some work accomplished. You couldn't lose.

Half of our misery *in our goal-driven lives* arises from our failure to thus have two alternative goals for a particular period. Again and again, we set only one goal. And then, if we fail to achieve it, as is so often the case, given the vagaries of human nature, we get depressed.

---

14. Such groups as *Experience Unlimited, Forty-Plus,* job-clubs, classes at your local Employment Office, or at your local Chamber of Commerce, etc.

For further details, see Cathy Beyer/Doris Pike/Loretta McGovern's *Surviving Unemployment: A Family Handbook for Weathering Hard Times.* 1993. Henry Holt and Company, Inc., 115 West 18th St., New York, NY 10011.

It is hardly a wonder, then, that when we get fired, sacked, terminated, or whatever, we approach unemployment in the same manner. We set ourselves only one goal for the period while we are unemployed: to find a *(meaningful)* job.

When we don't find a job -- *right away, at least* -- we get depressed. Real depressed. It is therefore important to face the activity problem here that may be contributing to that depression, and to fix it. How to fix it is obvious:

> You need to have more than one goal for your time of unemployment.

© Copyright 1981. Reprinted with permission of Universal Press Syndicate. All rights reserved.

You need to define this period of unemployment in some such terms as this: *"My goals during this time of unemployment are: (1) to find a good job; and (2)..."* Aye, there's the rub; what should (2) be? (Or, not to be.)

The most important characteristic of this second goal must be that it is *achievable*. It does our self-esteem no good, after all, to have two goals if we then fail to achieve either one of them. The second one *must* be achievable.

Certain goals which might at first suggest themselves to us, are therefore disqualified by this consideration: for example, a goal like determining to use this period of unemployment to lose 40 pounds permanently. That *is* a nice, admirable goal, except we all know by now that diets often have a yo-yo effect -- down, up; off again, on again. Consequently, very iffy goals such

as this may only increase your depressed feelings, when you
can't find a job *and* you can't lose weight, either.

What kind of goals, then, *are* achievable? Studying successful
job-hunters for some twenty or more years, it has become clear
to me that there are several, which vary in appropriateness
depending on how long you've been out of work. I'll summarize
them accordingly.

You should take the time-divisions on the following file cards
with a grain of salt. *Obviously,* if your money dictates that your
job-hunt *has to* proceed much faster, then you will want to speed
up all the time divisions on these cards, accordingly -- like, one
month, two months, three months, and four months.

IF YOU'VE BEEN OUT OF WORK TWO MONTHS OR LESS

Your goals for this time of unemployment are that you
are going to use this time (1) to find a (meaningful) job;
and (2) to work on what kind of person you are, and
what kind of person you would like to be.

Take an inventory, first of all, of all that you have already:
your skills (see Chapter 9), your knowledge (Chapter 10),
your values, your worldly goods, your spiritual blessings,
etc.

Then write out the kind of person you would like to
be, and what you would like to do with your family, friends,
etc. Write out a plan for starting to do this. Do a lot of
meditating on what you have written, preferably outdoors
amongst nature, or indoors with some of your favorite
music playing.

Does *a person who has no job* still matter, in the larger scheme
of things? That is the question which plagues many of us, when
we have been out of work for anything up to two months. If
that's the case with you, doubtless along about now you could
stand some reassurance that you still matter as a person. Doing
the paper-and-pen exercises mentioned on the file card, can
contribute *immensely* toward that end.

The truth is, who we are is more important than what we do. And who we are is: someone designed to be a blessing to this planet Earth.

IF YOU'VE BEEN OUT OF WORK FOUR MONTHS OR MORE

Your goals for this time of unemployment are to use this time (1) to find a (meaningful) job, and (2) volunteering to help others less fortunate than you are.

It is important to preserve four weekdays (say, Monday, Tuesday, Thursday, Friday) for your job-hunt, but one weekday (say, Wednesday) can be given to the work of helping others who are less fortunate.

You can volunteer your services:

- at places which feed or give shelter to the homeless;
- at places which give help to those afflicted with AIDS;
- at places which help battered women or abused children;
- at places which work with the disabled; and
- at places which work with the elderly or the dying.

If you have been out of work for four months or more, you will likely be hungering for some way in which to reassure yourself that you are still making a meaningful contribution to society. Volunteering one day a week can accomplish this. According to the Bureau of Labor Statistics, at least one person out of five, 16 years or older, does some volunteer work, without pay, during a typical year. It doesn't matter whether you are employed or unemployed. It's a way of occupying your time meaningfully, helping others, and incidentally picking up some new skills.

The crucial aspect of this particular activity is that it be work which puts you *face-to-face* with those who are in need, rather than doing administrative services at a desk or in an office. The latter is important, but it is not the kind of engagement that you most need at this juncture.

Your goal here is to avoid self-pity, and depression, by seeking greater compassion for those who are in need -- and particularly those who *(as the phrase has it)* are less fortunate than you. Incidentally, if your own particular misfortunes are making you feel there is no one in the whole world who is as bad off as you are, believe me, there are *always* others less fortunate than you are. As the old saying puts it, *"I cried for a lack of shoes, until I saw a man who had no feet. . . ."*[15]

---

15. If you're *really* feeling sorry for yourself, the best restorative is to turn off the TV, and sit down and read stories of others who have had a lot to deal with on their plate, in life, but refused to be beaten down by adversity. Such books as:

Diane Cole's *After Great Pain: A New Life Emerges* (Summit Books, 1992)

Arnold R. Beisser's *Flying Without Wings: Personal Reflections on Disability*. Doubleday, 1540 Broadway, New York, NY 10036. 1989. As one wise man said about his disability: "Every disabled person has the choice of either 'crying the blues' about their disability every day of their life, or realistically acknowledging what they have to do in order to have a successful, productive life." Beisser has ultimately opted for the latter, though it was not an easy battle, as this book reveals.

John Callahan's *Don't Worry, He Won't Get Far on Foot: The Autobiography of a Dangerous Man*. Random House, 201 E. 50th, 22nd Floor, New York, NY 10022. 1990. John became a quadriplegic at the age of 21, due to an automobile accident. However, he has a wicked sense of humor, and so has become a famous cartoonist. This book is John's autobiography, and it is graphic, funny, touching, and irreverent. Arnold Beisser (above) wrote a most relevant passage in his book, apropos of such 'disabled humor' as John's: "The able-bodied person is likely to be appalled by 'disabled humor' and find nothing funny at all about it. But . . . tragedy and comedy are but two aspects of what is real, and whether we see the tragic or the humorous is a matter of perspective." John's perspective is clearly that he prefers to see the humorous amid the tragedy.

    If you need more ideas of places where you might volunteer your services than are listed on the file card above, I refer you to the footnote below.[16] One important word of caution here: do not get so engrossed in this secondary goal for your time of unemployment, that you forget/neglect your primary goal: that of finding a job. The rule is: four days a week on your primary goal -- job-hunting; one day a week on your secondary goal -- volunteering.[17] You should stick like glue to that kind of division of your time. Let nothing tempt you to give four days a week to the volunteering, and only one day a week to your job-hunt,

---

16. Your first lead is to inquire whether or not there is an 'umbrella' volunteer organization in your community. Ask your county information center or social services department.

    Your second resource is/are the Yellow Pages in your local telephone book, to find individual places which may have paid staff, but also welcome volunteers. Look under "Social Service Organizations," "Handicapped & Disabled Services," "Hospitals," etc. for ideas. Also, your local churches or synagogues may know what facilities there are for helping those in need, where you might volunteer.

    Your third resource -- useful for ideas of *kinds* of places you might locate in your own community -- is that of books, which you search for in your local library, and if nothing is there, in your local bookstore. You will find such titles as the following (you can order them by mail if they are not in your local library); new titles keep appearing regularly:

    Golden Opportunities: A Volunteer Guide for Americans Over 50, by Andrew Carroll. 1994. Peterson's, P.O. Box 2123, Princeton NJ 08543-2123. 800-338-3282. While written for seniors, this is useful for all ages, as it is essentially an update of an earlier (now-out-of-print) book called *Volunteer USA.*

    The National Service Guide, by the editors of ACCESS. 1994. ACCESS, Networking in the Public Interest, 50 Beacon St., 4th Floor, Boston, MA 02108, 1-617-720-5627. Fax No.: 1-617-720-1318. Over 60 pages of volunteer opportunities and listings, listing hundreds of resources. $5.

    For our Canadian readers there is:

    Directory of Volunteer Opportunities, edited by Ellen Shenk, Career Information Centre, University of Waterloo, Waterloo, Ontario, N2L 3G1 Canada. 1986.

    For our older readers there is:

    Volunteerism and Older Adults, by Mary K. Kouri, ABC-CLIO, Inc., 130 Cremona Dr., P.O. Box 1911, Santa Barbara CA 93116-1911. 1990.

    You may also want to look at books about social service careers -- *if* they list places where you would be working directly with those in need, rather than doing administrative, legislative, or managerial work. Such books include:

    Good Works: A Guide to Careers in Social Change, 4th ed., edited by Jessica Cowan, Preface by Ralph Nader. Barricade Books Inc., Publisher, 61 Fourth Ave., New York, NY 10003; distributed by Publishers Group West, 4065 Hollis, Emeryville, CA 94608. 1991. It has a topical index, a geographical index, and an alphabetical index.

17. The weekend is for leisure, re-creation, sleep catchup, time with your family, friends, doing job-hunting homework, etc.

unless you have enough income to last for a long time, *and* the volunteering turns out to be the work you most love doing, in the whole world.

Otherwise, your *main* goal for this period -- finding meaningful, paid work -- still requires the lion's share of your time, no matter *how long* you've been out of work.

IF YOU'VE BEEN OUT OF WORK SIX MONTHS OR MORE

Your goals for this time of unemployment are to use this time (1) to find a (meaningful) job; and (2) to enroll at your local community college, or the adult education program in your town (if it has one) in order to learn something new.

This something new will be either:

• a subject that intrigues you, from past reading in newspapers or magazines; or
• a subject which upgrades your skills in your present (interrupted) career; or
• a subject which gives you skills or knowledge related to a possible new career that you are thinking about going into.

In a poll reported in *USA Today*,[18] where people were asked what they would do if they won one million dollars, 20% of them said they would go back to school. So, apparently this is a very common wish. It often gets lost, however, in the time-pressures we are under, when holding down a full-time job.

But, during this current period of unemployment, you are not holding down a full-time job, so now is a wonderful time to go back to school, and fulfill that longtime wish. Attending school is also a great way to keep your mind occupied with something other than your current misfortune.

---

18. 7/25/89.

One important word of caution here, as earlier: do not get so engrossed in this secondary goal for your time of unemployment, that you forget/neglect your primary goal, that of finding a job. The rule is the same as earlier: four days a week on goal #1 -- job-hunting; one day a week on goal #2 -- attending a class or two. Let nothing tempt you to give four days a week to school, and only one day a week to your job-hunt, unless you have enough income to last for the duration *and* you have decided this would be a good time to go back to school and get retrained for a new career. If that is the case, first read Chapters 9 and 10 very carefully, *please.*

Otherwise, your *main* goal for this period -- finding meaningful, paid work -- still requires the lion's share of your time, no matter *how long* you've been out of work. As far as your second goal is concerned, here, it should be a class, or two at the most, that you are dealing with, at this juncture. Agreed? Okay. If there is a nearby campus, go visit it, get their catalog, and see what they offer. If you can't afford the big college or university, look at a community college or local adult education program in your community.

If money is a problem, you should *always* talk to the Financial Aid office on the campus that interests you, to see what accommodations they can make to the fact that you are unemployed.[19]

If you are living out in the middle of *nowhere,* and there isn't any kind of adult education facility for a hundred miles around, you may want to consider a correspondence course *(now frequently called 'off-campus study program')* from some college that offers one.[20] (Even if you live in a metropolis, you may like this idea, though since the job-hunt is so often a lonely enterprise, I myself would elect to go sit in a classroom with other people.

---

19. Also see *(Bear's Guide to) Finding Money for College: The not-well-understood sources of unconventional and ordinary financial help and how to pursue them,* by John B. Bear and Mariah P. Bear. Ten Speed Press, Box 7123, Berkeley, CA 94707. 1993, revised ed.

20. The best books, by a long shot, about how to find a good correspondence course, are John Bear's. There is *Bear's Guide to Earning College Degrees Non-Traditionally,* available directly from the author, John Bear, P.O. Box 826, Benicia, CA 94510, 1-800-835-8535. 1992. Cost: $23. There is also a shorter version of it, John Bear's *College Degrees by Mail.* Ten Speed Press, Box 7123, Berkeley, CA 94707. 1991. $12.95. John's books deal with taking courses, as well as getting degrees. He covers *everything,* including schools overseas that offer correspondence degrees to Americans and Canadians, how to get a degree while in prison, and other subjects nobody but John would think of.

Anything you can do to make the job-hunt period of your life less lonely, is to be prized.)

IF YOU'VE BEEN OUT OF WORK EIGHT MONTHS OR MORE

Okay, this is beginning to drag on forever. You still want two goals for this period of unemployment, but now after eight months you're thinking they should be equal goals, rather than a primary and a secondary one.

The first remains the same as always, to find meaningful work, doing what you've done before. But the second goal is now equal: to consider some things you've never tried before: moving, starting your own business, etc. And that's what the next chapter is all about.

SUMMARY

When it looks like your job-hunt is going to stretch on for quite some time, you need to figure out how to avoid getting depressed. 'The blues,' sadness, discouragement, dejection, apathy, or feelings of being 'down,' all add up to the same thing: "I'm depressed."

Unemployment depression (*or, as some have called it, 'recession depression'*) is like a kind of phantom octopus, which has five tentacles: physical, emotional, mental, spiritual, and activity. If you would ward off feelings of depression, you must tackle all five, rather than just hacking away at one or two causes of it. As we know from studying thousands of job-hunters, the physical contribution toward depression, is the state of being very tired,

© Copyright 1980, Universal Press Syndicate.
All rights reserved. Used by special permission.

and out of shape. The emotional source of depression is stored-up anger. The mental source is the idea of meaninglessness. The spiritual source of depression resides in feelings of abandonment. And the activity side of our being contributes to our depression when we have only one goal, and that one goal is getting completely frustrated.

You tackle depression while you are out of work by staying physically fit, and rested, by getting the anger out of your system, by believing in the meaning of every event, by strengthening whatever relationship you have with God, and by setting at least two goals for your period of unemployment, only one of which should be that of finding meaningful work.

I do want to reiterate, however, that if you attack depression on all five fronts and it doesn't yield, you should immediately get yourself to a doctor or therapist, for further help. There are drugs and medicines, much as you may hate the idea, and there is also psychotherapy. The major point I'm making is that you should fight against accepting depression as though it were an inevitable and permanent part of your life. It isn't.

On the other hand, it will not do to view depression simply as a dark intruder into your life. When it arises in response to a crisis, like finding yourself unemployed, *and only then,* it often is a messenger bearing a gift. The gift is the announcement that the old center, around which your life used to revolve, is no longer sufficient. The depression is often a feeling of having abandoned the old center, but not yet finding the new. It's like an astronaut's journey from circling one planet to another. It's while you're *out there,* in between, that you feel depressed.

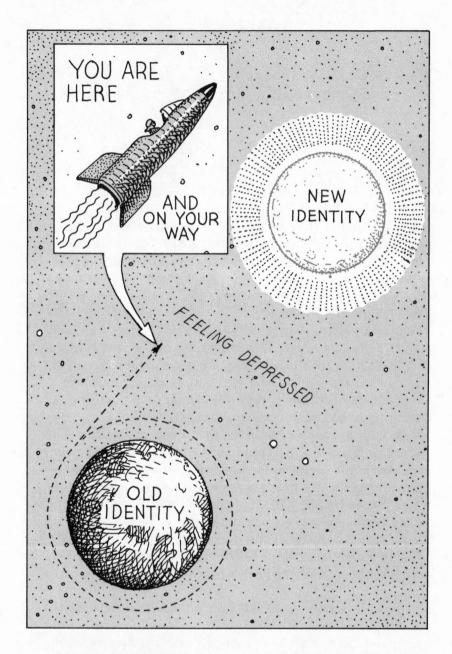

Hence, the depression is a wake-up call to your soul, telling you not just to stay out there, in the ozone. It is time to move on, time to look for a new destination, and find a new center, time to rethink your lifestyle, the way you typically do things, the goals you want to achieve, and the values (like honesty) that you want your life to enshrine.

You can use unemployment well, face the future rather than the past, and so, rebuild your life -- *if* you reject any picture you may have of yourself as passive, pitiable martyr, and opt instead for a picture of yourself as one who is actively at work, rebuilding your life, on new and stronger foundations.

Every human drama -- even *unemployment* -- is ultimately a drama about the survival of the spirit. Even in an unpredictable world. Even in a life that you wish were otherwise. You can be joyful in your daily living, even after considering all the facts. Your spirit *will* survive, and life can be even more triumphant than before.

Why should we be
in such desperate haste to succeed,
and in such desperate enterprise?
If a man does not keep pace
with his companions,
perhaps it is because he hears
a different drummer.
Let him step to the music
which he hears,
however measured
or far away.[1]

> Henry David Thoreau
> *Walden*, Chapter XVII, conclusion

---

1. I hope our readers will forgive Henry for using the masculine pronoun throughout. He wrote in terms of the sensitivities of *his* day, not *ours*.

CHAPTER SIX

New Ways to Work: Alternative Strategies When You Can't Find A Job (Or You Want to Try Something New)

Chapter 6

© 1982 NEA, Inc. Used by special permission.

YOU'LL LIKE THIS JOB, EXCEPT EVERY NOW AND THEN, WHEN THEY DUMP A LOT OF PAPER WORK ON YOU.

TEMPORARY WORK

In these difficult times, many many employers are cutting their staff to the bone. Trouble is, as time goes on, some extra work may then come their way, work which their reduced staff can't keep up with.

At that point, employers won't usually hire back the staff they cut, but they will turn to what are called "Temporary Help" agencies, for either full- or part-time work. If you are having trouble finding a long-term full-time job, you certainly want to go register at one or more of these agencies.

They may find for you: a full-time job that lasts for a number of days or weeks or even months.

Or they may find for you: a part-time job that lasts for a number of days or weeks or even months.

In the old days, temporary agencies were solely for clerical workers and secretarial help. But the field has seen an explosion of services in recent years -- according to the U.S. Bureau of Labor Statistics, temporary or part-time workers now number over 35 million, and represent 29% of the total civilian labor force.

Now there are temporary agencies *(at least in the larger cities)* for many different occupations. In your city you may find temporary agencies for: accountants, industrial workers, assemblers, drivers, mechanics, construction people, engineering people, management/executives, nannies (for young and old), health care/dental/medical people, legal specialists, insurance specialists, sales/marketing people, underwriting professionals, financial services, and the like, as well as for the more obvious specialties: data processing, secretarial, and office services. See your local phone book.

You will find the agencies listed in the Yellow Pages of your local phone book, under *Employment–Temporary*. Their listing or their ads will usually indicate what their specialities are.

If you want additional advice on how to use temporary agencies, new books are appearing every week, it seems. See your local library or bookstore; in desperation, order directly from the publisher.[2]

You realize, of course, that as with all employment agencies, there are many more job-hunters who list themselves with such agencies, than there are employers who come there looking for help. So, this cannot be your only strategy for finding work. But it is certainly worth a try.

---

2. Deborahann Smith, *Temp: How to Survive and Thrive in the World of Temporary Employment.* 1994. Shambhala Publications, Inc., Horticultural Hall, 300 Massachusetts Avenue, Boston, MA 02115.

Peggy O'Connell Justice, *The Temp Track: Make One of the Hottest Job Trends of the 90's Work for You.* 1994. Peterson's Guides,

Karen Mendenhall, *Making The Most of the Temporary Employment Market.* 1993. Betterway Books, 1507 Dana Avenue, Cincinnati, OH 45207.

Universal's *Job Guide: Your complete guide to finding temporary, part-time, contract and casual employment.* 1st ed., 1993. Universal Magazines, 64 Talavera Road, North Ryde 2113. 02 805 0399. Australia's guide to temporary work. A very detailed directory.

William M. Lewis and Nancy H. Molloy, *How To Choose and Use Temporary Services.* 1991. Amacom, a division of American Management Association, 135 West 50th St., New York, NY 10020. This is a book written for employers, but has useful points of view and directories that job-hunters may find helpful, so long as they keep in mind that the book was published in 1991.

You can increase the likelihood of the agency linking you up with a job, if you help them a little. For example, if you are in environmental engineering, and you know your field well, you can increase your chances of getting employment through a particular agency by compiling *for them* a list of the companies in your field, together with (if you know it) the name of the contact person there.[3] The temporary agency will do what it always does, initiate calls to those companies, soliciting their business; and if they uncover a vacancy, the odds are very great that it will be your name which is put forth for that job there.

PART-TIME WORK

If the temporary agencies never call, and you still can't find any full-time job, your next strategy for finding work is to look for part-time work. While there are many *involuntary* part-time workers these days[4] there are also many *voluntary* part-time workers. They don't *want* to work full-time. Period. End of story. And you of course may be among them.

But suppose you do want full-time work. Often you can put a couple of part-time jobs together, so as to make the equivalent of full-time work.

U.S. Statistics

Currently, the number of people having two careers, businesses, or jobs *(one or both of them part-time)* is at least 50% higher than it was ten years ago. This year one out of every 16 workers, will be holding down two or more jobs. That comes to 7,500,000 people. Half of them are holding down two part-time jobs just because they need to *make ends meet.* The other half are holding down two part-time jobs because they *want* to.

In some cases, you may even prefer this to one full-time job. Perhaps you feel yourself to be multi-talented and/or perhaps you have a couple of very different interests. You can sometimes find a part-time job in one of your fields of interest and a

---

3. I am indebted to one of our readers, Tathyana Pshevlozky, for this idea.

4. Involuntary part-time workers are those who want a full-time job, can't find one, so take a part-time job until a full-time job comes along.

second part-time job in another one of your fields of interest, thus allowing you to use *all* your favorite skills and interests -- in a way that no one full-time job might be able to do.[5]

You can put together two part-time jobs in a variety of ways. One can be a job where you work for someone else, the other can be your own business or consultancy -- which I discuss later in this chapter.

One can be a job advertised in a newspaper (or agency) or *online*, and the other can be a job that you create for yourself by approaching someone you'd really like to work with (or for), and asking what kind of help they need.

One can be a job with someone you never met before, and the other can be a job with your father, mother, brother, sister, aunt, uncle, or your best friend.

One can be a job during the day-time, on weekdays, and the other can be a job you do on weekends, or on certain evenings.

How you find such jobs, will depend on the nature of the job. If it's with a family member or friend, you ask them. If one of the jobs involves starting your own business, you start it. Newspaper ads also are a way of finding part-time jobs. If they want part-time workers, they will say so. Experience usually dictates that these jobs will either be at places you like, for much less money than you want, or they will be at places you hate, for a lot more money (e.g., toll-booth collectors, check-out people at supermarkets, etc.). The general rule is: the more boring the job, the higher the pay. You decide.

---

5. *The* classic textbook on this is Jay Conrad Levinson, *Earning Money Without A Job.* Revised for the '90s. Henry Holt and Company, Inc., 115 W. 18th St., New York, NY 10011. 1991. One of my favorite books. The first part of this excellent book is devoted to his story, and his idea of "modular economics" -- putting together several small jobs, rather than one big one. The second part of the book lists actual businesses that can thus be put together.

Also by the same author: *Guerrilla Marketing: Secrets for Making Big Profits from Your Small Business.* Completely revised and updated for the '90s. 1993. And: *Guerrilla Marketing for the '90s: The New Secrets for Making Big Profits from Your Small Business.* Completely revised and updated. 1993. Very useful little book. And: *Guerrilla Marketing Excellence: The Fifty Golden Rules for Small Business Success.* 1993. All three from Houghton Mifflin Company, 222 Berkeley St., Boston, MA 02116.

Barbara J. Winter teaches a concept similar to Jay Levinson's idea of 'modular economics.' She calls it 'Multiple Profit Centers.' See her book: *Making A Living Without A Job: Winning Ways for Creating Work That You Love.* 1993. Bantam Books, 1540 Broadway, New York, NY 10036.

If you're real picky about what kind of part-time job you take, your refuge is to do Chapters 9–11, and identify a job you would *love to do,* even if it is only part-time.

JOB-SHARING

You're looking for part-time work. But one day, while you're looking through the ads or talking to some friends, you discover a full-time job that you are really interested in, and it's at just the kind of place where you would like to work. But they want someone full-time, and you only want to work part-time. There is a *possible* solution.

You can sometimes sell the organization on the idea of letting *two* of you fill that one job *(one of you from 8–12 noon, say, and the other from 1–5 p.m)*. Of course in order to do this, you have to find someone else -- a relative, friend, or acquaintance -- who is also looking for part-time work, *and* is very competent, *and* would be willing to share that job with you. And you have to find them *first,* and talk them into it, before you approach the boss at that place that interests you. This arrangement is called *job-sharing,* and there are a number of books and places you can write to, if you need some further guidance about how to do it, and how to sell the employer on the idea.

Incidentally, don't omit larger employers, from this particular search just because they would seem to you to be too bound by their own bureaucratic rules -- *some* of them are very open to the idea of job-sharing. *On the other hand, of course, a lot of them aren't.* But it never hurts to ask.

WORKING FOR OTHERS
AT HOME

One new way to work, if you already have a job, is to talk your boss into letting you do at least *some* of your work at home.

Your boss, of course, may take the initiative here, before it has even occurred to you, and he or she may *ask* you to work at home, connected to the office by computer-network telephone lines. This new way to work is called 'telecommuting,' and people who do it are called 'telecommuters' -- a term coined by Jack Nilles in 1973.

U.S. Statistics

Surveys indicate that currently 39 million people (nearly a third of the U.S. work force) do at least some work out of their homes. Advancing technology, such as fax machines, computer notebooks, modems, software that effortlessly connects home computers to office networks, have caused their numbers to increase dramatically -- sometimes on the order of 20% per year, in the U.S. Currently these 39 million are divided as follows:

23.8 million work at home running their own business. 12.1 million of these are *full-time;* 11.7 million are *part-time.*

8.6 million work outside the home during office hours, but take work home for their employers, *after* office hours.

And, 6.6 million[6] work at home for their employers (businesses or government agencies) *during* office hours; these are the ones officially called 'telecommuters.' 3.5 million of these are men, 3.1 million, women.[7] Telecommuters usually put in at least *some* time at the office or place of work each week; typically they work at home between 2 to 4½ days a week.[8]

---

6. Link Resources, reported in *The New York Times,* Section 3, 4/18/93. The statistic is for the most recent year available (1992), as I write.

7. *The New York Times,* Section 3, 4/18/93.

8. Note well, if you are thinking about telecommuting, that it is definitely a mixed bag -- depending a great deal on the disposition, self-discipline, and home conditions of the individual concerned. Some telecommuters boost their output and productivity by 3–5%, due to lack of interruption from co-workers, and the consequent ability to concentrate on the task at hand -- *not to mention their desire to prove that they aren't goofing off.* A few telecommuters, however, experience a fall-off in productivity, due to childcare demands, and other interruptions. Other downsides are: sometimes having uneven work flow, or when the work flow is heavy, working nonstop at all hours, your mate's feeling that they need their own space, a lack of social contact and interaction with other workers, resentment from colleagues at the office who feel you're just taking days off, and the feeling that you are often passed over when it comes time for promotion. Therefore, if telecommuting is of any interest to you, be sure that before you talk to your boss about the possibility, you talk to some experienced telecommuters -- at your place or elsewhere -- to find out what telecommuting is *really* like. If you want to *read* further about this idea, see Brad Schepp, *THE TELECOMMUTER'S HAND-BOOK: How to Work for a Salary–Without Ever Leaving the House.* Pharos Books, Funk & Wagnalls, One International Blvd., Suite 444, Mahwah, NJ 07495. 1990. It describes the jobs best suited for telecommuting, names and addresses of more than 100 companies that allow employees to work at home, pros and cons of telecommuting for both employee and employer. In order for this to work, you will need a sympathetic, supportive boss or supervisor, and you will need a reputation as a mature and responsible individual. In the end, you will probably have to be *more* productive than those who work in the office full-time, to continue to justify their faith in you, if they give you a trial *go-ahead.*

WORKING FOR YOURSELF
AT HOME

Sure, you've thought about it, a million times. Hasn't everyone? Every time you're tied up in traffic going to or from

work. You've toyed with the idea of not having to go to an office or other place of business, but of running your own business, out of your own home, making your own product or selling your own services, being your own boss, and keeping all the profits for yourself. It's called 'the world's fastest commute,' or 'going downstairs, instead of downtown.'[9]

Great idea! *But,* nothing's ever come of it. Until now. Now, you're out of work, or you're fed up with your job, and you're thinking to yourself: *Maybe it's now, or never. Maybe I ought to just do it.*

---

9. Coined by Robert E. Calem in *The New York Times,* 4/18/93.

Three hundred years ago, of course, nearly everybody did it. They worked at home or on their farm. But then the industrial revolution came; and the idea of working *away from* home became normal. In recent times, however, the idea of working at home has been finding new life, due to congestion on the highways, and the development of new technologies. If you can afford them, a fax machine, the telephone,[10] a computer with a modem, e-mail, online services, mail order houses, and the like, all make a home business feasible, as never before.

It's called *self-employment,* or being *an independent contractor,* or *free-lancing* or *contracting out your services.*[11]

---

10. This family includes cellular telephones, 'call-forwarding' -- the technology where people call your one fixed telephone number, and then get automatically forwarded to wherever you have told the phone company you currently are -- and voice/electronic mail.

11. If you decide to launch yourself on this path, be sure to talk to people who have been free-lancers, until you know the name of every pitfall and obstacle in *free-lancing.* Where do you find such people? Well, free-lancers are *everywhere.* Independent screenwriters, copy writers, artists, songwriters, photographers, illustrators, interior designers, video people, film people, consultants, and therapists, are only *some* examples of the type of people who must free-lance, in the very nature of their job. Talk with enough of them, even if they're not free-lancing in the same business you have in mind, until you learn all the pitfalls of free-lancing. For further exploration of launching out on your own, see:

Jeffrey Lant's: *The Consultant's Kit: Establishing and Operating Your Successful Consulting Business* (208 pages, $38.50) and *How To Make At Least $100,000 Every Year As A Successful Consultant in Your Own Field: The Complete Guide to Succeeding in the Advice Business* (315 pages, $39.50). Jeffrey Lant Associates, 50 Follen Street, Suite 507, Cambridge, MA 02138. 617-547-6372.

So, if you are thinking about working at home *for yourself,* you would be joining the more than 23.8 million, in the U.S. who already do that, plus the estimated 25 million additional workers who are *thinking* about doing it.

THE THREE MAJOR PROBLEMS OF HOME BUSINESSES

(1) The first major problem of home businesses, according to experts, is that on average home-based workers *(in the U.S. at least)* only earn 70% of what their full-time office-based equals do. So, you must think carefully whether you could make enough money to survive -- *or prosper.*

(2) The second major problem of home businesses is that it's often difficult to maintain the balance between business and family time. Sometimes the *family* time gets short-changed, while in other cases the demands of family (particularly with small children) may become so interruptive, that the *business* gets short-changed. So, do investigate thoroughly, ahead of time, *how* you would go about doing this *well.* There are books that can help.[12]

(3) Lastly, a home business puts you into a perpetual job-hunt.

Some of those of us who are unemployed *hate* job-hunting,

---

12. Books to help you do this, include:

Barbara Brabec, *Homemade Money: Your Homebased Business Success Guide:* 4th ed. Betterway Books, 1507 Dana Avenue, Cincinati, OH 45207. 1992. A very fine book, with an A to Z business section, and a most helpful summary of which states have laws regulating (or prohibiting) certain home-based businesses; it is updated regularly. Barbara also publishes a newsletter, *National Home Business Report.* If you wish more information, you can ask for her catalog, by writing to National Home Business Network, P.O. Box 2137, Naperville, IL 60567.

Lynie Arden, *The Work-at-Home Sourcebook.* 5th ed. 1994. Live Oak Publications, P.O. Box 2193, 1515 23rd St., Boulder, CO 80306.

Paul and Sarah Edwards, *Working from Home: Everything You Need to Know about Living and Working under the Same Roof.* 3rd ed. J.P. Tarcher, Inc., 200 Madison Avenue, New York, NY 10016. Now revised and expanded. 440 pages. Has a long section on computerizing your home business, and on telecommunicating.

Homeworking Mothers, a quarterly newsletter for women who want to start their own businesses and work from their homes. Mother's Home Business Network, Box 423, East Meadow, NY 11554.

Frank and Sharon Barnett, *Working Together: Entrepreneurial Couples.* Ten Speed Press, P.O. Box 7123, Berkeley, CA 94707. 1989.

and are attracted to the idea of a home business because this seems like an ideal way to cut short their job-hunt. The irony is, that a home business makes you in a very real sense a *perpetual* job-hunter -- because you have to be *always* seeking new clients or customers -- which is to say, new *employers*. (I call them *employers*, because they *pay* you for the work you are doing. The only difference between this and a full-time job is that here *the contract is limited*. But if you are running your own business, you will have to *continually* beat the bushes for new clients or customers -- who are in fact short-term employers.)

Of course, the dream of most home business people is to become so well known, and so in demand, that clients or customers will be literally beating down your doors, and you will be

able to stop this endless job-hunt. But that only happens to a relative minority, and your realistic self must know that.

The greater likelihood is that you will *always* have to beat the bushes for employers/clients. It may get easier as you get better at it, or it may get harder, if economic conditions take a severe downturn. In any event, it will probably be the one aspect of your work that you will *always* cordially dislike. If you're going to go this route, you must learn to make your peace with it -- however grudgingly.

If you can't manage that, if you avoid that task like the plague until there's literally no bread on the table, you're probably going to find *a home business* is just a glamorous synonym for *'starving.'* I know *many* home business people to whom this has happened, and it happened precisely because they couldn't stomach going out to beat the bushes for clients or customers. If that's true for you, you should plan to start out by *hiring, co-opting, volunteering* somebody part-time, who is willing to do this for you -- one who, in fact, 'eats it up.'

WHAT KIND OF HOME BUSINESS?

If you're not deterred by the downside of having your own home business, then you need to begin by deciding what kind of home business you want to be in. Perhaps you haven't the foggiest notion.

Or, perhaps you know exactly *what,* because you've been thinking about it for *years,* and may even have been *doing* it for years -- in the employ of someone else.

Now you are thinking about doing it on your own, whether it be business services, or consultancy, or repair work, or some kind of craft, or the making of some kind of product, or teaching, or offering of home services, such as childcare or delivery by night. Some sorts of jobs are just made for working out of one's home, as when you are already some kind of writer, artist, performer, business expert, lawyer, consultant, craftsperson, or the like.

Be prepared for the fact that your present home may not be big enough for the kind of thing you're dreaming of. For example, your dream may be: *I want a horse ranch, where I can raise and sell horses.* Or *I want to run a bed-and-breakfast place.*[13] Stuff like that.

Well, the nice thing about deciding to work out of your home is that you get to define what *home* is. Given today's technology, you could *literally* work wherever your preferred environment in the whole world is -- whether that be out in nature, or at your favorite vacation spot,[14] or skiing chalet, or in some other country altogether.

The only rule is, if it involves a possible move, be sure to go talk to other people who have already done that. Pick their brains for everything they're worth. No need for you to step on the same *landmines* that they did.

WHEN YOU'VE
INVENTED SOMETHING

If you are inclined toward invention or tinkering, you might want to start by improving on an idea that's already *out there.* Start with something you like, such as bicycles. You might experiment with making -- let us say -- a folding-bicycle. Or, if you like to go to the beach, and your skills run to sewing, you might think about making and selling beach towels with weights sewn in the corners, against windy days.

If you've already invented something, and it's been sitting in your drawer, or the garage, but you've never attempted to duplicate or manufacture it before, now might be a good time to try. Think out very carefully just how you are going to get it manufactured, advertised, and marketed, etc. There are firms out there which claim to specialize in promoting inventions such as yours, for a fee. However, according to the Federal Trade Commission, in a study of 30,000 people who paid such promoters, not a single inventor ever made a profit after giving their invention to such firms.[15] If you want to gamble some of your hard-earned money on such firms, consider whether you might better drop it at the tables in Las Vegas. I think the odds are *better* there.

You're much better off, *of course,* doing your own research as to how one gets an invention marketed. Through the copyright office, and your library, locate other inventors, and ask if they

---

13. Barbara Notarius and Gail Sforza Brewer, *Open Your Own Bed & Breakfast.* 2nd ed. John Wiley & Sons, Inc., Business/Law/General Books Division, 605 Third Ave., New York, NY 10158-0012. 1992.

14. Jeffrey Maltzman, *Jobs in Paradise: The Definitive Guide to Exotic Jobs Everywhere.* Perennial Library, HarperCollins, 10 East 53rd Street, New York, NY 10022. 1993. Describes jobs at lakes, rivers, coasts and beaches, snow & skiing, tropical islands, mountains, deserts, and so forth. You will probably not want to look so much at the *jobs* described here, as at the *categories,* to help you think out just what *kind* of place you might like to be a telecommuter from. As a place to *start* some informational interviewing, this is a great book -- *if* you're interested in working exactly where you'd also like to spend your leisure time.

15. *San Francisco Chronicle,* 1/26/91.

were successful in marketing their own invention. When you
find those who were, pick their brains for everything they're
worth. Of course one of the first things they're going to tell you
is to go get your invention copyrighted or trademarked or pat-
ented.[16]

WHEN YOU DON'T KNOW
WHAT KIND OF HOME
BUSINESS TO START

Maybe you like the idea of working at home. Maybe you love
the idea of running your own business. But maybe you haven't
the foggiest notice of what kind of business to start. *Minor little
detail!*
There are several steps you can take, to nail this down.

First, read. There are oodles of books out there that are *filled*
with ideas for home businesses.[17] Browse your local library, or
bookstore.
Secondly, look around your own community, and ask yourself
what services or products people seem to need the most. Or
what service or product already offered in the community could
stand a lot of *improving*? There may be something there that
grabs you.
The underlying theme to 90% of the businesses that are *out
there* these days is *things that save time.* It's what single parents,
families where both parents work, and singles who have over-
crowded lives, most want.
If none of the books you look at have any ideas that grab you,
here are some other ideas that you might consider: offering
home deliveries of local restaurants' dinners, or home delivery
of grocery orders from any downtown supermarket. Evening
delivery services of laundry, etc. Daytime or evening office cleaning services and/or home cleaning services. Home repairs, especially in the evening or on weekends, of TVs, radios, audio
systems, laundries, dishwashers, etc. Lawn care. Care for the
elderly in their own homes. Childcare in their own homes.
Pickup and delivery of things (even personal stuff, like cleaning) at the office. Automobile care or repair services, with
pickup and delivery. Offering short-term business consultancy

in various fields. Other successful businesses these days deal with leisure activities.

Third, consider mail order. If you find no needs within your own community, you may want to broaden your search, to ask what is needed in this country -- or the world. After all, mail order businesses can be started *small* at home, and catalogs can be sent *anywhere*. If this interests you, read up on the subject.[18] Also, for heaven's sakes, go talk to other mail order people (for names, just look at the catalogs you're already likely receiving).

Fourth, dream. In evaluating any ideas that you pick up, the first thing you ought to look at are your dreams. What have you always dreamed about doing? Since childhood? Since last week? Now is the time to dust off those dreams.

And please don't pay any attention, for now, to whether those dreams represent *a step up* for you in life, or not. Who cares? Your dreams are yours. You may have been dreaming of earning *more* money. But then again, you may have been dreaming of doing work that you really love, even if it means a lesser salary or income than you have been accustomed to. Don't *judge* your dreams, and don't let anyone else judge them either.

Fifth, consider a franchise.

16. Richard C. Levy, *The Inventor's Desktop Companion: A Guide to Successfully Marketing and Protecting Your Ideas.* Visible Ink Press, a division of Gale Research Inc., 835 Penobscot Bldg., Detroit, MI 48226-4094. 1991. From securing a patent for it, to selling it, a very complete compendium.

Fred Grissom & David Pressman, *The Inventor's Notebook.* Nolo Press, 950 Parker St., Berkeley, CA 94710. 1987. A manual to help you keep records about your invention.

17. Entrepreneur Magazine's *184 Businesses Anyone Can Start and Make a Lot of Money.* 2nd ed., Bantam Books, 1540 Broadway, New York, NY 10036. 1990. Ideas related to Personal Services, Business Services, Food, Retail, Sports and Entertainment, Automotive Businesses, Publishing, and miscellaneous.

Entrepreneur Magazine's *168 More Businesses Anyone Can Start and Make a Lot of Money.* 2nd ed., Bantam Books, 1540 Broadway, New York, NY 10036. 1991. Same categories as above, plus Computer Businesses.

Sharon Kahn, *101 Best Businesses to Start.* Doubleday, 1540 Broadway, New York, NY 10036. 1988. The categories here are the same as above, plus Healthcare and Fitness, Household Services, Real Estate, Sales and Marketing, and Travel.

Paul and Sarah Edwards, *The Best Home-based Businesses for the 90s: The Inside Information You Need to Know to Select A Home-based Business That's Right For You.* Jeremy P. Tarcher, 200 Madison Avenue, New York, NY 10016. 1991. The book profiles their choices for the 70 top businesses.

18. Cecil C Hoge, Sr., *Mail Order Moonlighting.* 2nd ed. Ten Speed Press, Box 7123, Berkeley, CA 94707. 1988.

FRANCHISES

Franchises are for people who want their own business, but don't care if it's not *in the home*. (Though some franchises can be done from your home,[19] the majority require an outside site.)

Franchises exist because some people want to have their own business, but don't want to go through the agony of starting it up. They want to *buy in* on an already established business, and they have the money in their savings with which to do that (or they know where they can get a bank loan). Fortunately for them, there are a lot of such franchises. In the U.S., for example, there are more than 2,100 franchised businesses, with more than 478,000 outlets, employing more than 6 million people. Your library or bookstore should have books that list many of these, in this country and elsewhere.[20]

In the U.S., the overall failure rate for franchises is less than 4%.[21] You want to keep in mind that some *types* of franchises have a failure rate *far* greater than that. The ten *riskiest* small businesses, according to experts, are local laundries and dry cleaners, used-car dealerships, gas stations, local trucking firms, restaurants, infant clothing stores, bakeries, machine shops, grocery or meat stores, and car washes -- though I'm sure there will be some new nominees for this list, by the time you read this. *Risky* doesn't mean you can't make them succeed. It only means the odds are greater than they would be with other small businesses.

You want to keep in mind also that some individual franchises are *terrible* -- and that includes well-known names. They charge too much for you to *get on board,* and often they don't do the advertising or other commitments that they promised they would.

There isn't a franchising book that doesn't warn you eighteen times to go talk to people who have *already* bought that same franchise, before you ever decide to go with them. And I mean *several* people, not just one. Most experts also warn you to go talk to *other* franchises in the same field, not just the kind you're thinking about signing up with. Maybe there's something better, that such research will uncover.

If you are drawn to the idea of a franchise, because you are in a hurry, and you don't want to do any homework first, *'cause it's just too much trouble,* you will deserve what you get, believe me. That way lies madness.

YOUR OWN BUSINESS OR FRANCHISE: WHAT ARE YOUR CHANCES OF 'MAKING A GO' OF IT?

If you investigate the odds of succeeding at your own business -- whether it be at home or downtown, whether it be of your own devising or a franchise -- the first thing you will come across are some *intimidating* statistics. Hidden in them is not just bad news, but also some good news.

---

19. Lynie Arden, *101 Franchises You Can Run From Home,* John Wiley & Sons, Professional and Trade Division, 605 Third Ave., New York, NY 10158-0012. 1990.

20. *Franchise Opportunities Handbook,* 22nd ed., Sterling Publishing Co., Inc., 387 Park Ave. S., New York, NY 10016. 1991. This is a reprint of the 22nd edition of *Franchise Opportunities Handbook,* issued by the U.S. Government Printing Office. An immensely thorough book, together with a good introductory section about how to investigate a franchise.

Erwin J. Keup, *Franchise Bible: A Comprehensive Guide.* 2 vol. The Oasis Press®/PSI Research, 300 N. Valley Dr., Grants Pass, OR 97526. 1991. Mr. Keup is a lawyer who has specialized in franchise law and franchise consulting for the past 32 years. He covers 'buying an existing business,' as well as franchises. Also, if you have a successful business already, he discusses the pros and cons of turning it into a franchise.

Ray Bard and Sheila Henderson, *Own Your Own Franchise: Everything You Need to Know about the 160 Best Opportunities in America.* A Stonesong Press Book, Addison-Wesley Publishing Co., Inc., Route 128, Reading, MA 01867. 1987.

Robert Laurance Perry, *The 50 Best Low-Investment, High-Profit Franchises.* 1990. Prentice-Hall, Order Dept., 200 Old Tappan Road, Old Tappan, NJ 07675. 1-800-223-2348. Since there is a disturbing trend in franchises these days toward higher and higher start-up fees, up in the $150,000 category or higher, Perry attempts to list ones which people can afford; most of them are less than $20,000, some less than $5,000.

The 220 Best Franchises to Buy. Philip Lief Group's Editors, Bantam Books, 1540 Broadway, New York, NY 10036. 1993. A sourcebook for evaluating the best franchise opportunities.

21. Ray Bard and Sheila Henderson, *Own Your Own Franchise,* page one.

U.S. Statistics

The following figures are for the U.S., but similar statistics probably can be found in every industrialized country of the world. Currently, in the U.S., 10,200,000 people -- or one out of every twelve people in the work force -- have started their own business. *But,* at least 65% of all new businesses fail within their first five years of operation -- that's more than one out of every two. A well-known statistic, and the only debate you'll get on it from experts is whether or not the figure is *too low.* 96,100 businesses went bankrupt in 1992.[22] So, if you want to go into business for yourself, there's a great risk that it's going to go belly-up[23] *early on.* That is, as they say, the bad news.

The good news is that *if* you survive this early-on period, things start to look up. The risk decreases. There are two evidences for saying this.

First, only about 25% of new businesses fail *in any given year;* so, taking it on just a year to year basis, you have a 75% chance of *not* going belly-up *that* year.[24] Secondly, there are about 28 *old* businesses in the U.S. for every new business that starts up. So, the national bankruptcy/failure rate -- taking *all* businesses into account -- is *much* lower than most people think. In one year recently, out of each 10,000 businesses in the U.S., only 120 failed.[25] That means that 9,880 out of each 10,000 businesses survived.

What these statistics add up to, is that *if* you can make it through the first few years in your home business, you'll probably survive thereafter.

That leaves the BIG question: how do you survive those first few difficult years? The answer is: *Research. Homework. Interviewing people.* Before you commit yourself to this new thing, you need to find out something. That *something* can be summarized in the following formula:

---

22. *San Francisco Chronicle,* Thursday, 1/21/93, p. C1.

23. If any of my readers outside the U.S. do not understand the slang phrase "belly-up," other more familiar synonyms would be: bankrupt, out of business, kaput.

24. These figures are from David Birch's *Job Creation In America.* The Free Press, 866 Third Ave., New York, NY 10022. 1987. David is an excellent researcher, and knows more about small businesses than anyone else in the country that I know of; I recommend this book, highly. It describes at length where the new jobs are coming from, and how our smallest companies put the most people to work.

25. 1986, the most recent year for which I have statistics.

A, MINUS B,
EQUALS C

By way of introduction to this subject, in the past twenty-five years I have found it *mindboggling* to discover how many people start a new business, at home or elsewhere, without ever going to talk to anybody else in the same kind of business.

One job-hunter told me she started a homemade candle business, without ever talking to anyone else who had tried a similar endeavor. Her business went belly-up within a year and a half. She concluded: no one should go into such a business. I concluded: she hadn't done her homework, before she started.

To avoid her fate, here are the rules for homework you *must* do, before starting your own home business -- or any kind of new venture. Please *memorize* them:

A – B = C

1. You write out exactly what kind of business you are thinking about starting.

2. You identify towns or cities that are at least twenty-five miles away, and you try to get their phone books, addresses of their Chambers of Commerce, etc.

3. By using the phone book and the Chambers, you try to identify names of three businesses in those towns, that are identical or similar to the business you are thinking of starting. You journey to that town or city, and talk to the founder/owner of same.

4. When you talk to them, you ask them what pitfalls or obstacles they ran into. You ask them how they overcame them. You ask them what skills or knowledges do they think are necessary to running this kind of business

successfully. You make a list of the latter. When you've finished talking to all three owners, you put together a list of the skills and knowledges they agreed on, as necessary to running the business. We'll call this list "A."

5. Back home you sit down and inventory your own skills and knowledges, perhaps using Chapters 9 and 10 in this book. We'll call this list "B."

6. Finally, you subtract "B" from "A," and this results in a list we will call "C." That's the list of the skills or knowledges you don't have, but must find -- either by taking courses, or by getting volunteers with those skills, or by hiring someone with those skills.

Why twenty-five miles away? Well, actually, that's a minimum. You want to interview businesses which, *if they were in the same town* with you, would be your rival. And if they were in the same town with you, wouldn't likely tell you how to get started. After all, they're not going to train you just so you can then take business away from them.

But, when a guy, a gal, or a business is twenty-five miles away -- even better, fifty miles away -- you're not as likely to be perceived as a rival, and therefore they're much more likely to tell you what you want to know about their own experience, and how *they* got started, and where the landmines are hidden.

Doubtless at this point you would like an example of this whole process. Okay. Our job-hunter is a woman who has been

making harps for some employer, but now is thinking about going into business for herself, not only *making* harps at home, but also *designing* harps, with the aid of a computer. After interviewing several homebased harpmakers and harp designers, and finishing her own self-assessment, her chart of A – B = C came out looking like the one on the next page.

If she decides to try her hand at becoming an independent harpmaker and harp designer, she now knows what she needs but lacks: *computer programming, knowledge of the principles of electronics, and accounting.* Column **C.** These she must either go to school to acquire for herself, OR enlist from some friends of hers in those fields, on a volunteer basis, OR go out and hire, part-time.

These are the essential steps for any new enterprise that you are considering: A – B = C. If you want to start up more than one venture, you need to interview people *in each line of work* to find out A – B = C for both jobs.

You may also want to talk to people who have juggled two (or more) careers, at the same time.

HOW CAN YOU DO A – B = C, IF YOU'VE THOUGHT OF A BUSINESS OR CAREER THAT NO ONE'S EVER HEARD OF BEFORE

No matter how inventive you are, you're probably *not* going to invent a job that *no one* has ever heard of, before. You're only going to invent a job that *most* people have never heard of, before. But the likelihood is *great* that someone, somewhere, in this world of endless creativity, has already put together the kind of job you're dreaming about. Your task: to find her, or him, and interview them thoroughly. And then . . . well, you know the drill: A – B = C.

A − B = C

Skills and Knowledges Needed to Run This Kind of Business Successfully	Skills and Knowledges Which I Have	Skills and Knowledges Needed, Which I Do Not Have, and Which I Will Therefore Have to Get Someone to Volunteer, or I Will Have to Go Out and Hire
Precision-working with tools and instruments	Precision-working with tools and instruments	
Planning and directing an entire project	Planning and directing an entire project	
Programming computers, inventing programs that solve physical problems		Programming computers, inventing programs that solve physical problems
Problem solving: evaluating why a particular design or process isn't working.	Problem solving: evaluating why a particular design or process isn't working.	
Being self-motivated, resourceful, patient, and persevering, accurate, methodical, and thorough	Being self-motivated, resourceful, patient, and persevering, accurate, methodical and thorough	
Thorough knowledge of: Principles of electronics	*Thorough knowledge of:*	*Thorough knowledge of:* Principles of electronics
Physics of strings	Physics of strings	
Principles of vibration	Principles of vibration	
Properties of woods	Properties of woods	
Computer programming		Computer programming
Accounting		Accounting

If there isn't someone doing *exactly* what you are dreaming of, there is at least someone who is *close*. This is how you find them:

WHEN NO ONE HAS DONE WHAT YOU WANT TO DO

You can always find someone who has done something that at least approximates what you want to do. The rules are:

1. Break down your projected business or career into its parts.

2. Then take any two of those parts at a time. See what kind of person that describes.

3. Find out the names of such persons, preferably two or more.

4. Go see, phone, write him or her; you will learn a great deal, that is relevant to your dream.

5. They, in turn, may be able to give you a lead to someone whose business is even closer to what it is you want to do. And then you can go interview them. And so on, and so forth.

For example, let's suppose your dream is -- here we take a ridiculous case -- to use computers to monitor the growth of plants at the South Pole. And suppose you can't find anybody who's ever done such a thing. The way to tackle this seemingly insurmountable problem, is to break the proposed business down into its parts, which -- in this case -- are: *computers, plants,* and *the Antarctic.*

Then you try combining any two parts, together, to define the person or persons you need to talk to. In this case, that would mean finding someone who's *used computers with plants here in the States,* or someone who's *used computers at the Antarctic,* or someone who has *worked with plants at the Antarctic,* etc. You go talk to them, and along the way you may discover there *is* someone who has used computers to monitor the growth of plants at the South Pole. Then again, you may not. In any event, you will learn most of the pitfalls that wait for you, by hearing the experience of those who are in *parallel* businesses or careers.

Thus, it is *always* possible -- with a little blood, sweat and imagination -- to find out what A – B = C is, for the business you're trying to design.

NEW WAYS TO WORK

Well, we've about covered now some new ways to work. If you're at a turning point in your life, all of these are worth weighing and considering.

Of course, none of the strategies in this chapter are actually *new* ways to work. They are only *new to you.* Even so, it takes a lot of guts to try something new *for you* in today's economy. It's easier, however, if you keep three rules in mind:

---

1. There is always some risk, in trying something new. Your job is not to avoid risk -- there is no way to do that -- but to make sure ahead of time that the risks are *manageable.*

2. You find this out before you start, by first talking to others who have already done what you are thinking of doing; then you evaluate whether or not you still want to go ahead and try it.

3. Have a Plan B, already laid out, *before you start,* as to what you will do if it doesn't work out; i.e., know where you are going to go, next. Don't wait, *puh-leaze!* Write it out, now. *This is what I'm going to do, if this doesn't work out:*

These rules always apply, no matter where you are in your life: just starting out, already employed, unemployed, in mid-life, recovering after a crisis or accident, facing retirement, or whatever. Do take them very seriously.

If you're sharing your life with someone, sit down with that partner or spouse and ask what the implications are *for them* if you try this new thing. Will it require all your joint savings? Will they have to give up things? If so, what? Are they willing to make those sacrifices? And so on.

If you aren't out of work, you will need to debate the wisdom of quitting your job before you start up the new company, or business. And what do the experts say, here? In a word, they say, if you have a job, *don't* quit it. Better by far to move *gradually* into self-employment, doing it as a moonlighting activity first of all, while you are still holding down that regular job somewhere else. That way, you can test out your new enterprise, as you would test a floorboard in an old run-down house, stepping on it cautiously without at first putting your full weight on it, to see whether or not it will support you.[26]

If your investigation revealed that it takes good accounting practices in order to turn a profit, and you don't know a thing about accounting, you go out and hire a (part-time) accountant *immediately* -- or, if you absolutely have no money, you talk an accountant friend of yours into giving you some volunteer time, for a while.[27]

It is up to you to do your research thoroughly, weigh the risks, count the cost, get counsel from those intimately involved with you, and then if you decide you want to do it (whatever *it* is), go ahead and try -- no matter what your well-meaning but pessimistic acquaintances may say.

You only have one life here on this earth, and that life (under God) is *yours* to say how it will be spent, or not spent.

THE LAST PARACHUTE:
STOP-GAP JOBS

When I first started out in this field, twenty-five years ago, I read every book there was, on job-hunting and career-change. One thing that frustrated me was that they would offer some recommended strategies, and then act as though, *Well, of course this will solve all your problems.*

I always wondered, as I read, *"But what if they don't?"* So, I am concerned for my own readers, in case any of you tries *everything*

---

26. See Philip Holland, *How To Start A Business Without Quitting Your Job: The Moonlight Entrepreneur's Guide.* Ten Speed Press, P.O. Box 7123, Berkeley, CA 94707. 1992.

27. There are also books that may help you out of the financial thicket, such as James D. Schwartz's *"ENOUGH" A Guide to Reclaiming Your American Dream.* Labrador Press, distributed by RE/MAX International, Inc., 5445 DTC Pkwy., Suite 1200, Englewood, CO 80111. 1992.

in this chapter, and previous chapters, and you're still out of work, and the money is getting to the crisis stage.

You know about welfare, of course. It varies from country to country, but it is a safety net that most countries have constructed.

But what if . . . ? What if: none of this is available, for whatever reason, to you? Then what do you do?

The answer is: *a stop-gap job.* This phrase, used by many experts, refers to the situation where your money is about gone, and you have exhausted all job-hunting strategies. At this point, the advice of every expert is to take *any kind of work you can get.* That fills, or stops-up, the gap in your money situation -- hence, it is called a *stop-gap job.*

The mark of a stop-gap job is simple: it's a short-term job that you would *hate* if it was anything but short-term. It isn't supposed to be anything you really *like* to do. Its only requirement is that it be honest work, and that it bring in some money. It will probably be less money than you are used to making, per hour. It will probably also be hard work; or boring work. *But,* who cares? Its sole purpose is to put some honest money on the table, so you can eat. And pay the rent. And that's *it.*

The way you go about finding a stop-gap job is simple. You get your local newspaper, you look at the help-wanted ads, and you circle *any* and *every* job that you could see yourself doing *for a short time,* simply for the money. Then you go and apply for those jobs.

You also go to employment agencies, and say, "I'll do *anything;* what have you got?"

Unhappily, this spirit -- "I'll do anything" -- is rarer than it ought to be. Many job-hunters refuse to even consider a stop-gap job; they'd rather go on welfare, first. One reason for this financially-suicidal feeling is the conviction that 'such jobs are *beneath* me.' You know: *"I wouldn't be caught dead washing dishes."*

I need to state the obvious here: namely, that any honest hard work neither demeans you, nor makes you less important as a person. The 'you' who is doing that work, remains the same. Except that it is a 'you' that *needs this money.* I should also add, while I'm at it, that there are many salutary lessons for the soul, to be learned from temporarily taking a stop-gap job. And this is especially true if that job is at a different level and in a different world than you have been accustomed to.[28]

Many of us delay in seeking a stop-gap job for a somewhat higher reason: namely, the conviction that we must have full-time to devote to our job-hunt. Well, that's important, of course; but so is eating. You may want to consider a part-time stop-gap job, in order to address both concerns, fairly. (Also you might want to keep a *time-log* for two weeks, to see just how much time you actually *are* spending on your job-hunt. The easiest person in the world to deceive is *ourselves*.)

A final reason many refuse to seek a stop-gap job is that they are receiving unemployment benefits, which of course would be cut off, if they took a job of any kind. But, needless to say, unemployment benefits do run out, and should they run out before you have found a job, then it is a very different story. Run, do not walk, to find a job, any job, find it and take it -- as a stop-gap measure . . . only. And keep working on Chapters 9–11. And keep looking.

For, as the birds say *(I overheard them just the other day):* "A stop-gap job is like a frail branch of a tree: a lovely place to stop and catch your breath, but a lousy place to build a permanent nest."

---

28. At one point in my life, I took a stop-gap job which involved cutting grass, helping lay cement sidewalks, and building retaining walls. It was one of the most educational experiences of my life. It also brought in exactly the money that I so badly needed.

Two roads diverged in a yellow wood,
And sorry I could not travel both
And be one traveler, long I stood
And looked down one as far as I could
To where it bent in the undergrowth;

Then took the other, as just as fair,
And having perhaps the better claim,
Because it was grassy and wanted wear;
Though as for that the passing there
Had worn them really about the same,

And both that morning equally lay
In leaves no step had trodden black.
Oh, I kept the first for another day!
Yet knowing how way leads on to way,
I doubted if I should ever come back.

I shall be telling this with a sigh
Somewhere ages and ages hence:
Two roads diverged in a wood, and I—
I took the one less traveled by,
And that has made all the difference.

Robert Frost (1874–1963)[1]

---

1. The title of this poem is "The Road Not Taken," from The Poetry Of Robert Frost edited by Edward Connery Lathem. Copyright 1916, © 1969 by Holt, Rinehart & Winston. Copyright 1944 by Robert Frost. Henry Holt and Company, Publisher. Used with permission. Incidentally, Scotty Peck's modern classic, *The Road Less Traveled*, takes its title from this poem.

CHAPTER SEVEN

Retiring
Or Moving
To A New Place

Chapter 7

Reprinted with special permission of King Features Syndicate, Inc.

WHEN YOU WANT TO PULL UP STAKES, MOVE, AND RELOCATE

In the U.S., surveys reveal that the average person moves eleven times between birth and death. Sometimes that's within the same town.[2] Other times it's to a faraway place. Similar patterns of mobility often occur in other countries, as well.

There are two reasons, above all else, why you might decide to relocate:

(1) You may have reached the point where you decide that where you live is more important to you than any other consideration. Maybe you're living in some city, town, or rural area that you detest more, every day you are there. Finally you decide you can't stand it any longer. You've only one life to live, on this earth, and you want to spend the rest of it in a place you really enjoy. This crisis can occur when you're twenty, forty, or sixty. Or, perhaps you're retiring, and you want a place where it's always warm, or a place where you can always ski, or whatever.

(2) You like where you're living, but you just can't find any work -- decent–paying work, anyway -- there. It seems as though every job there is filled, numbered, and has a waiting list besides. You've decided you've *got* to move.

---

2. While I was growing up in Teaneck, New Jersey, my parents could only afford to rent, and when rents changed, we moved. Between the time I was five and eighteen years old, we moved seven times, within the same town. This is a typical experience for many urban dwellers who rent.

HOW TO CHOOSE
A NEW PLACE

When facing a move, some people already know *where to:*

You may choose a town or city where you already have friends, or family. You decide to move *there,* because you will have their support and help. Or you may choose a town or city where you've always *dreamed* of living. You're confident you'll be able to find a job there, somehow, somewhere, once you get there. You'll *make it work,* some way, somehow.

In such a case, where you *know* where you're going (and you know who's going with you), you need no advice from me.

But there are those other times, when you need or want to move, but you have no idea where to move to.

At such a time, you have one of two choices:

a) Your first consideration is that it be a place you could love. And you want some help in figuring *that* out. You're pretty confident you'll be able to find a job there, some way, somehow.

b) Your first consideration is that it be a place where it is easy to find the kind of work you do, or want to do. And you want some help in figuring *that* out. You're pretty sure that you'll get used to living there, once you settle in.

Let's look at these two scenarios, taking the second first:

CHOOSING A PLACE BY
WHETHER OR NOT IT HAS JOBS

If jobs are the first thing on your mind, you have two ways to go. One is to move where the unemployment rate is low for *all* jobs. In the U.S., your local Federal/State employment office can usually give you the current statistics about all 50 States. You look for the States with the lowest unemployment rate. Then you pick one or more metropolitan areas in those States, and write to their Chambers of Commerce (pick up your phone and ask *Information* for their phone numbers, in each city). You ask those Chambers for all the information they have in writing about businesses which deal with your trade or specialty, and you ask that these lists be sent to you.

Send them a thank-you note *the day* the stuff arrives, *please.* You may need to contact them again later, perhaps when you're actually in the area, and it will help you a lot if they can say, *"Oh yes, you're that nice person who sent us a thank-you note when we sent you our materials. First thank-you note we've gotten in three years."* Chances are, they will bend over *backwards* to help you.

Your other strategy for choosing a place by whether or not it has jobs, is to find out what places throughout the country have a particular need for your kind of skills. This is hard to do in the case of some jobs -- like that of a writer, say, but easier to do if you are a craftsperson or practice a particular trade. In the latter case, go to your local library, and ask the librarian to help you find a trade association directory, or directories. (See Appendix B.) You then look up the association that deals with your occupation, and jot down the address of their national headquarters. Then write or phone them and ask if they know where the demand is greatest, in that industry, nationwide. If their answer turns out to be 'several places,' then you can fall back on such books as Richard Boyer's and David Savageau's *Places Rated Almanac,* to decide which of those is your first choice, which is your second, etc.

CHOOSING A PLACE
BY WHETHER OR NOT
YOU LOVE IT THERE

It is relatively easy to figure out a place you could love. First of all, you can interview all your friends and acquaintances, to ask them what places *they* have loved the most, in the U.S. or in whatever country you live. And *why.* This task can be a lot of fun. And then, out of all the *candidates* they propose, you can choose two or three places for further investigation.

Secondly, you can turn to books. In the U.S., there are quite a number of them that rate various cities and towns according to *factors* that may be important to you, such as *weather, crime, educational system, recreational opportunities,* etc.[3] The best of these, by a long shot, is Richard Boyer's and David Savageau's aforementioned *Places Rated Almanac.* If you live in another country, you may find similar resources for your own country; visit a large bookstore, and ask. One word of caution: do remember, in all these books, that a computer was usually used to sum up, and rate, all the factors. You may find that *the whole* is less than the sum of its *parts.*

Thirdly, you can do a thorough-going analysis of all the places you have ever lived, to come up with *descriptors* -- and then *names* -- of places that combine all the factors that were ever important to you in any town or city from your past.[4]

In the end, you want to try to come up with three names, because if your first choice doesn't pan out for some reason, you will have a backup, and also a backup to that backup.

WHEN YOU WANT TO 'GO RURAL'

It may be you will discover, as you go about this task, that your idea of *paradise* is to 'go rural' -- to move, at last, to 'the country.' Sometimes it's the desire for a simpler life; sometimes, it's the desire for a less expensive cost of living. Whatever the reasons, if this is your vision, take this vision seriously. You only have one life to live, on this earth.

---

3. Richard Boyer and David Savageau, *Places Rated Almanac: Your Guide to Finding the Best Places to Live in North America.* Revised ed. 1993. Prentice-Hall, Order Dept., 200 Old Tappan Road, Old Tappan, NJ 07675. 1-800-223-2348. A marvelous book. Immensely helpful for anyone weighing where to move next. All 343 metropolitan areas are ranked and compared for living costs, job outlook, crime, health, transportation, education, the arts, recreation, and climate. Has numerous helpful diagrams, charts, and maps, showing (for example) earthquake risk areas, tornado and hurricane risk areas, the snowiest areas, the stormiest areas, the driest areas, and so on. Don't leave home without it.

David Savageau, *Retirement Places Rated.* 3rd ed. 1990. Prentice-Hall, Order Dept., 200 Old Tappan Road, Old Tappan, NJ 07675. 1-800-223-2348. Although purportedly about retirement, it is useful information for anyone. Compares 151 top geographical areas in the U.S.

G. Scott Thomas, *The Rating Guide to Life in America's Small Cities.* Prometheus Books, 59 John Glenn Dr., Buffalo, NY 14228. 1990. Compares 219 small cities in areas of climate, economics, education, health care, housing, public safety, transportation, proximity to urban centers, sophistication, and diversions.

Norman D. Ford, *50 Healthiest Places to Live and Retire in U.S.,* Mills & Sanderson, 41 North Rd., Suite 201, Bedford MA 01730-1021.

Lee & Saralee Rosenburg, *50 Fabulous Places to Raise Your Family,* Career Press, 1-800-CAREER-1.

Jill Andresky Fraser, *The Best U.S. Cities for Working Women.* Plume Books, New American Library, 1633 Broadway, New York, NY 10019. 1986.

4. Detailed instructions on how to do this are to be found in my workbook entitled *How To Create A Picture of Your Ideal Job.* You can order it from the publisher, Ten Speed Press, Box 7123, Berkeley CA 94707. It costs $5.95.

Just be sure to investigate it *thoroughly*. "Look before you leap" is always a splendid caution, and it means -- in this particular case -- that if there's a place that sounds good to you, *be sure* to go visit it as a tourist before you up and move there. I mean, *go there*, and talk to *everyone*. Get the good side, and the bad. Interview anyone you know, who has moved from urban to rural, and ask them what they like most about the move, and what they miss the most about their former locale. Then weigh what you learn.

Fortunately, there are a number of books that you can use to explore this idea, if it interests you.[5]

WHEN YOU WANT TO
WORK OVERSEAS

On the other hand, if you've always wanted to live and work overseas, then that too is a dream you should explore. I will assume here that we are talking about job-hunters in the U.S. who want to move to Europe, Africa, Asia, Canada, or South America. However, there are readers of this book who live in those places and want to move to the U.S. Much of what I have to say here will apply, as general principles, to them.

First of all, be sure you're not going overseas in order to find Utopia. Utopia rarely lives up to expectations. Even if (big *if*) you do not find the same things that irritate you about your present country, I guarantee you that you will find some brand new things to irritate you.

Regarding the mechanics of going overseas: many people assume you find an overseas job by packing a bag, buying a ticket and passing out resumes once you reach your foreign

---

5. The resources which follow are for the U.S. You may find similar resources in your own country, if you do not live in the U.S.

William L. Seavey, ed., *The Eden Seeker's Guide.* 1989. Loompanics Unlimited, PO Box 1197, Port Townsend, WA 98368, or from the author (see below). What kinds of places offer optimum quality of life. The author also has a business called *Greener Pastures Institute,* which publishes a newsletter entitled *Greener Pastures Gazette* (Sample back issue: $3). They also have a pamphlet which tells you the basic resources for moving to the country or a small town. Greener Pastures Institute, P.O. Box 2190, Henderson, NV 89009-7009, 800-688-9017, or 818-355-1670.

John F. Edwards, *Starting Fresh: How to Plan for a Simpler, Happier, and More Fulfilling New Life in the Country.* Prima Publishing, Sierra Gardens, Suite 130, Roseville, CA 95661. 1988.

Frank Levering and Wanda Urbanska, *Simple Living.* Viking Penguin, 375 Hudson St., New York, NY 10014. 1992.

Frank Kirkpatrick, *How to Find and Buy Your Business in the Country.* Storey Communications, Inc., Schoolhouse Road, Pownal, VT 05261. 1985. How to find a simpler lifestyle, away from the hustle and bustle of the city.

The Caretaker Gazette, published by Gary C. Dunn, 221 Wychwood Road, Westfield, NJ 07090. 908-654-6600. $18 for a one-year subscription (six issues). Landowners searching for caretakers advertise in this *Gazette.* Caretaking is an inexpensive way for you to experience life in a specific geographic area, particularly rural ones. While the majority of the jobs listed are in the U.S., some international positions are also included. A map on the front page of each issue indicates where the employment opportunities are. The June 1994 issue, by way of example, had 50 job listings in 26 states and five countries.

Marilyn and Tom Ross, *Country Bound!™ Trade Your Business Suit Blues For Blue Jean Dreams™.* Communication Creativity, P.O.Box 909, Buena Vista, CO 81211. 1992.

destination. No, no, no. Work-permit requirements and high unemployment make finding jobs at foreign destinations often difficult, and sometimes impossible.

For example, if you were to study employment classifieds in, say, a newspaper from London, England, you would at first sight think you had found some grand opportunities for yourself. *Unfortunately,* these are in most cases job opportunities open only to British nationals or citizens of EEC nations. What is true in England is true elsewhere. Your U.S. citizenship will actually preclude you from working in a foreign country -- even Canada -- unless your employer can prove that a local national is unavailable to take the job, and thus secure a work permit for *you.*

Your wisest approach to overseas employment is to conduct your job-hunt for an overseas job while you are still here in the U.S. How do you go about it? Well, first of all, research the country or countries that interest you, as to living conditions, conditions of employment, et cetera. Talk to everyone you possibly can who has in fact been overseas, most especially to those country or countries. A nearby large university will probably have such faculty or students *(ask).* Companies in your city which have overseas branches *(your library should be able to tell you which they are)* should be able to lead you to people also -- possibly to the names and addresses of personnel who are still "over there" to whom you can write for the information you are seeking. Alternatively, try asking every single person you meet for the next week (at the supermarket checkout, at your work, at home, at church or synagogue, etc.) if they know someone who used to live overseas and now lives here in your city or town. You may be amazed at how many normal-looking people are actually world travelers. By doing research with such people, you will learn a great deal. Find out what they liked and didn't like, about the country which interests you. Find out what they know about the conditions for working over there.

Next, you need to research what kinds of job possibilities exist in that country. Every *successful* overseas search starts with *some* sources of information on "who's hiring now." *Which* sources you access, and how you make use of them, will greatly affect your chances of landing an overseas assignment.[6]

What do I mean? Well, for openers, beware of such sources as employment agencies that promise to find you an overseas job for an advance fee. 98% of their clients *do not* find an overseas job. This fleecing industry has flourished for years, with a few individuals often running scores of companies under an assortment of names. Such companies regularly go out of business or file for bankruptcy *once they've fleeced enough suckers.*[7]

Beware also of directories advertised in newspapers, etc. as *listing overseas employers.* Many, though not all, of these job listings are out of date and tend to report on "who *was* hiring" rather than "who is hiring *now.*"

You can still make effective use of any such directory by taking care that *if* you contact an organization listed therein, you include a cover letter which requests that your resume be

---

6. As for the general facts about living overseas, books get outdated very fast; but currently the live ones are:

International Business Travel and Relocation Directory, 6th ed. Gale Research, Inc., 835 Penobscott Bldg. Detroit, MI 48226-4094. It presents all the relevant details for every country in the world.

Robert Sanborn, Ed.D., *How To Get A Job in Europe: The Insider's Guide.* 2nd ed. Surrey Books, 230 E. Ohio St., Suite 120, Chicago, IL 60611. 1993. Includes tips on how to find a job in the New Europe.

Dale Chambers, *Passport to Overseas Employment: 100,000 Job Opportunities Abroad.* Prentice-Hall, Order Dept., 200 Old Tappan Road, Old Tappan, NJ 07675. 1-800-223-2348. 1990. Deals with overseas study programs, international careers, temporary employment, airlines and cruises, embassies and consulates, United Nations, and volunteer programs.

Howard Schuman, *Making It Abroad–The International Job Hunting Guide.* John Wiley & Sons, 605 Third Ave., New York, NY 10158-0012. l988.

Susan Griffith, *Work Your Way Around the World.* 6th ed. Peterson's Guides, P.O. Box 2123, Princeton, NJ 08543. 1993.

Mary Green and Stanley Gillmar, *How to Be an Importer and Pay for Your World Travel.* 2nd ed. Ten Speed Press, Box 7123, Berkeley, CA 94707. 1993.

For teachers wishing to work overseas, the Department of Defense publishes a pamphlet, with application, entitled *Overseas Employment Opportunities for Educators.* Write to U.S. Department of Defense Dependent Schools, Recruitment and Assignments Section, Hoffman Bldg. I, 2461 Eisenhower Ave., Alexandria, VA 22331-1100, for the pamphlet/application.

Your library should also have books such as Juvenal Angel, *Dictionary of American Firms Operating in Foreign Countries* (World Trade Academy Press).

And to research overseas public companies which sell stock in this country, the Securities Exchange Commission will have their Form 6-K, which they filed in order to be able to sell that stock.

If you want more books about overseas work (or study), write to WorldWise Books, P.O. Box 3030, Oakton, VA 22124, and/or Writer's Digest Books, 1507 Dana Ave., Cincinnati, OH 45207, and ask for their catalogs.

7. Write to Stuart Alan Rado, 1500 West 23rd St., Sunset Island #3, Miami Beach, FL 33140, if you wish to know more.

kept on file 'for further consideration *if there are no current openings.*' As I have emphasized elsewhere in this book, pure dumb luck -- which means, having your name in 'the right place at the right time' -- plays a crucial role in finding most jobs. Since you can't get *over there*, at the moment, you will have to rely more heavily on resumes here than I would normally advise, to keep your name in the right place. In the case of overseas employment, the more employers who have your resume, the better.

Rather than the kind of resources mentioned above, I think your best bet for job leads are authoritative directories such as those listed on the next page.[8] Also, in your job-search do not forget that the U.S. Government is a heavy overseas employer. Understandably, in the post-USSR world, with the end of the cold war, there are numerous cutbacks going on overseas. Nonetheless, this possibility is still well worth exploring. *How* you explore it, is described in the book listed.[9]

If you run into an absolute stonewall in your search for an overseas job, there are two backup strategies for you to consider. The first is to seek an international internship. The second strategy begins with the fact that many companies operating in this country, both domestic and foreign-owned, *have branches overseas.* Thus, *sometimes* your ticket to getting overseas may be to start working here in the U.S. for such a company, hoping they will eventually send you overseas. It *does* happen. And if it happens, they will likely take care of the visa and work permit red tape, pick up your travel bill, and provide other helpful benefits. Unfortunately, however, you can't *count* on their ever sending you overseas. In other words, it's a big fat gamble. *You* have to decide whether you're willing to take it, or not.

If you decide to do either of the above strategies, you'll find the names of organizations by going to your local library and asking the reference librarian to help you find such directories as these: *Principal International Businesses,* published by Dun's Marketing Service; *International Directory of Corporate Affiliations,* published by Corporate Affiliations Information Services, of the National Register Publishing Company; and *International Organizations, revised annually,* published by Gale Research, Inc.

Lastly, contact every friend you have who already lives overseas -- even if it's not in the country that is your target. Ask for their counsel, advice, help, and prayers. They went before you; hopefully they can now be your guide, and door-opener.

One final word about hunting for an overseas job: above all, be patient. The search for an overseas job takes *more* time than looking for a job in this country. Don't expect to be in an exotic foreign capital within 90 days. Perseverance is the key.

EXPLORING THE FARAWAY
PLACE OF YOUR CHOICE

And now, whether your choice is overseas or here in your own country, whether your choice is urban or rural, there is the $64,000 question: how do you go about finding out about *jobs* in your chosen target city or town? Naturally, there are *ways*.

If it has a local newspaper, *subscribe*, even while you are still living *here*. Read the whole paper, when it comes, however long delayed. Look particularly for: news of companies that are *expanding*, news of *promotions* or *transfers* (that creates vacancies *down below* in 'the company store'), and the like.

If you can get the Chamber of Commerce there, or someone you know there, to send you their phone book, particularly the Yellow Pages, by all means do so.

---

8. *International Employment Hotline*, Box 3030, Oakton, VA 22124. Published monthly since 1980, this newsletter provides job-search advice and names and addresses of employers currently hiring for international work in government, nonprofit organizations, and private companies. They also have other titles on overseas work, which you can ask them about. Incidentally, do *not* confuse this reputable firm with International Employment Hotline in Amsterdam, Holland, or London; there is *no* connection whatsoever.

9. Will Cantrell and Francine Modderno, *How To Find an Overseas Job with the U.S. Government*. 1992. Worldwise Books, P.O. Box 3030, Oakton, VA 22124. Comprehensive guide to finding work with the organization that hires the greatest number of Americans abroad. In-depth job descriptions and application procedures are provided for over 17 individual government agencies, along with information on how to complete the government's standard application for employment (SF-171), and how to prepare for and pass the Foreign Service exam. Highly recommended. They also have authored *International Internships and Volunteer Programs*. 1992. Worldwise Books, P.O. Box 3030, Oakton, VA 22124. Information on programs serving as 'stepping-stones' to international careers, for both students and professionals. Positions include salaried and volunteer opportunities, both abroad and also here in the U.S.

Frances Bastress, *The New Relocating Spouse's Guide to Employment: Options & Strategies in the U.S. and Abroad*. 4th ed. 1993. Impact Publications, 9104-N Manassas Drive, Manassas Park, VA 22111.

And finally, when you're ready to go visit that town or city *in person* (on your summer vacation, perhaps) try to line up contacts and interviews *ahead of time,* before you go there. If you have trouble connecting with someone, see if that town has any church, synagogue, or national organization that you belong to here. Write, tell them of your local affiliation, and ask for their help in finding the person you're trying to connect with.

If you have a spouse or partner, who works, they should be doing the same kind of research, and setting up the same kinds of interviews, as you are.

When you get there, in addition to interviewing about jobs, you will want to explore (of course) the issues of apartment vs. house, of rental vs. buying, and the like. Back home again, you will want to weigh what you have learned, and weigh whether or not it will be easy to sell your present home, if you own one -- or are on your way toward owning one.

WHAT TO DO
WHEN YOU CAN'T GET THERE,
TO VISIT OR INTERVIEW

If your finances are tight, it may not be possible for you to go there, at least in the forseeable future. In which case, you do your best to research the place from a distance, as described above. And when that research seems complete, and you have discovered some organizations that, at a distance, look like *possibles*, you then contact them by mail or through whatever contacts you have developed in that city or town, as I am about to describe.

You will first want to research each organization that you are planning to approach by mail, so that you know *who* to address the letter to, *by name*. And then you want to keep in mind that that letter will carry a lot more weight if you can mention, in it, the name of *a mutual friend or acquaintance.*

Toward that end, it is important that you have previously discovered people in that city or town who can be your *contacts*. For example, if you went to college, find out if any graduates of that college live in this new city or town. (Contact the alumni office of your college, and ask.) Also any church, synagogue or national organization you belong to, that has a presence there -- as mentioned above. Also ask your friends locally, if they know of anyone who lives in that city or town. Use these names *only if* they know the employer to whom you are writing.[10]

Should you also enclose a resume? Professional opinions vary widely. *Everything* depends on the nature of the resume, and the nature of the person you are sending it to. With some employers I know, a resume is *death*. It will *ensure* that your letter is merely tossed aside. Other employers like to see one. Just to play it safe, I think a well-composed letter summarizing all you would say in a resume, may be your best bet; with a footnote indicating your resume is available, should they wish it.

---

10. Unless -- the job-hunter's nightmare -- your mutual "friend"/contact has *misrepresented* how close he or she is to your target employer, and as a matter of fact said employer can't stand the sight of this "mutual friend." *It has happened*. It is to die. Asking a question beforehand, of the "mutual friend," like "How *well* do you know him -- or her?" may help avoid this.

CONCLUSION

There is a great joy in moving to a new place, particularly if it is to a place that you love. One job-hunter described this joy to me, in words which many other job-hunters could echo:

"In 1990, my wife and I took a trip out to the Southwest from our home in Annapolis, Maryland, to see the Grand Canyon and sights like that. We both fell in love with the Southwest, and said, 'Wouldn't it be great if I could get a job out here as a highway engineer, and maybe we could work with the Native Americans.' Back in Annapolis, I purchased Parachute *and read it with extreme interest. So I started some network planning, and scheduled another upcoming trip to Arizona in February of 1992, planning to visit various engineering offices and check out living conditions.*

"Meanwhile, I visited the U.S.G.S. Headquarters in Reston, Virginia. On the way out, I noticed an ad on the bulletin board for 'Highway Engineer–Bureau of Indian Affairs, Gallup, New Mexico.' Naturally, I applied for the job but received notice that the position had been cancelled. Disappointed, my wife and I decided to each spend a day in prayer. On the following day I received a call from that office in Gallup informing me there was another position for Highway Planner now open; was I still interested? Still interested?!

"Using your advice, I called the Bureau in Gallup and got the names of the bosses of the various divisions or sections that would impinge upon my application. I sent in the application to the person by name who was the chief decision-maker. In February of 1992 we carried out the trip I had been planning, now including a visit to Gallup. We visited headquarters there, though they weren't yet ready to formally interview, since not all applicants had yet been screened. However, it was a useful visit, and on returning, I wrote Thank You notes to all the people I had met, and hoped for the best.

"In March I received another phone call, asking for further information; I used this to invite myself out for an actual interview, at my expense. My offer was accepted, I was out there in two days, the interview went well, and I received official notice to report for work in May. We were ecstatic! And we found a house in Gallup, through a friend in Annapolis who had a friend in Gallup, who knew of a co-worker who was moving out.

"In short, ours is a wonderful story. Who would think a 66 year old man could leave one job and move into another full-time job, at a salary almost equal to his present one, in a place 2600 miles away, that he and his wife truly love! What a blessing! And what you said has stuck with me all this time: I've remembered to write my Thank You notes."

*Pray, as though everything
    depended on God;
then work, as though everything
    depended on you.*

CHAPTER EIGHT

How to Choose
Or Change
A Career

Chapter 8

ARLO & JANIS reprinted by permission of NEA, Inc.

U.S. Statistics

The average person currently can expect to have three different careers during their lifetime.

In the most recent year surveyed, 1986, it was discovered that 10 million workers changed careers[1] that year.

5.3 million of them changed careers *voluntarily,* and in 7 out of 10 cases their income went up;

3.4 million of them changed careers for a *mixture* of voluntary and involuntary reasons (such as needing to go from part-time to full-time work, etc.);

1.3 million of them changed careers *involuntarily,* because of what happened to them in the economy, and in 7 out of 10 cases, their income went down.

Despite the *myth* that people only contemplate career-change in mid-life, in point of fact *only one million* out of the ten were in mid-life. People can and do change careers at *all* ages.

Many experts think, however, that the remainder of the '90s will see a lot more 'mid-life career-change,' since this is the decade when a whopping number -- the U.S.'s 76 million 'baby boomers' -- are entering mid-life. In a 1992 survey by the Roper Organization, 45% of U.S. workers said they would change their careers if they could.[2]

Whether you're employed or unemployed, the basic question you always have to ask yourself about your current (or most recent) job is: "Is this *really* what I want to do for the rest of my life?"

The answer often is "No," -- for millions and millions of workers. And maybe for you. This doesn't necessarily mean that you made a big fat mistake in ever taking your current job (though that happens often enough, Heaven knows).

But even if it *was* a good choice, it is a law of the '90s that jobs can alter profoundly in a day and a night. You are given new additional responsibilities, without any raise in salary. Or your much-beloved supervisor moves on, leaving you working for a jerk. Or, your workplace comes under stringent budget cuts. Or your funding is lost, entirely. Whatever. The job which was a perfect match for you just a year ago, is now 'the job from hell.'

You may want to change careers for other reasons, too. When we are very young, work is largely a matter of how to find bread to eat, and clothes to wear, and how to put a roof over our head. But as we move through the various stages of our life, our work becomes increasingly a matter *also* of how our soul lives out its dreams. For example, if we have been working too hard, we want to figure out how we can take more time 'to smell the roses.'

And, through each of our *work* choices during our lifetime, we increasingly find ourselves looking for the work we feel we were *born* to do. This is what we mean when we speak of looking

---

1. The word **career** remains a very fuzzy word in the English language, but there are three principal senses in which it is used. It is used, first of all, to mean *work* in contrast to *learning* or *leisure*. Thus when clothing ads speak of "a career outfit," they are referring to clothes which are worn primarily at work, rather than during learning-activities or leisure-activities. It is used, secondly, to sum up *a person's whole life in the world of work.* Thus when people say of someone at the end of their life, "He or she had a brilliant career," they are not referring to a particular occupation, but to *all* the occupations this person ever held, and all the work this person ever did. Thirdly, in its most common sense, as I indicated above, it is used as a synonym for the word *occupation* or *job* -- particularly where that occupation or job offers opportunity for promotion and advancement, toward the top. (This *movement toward a goal* is its most primitive meaning, as it dates from the origin of the word. *Career* comes from the Latin *carrus*, referring to a racetrack where horses compete in an effort to win a race.) *Adapted from the article on "Careers" in* Collier's Encyclopedia, *written by the author. Copyright © 1991 by Macmillan Educational Company.*

2. The survey was done for Shearson Lehman Brothers, in 1992. Should you wish further resources dealing with career-change at mid-life, these include:

Betsy Jaffe, Ed.D., *Altered Ambitions: What's Next in Your Life? Winning Strategies To Reshape Your Career.* Donald I. Fine, Inc., 19 W. 21st St., New York, NY 10010. 1991.

Godfrey Golzen and Philip Plumbley, *Changing Your Job After 35.* Kogan Page Ltd., 120 Pentonville Rd., London Nl 9JN. 1988.

for **our vocation**, or **calling**. By *vocation* we mean work which is the deepest fulfillment of our being, reflecting who we most truly are. By *calling* we mean *from God* -- in whom over 94% of us believe (see the Epilogue).

Most of us are engaged in a life-long search for, and journey toward, *meaning* -- a process in which career-change plays an important part.

IS THIS THE RIGHT TIME
TO CHANGE CAREERS?

Whenever we are unhappy in our present job or career, we usually can hear two voices raging back and forth within our mind:

Is this what you want to do for the rest of your life?

"No."

Then what are you going to do about it?

"I don't know. Perhaps this just isn't the right time."

And so the dialogue goes -- while in our inmost spirit we know that waiting for 'the right time' is *often* just another name for *procrastination*.

Friend, there will probably never be *a right time*. Conditions will always be *difficult*. Obstacles will always be *in your way*, which you must overcome. It will always be a challenge, if you decide to launch out into the deep and mysterious destiny to which you feel called, by the dreams of your soul.

Yet a time comes in each of our lives when we *know* we simply *must* accept that challenge. When we know we must go do what we really want to do with our life -- no matter how hard the times, and no matter how difficult the struggle may be. We know that there is always a chance that we may not succeed at it. But we know we will never feel we have really lived our life, until we at least *try*.

And, in some ways, it is a journey in which we cannot fail. Even if we are not able to *pull it off*, in any way that the world calls 'successful,' we know we will at the very least be a better man or woman, for having tried. There is something about *adversity* and *challenge* that tests and refines *character*, even as the fire tempers steel. A challenge toward growth and change -- willingly accepted -- can often bring out the very best in us.

If nothing else, it brings *clarity of vision*. As the late Sylvia Sims[3], the legendary singer, once said about adversity, "I'm down to the bottom of my sound, but I'm up to the clearest understanding of my life."

THE EIGHT PARTS
OF A JOB OR CAREER

There are eight parts to a career (or job), and career-change involves changing one or more of those eight parts.

We can illustrate those eight parts with an occupation most people are familiar with, namely that of a waiter or waitress at a restaurant: (1) *the workplace:* here it is the restaurant, an indoor place (usually) with lots of supervision; (2) *the stated goal:* here it is to wait on customers, keep them happy, and make a profit for the restaurant owners; (3) *the tasks assigned:* here they may include: to clean and set tables, to bring the customers a menu,

3. Born in 1918, died in 1992.

water, and bread; to take their orders; to hand the orders in to the kitchen; to serve the orders, when ready; to stay alert to any additional service the customers may require; to bring them their check when done; and to clear off and set the table again; (4) *the tools:* here they are the uniform (if there is one), cleaning-rags, silverware, napkins, plates, menus, food, checks, pen or pencil, and perhaps a calculator; (5) *the salary:* here it is whatever the boss and waiter/waitress agree upon, plus tips, of course; (6) *the time involved:* here it is whatever number of hours there are on the worker's shift; (7) *the talents or skills needed:* here they are: *punctuality* -- being able to get to work on time; *taking instructions* from both boss and customer; *advising* (customers on what is good on the menu, if they ask); *empathy* (conveying warmth); *memory* (remembering who ordered what); *finger-dexterity* (being skillful at handling dishes); *copying* (prices on to the check); *computing* (the total on the check); and *problem-solving* (when problems arise, with the customer); (8) *the fields of knowledge needed:* here they include: *food* (what the items on the menu mean); *mathematics* (addition and subtraction, at least); *machine operation* (knowing how to operate a cash register and/or calculator).

If you're contemplating a new career because you've been unhappy in your previous job or career, it is useful to sit down and figure out *which* of these eight areas you were *most* unhappy with.

'THE ESSENCE'
OF CAREER-CHANGE

As I said, career-change can involve changing any, or all, of these eight parts.

But *in its essence* it is always a change in just *two* of these areas, above all. Those are: the skills you want to use, and the fields of knowledge or interest, that you want to use them with.

It will help you to understand this, if you memorize two simple equations:

1. Skills ≈ general job-titles.   Job-titles ≈ skills. *and*
2. Knowledges ≈ field of interest.   Field of interest ≈ knowledges.

Note that in the equations above we use the sign for *correspond to* ($\approx$) instead of the *equals* (=) sign. The equation is *approximate*, not *exact*.

The *essence* of a career-change is that you change one or both of these: your general job-title, *and* the field you operate in. You do this by *redefining* what skills you most want to use, and/or by *redefining* what knowledges you most want to use them with.

Types of Career Change Visualized

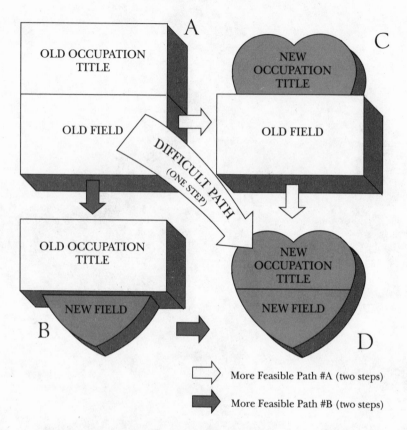

© Copyright 1991 by D. Porot. Adapted by special permission. Not to be reproduced without permission in writing from D. Porot.

You may change just the field, but not your general job-title (**A** to **B** in the diagram on this page). Or you may change just your general job-title, but not your field (**A** to **C** in the diagram). Or, for the completest and most *dramatic* career-change you may change *both* (**A** to **D** in the diagram).

To illustrate, let's say you're an accountant, and you work for a television station. If you move to a new field, but keep the same general job-title, (**A** to **B**) then you might, let us say, become an accountant with a medical firm. If you keep the same field, but move to a new general job-title (**A** to **C**), you

Types of Career Change Visualized

© Copyright 1991 by D. Porot. Adapted by special permission. Not to be reproduced without permission in writing from D. Porot.

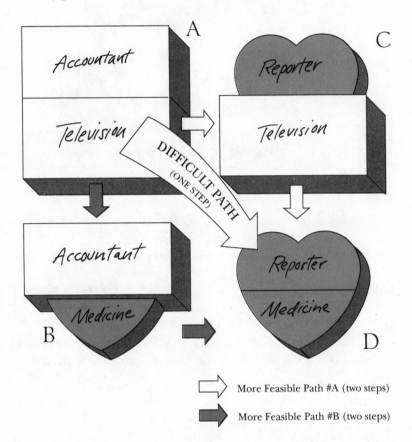

⇨ More Feasible Path #A (two steps)

➡ More Feasible Path #B (two steps)

might become a reporter at that television station. And if you change both title and field (**A** to **D**), you might become a reporter for a medical journal. So, the completest and most dramatic career-change would, in this case, be that of moving from being an accountant at a television station, to a reporter for a medical journal. New general job-title, new field.

Note, in the diagram above, that were you to pursue this profoundest career-change (**A** to **D**), there are three ways you can move into your new career -- gradually or abruptly, in steps or all at once -- as shown by the arrows.

MUST I GO BACK TO SCHOOL?

When people change careers, voluntarily or involuntarily, it is widely assumed that there is only *one* way to go about it: *go back to school, for retraining.* With this approach, you look at the diagram above, and you see that career-change involves a field and a general job-title -- so you *choose* a field or general job-title -- often on the basis of very little knowledge -- and then go major in that field at some nearby college or university.

This is the way that 98% of all career-choice or career-change is done. But there are four problems with this approach to career-change.

Problem #1: There's a bewildering menu of choices out there. In the U.S., for example, experts can *name* at least 12,860 different occupations or careers that you might choose between, and these have 8,000 alternative job-titles, for a total of over 20,000. A description of all these 20,000 occupations or careers is to be found in the *Dictionary of Occupational Titles,* familiarly known as the *D.O.T.,* published by the U.S. Department of Labor's Bureau of Labor Statistics.[4] Similar volumes exist in a number of other countries.

Most people, however, find that trying to choose between 20,000 of anything, is virtually impossible. That's why, as it's turned out, 90% of the U.S. workforce of 119 million workers are employed in 300 job-titles, and 50% are employed in just 50 job-titles.[5] A lot of these careers don't require you to go back to school for retraining. On the other hand, even for those that do, if none of them really interest you, then what's the point?

Problem #2: Many times, if you enroll in a particular degree program, you spend *a lot of time* learning knowledges and skills you really already have. I once spent a weekend with a group of graduate students in Spokane, Washington, who asked me to help them identify the skills and fields of knowledge which they already possessed; when they saw that they already had the skills they were allegedly trying to pick up in their graduate school program, they were more than just a little *mad.* And who can blame them? Why work so hard to acquire what you already possess?

Problem #3: You *think* that *if* you get this degree, you will be much more *marketable* and able to command a higher salary -- but unfortunately there is no guarantee, *whatsoever,* that this is true. Every year thousands and thousands of people finish a degree program, and then find out they *still* cannot find a job. The degree does *not* come with a job automatically attached. If you could see my mail, from dejected adult-graduates, 22 years of age, 30 years of age, 40 years of age, 50 years of age, who

---

4. The *D.O.T.* is updated periodically -- most recently in 1991, with the previous revision 1977, supplemented in 1982, 1986, and 1987. While vocational experts always recommend using this directory, our readers have testified that they find it a *terribly unhelpful* book. As one reader, a chemist, wrote: "While it claims to be updated to 1991, I found that *every* description I looked up was last updated in 1977! . . . I read the description of my present occupation and it sounds quite good. I wish I was doing what it described. That may have been what a chemist did 20 years ago but with most companies de-emphasizing research it is hardly what they do today."

5. These 50 job-titles are: automobile mechanics, carpenters, electricians, light- or heavy-truck drivers, construction laborers, welders & cutters, groundskeepers & gardeners, electrical and electronic engineers, freight, stock, and material movers or handlers, guards and police, production occupations supervisors, farmers, commodities sales representatives, laborers, lawyers, farm workers, stockhandlers & baggers, insurance sales, janitors & cleaners, managers & administrators, supervisors & proprietors, machine operators, teachers -- university, college, secondary and elementary school, stock & inventory clerks, accountants & auditors, underwriters and other financial officers, secretaries, receptionists, childcare workers, registered nurses, typists, bookkeepers, textile sewing machine operators, nursing aides, orderlies & attendants, hairdressers & cosmetologists, waiters & waitresses, maids and housemen, cashiers, general office clerks, administrative support occupations, sales workers, computer operators, miscellaneous food preparation occupations, production inspectors, checkers & examiners, cooks, real estate sales, and assemblers.

lament that their new degree *(bought with blood, sweat and tears)* hasn't improved their chances of finding a job in their new career *one bit,* you would cry. In their letters, they are still unemployed, a year or two after graduation, or hired only for a pittance, often in occupations totally unrelated to their hard-won degree. They feel our culture lied to them, and they are depressed, and often very bitter. Thus they illustrate the unwitting irony in the phrase, *"Getting a job by degrees."*

Problem #4: Even if you do find a job, there's often a dramatic chasm (the size of the Grand Canyon) between the skills and fields of knowledge that you *thought* you were going to get a chance to use in this career, vs. the reality.[6] *Oops!* Incidentally, this happens to many first-time college graduates, as well as to those who go back later in life. And so it is, that your new career may turn out to be just as unfulfilling as your old career. You will be just as miserable, only in a different environment. (This will remind some people of jumping into a second marriage without having first taken time to learn the lessons from the first).

The moral here is: don't assume that the only way to make a career-change is by going back to school. That takes a lot of your time, a lot of your money, and doesn't do *a thing* to guarantee you a job in your new career. It *can't* be the only way.

OKAY, WHAT'S 'THE OTHER WAY'? (THERE MUST BE ONE)

The other way -- the creative way -- involves forgetting about going back to school, at least for the time being, and forget about *starting with* a field and a general job-title.

You start instead by doing some hard homework on yourself, first doing a thorough inventory of *What* skills you most enjoy using; and then doing a thorough inventory of *Where* you want to use those skills, in terms of your favorite knowledges which you already have or want to acquire. Then you let those *point to* a new career, whose name you discover through some investigation, interviews, and research.

This alternative approach looks like this, and will be the subject of our next three chapters:

The Creative Process of Career Change

© Copyright 1991 by D. Porot. Adapted by special permission. Not to be reproduced without permission in writing from D. Porot.

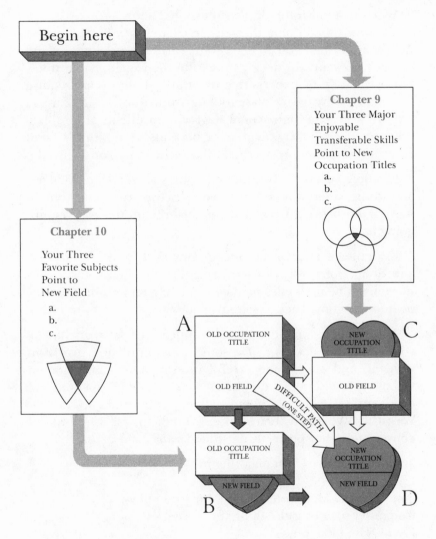

Then, you do interviewing and some library research to discover what title, and what field, your skills and knowledge point to. (Chapter 11)

---

6. See footnote 4, on page 163.

LET'S NOT BE SILLY:
SOMETIMES SCHOOL WILL
TURN OUT TO BE NECESSARY

When you finish the process illustrated above -- that is, when you have finished doing the work in Chapters 9, 10, and 11 -- it may turn out that you *do* need some further schooling, for the career you eventually decide upon. But then again, it may not.

It is claimed by experts that one-third of all careers require less than twelve years of schooling[7]; one-third of all careers require at least a high school degree; and one-third of all careers require a college degree, or beyond. So, two-thirds of all careers *don't* require you to go back to school. *But,* one-third do.

Example: if after inventorying your skills and knowledges, and doing your own research, you discover that you want to move from being a typist to being a surgeon, this *will* require going back to school.

Example: if after inventorying your skills and knowledges, and doing your own research, you discover that you want to move from being a sales manager to being an author, this may *not* require going back to school at all.

The point is, with the creative approach to career-change, you make this decision *after* some thoughtful homework on yourself, and after some careful investigation -- and not on whim or impulse. What do I mean by *whim and impulse?* Once, I overheard two college students talking, in Central Park in New York City. We'll call them Jim and Fred. In half a minute of conversation they perfectly illustrated *whim and impulse:*

Jim: Hey, what are you majoring in?
Fred: Physics.
Jim: Physics? Man, you shouldn't major in physics.
Computer science is the thing these days.
Fred: Naw, I like physics.
Jim: Man, physics doesn't pay much.
Fred: Really? What does?
Jim: Computer science. You should switch to computer science.
Fred: Okay, I'll look into it tomorrow.

You see my point. Huge life-decisions often are made in the whim of a moment. This is, indeed, the way most career choices (and career-changes) are made. No wonder surveys of worker dissatisfaction find that up to 80%, or four out of every five workers, are dissatisfied with some important aspects of their jobs or careers. *It's not a pretty picture.*

The alternative to *whim and impulse* is *planning,* and *hard thinking* and *work.* For the lazy, this is not good news. But as we grow older, and hopefully wiser, most of us begin to see the merit of this kind of homework.

Choices made intelligently, based on the sure knowledge of who we are, almost always turn out to be far superior to choices made by a roll of the dice.

This is why it is so important for you to do your homework, identifying your favorite and strongest skills, and your favorite fields of knowledge, before you choose a career, change a career, or go out to pound the pavement.

---

7. *The Guide To Basic Skills Jobs:* 2nd ed., *Vols. 1 and II.* RPM Press, Inc., P.O. Box 31483. Tucson, AZ 85751. 602-886-1990. 1993. A catalog of viable jobs for individuals with only basic work skills and/or limited education and/or limited general aptitudes -- such as persons with physical impairments, limited English proficiency, migrant workers, welfare recipients, persons with mental illness, etc. The database is *broken out* from the D.O.T., but a concise, easy-to-use classification system is added. This volume identifies over 5,000 major occupations which require no more than an eighth-grade level of education, and no more than one year of specific vocational preparation. Based upon research originally done by occupational analysts at North Carolina State University, and U.S.E.S. *Immensely useful book* if you counsel any of the above populations.

Herein lies your safety, for as Jim and Fred made clear:

> You have got to know what it is you want, or else someone is going to sell you a bill of goods somewhere along the line that can do irreparable damage to your self-esteem, your sense of worth, and your stewardship of the talents that God gave you.

Okay, let's take a *first fling* at identifying a new career for you. It's called the RIASEC theory, and was invented by John L. Holland.[8]

R for "Realistic"

People who have athletic or mechanical ability, prefer to work with objects, machines, tools, plants, or animals, or to be outdoors.

I for "Investigative"

People who like to observe, learn, investigate, analyze, evaluate, or solve problems.

The Party

C for "Conventional"

People who like to work with data, have clerical or numerical ability, carrying things out in detail or following through on others's instructions.

A for "Artistic"

People who have artistic, innovating or intuitional abilities, and like to work in unstructured situations, using their imagination or creativity.

E for "Enterprising"

People who like to work with people -- influencing, persuading or performing or leading or managing for organizational goals or for economic gain.

S for "Social"

People who like to work with people-- to inform, enlighten. help, train, develop, or cure them, or are skilled with words.

THE PARTY EXERCISE

In John's system, all jobs, careers, skills, and personality types are reduced to just six clusters or *families:* **R**ealistic, **I**nvestigative, **A**rtistic, **S**ocial, **E**nterprising, or **C**onventional. Hence, **R I A S E C**. You are asked to figure out your 'Holland Code,' which consists of three of the six letters.

The most thorough way to do this is to get your hands on a copy of John's instrument called 'The Self-Directed Search (SDS).'[9] The SDS is a self-marking test, which takes about 30–40 minutes. You score it yourself, and it will tell you *exactly* what your 'Holland code' is.[10]

If you want an immediate but not quite so accurate way of identifying your 'Holland Code,' take this 'Party Exercise' which follows:[11]

Above is an aerial view of a room in which a *two-day* party is taking place. At this party, people with the same or similar interests have (for some reason) all gathered in the same corner of the room. It is a six-sided room, and all six corners are filled with babbling people. What they are babbling about, I have made clear by each corner. Now, the questions:

• Which corner of the room would you instinctively be drawn to, as the group of people you would most *enjoy* being with for the longest time? (Leave aside any question of shyness, or whether you would have to talk with them.)

Write the *letter* for that corner here: ☐

• After fifteen minutes, everyone in the corner you have chosen leaves for another party crosstown, except you. Of the groups *that still remain* now, which corner or group would you be drawn to the most, as the people you would most *enjoy* being with for the longest time?

Write the letter for that corner here: ☐

• After fifteen minutes, this group too leaves for another party, except you. Of the corners, and groups, which remain now, which one would you most enjoy being with for the longest time?

Write the letter for that corner here: ☐

These three letters, in the order in which you wrote them --
such as 'S I A' -- are a quick guess at your 'Holland code.'

Once you know your 'Holland code,' whether from this Party
Exercise, or from the more thorough and trustworthy *Self-
Directed Search,* you then want to look up *what* jobs or careers
match that 'code.'

The way to do this is to buy, borrow, or go to your local library
to consult a copy of the *Dictionary of Holland Occupational Codes:
A Comprehensive Cross-Index of Holland's RIASEC Codes with 12,000
DOT Occupations,* by John L. Holland and Gary D. Gottfredson.
1989. 2nd ed., revised and expanded. If you can't find it *anywhere,* it is available from the same publisher listed in footnote
#9, but be aware that it costs $35. *Do not use the brief Occupations
Finder, that is included in the SDS Specimen Set, as an attempted
substitute for Holland's 640-page* Dictionary. *The Occupations Finder's
list is so short, that you can easily be depressed when you find little or
nothing that matches your code.*

Use the *Dictionary,* instead, and try all six 'permutations' of
your code, when you look it up in that *Dictionary.* What do I
mean by 'permutation?' Well, if your code is, say, S I A, then you
rearrange it in every way you can, thus:

```
S I A      A S I
S A I      A I S
I S A
I A S
```

Then look up all these codes, in Holland's *Dictionary,* and jot
down, for your future exploration, any careers that sound interesting to you, under any of the six codes.

What do you do, then, with those careers? Well, you'll be
tempted to go to the U.S. *Dictionary of Occupational Titles* (not to
be confused with Holland's *Dictionary*) and look up those careers there -- especially since Holland gives the *D.O.T.* number
for each of 12,860 occupations. *But,* one of the reasons this
temptation should be resisted is that the *D.O.T.* can be a hope-
lessly confusing not to mention unhelpful reference book *(see
footnote #4, on page 163).* Many career-changers have fallen exhausted on the battlefield of trying to wrestle something useful
out of the *D.O.T.* The *D.O.T.* didn't 'give.'

So, if you get tired of trying to make sense out of the *D.O.T.,* or if you decide to avoid it altogether, you will be glad to know that there is a better way of gathering information about careers that interest you, and that way is described at length in Chapter 11.

8. John Holland developed this more than twenty years ago, and has continually updated it since then. It has been used by more than 15 million people, thus far.

9. You can order an SDS Specimen Set from the publisher, PAR (Psychological Assessment Resources, Inc.), Box 998, Odessa, FL 33556, (1-800-331-8378, or in Florida 1-813-968-3003). The cost is about $11 *(at this writing)* -- which includes handling and shipping by UPS. This set contains not only the SDS, Form R, but also a brief *Occupations Finder* and a booklet 'You and Your Career.' There are many other versions of the SDS available: there is a version for people with limited English, a version for junior high students, a version for senior high and college students, etc., a Braille version, Canadian versions in either English or French, a Spanish version, a Vietnamese version, and a 'career planning' version. You can ask PAR for their catalog. If you want a different approach to Holland 'codes,' there is *Your Career: Choices, Chances, Changes* by David C. Borchard, John J. Kelly, and Nancy-Pat K. Weaver. Kendall/Hunt Publishing Company, Dubuque, Iowa. 1992. Fifth Edition. Pages 64–104 deal with Holland exercises.

10. Holland codes are useful for other purposes than identifying interesting jobs or careers. They can also be used for choosing one's major in college, and for choosing one's leisure activities.

If you are just starting college, and are puzzled about what to major in, you may want to get your hands on the *College Majors Finder.* It helps identify the college majors that match your Holland 'code.' Over 900 college majors are listed. Psychological Assessment Resources, Inc., P.O. Box 998, Odessa, FL 33556.

If you want to choose leisure activities that are the *opposite* of the skills you use all week long at work, see: *The Leisure Activities Finder: For Use with the Self-Directed Search and the Vocational Preference Inventory.* 1990. Psychological Assessment Resources, Inc., P.O. Box 998, Odessa, FL 33556. This takes your Holland Code and relates it to leisure activities. We recommend, however, that instead of taking your *favorite* corner, e.g., 'S,' you go *across the hexagon* (as in The Party exercise, page 168) -- which in this example, would be 'R,' and look up *those* leisure activities. The reason for this advice, is that leisure is best when it is an *alternating rhythm* to the stuff you do, and the skills you use, when you are at work.

The background theory for Holland's 'codes' is carefully explained in: John L. Holland, *Making Vocational Choices. A Theory of Vocational Personalities and Work Environments,* 2nd ed., Prentice-Hall, Inc., Sylvan Ave., Englewood Cliffs, NJ 07632. 1985. You can order it from Psychological Assessment Resources, Inc., Box 998, Odessa, FL 33556, (1-800-331-TEST, or in Florida 1-813-968-3003). $19.95, at this writing.

11. I am the inventor of the Party exercise. I mention this because we receive *many* inquiries from career counselors each year as to who invented it, and how can one get permission to buy or make multiple copies of it. The answer is, that in order to avoid competing with my friend John Holland's SDS, which I don't want to do, the Party Exercise is not available separately, nor can it be reproduced by itself. It *is* available in a relatively cheap form, namely *The Beginning Quick Job-Hunting Map,* available from Ten Speed Press, Box 7123, Berkeley CA 94707, at $1.95 a piece.

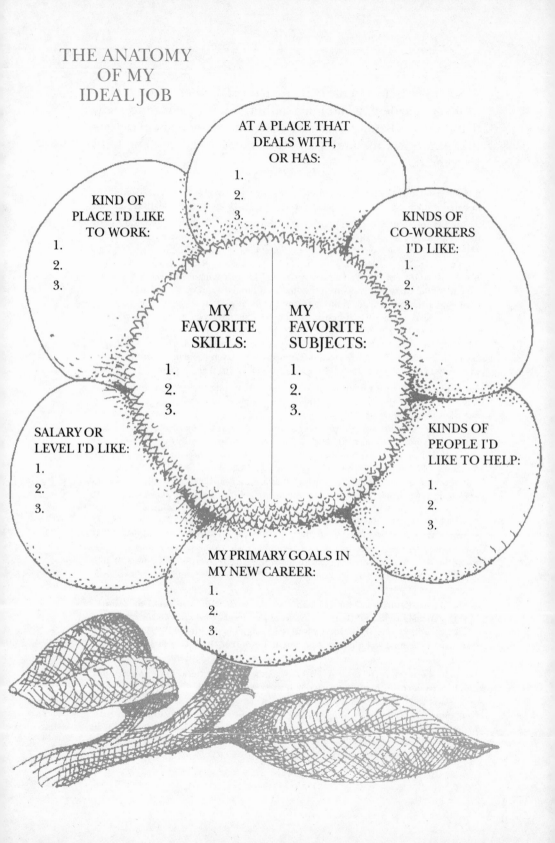

THE ANATOMY
OF MY
IDEAL JOB

AT A PLACE THAT
DEALS WITH,
OR HAS:
1.
2.
3.

KIND OF
PLACE I'D LIKE
TO WORK:
1.
2.
3.

KINDS OF
CO-WORKERS
I'D LIKE:
1.
2.
3.

MY
FAVORITE
SKILLS:
1.
2.
3.

MY
FAVORITE
SUBJECTS:
1.
2.
3.

SALARY OR
LEVEL I'D LIKE:
1.
2.
3.

KINDS OF
PEOPLE I'D
LIKE TO HELP:
1.
2.
3.

MY PRIMARY GOALS IN
MY NEW CAREER:
1.
2.
3.

'QUICK AND DIRTY' VS.
SLOW AND CLEAN

Your Holland code is the 'quick and dirty' way of approaching career change. It will sometimes be very helpful; it will sometimes lead nowhere. It can sometimes be elating; it can sometimes be depressing, for career-changers.

Fortunately, there is a more thorough way to approach career change, the **WHAT**, **WHERE**, and **HOW** method, which we now turn to, in our next three chapters.

Work is Love made visible.
And if you can't work with love but only with distaste,
It is better that you should leave your work
and sit at the gate of the temple and
take alms of the people who work with joy.

Kahlil Gibran, *The Prophet*

CHAPTER NINE

The Systematic Approach To
The Job-Hunt and Career-Change:

PART I

What

Skills Do You Most Enjoy Using?

Chapter 9

PEANUTS reprinted by permission of UFS, Inc.

SHOULD I DO THE HOMEWORK IN THESE NEXT THREE CHAPTERS IF I'M NOT THINKING ABOUT CHANGING CAREERS?

Oh yes. This WHAT, WHERE, and HOW method was originally devised by 'the creative minority'[1] as a *job-hunting* method -- one which turned out to have the highest rate of success (86%) of any job-hunting method ever devised.

But because, in its essence, it requires you as job-hunter to go back to 'square one,' and inventory all over again what gifts you have been given, and what knowledges you have acquired, it is also the best *career-change* method ever devised.

It is both things, at the same time. This is your 'Plan B' when the normal job-hunting process just isn't working for you. And this is also your 'Plan B' when you want to change careers.

Indeed, even those who are happily employed find these chapters (9 and 10 in particular) immensely helpful, when they want to get a fresh view of their skills and talents. As one worker wrote,

---

1. John Crystal, Sidney Edlund, Richard Lathrop, Bernard Haldane, Tom Jackson, and Arthur Miller were the original creators of one or more parts of this approach, though it was the late John Crystal who gave it its name.

"I like my present job a lot. Still, the skills inventory you have people do in your book is something I do every two or three years. Each time I do it, I find out more specific things about what I do well. This information tells me what to watch for in the world -- what kind of tasks I can volunteer for and do very well at. I know more about the *kind* of thing I want to be, do, be surrounded by. I am now sensitized and ready to recognize them when they swim by."

It is time for us, then, to describe what this process is, and how you go about doing it.

AN OUTLINE OF THE
CREATIVE APPROACH

The creative approach to career-change has three parts to it. These parts are in the form of three questions: *What, Where* and *How.*

1. **WHAT?** The full question here is *what are the skills you most enjoy using?* To answer this question, you need to identify or inventory what **skills/gifts/talents** you have; and then you need to prioritize them, in their order of importance and enjoyment for you. Experts call these transferable skills, because they are transferable to any field/career that you choose, regardless of where you first picked them up, or how long you've had them.

2. **WHERE?** The full question here is *where do you most want to use those skills?* This has to do *primarily* with the **fields of knowledge** *you have already acquired,* which you most enjoy using. But *where* also has to do with your preferred working conditions, what kinds of data or people or things you enjoy working with, etc.

3. **HOW?** The full question here is *how do you find such jobs, that use your favorite skills and your favorite fields of knowledge?* To answer this question, you need to do some interviewing of various people in order to find out the information you are looking for, here. You begin this interviewing with the awareness that *skills* point toward job-titles; and knowledges help define your *field,* where you will use those skills. Beyond identifying a job-title in a particular field, you want also to find out the names of *organizations* in your preferred geographical area which have such jobs to offer. *And,* the names of the people or person

there who actually has the *power* to hire you.

With this overview in mind, we must now proceed to describing each of these three steps in some detail.

This chapter will be devoted to **What**. Chapter 10 will be devoted to **Where**. And Chapters 11 and 12 will be devoted to **How**.

So, let us begin.

THE MOST MISUNDERSTOOD
WORD IN THE WORLD OF WORK:
SKILLS

You begin career-change (or a thorough job-hunt) by first identifying your transferable, functional, skills. Here you are looking for the basic building-blocks of your work.

Unfortunately, many people totally misunderstand this word 'skills,' and consequently are always putting themselves *down*, by their use of it. This habit begins early: "I haven't really got any skills," high school graduates will say. It continues with college students: "I've spent four years in college, studying my (head) off; I haven't had time to pick up any skills." And it lasts through the middle years, especially when a person is thinking of changing his or her career: "I want to change careers, but all my skills are in my old career." This misunderstanding is shared, we might add, by altogether too many employers, human resource departments, personnel people, and other so-called 'vocational experts.'

The most common misunderstanding about skills is to think they are such things as: *has lots of energy, gives attention to details, gets along well with people, shows determination, works well under pressure, is sympathetic, intuitive, persistent, dynamic, dependable*, etc. Popular tests, such as the *Myers-Briggs*, measure this sort of thing.[2]

However, these are not functional/transferable skills -- which is what we are looking for. Rather, these are **traits** or **temperaments**. Traits are the *style* with which you do a particular skill. For example, let's take *"gives attention to details."* And let us say that one of your *transferable skills* might be something like *"conducting research."* In which case, your *trait -- "gives attention to details"*-- describes the manner or style with which you do that research.

All right, then, let's see what transferable skills *are*.

A CRASH COURSE ON
TRANSFERABLE SKILLS

Here are the most important truths you need to keep in mind about transferable, functional, skills:

1. Your transferable *(functional)* skills are the most basic unit -- the atoms -- of whatever career you may choose.

You can see this from this diagram:

---

2. Myers-Briggs measures what is called *psychological type*. For further reading about this, see:

Paul D. Tieger & Barbara Barron-Tieger, *Do What You Are: Discover the Perfect Career for You Through the Secrets of Personality Type*. 1992. Little, Brown & Company, Inc., division of Time Warner Inc., 34 Beacon St., Boston MA 02108. Includes the TAPT (Tieger Assessment of Personality Types) for those who cannot obtain the MBTI® (Myers-Briggs Type Indicator) -- registered trademarks of Consulting Psychologists Press.

David Keirsey and Marilyn Bates, *Please Understand Me: Character & Temperament Types*. 1978. Includes the Keirsey Temperament Sorter -- again, for those who cannot obtain the MBTI® (Myers-Briggs Type Indicator) -- registered trademarks of Consulting Psychologists Press.

A publication list of other readings about psychological type can be obtained from the Center for Application of Psychological Type, 2720 N.W. 6th St., Gainesville, FL 32609. 904-375-0160.

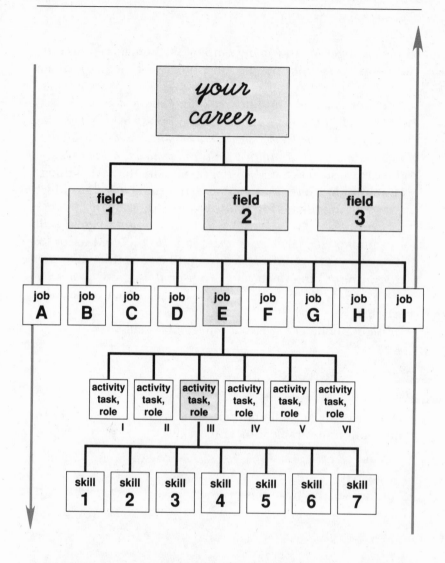

Skills are the one thing that all jobs, and all careers, have in common. Thus skills serve as a bridge from one job to another, or one career to another. Once you have demonstrated or mastered a skill in one career, you can easily *transfer* it from one job to another, from one field to another, from one career to another. That is why they are called *transferable* skills.

The essence of career-choice or career-change is the rearrangement of your *old* transferable skills into new patterns, by establishing new *priorities*.

It is most akin to the rearranging of *building blocks* that we used to do, as a child. Change the order of these building blocks *(which skills you now decide are most important to you)*, and you have defined a new career.

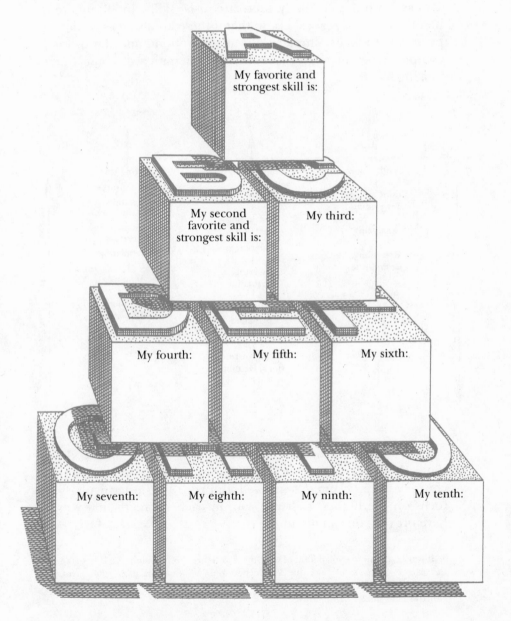

My favorite and strongest skill is:

My second favorite and strongest skill is:

My third:

My fourth:

My fifth:

My sixth:

My seventh:

My eighth:

My ninth:

My tenth:

2. You should always claim the *highest* skills you legitimately can, on the basis of your past performance.

Your skills break down into three *families,* according to whether you use them with **Data (Information)**, or **People** or **Things**. Within each family, there are *simple* skills, and there are higher, or *more complex* skills, so that if these are listed as vertical pyramids, with the simpler skills at the bottom, and the more complex ones in order above it, the diagram will come out looking like this:

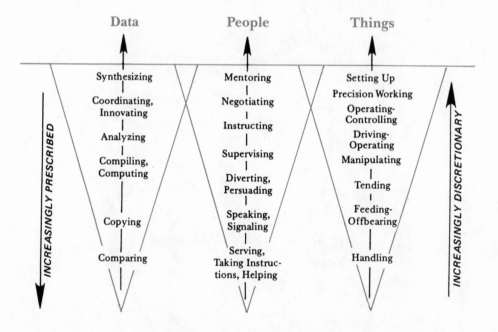

Each higher skill *usually* requires you to be able also to do those skills listed below it (on the pyramid diagram) -- so of course you can claim *those,* as well. But you want to particularly focus on the highest skill you can, in each pyramid, that you have proven you can do, in the past.[3]

---

3. If you desire more explanation of what these skills are, I refer you in the U.S. to the *Dictionary of Occupational Titles,* the 1991 revised fourth edition, pp. 1005–1006 in vol. II. It should be available in any public library in the U.S. Other countries (such as Canada) have similar dictionaries.

3. **The higher your transferable skills, the more freedom you will have on the job.**

Simpler skills can be, and usually are, heavily *prescribed* (by the employer), so if you claim *only* the simpler skills you will have to *'fit in'* -- following the instructions of your supervisor, and doing exactly what you are told. The *higher* the skills you can legitimately claim, the more you will be given discretion to carve out the job the way you want to -- so that it truly fits you.

"*. . . and give me good abstract-reasoning ability, interpersonal skills, cultural perspective, linguistic comprehension, and a high sociodynamic potential.*"

4. **The higher your transferable skills, the less competition you will face for whatever job you are seeking, because jobs which use such skills will rarely be advertised through normal channels.**

Not for you the way of classified ads, resumes, and agencies. No, if you can legitimately claim higher skills, then to find such jobs you *must* follow the creative job-hunting methods described in Chapters 11 and 12.

Drawing by Ed Fisher; © 1981 The New Yorker Magazine, Inc. Used by permission.

The essence of this creative approach to job-hunting or career-change is that you approach *any organization that interests you, whether they have a known vacancy or not.* So of course, at whatever place you visit -- and particularly at those which have not advertised any vacancy -- you will find far fewer job-hunters that you have to compete with.

In fact, if the employers you visit happen to like you well enough, they may be willing to create for you a job that does not presently exist. *In which case, you will be competing with no one, since you will be the sole applicant for that newly created job.*

While this doesn't happen all the time, it is amazing how many times it does happen. *The reason* it does is that the employers you visit may have been *thinking* about creating such a job within their organization, for quite some time -- but with this and that, they just never got around to *doing* it. Until they saw you. Then they decided they didn't want to let you get away, since *good employees are as hard to find as are good employers.* Voila! It is now time to create that job they have been thinking about for many weeks or months. That new job which is not only what they need, but is exactly what you were looking for. Match-match. Win-win.

Note well: you have not only gotten a job, but by this job-hunting initiative of yours, have helped *accelerate* the creation of more jobs in your country, which is so much on everybody's mind here in the '90s. How nice to help your country, as well as yourself!

> And so, the paradoxical moral of all this: The less you 'stay loose,' and the higher you legitimately can define your skill level with *Data/Information* and/or *People* and/or *Things*, **the more likely you are to find a job.** Just the opposite of what the typical career-changer starts out believing.

From *The Saturday Review*, 8/8/77. Reprinted by special permission.

"Let's put it this way — if you can find a village without an idiot, you've got yourself a job."

"I WOULDN'T RECOGNIZE MY SKILLS IF THEY CAME UP AND SHOOK HANDS WITH ME"

Well, now that you know what skills technically *are*, the problem is figuring out your own. If you are one of the few lucky people who already know what your transferable skills are, blessed are you. Write them down, and put them in the order of preference, for you.

If, however, you don't know what your skills are (and 95% of all workers *don't*), then you will need to write out some stories about yourself. Generally speaking, they should not be stories about your **feelings** (ecstasy or sorrow), or stories about things that happened **to** you.

Rather, they should be stories about your own **actions** or achievements when you were most enjoying yourself, or doing something you felt good about. Each story should be about a paragraph long, two paragraphs at the most. The most useful stories will be those that include, in one order or another, these five parts:

Column I Your Goal: What You Wanted To Accomplish	II Some Kind of Hurdle or Restraint You Faced	III What You Did Step by Step *(Use your verb, plus other verbs)*	IV Description of the Result *(What you accomplished)*	V Any Measure or Quantities To Prove Your Achievement

Here is a specific example, so you can see how it is done:

"I wanted to be able to take a summer trip with my wife and four children. I had a very limited budget, and could not afford to put my family up, in motels. I decided to rig our station wagon as a camper.

"First I went to the library to get some books on campers. I read those books. Next I designed a plan of what I had to build, so that I could outfit the inside of the station wagon, as well as topside. Then I went and purchased the necessary wood. On weekends, over a period of six weeks, I first constructed, in my driveway, the shell for the 'second story' on my station wagon. Then I cut doors, windows, and placed a six-drawer bureau within that shell. I mounted it on top of the wagon, and pinioned it in place by driving two-by-fours under the station wagon's rack on top. I then outfitted the inside of the station wagon, back in the wheelwell, with a table and a bench on either side, that I made.

"The result was a complete homemade camper, which I put together when we were about to start our trip, and then disassembled after we got back home. When we went on our summer trip, we were able to be on the road for four weeks, yet stayed within our budget, since we didn't have to stay at motels.

"I estimate I saved $1900 on motel bills, during that summer's vacation."

You will notice this sample story has all the parts outlined above:

I.) **Your goal: what you wanted to accomplish:** *"I wanted to be able to take a summer trip with my marriage partner and four children."*

II.) **Some kind of hurdle, obstacle, or constraint that you faced** (self-imposed or otherwise): *"I had a very limited budget, and could not afford to put my family up, in motels."*

III.) **A description of what you did, step by step** (how you set about to ultimately achieve your goal, above, in spite of this hurdle or constraint): *"I decided to rig our station wagon as a camper. First I went to the library to get some books on campers. I read those books. Next I designed a plan of what I had to build, so that I could outfit the inside of the station wagon, as well as topside. Then I went and purchased the necessary wood. On weekends, over a period of six weeks, I . . ." etc., etc.*

IV.) **A description of the outcome or result:** *"When we went on our summer trip, we were able to be on the road for four weeks, yet stayed within our budget, since we didn't have to stay at motels."*

V.) **Any measurable/quantifiable statement of that outcome, that you can think of:** *"I estimate I saved $1900 on motel bills, during that summer's vacation."*

So write out your first story, in keeping with this model.

My transferable skills dealing with

THINGS

I am good at

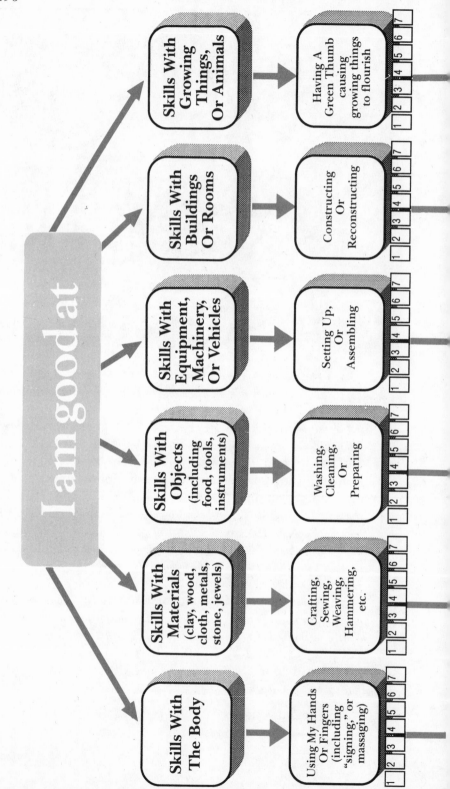

Skills With The Body

Using My Hands Or Fingers (including "signing," or massaging)
1 2 3 4 5 6 7

Skills With Materials (clay, wood, cloth, metals, stone, jewels)

Crafting, Sewing, Weaving, Hammering, etc.
1 2 3 4 5 6 7

Skills With Objects (including food, tools, instruments)

Washing, Cleaning, Or Preparing
1 2 3 4 5 6 7

Skills With Equipment, Machinery, Or Vehicles

Setting Up, Or Assembling
1 2 3 4 5 6 7

Skills With Buildings Or Rooms

Constructing Or Reconstructing
1 2 3 4 5 6 7

Skills With Growing Things, Or Animals

Having A Green Thumb causing growing things to flourish
1 2 3 4 5 6 7

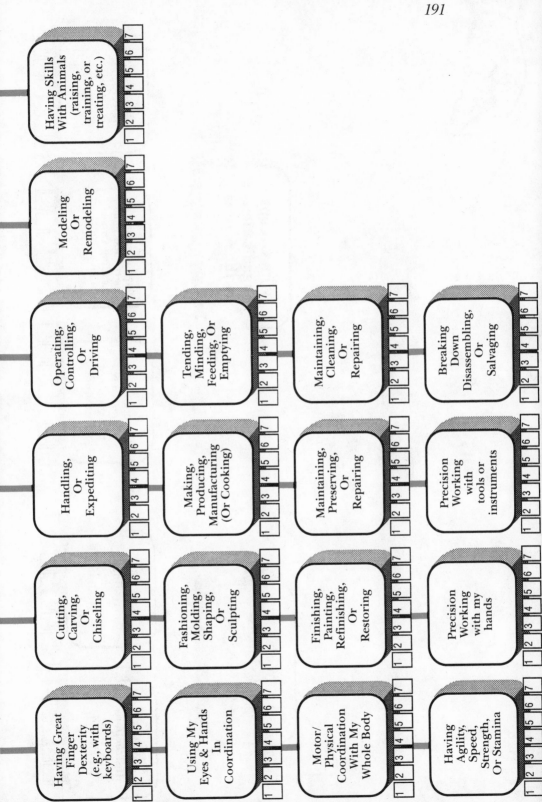

My transferable skills dealing with

PEOPLE

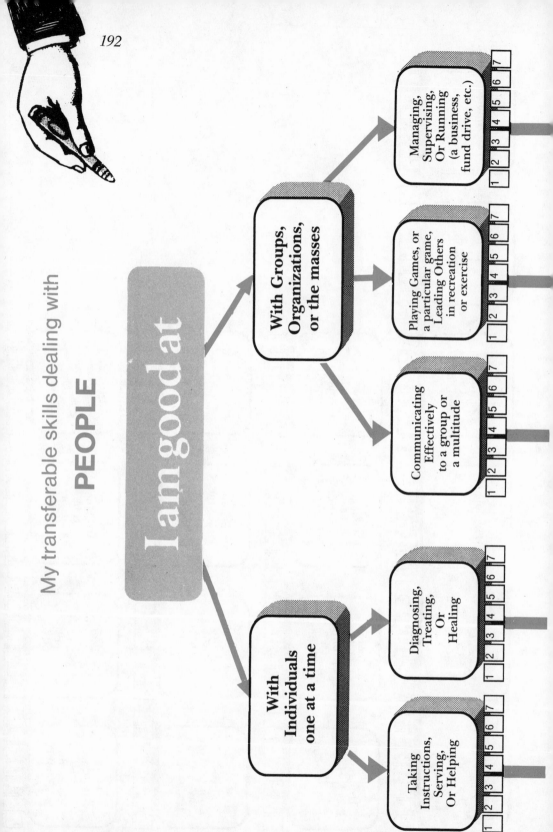

I am good at

With Groups, Organizations, or the masses

Managing, Supervising, Or Running (a business, fund drive, etc.)

1 2 3 4 5 6 7

Playing Games, or a particular game, Leading Others in recreation or exercise

1 2 3 4 5 6 7

Communicating Effectively to a group or a multitude

1 2 3 4 5 6 7

With Individuals one at a time

Diagnosing, Treating, Or Healing

1 2 3 4 5 6 7

Taking Instructions, Serving, Or Helping

1 2 3 4 5 6 7

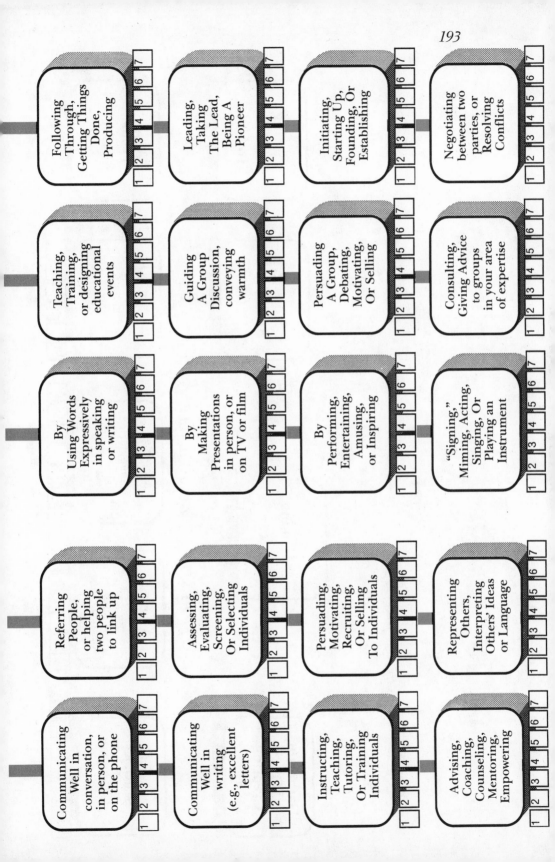

Communicating
Well in
conversation,
in person, or
on the phone
`1` `2` `3` `4` `5` `6` `7`

Referring
People,
or helping
two people
to link up
`1` `2` `3` `4` `5` `6` `7`

By
Using Words
Expressively
in speaking
or writing
`1` `2` `3` `4` `5` `6` `7`

Teaching,
Training,
or designing
educational
events
`1` `2` `3` `4` `5` `6` `7`

Following
Through,
Getting Things
Done,
Producing
`1` `2` `3` `4` `5` `6` `7`

Communicating
Well in
writing
(e.g., excellent
letters)
`1` `2` `3` `4` `5` `6` `7`

Assessing,
Evaluating,
Screening,
Or Selecting
Individuals
`1` `2` `3` `4` `5` `6` `7`

By
Making
Presentations
in person, or
on TV or film
`1` `2` `3` `4` `5` `6` `7`

Guiding
A Group
Discussion,
conveying
warmth
`1` `2` `3` `4` `5` `6` `7`

Leading,
Taking
The Lead,
Being A
Pioneer
`1` `2` `3` `4` `5` `6` `7`

Instructing,
Teaching,
Tutoring,
Or Training
Individuals
`1` `2` `3` `4` `5` `6` `7`

Persuading,
Motivating,
Recruiting,
Or Selling
To Individuals
`1` `2` `3` `4` `5` `6` `7`

By
Performing,
Entertaining,
Amusing,
or Inspiring
`1` `2` `3` `4` `5` `6` `7`

Persuading
A Group,
Debating,
Motivating,
Or Selling
`1` `2` `3` `4` `5` `6` `7`

Initiating,
Starting Up,
Founding, Or
Establishing
`1` `2` `3` `4` `5` `6` `7`

Advising,
Coaching,
Counseling,
Mentoring,
Empowering
`1` `2` `3` `4` `5` `6` `7`

Representing
Others,
Interpreting
Others' Ideas
or Language
`1` `2` `3` `4` `5` `6` `7`

"Signing,"
Miming, Acting,
Singing, Or
Playing an
Instrument
`1` `2` `3` `4` `5` `6` `7`

Consulting,
Giving Advice
to groups
in your area
of expertise
`1` `2` `3` `4` `5` `6` `7`

Negotiating
between two
parties, or
Resolving
Conflicts
`1` `2` `3` `4` `5` `6` `7`

My transferable skills dealing with

INFORMATION, DATA, AND IDEAS

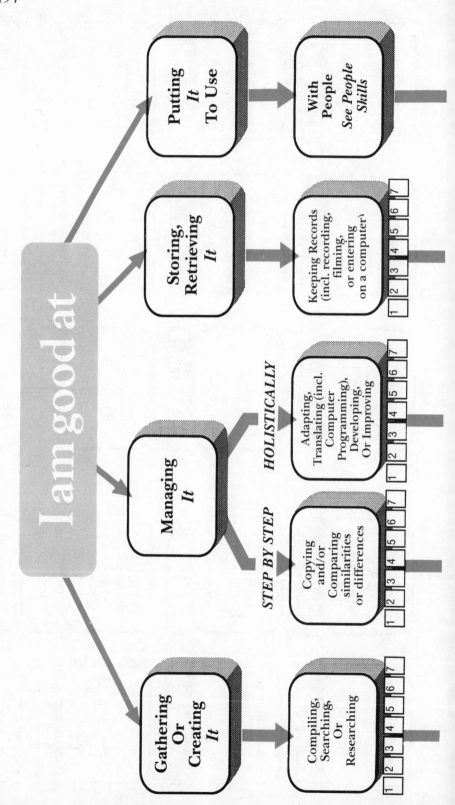

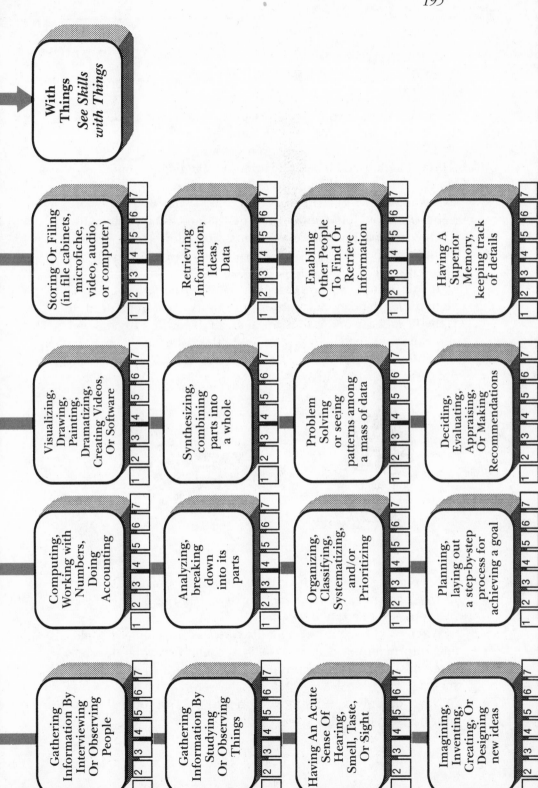

With
Things
*See Skills
with Things*

Storing Or Filing
(in file cabinets,
microfiche,
video, audio,
or computer)
1 2 3 4 5 6 7

Retrieving
Information,
Ideas,
Data
1 2 3 4 5 6 7

Enabling
Other People
To Find Or
Retrieve
Information
1 2 3 4 5 6 7

Having A
Superior
Memory,
keeping track
of details
1 2 3 4 5 6 7

Visualizing,
Drawing,
Painting,
Dramatizing,
Creating Videos,
Or Software
1 2 3 4 5 6 7

Synthesizing,
combining
parts into
a whole
1 2 3 4 5 6 7

Problem
Solving
or seeing
patterns among
a mass of data
1 2 3 4 5 6 7

Deciding,
Evaluating,
Appraising,
Or Making
Recommendations
1 2 3 4 5 6 7

Computing,
Working with
Numbers,
Doing
Accounting
1 2 3 4 5 6 7

Analyzing,
breaking
down
into its
parts
1 2 3 4 5 6 7

Organizing,
Classifying,
Systematizing,
and/or
Prioritizing
1 2 3 4 5 6 7

Planning,
laying out
a step-by-step
process for
achieving a goal
1 2 3 4 5 6 7

Gathering
Information By
Interviewing
Or Observing
People
1 2 3 4 5 6 7

Gathering
Information By
Studying
Or Observing
Things
1 2 3 4 5 6 7

Having An Acute
Sense Of
Hearing,
Smell, Taste,
Or Sight
1 2 3 4 5 6 7

Imagining,
Inventing,
Creating, Or
Designing
new ideas
1 2 3 4 5 6 7

ANALYZE THE STORY
USING THE 'SKILLS KEYS'
DIAGRAMS

Once you have your first story thus written, put a title at the top. In this case, "Story/Achievement #1."

Then, go to the *skills* diagrams, found on pages 190–195. These diagrams are a *rhapsody* upon the *Data, People,* and *Things* skills that we saw earlier, on page 184. And they are here laid out as *mock typewriter keys* (hence we call them *skills keys*). They are generally, though not always, in order of increasing complexity.

On each page of those diagrams, work down each vertical column of the *skills keys*. Ask yourself, as you look at each *key*, "Did I use this transferable skill *in this story?*"

If you decide you probably did, color in the *little box* that is right under that key. Since this is your Story/Achievement #1, it is the #1 *little box* under that key, that you color in. I suggest you use a **red** pen, pencil, or crayon, to do this coloring.

Precision
Working
with my
hands

Keep going down each vertical column, in turn, on each of the *skills keys* pages. Under each key, color in box #1 *only if* you feel you used that skill *in this story*.

When you have gone over all the *skills keys,* for Things, People, and Information, once, you will have identified your transferable skills. Or, at least, *those* transferable skills which you used in story #1.

Now, you only have six more stories to go, and you will know your transferable skills.

HELP ME MAKE IT
THROUGH MY LIFE

You may know exactly what six stories from your life you want to select at this point. In which case, just jump to page 202.

But our experience has been that most people run into trouble when they try to think of six more stories. So, we need some help here, and it turns out the best way of approaching the problem is to write a summary of your life. There are two ways of doing this. We'll call them: Plan A, and Plan B.

Plan A

The preferred way of doing this, by far, is to write an *outline* of your life, which we call *A Memory Net*. It is faster than writing the autobiography suggested in Plan B, below; it usually takes three hours or less, even allowing for heavy thinking, and a couple of long walks.

The Net is on the next two pages. The first three columns are alternative ways of establishing *pegs* on which to hang your memories. You can use five-year periods of your life (Column 1), *or* jobs you have held (Column 2), *or* places you have lived (Column 3). *Naturally,* you can use alternative *pegs* if you wish: people who were influential in your life at various times, schools you attended, etc., etc.

As you continue across the Memory Net, after Column 3, you should fill out Columns 4, 6, and 8 first *(Activities)*. Then go back and fill in Columns 5, 7, and 9 *(Accomplishments)*. The Activities are more general, and easier to recall. The Accomplishments are more specific, and can use some memory-jogging -- which the *Activities* furnish. In all the columns, put down just a few words, to jog your memory, rather than attempting a more detailed description, *at this time.*

Memory

| Column 1 | Column 2 | Column 3 | Column 4 | Column 5 |

Jogging Your Memory   Leisure

In Terms of Five-Year Periods	In Terms of Jobs You Have Held	In Terms of Places You Have Lived	Activities	Accomplishments
e.g. 1995–				
1990–1994				
1985–1989				
1980–1984				
1975–1979				
1970–1974				
1965–1969				
1960–1964				
1955–1959				
1950–1954				
1945–1949				
1940–1944				

Net

Column 6	Column 7	Column 8	Column 9
Learning		**Labor**	
Activities	Accomplishments	Activities	Accomplishments

Plan B

If you just draw a blank when trying to construct an *outline* of your life, then you will probably have to take the longer way, and write out a detailed mini-autobiography of your entire life. An informal summary for your eyes only -- *who cares about your spelling or grammar?* -- of

where you've ever been, and
what you've ever done,
where you were ever working, and
what you did there (not in terms of job titles -- *forget them* -- but **in terms of what you feel you accomplished** there).

As you write this, take the time to describe **your spare time**, in each place where you lived. What did you do? What did you most enjoy doing? Any hobbies? Avocations? Great. Were there any activities in your work that paralleled the kinds of things you enjoyed doing in your leisure?

Concentrate both on the things you have done, and also on the particular characteristics of your surroundings that were important to you, and that you really enjoyed: green grass, the theater, tennis, warm climate, skiing, or whatever.

Keep yourself open and sensitive to whatever insights may pop up, about your life outside the workplace. Notice particularly as you go, what values keep surfacing. Truth, beauty, color, light, nature, justice, spirituality, righteousness, ambition, compassion, security, service, popularity, status, power, friends, achievement, love, authority, freedom, glamor, giving, integrity, honesty, loyalty, sensitivity, caring -- which of these holds the most meaning and importance for you? Stay alert and sensitive to questions such as this. You will get much clearer about who you are willing to work with and for, and who you are not.

Sift later. For now, put down anything that helped you to enjoy a particular moment or period of your life. Keep your eye constantly on: *enjoyable*. It's not *always* a guide to what you should be putting down, but it sure is more reliable than any other key that people have come up with.

Don't be afraid if at times it sounds, to your modest ears, like boasting. Who's going to see this document besides you, God, and any loved one that you choose to show it to? So, let it rip.

Just be *sure* to back up your elation and sense of pride with concrete examples, and figures.

Don't try to make this mini-autobiography very structured. You can bounce back and forth in time, if that's more congruent with *your* way of doing things.

When your mini-autobiography is all done, you may have a small book -- it can run 30 pages or more. *(My, you've done a lot of living, haven't you?)* Now, you have something to search, looking for evidences of your skills.

Once you have finished this overview of your life, whether through the mini-autobiography, or the Memory Net, you are ready to choose your next story.

SELECTING STORY #2

Look over the Memory Net or your mini-autobiography, and select the story you are going to use as your Story #2 -- some time you felt good about, when you were achieving something, and enjoying yourself. If you are using the Memory Net, study particularly columns 5, 7, and 9.

Choose, if possible, an entirely different kind of story/ achievement than Story #1 -- perhaps from another time in your life, or in another arena *(work/leisure/learning)*.

Once you have selected this story, write it out in detail, following the same procedures as you did with Story/Achievement #1.

Back to the *skills keys,* back to the same question -- different box -- for each *skill key:* "Did I use this skill *in this story* (#2)?" If the answer is "Yes," or even "I think so," color in the little box right under that *key,* that has the number 2 in it.

You're beginning to get the hang of it. Continue through all the *keys* in the same fashion as before.

AND ANOTHER,
AND ANOTHER

Repeat the same process five more times, choosing a new story each time -- until you have been through Story/Achievement #7, and the little boxes under each *skill key* that are numbered.

LOOK BACK,
FOR PATTERNS

You will now want to ask yourself these questions, as you study the completed *skills keys* pages, with their filled-in little red boxes:

1) Which transferable skills are *most* colored-in -- those on the Things page, or those on the People page, or those on the

Data/Information page? Which of the three families are my personal favorites -- regardless of whether the little boxes are colored-in under them, or not? Is my strong-suit with Things, or People, or Data? And if the answer is *More than one,* in what order of priority?

2) Looking at all the *skills keys* pages, which are my eight favorite skills, regardless of which *family* they belong to? Are they the *skills keys* that got the most little boxes colored-in under them, or does my intuition tell me I chose bad stories, and my really favorite skills include some that are not well colored-in? (If so, write some new stories, that demonstrate you have those skills that are your favorites.)

3) Do I see any *patterns* -- where the same transferable skills *popped up* again and again, in most of my stories? (Experts call this *the irresistibility* of skills -- some skills, in each of us, *insist* on getting used.)

PRIORITIZE, PRIORITIZE

As I mentioned previously, every full-fledged career-change requires that you *rearrange* the 'building blocks' of your skills, into a new order of priority. The priority is *everything.* It will ultimately help determine *what* career you choose.

Also, in the best of all possible worlds, it is not always possible to get a job that uses *all* your transferable skills. But you want to take care that you are pursuing a job which at least allows you to use *the most important of your skills.*

Furthermore, down the line this prioritizing will help you to better describe yourself during a job-interview. Instead of saying, in effect, "I have some skills," you will be prepared to say, "This is my greatest strength or talent, this is my next greatest, etc."

Hence the absolute importance, once you have fleshed out your skills, of putting them in order of importance or priority to you. If you skip over this step, you are essentially committing job-hunting suicide.

Take your eight favorite skills, and put them in absolute order of importance to you. You can do this *prioritizing* either by guess and by gosh, *or* you can use the prioritizing grids on the following pages.

How to Prioritize Your Lists of Anything

On the next page is a method for taking up to ten[4] items, of any kind, and figuring out which one is the most important to you, which one is next most important, and so forth.

• Insert the items to be prioritized, in any order, in Section A, on the following page. Then, in Section B, compare just the *two* items that are in each small box. For example, the first little box has a *1 and a 2 in it,* standing for whatever you listed as item #1 and item #2 in Section A. Which one of these is more important to you? You might ask it in some such form as this: "If I were offered two jobs, and the first job gave me a chance to use the skill in item #1, but *not* the skill listed in item #2 -- while the second job gave me just the opposite: a chance to use the skill listed in item #2, but *not* the skill listed in item #1 -- which job (other things being equal) would I take?" You then circle, in that first box in Section B, whichever skill you preferred *in that pair.* Then go on to the next pair in the next little box of Section B, which has *1 and 3 in it,* and ask the same *kind* of question.

• When you have finished circling one number in each small little box, turn to Section C. The first question there is: "How many times circled?" -- referring to the items, by number, immediately above. So, count how many times item #1 got circled, and enter that total immediately under the "1" in Section C. Then count how many times item #2 got circled, etc., through all ten items. The next question in Section C is: "Final rank?" The one with the most circles is counted as first (copy it down as *new* number 1 in Section D). The one next most circled is counted as second (*new* number 2 in Section D). And so forth.[5]

A similar prioritizing grid for a larger number of items (twenty-four) appears on the page following the ten-item prioritizing grid.

---

4. The reason the grid deals with ten items, not eight, is that while you are only dealing with your *eight* top skills at the present, you will be dealing with ten items, in other categories, in the next chapter.

5. Each time you use this grid, make a photocopy of it, and fill in the photocopy rather than the original. (You will need to photocopy this grid many times as you go through this map. If you don't want to do that, and you have a personal computer that is an IBM or IBM-compatible, there is a computer program that prints this Grid for you. You can order it, for an $11 check ($10 + $1 shipping) made out to Ron Grossman, 9 Union Sq., Suite 110, Southbury, CT 06488. Specify whether you want the DOS or Windows version, and whether you want it on a 3.5" or 5.25" floppy disk.)

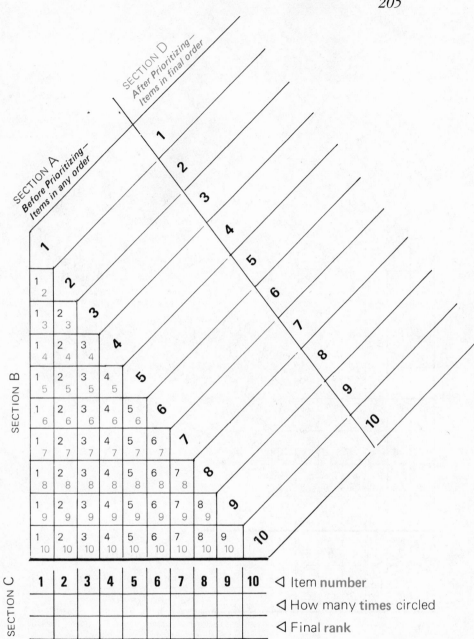

SECTION D—
*After Prioritizing—
Items in final order*

SECTION A
*Before Prioritizing—
Items in any order*

SECTION B

SECTION C

◁ Item **number**

◁ How many **times** circled

◁ Final **rank**

Prioritizing Grid
for 10 Items

Copyright © 1989 by Richard N. Bolles. All rights reserved.

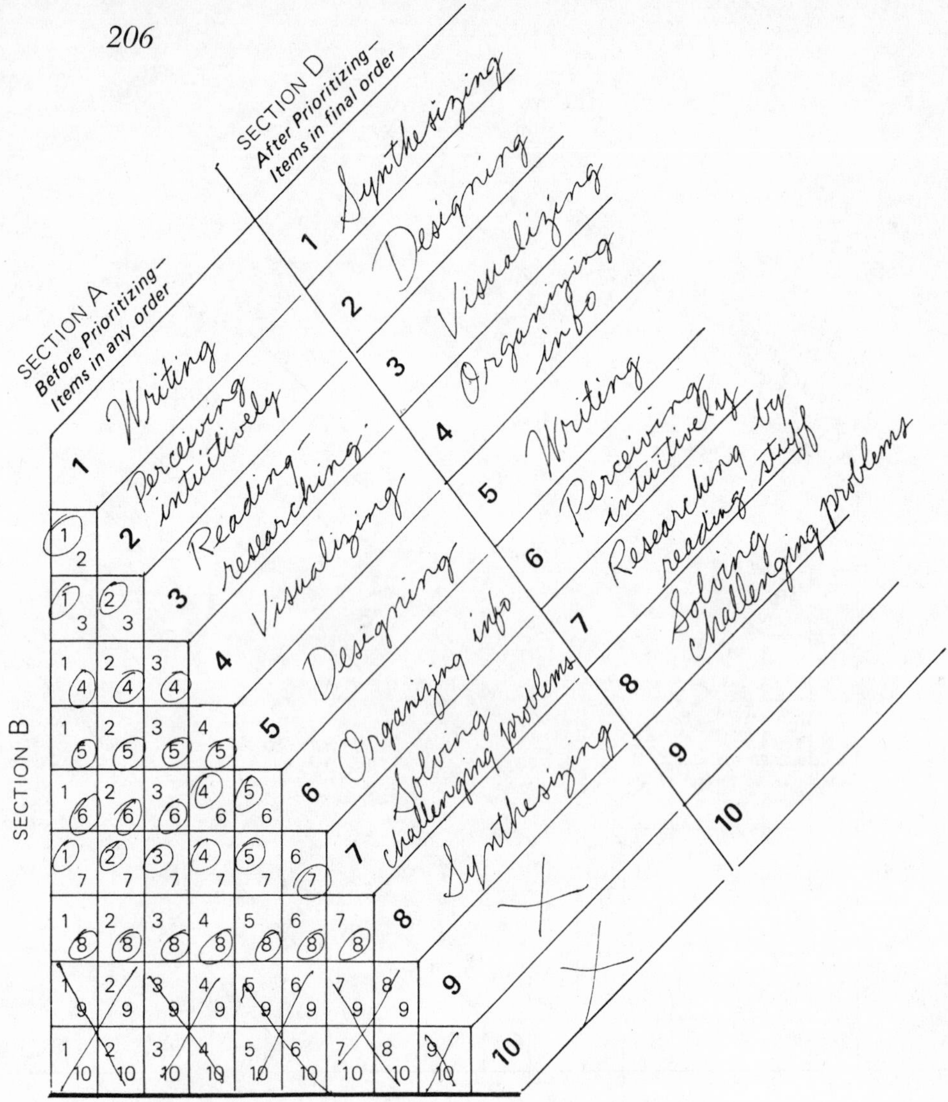

SECTION D
After Prioritizing—
Items in final order

SECTION A
Before Prioritizing—
Items in any order

SECTION B

SECTION C

Writing
Perceiving intuitively
Reading-researching
Visualizing
Designing
Organizing info
Solving challenging problems
Synthesizing

1 Synthesizing
2 Designing
3 Visualizing
4 Organizing info
5 Writing
6 Perceiving intuitively
7 Researching by reading stuff
8 Solving challenging problems

*	1	2	3	4	5	6	7	8	9	10	◁ Item **number**
	3	2	1½	5	6	3½	1	7			◁ How many **times** circled
	5	6	7	3	2	4	8	1			◁ Final **rank**

Example

*A tie; but when 1/6 were compared (above), 6 was preferred -- hence gets an extra ½ point here.

Prioritizing Grid
for 10 Items

Copyright © 1989 by Richard N. Bolles. All rights reserved.

```
1  1  1  1  1  1  1  1  1  1  1  1  1  1  1  1  1  1  1  1  1  1  1
 2  3  4  5  6  7  8  9 10 11 12 13 14 15 16 17 18 19 20 21 22 23 24

2  2  2  2  2  2  2  2  2  2  2  2  2  2  2  2  2  2  2  2  2  2
 3  4  5  6  7  8  9 10 11 12 13 14 15 16 17 18 19 20 21 22 23 24

3  3  3  3  3  3  3  3  3  3  3  3  3  3  3  3  3  3  3  3  3
 4  5  6  7  8  9 10 11 12 13 14 15 16 17 18 19 20 21 22 23 24

4  4  4  4  4  4  4  4  4  4  4  4  4  4  4  4  4  4  4  4
 5  6  7  8  9 10 11 12 13 14 15 16 17 18 19 20 21 22 23 24

5  5  5  5  5  5  5  5  5  5  5  5  5  5  5  5  5  5  5
 6  7  8  9 10 11 12 13 14 15 16 17 18 19 20 21 22 23 24

6  6  6  6  6  6  6  6  6  6  6  6  6  6  6  6  6  6
 7  8  9 10 11 12 13 14 15 16 17 18 19 20 21 22 23 24

7  7  7  7  7  7  7  7  7  7  7  7  7  7  7  7  7
 8  9 10 11 12 13 14 15 16 17 18 19 20 21 22 23 24

8  8  8  8  8  8  8  8  8  8  8  8  8  8  8  8
 9 10 11 12 13 14 15 16 17 18 19 20 21 22 23 24

9  9  9  9  9  9  9  9  9  9  9  9  9  9  9
10 11 12 13 14 15 16 17 18 19 20 21 22 23 24

10 10 10 10 10 10 10 10 10 10 10 10 10 10
11 12 13 14 15 16 17 18 19 20 21 22 23 24

11 11 11 11 11 11 11 11 11 11 11 11 11
12 13 14 15 16 17 18 19 20 21 22 23 24

12 12 12 12 12 12 12 12 12 12 12 12
13 14 15 16 17 18 19 20 21 22 23 24

13 13 13 13 13 13 13 13 13 13 13
14 15 16 17 18 19 20 21 22 23 24

14 14 14 14 14 14 14 14 14 14
15 16 17 18 19 20 21 22 23 24

15 15 15 15 15 15 15 15 15
16 17 18 19 20 21 22 23 24

16 16 16 16 16 16 16 16
17 18 19 20 21 22 23 24

17 17 17 17 17 17 17
18 19 20 21 22 23 24

18 18 18 18 18 18
19 20 21 22 23 24

19 19 19 19 19
20 21 22 23 24

20 20 20 20
21 22 23 24

21 21 21
22 23 24

22 22
23 24

23
24
```

Total times each number got circled

1	2	3	4	5	6
7	8	9	10	11	12
13	14	15	16	17	18
19	20	21	22	23	24

Prioritizing Grid
for 24 Items

Each time you use this grid, make a photocopy of it, and fill in the photocopy rather than the original. (You will need to photocopy this grid many times as you go through this process.)

Copyright © 1989 by Richard N. Bolles. All rights reserved.

Reproduced by special permission of Playboy Magazine.
Copyright © 1979 by Playboy.

"I'll tell you why I want this job. I thrive on challenges. I like being stretched to my full capacity. I like solving problems. Also, my car is about to be repossessed."

'FLESH OUT' YOUR TOP EIGHT

Once you have identified your eight top favorite transferable skills *(or however many you wish),* you need to *flesh out* your skill-description for each of those eight. Currently, each one is basically only *one word.* One word is a good place to *begin,* but a poor place to *end.* For, in the end, you want to be able to describe each of your talents or skills in more than just one word.

Let me give an example. Let's say one of your skills is *organizing.* "I'm good at *organizing*" doesn't tell us much. Organizing what? People, as at a party? Nuts and bolts, as on a workbench? Or lots of information, on a computer? Those are three entirely different skills. The one word *"organizing"* doesn't tell us which one is *yours.*

So, *please* go back over the transferable skills you identified as your eight favorites, and make sure that each one-word definition gets *fleshed out* with an object -- some kind of *Data/Information,* or some kind of *People,* or some kind of *Thing.* Add an adverb or adjective, too.

Why adjectives? Well, "I'm good at organizing information *painstakingly and logically*" and "I'm good at organizing information *in a flash, by intuition,*" are two *entirely different* skills. The difference between them is spelled out not in the verb, nor in the object, but in the adjectival or adverbial phrase there at the end.

> When you are face-to-face with an employer, you want to be able to explain what makes you different from nineteen other people who can basically do the same thing that you can do. It is often the adjective or adverb that will save your life, during that explanation.

So, expand each definition of your eight favorite skills, in the fashion I have just described.

A PICTURE IS WORTH A THOUSAND WORDS

When you have your eight top favorite skills, in order, and *fleshed out*, it is time to put them on the diagram on page 211, called as you can see *My Favorite Tasks/Transferable Skills*.

It is part of a larger diagram, which we call *The Flower Diagram*, that you will find on the following page.

Over the years, we have found it useful to enroll *all* the information you gather about yourself, in these chapters, on one unifying diagram, a kind of *picture of yourself*. We have tried a variety of graphic images over the years, but the one which has proved the most popular has been a picture of each of us as *a flower*. It is an interesting and accurate metaphor, because in the world of work there *are* certain environments in which we blossom, and there are environments which practically kill us. As is true of a flower.

Anyway, this is the picture we'll be working on throughout the next chapter, and for right now, we have one of the *petals* from that Flower, on page 211.[6]

Copy on to this *petal*, the list of your eight favorite skills, in order, as you have fleshed them out. *(If you wish, you may of course copy the petal onto a larger piece of paper, so that it is easier to read.)*

---

6. The whole process discussed in Chapters 9, and 10, is available from Ten Speed Press, Box 7123, Berkeley, CA 94707, as a workbook -- with the Flower Diagram and the other exercises appearing on larger, 8½ × 11" sheets. It is called "How to Create A Picture of Your Ideal Job," and you can order it directly from them ($5.95). If all you want is just a larger size picture of the Flower diagram, that is available from them, also, as a poster you can write on. The *skills keys*, enlarged, appear on the reverse side ($4.95).

The Flower Diagram

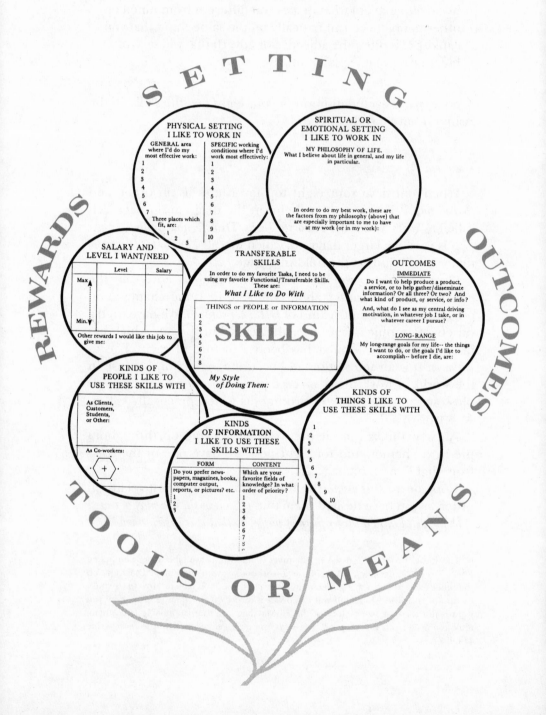

SETTING

PHYSICAL SETTING I LIKE TO WORK IN

GENERAL area where I'd do my most effective work:
1
2
3
4
5
6
7

SPECIFIC working conditions where I'd work most effectively:
1
2
3
4
5
6
7
8
9
10

Three places which fit, are:
1
2
3

SPIRITUAL OR EMOTIONAL SETTING I LIKE TO WORK IN

MY PHILOSOPHY OF LIFE.
What I believe about life in general, and my life in particular.

In order to do my best work, these are the factors from my philosophy (above) that are especially important to me to have at my work (or in my work):

OUTCOMES

SALARY AND LEVEL I WANT/NEED

	Level	Salary
Max.		
Min.		

Other rewards I would like this job to give me:

REWARDS

TRANSFERABLE SKILLS

In order to do my favorite Tasks, I need to be using my favorite Functional/Transferable Skills. These are:
What I Like to Do With

THINGS or PEOPLE or INFORMATION
1
2
3
4
5
6
7
8

SKILLS

My Style of Doing Them:

OUTCOMES

IMMEDIATE
Do I want to help produce a product, a service, or to help gather/disseminate information? Or all three? Or two? And what kind of product, or service, or info?

And, what do I see as my central driving motivation, in whatever job I take, or in whatever career I pursue?

LONG-RANGE
My long-range goals for my life-- the things I want to do, or the goals I'd like to accomplish-- before I die, are:

KINDS OF PEOPLE I LIKE TO USE THESE SKILLS WITH

As Clients, Customers, Students, or Other:

As Co-workers:

KINDS OF THINGS I LIKE TO USE THESE SKILLS WITH
1
2
3
4
5
6
7
8
9
10

KINDS OF INFORMATION I LIKE TO USE THESE SKILLS WITH

FORM	CONTENT
Do you prefer newspapers, magazines, books, computer output, reports, or pictures? etc.	Which are your favorite fields of knowledge? In what order of priority?
1	1
2	2
3	3
	4
	5
	6
	7
	8
	9

TOOLS OR MEANS

My Favorite
Transferable Skills / Tasks

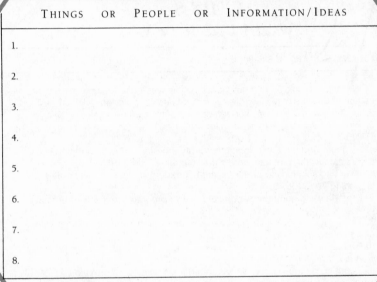

In order to do my favorite Tasks/Skills,
I need to be using my favorite
Functional/Transferable Skills.
These are:

What I Like to Do With

THINGS	OR	PEOPLE	OR	INFORMATION/IDEAS
1.				
2.				
3.				
4.				
5.				
6.				
7.				
8.				

My Style
of Doing Them: (so-called "traits" or "self-management skills")
e.g., "quickly," "thoroughly," "painstakingly," etc.

Example

Object

Modifying Phrase

Verb

In order to do
my favorite tasks
I need to be using my
favorite Functional/Transferable
SKILLS
What I Like to Do With.

TʜɪNGS ᴏʀ Pᴇᴏᴘʟᴇ ᴏʀ Iɴꜰᴏʀᴍᴀᴛɪᴏɴ/Iᴅᴇᴀꜱ

1. Writing, particularly with humor, for people who need to know more information about one of my favorite fields of interest/knowledge   INFORMATION
2. Crafting, with precision, wooden objects of my own design   THINGS
3. Precision working with my own tools and instruments to do woodcrafting THINGS
4. Planning and directing an entire activity (physical project), bringing it to completion, with great attention to the last detail   INFORMATION
5. Inventing solutions to problems in the physical world, by creating new technologies   IDEAS
6. Programming computers, particularly with programs that solve particular problems in the physical world   IDEAS
7. Laying out a step-by-step process for achieving the implementation of a design of my own devising   IDEAS
8. Evaluating why a particular design or process in the physical world isn't working   INFORMATION
9. Teaching a group of people who need to know more information about one of my favorite fields of interest/knowledge   INFORMATION
10. Starting, initiating new physical projects involved with design, problem-solving, and the employment of electronics   IDEAS

My Style of Doing Them:

I am a person who is self-motivated, takes lots of initiative, is resourceful and creative, patient and persevering despite obstacles. I enjoy a challenge, maintain neatness and order in my workplace, am accurate, methodical, thorough, particularly with details, and achievement oriented.

THE 'STYLE' WITH WHICH
YOU USE YOUR SKILLS

There is one final task, left, in your skill-identification. You will notice on the petal above, that there is a space at the bottom called 'My Style of Doing Them *(The Skills).*' This serves as a kind of *catch-basin* for what people traditionally call *Traits*, as I mentioned earlier in this chapter. When you are face-to-face with an employer, they will be useful, as you try to describe what makes you different from nineteen other people who can do the same thing that you do.

You know what traits are. Such things as: *accurate, adaptable, diligent, energetic, enthusiastic, innovative, methodical, patient, persevering, punctual, work quickly, responsible, self-reliant, tactful, thorough, versatile,* and the like. Figure out what your traits are, and enroll them at the bottom of this petal diagram.

And that's it, for this chapter.

Voila! You now have finished with **WHAT**.

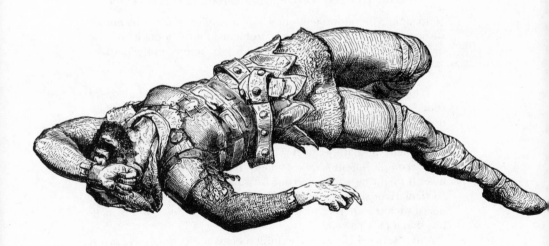

ADDENDUM **TO CHAPTER 9:**

SOME PROBLEMS YOU MAY RUN INTO,
WHILE DOING YOUR SKILL-IDENTIFICATION

In doing the aforementioned skill-identification, it will not be surprising if you run into some problems. Let us look at the five more common ones that have arisen for job-hunters, in the past:

1. "I don't know exactly what is an achievement."

When you're looking for a story/achievement to illustrate one of your skills, you're *not* looking for something that only you have done, in the history of the world. What you're looking for is a lot simpler than that. You're looking for *any* time in your life when you did something that was, at that time of your life, a source of pride and accomplishment *for you*. It might have been learning to ride a bike. It might be achieving your first quota, at work. It might be a particularly significant project that you designed, in mid-life. It doesn't matter whether or not it pleased anybody else; it only matters that it pleased you.

I like Bernard Haldane's definition of an achievement. He says it is: something you yourself feel you have done well, that you also enjoyed doing and felt proud of. In other words you are looking for an accomplishment which gave you two pleasures: enjoyment while doing it, and satisfaction from the outcome. That doesn't mean you may not have sweated as you did it, or hated *some parts* of the process, but it does mean that basically you enjoyed *most of* the process. The pleasure was not simply in getting it done.

Generally speaking, an achievement will have all the parts outlined on page 188.

2. "I don't see why I should look for skills I enjoy; it seems to me that employers will only want to know what skills I do well. They will not care whether I enjoy using the skill or not."

Well, sure, it is important for you to find the skills you do well, above all else. But, generally speaking, that is hard for you to evaluate about yourself. Do I do this well, or not? Compared to whom? Even aptitude tests can't resolve this dilemma for you. So it's better to take the following reverse equations, which experience has shown to be true:

If it is a skill you do well, you will generally enjoy it.

If it is a skill you enjoy, it is generally because you do it well.

Experience has shown that people rarely enjoy something they do very badly. There are occasional exceptions, usually when you are engaged in amateur athletics or leisure. But that's all.

With these equations in hand, you will see that -- since they are equal anyway -- it is much more useful to ask yourself, "Do I enjoy doing it?" instead of hunting for the elusive "Do I do it well?" I repeat: listing the skills you most enjoy is -- in most cases -- just another way of listing the skills you do best.

The reason why this idea -- of making enjoyment the key -- causes such feelings of uncomfortableness in so many of us is that we have an old historical tradition in this country which insinuates you shouldn't really enjoy yourself in life. To suffer is virtuous.

Sample: Two girls do babysitting. One hates it. One enjoys it thoroughly. Which is more virtuous in God's sight? According to that old tradition, the one who hates it is more virtuous. Some of us feel this instinctively, even if more logical thought says, Whoa!

We have this subconscious fear that if we are caught enjoying life, punishment looms. Thus, the story of two Scotchmen who met on the street one day: "Isn't this a beautiful day?" said one. "Aye," said the other, "but we'll pay for it."

We feel it is okay to talk about our failures, but not about our successes. To talk about our successes appears to be boasting, and that is manifestly a sin. Or so we think. We shouldn't be enjoying so much about ourselves.

But look at the birds of the air, or watch your pets at play. You will notice one distinctive fact about that part of God's creation: when a bird or a pet does what it is meant to do, by God and nature, it manifests true joy.

Joy is so clearly a part of God's plan for us. God wants us to eat; therefore He made eating enjoyable. God wants us to sleep; therefore He made sleeping enjoyable. God wants us to procreate, love, and make love; therefore He made sex enjoyable, and love even more so.

Likewise, God gives to each of us unique combinations of skills and talents which He wants us to contribute to His general plan -- to the symphony of the world, and the music of the spheres. Therefore, **when we use the talents He most wants each of us to use, He attends it with a feeling of great joy.** Everywhere in God's plan for His creation, joy rewards right action.

You need to identify the skills you enjoy using -- not only now, as you are in the process of choosing a new career, but also later when you are face-to-face with an employer. True, bad employers will not care whether you enjoy a particular task, or not. But good employers will care greatly. They know that unless a would-be employee has **enthusiasm** for his or her work, the quality of that work will always suffer.

3. "I have no difficulty finding stories to write up, from my life, that I consider to be enjoyable achievements; but once these are written, I have great difficulty in seeing what the skills are -- even if I stare at the skills keys diagram for hours. *I need somebody else's insight."*

You will want to consider getting two friends or two other members of your family to sit down with you, and do skill identification through the practice of 'Trioing' which I invented some twenty years ago to help with this very problem. This practice is fully described in my book, *Where Do I Go From Here With My Life?* But to save you the trouble of reading it, here is -- in general -- how it goes:

a. Each of the three of you quietly writes up some story of an accomplishment in their life that was enjoyable.

b. Each of the three of you quietly analyzes just your own story to see what skills you see there; you jot these down.

c. One of you then volunteers to go first. You read your story aloud. The other two jot down on a piece of paper whatever skills they hear you using. They ask you to pause if they're having trouble keeping up. You finish your story. You read aloud the skills *you* picked out in that story.

d. Then the second person tells you what's on their list: what skills *they* heard you use in your story. You copy them down, below your own list, even if you don't agree with every one of them.

e. Then the third person tells you what's on their list; what skills *they* heard you use in your story. You copy them down, below your own list, even if you don't agree with every one of them.

f. When they're both done, you ask them any questions for further elaboration that you may have. *"What did you mean by this skill? Where did you think you heard me using it?"*

g. Now it is the next person's turn, and you repeat steps 'c' through 'f' with them. Then it is the third person's turn, and you repeat steps 'c' through 'f' with them.

h. Now it is time to move on to a second story for each of you, so you begin with steps 'a' through 'g' all over again, except that each of you writes a new story. And so on, through seven stories.

4. "How do I know if I've done this all correctly? What if I just think I understood what I was supposed to do, but I really didn't? I want to be sure the stuff I've identified is really going to help me in my job-hunt."

It will, if you've followed *all* the directions above *(no shortcuts)* and *if* you avoided stating your skills in the jargon or language of your past career. This is a point on which some professions fall down: people who formerly were in professions filled with a lot of jargon. Let us take clergy as an example. It is not useful to conclude, from your skill-identification, *"I am good at preaching."* If you are going to choose a new career, out there in what you call the secular world, you must not use language that locks you into the past. Or suggests that you can do one field and one field only. So, in the case of preaching, for example, ask yourself, what is its larger form? *"Teaching?"* Perhaps. *"Motivating people?"* Perhaps. *"Inspiring people to the depths of their being?"* Perhaps. *Only you can say what is true, for you.* But in one way or another be sure to get your skills out of *any jargon that locks you into your past career.*

Let's look at a few other questions, to be sure you've done the job of skill-identification *well.* Have you thus far steered clear of putting a job title on what you're aiming toward? Skills can point to many different jobs, which have a multitude of titles, as we shall see in Chapter 11. Don't lock yourself in, prematurely.

"I'm looking for a job where I can **use** the following skills," is fine. But, "I'm looking for a job where I can **be** a (job title)" is a no-no, at this point in the process of career-change.

Are you willing to look at a number of alternatives, as you move through Chapters 10 and 11? Or is your desire to finish this off *fast* leading you to push prematurely for just one way to go? *Stay loose.* Keep *all* your options open.

5. "I don't want to do the lengthy process you described, writing out seven stories, and working through the skills keys, etc. Is there any shortcut to the process of identifying your skills?"

Sure. Following is a sampler of *skill-verbs.* The way in which this list is typically used by career-changers or job-hunters is to put a check-mark in front of each skill that: a) you believe you possess; b) you enjoy doing; and c) you believe you do well.

A List of 247 Skills as Verbs

achieving
acting
adapting
addressing
administering
advising
analyzing
anticipating
arbitrating
arranging
ascertaining
assembling
assessing
attaining
auditing
budgeting
building
calculating
charting
checking
classifying
coaching
collecting
communicating
compiling
completing
composing
computing
conceptualizing
conducting
conserving
consolidating
constructing
controlling
coordinating
coping
counseling
creating
deciding
defining
delivering
designing

detailing
detecting
determining
developing
devising
diagnosing
digging
directing
discovering
dispensing
displaying
disproving
dissecting
distributing
diverting
dramatizing
drawing
driving
editing
eliminating
empathizing
enforcing
establishing
estimating
evaluating
examining
expanding
experimenting
explaining
expressing
extracting
filing
financing
fixing
following
formulating
founding
gathering
generating
getting
giving
guiding

handling
having
 responsibility
heading
helping
hypothesizing
identifying
illustrating
imagining
implementing
improving
improvising
increasing
influencing
informing
initiating
innovating
inspecting
inspiring
installing
instituting
instructing
integrating
interpreting
interviewing
intuiting
inventing
inventorying
investigating
judging
keeping
leading
learning
lecturing
lifting
listening
logging
maintaining
making
managing
manipulating
mediating

meeting
memorizing
mentoring
modeling
monitoring
motivating
navigating
negotiating
observing
obtaining
offering
operating
ordering
organizing
originating
overseeing
painting
perceiving
performing
persuading
photographing
piloting
planning
playing
predicting
preparing
prescribing
presenting
printing
problem
 solving
processing
producing
programming
projecting
promoting
proof-reading
protecting
providing
publicizing
purchasing
questioning

raising
reading
realizing
reasoning
receiving
recommending
reconciling
recording
recruiting
reducing
referring
rehabilitating
relating
remembering
rendering
repairing
reporting
representing
researching
resolving
responding
restoring
retrieving
reviewing
risking
scheduling
selecting
selling
sensing
separating
serving
setting
setting-up
sewing
shaping
sharing
showing
singing
sketching
solving
sorting
speaking

studying
summarizing
supervising
supplying
symbolizing
synergizing
synthesizing
systematizing
taking
taking
 instructions
talking
teaching
team-building
telling
tending
testing and
 proving
training
transcribing
translating
traveling
treating
trouble-
 shooting
tutoring
typing
umpiring
understanding
understudying
undertaking
unifying
uniting
upgrading
using
utilizing
verbalizing
washing
weighing
winning
working
writing

A Friendly Word to Procrastinators

If two weeks have gone by, and you haven't even *started* doing the inventory in this chapter, then -- I hate to tell you this -- you're going to have to get someone to help you. Choose a helper for your job-hunt -- a friend rather than family, if possible. A *tough* friend. You know, *taskmaster.* Ask them if they're willing to help you. Assuming they say yes, put down in *both* your appointment books a regular *weekly* date when you will guarantee to meet with them, and they will guarantee to meet with you, check you out on what you've done already, and be very stern with you if you've done little or nothing since last week's meeting. Tell them that it is at least a 20,000-hour, $200,000 project. It's also responsible, concerned, committed Stewardship of the talents God gave you.

Where did we get the figure of 20,000 hours? Well, a forty-hour-a-week job, done for fifty weeks a year, adds up to 2,000 hours annually. So, how long are you going to be doing this new career that you are looking for? How many years do you plan to stay in the world of work? Ten years? That means 20,000 hours. Twenty years? That's 40,000 hours. So, it's at least a 20,000-hour project.

Where did we get the figure of $200,000? Well, figure it out for yourself. If you earned, let us say, at least $10 an hour in your new career, that *times* 20,000 hours adds up to $200,000. If by chance you were to earn $20 an hour, that would be $400,000.

So, in working through this chapter and the two following ones, you're working on a 20,000 hour, $200,000 project, at least. It's *worth* giving the time to, believe me.

And if you don't have the self-discipline to stick at it, it's worth enlisting a friend to help you.

If you have no friend who will help you, then you're probably going to want to think about professional help. Read, study, memorize, Appendix A in the back of this book. Go talk to several career-counselors. Choose the one you like best, and *get on with it.*

You've only one life to live, my friend. And every day is precious.

How far you go in life
Depends on your being
Tender with the young,
Compassionate with the aged,
Sympathetic with the striving, and
Tolerant of the weak & strong;
Because someday in your life,
You will have been all of these.
George Washington Carver

CHAPTER TEN

The Systematic Approach To
The Job-Hunt and Career-Change:

PART II

Where

Do You Want To
Use Your Skills?

222

Chapter 10

"WHILE YOU'RE WAITING FOR YOUR SHIP
TO COME IN, WHY DON'T YOU DO SOME
MAINTENANCE WORK ON THE PIER ?"

© Copyright, 1980, King Features Syndicate, Inc. Used by special permission.

THE LANGUAGE OF YOUR CAREER

Suppose you had a dream, one night, where you found your-self working at a fast-food place which had twelve other em-ployees -- none of whom spoke any language except Portuguese. All the customers, also, spoke nothing but Portuguese. And, in this dream, you spoke nothing but English. You can imagine how difficult it would be, in the dream, for you to enjoy that job.

The *language* spoken at your workplace is crucial. Except that in real life, *language* is not merely a question of whether a place's employees speak English or Portuguese. There are other languages *at work*. I myself once worked as *a secretary,* so let us take that job-title as an example, and see how this truth works out.

If you work as a legal secretary, there's a lot of talk there, all day long, about legal procedures. Therefore, Law is the *language* you have to live with, all day, at that workplace.

If you work as a secretary at a gardening store, there's a lot of talk there, all day long, about gardens and such. Therefore, Gardening is the *language* you have to live with, all day, at that workplace.

If you work as a secretary at an airline, there's a lot of talk there, all day long, about airlines procedures. Therefore, Airlines is the *language* you have to live with, all day, at that workplace.

If you work as a secretary at a church, there's a lot of talk there, all day long, about church procedures and matters of faith. Therefore, Religion is the *language* you have to live with, all day, at that workplace.

If you work as a secretary in a photographic laboratory, there's a lot of talk there, all day long, about photographic procedures. Therefore, Photography is the *language* you have to live with, all day, at that workplace.

If you work as a secretary at a bank, there's a lot of talk there, all day long, about banking procedures. Therefore, Banking is the *language* you have to live with, all day, at that workplace.

If you work as a secretary at a chemical plant, there's a lot of talk there, all day long, about chemicals manufacturing. Therefore, Chemistry is the *language* you have to live with, all day, at that workplace.

If you work as a secretary for the Federal government, there's a lot of talk there, all day long, about government procedures. Therefore, Government is the *language* you have to live with, all day, at that workplace.

You may object that what I am here calling *languages* are, in reality, **Fields -- Fields of interest,** or **Fields of knowledge,** or **Subjects** -- and so they are. But the *field* you choose for your next job or career determines the *language* you have to listen to, speak, and work in, all day long.

If you enjoy the *field,* you will enjoy the language you are dealing with all day long, and therefore you will be happy in that career. However, if you don't enjoy the *field* -- if, say, *gardening* is one of your favorite subjects, but you work at a place where *law* is the language you have to listen to, and work in, all day long, and you *hate* that field and language -- then you are not going to be happy in that career.

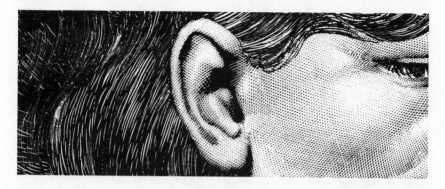

So, if you want to be happy in your next job or career it is important for you to begin your consideration of "*Where* do I want to use my (favorite) skills?" by making a list of your **Favorite Subjects** -- interests, fields of knowledge, favorite discussion topics, etc., that you know and care about. For this determines the language you must listen to, all day long.

"THIS MUCH I DO KNOW"

As this old expression implies, there are a lot of things that you know *something* about. This is where you begin, in identifying your favorite subjects.

What you need is a list of the subjects that:

a) You *already* know quite a bit about[1] -- though it is *not* necessary that you have a *mastery* of them; *and* that

b) You love.

School, Schmool

It doesn't have to be subjects you studied in school -- *e.g.,* psychology, electronics, business science, law, theology.

It could be some knowledge you've just picked up along the way in life -- say, *antiques,* or *cars,* or *interior decorating,* or *music* or *movies* or *psychology,* or *the kind of subjects that come up on television 'game shows.'* It is sufficient that you *like* the subject a lot, and that you picked up a working knowledge of it -- who cares where or how? As the late John Crystal used to say, it doesn't matter whether you learned it in college, or sitting at the end of a log.

Let's take *antiques* as an example. Suppose it's one of your favorite subjects, yet you never studied it in school. You picked up your knowledge of antiques by going around to antique stores, and asking lots of questions. And you supplemented this by reading a few books on the subject, and you subscribe to an antiques magazine. You've also bought a few. That's enough, for you to put *antiques,* on your list of fields/interests/languages.

Your degree of *mastery* of that language is irrelevant -- *unless you want to work at a level in that field that demands and requires mastery.* We'll come to *that,* later.

FIRST, REMEMBER;
THEN, EVALUATE

To figure out *your favorite subjects* I recommend you begin with the table on the next page.

This table calls for you to put down every subject you have ever had any interest in, or learned about. Do not list just your *favorite* subjects. That requires you to try to do two things at once -- *remember* and *evaluate.* You'll be like a bareback rider trying to stand astride two horses which are starting to go in different directions. Don't do it! First, *remember.* Later on, we'll get to the *evaluating* (which ones are your favorites).

So, to begin with, take time just to *remember,* by filling out the table. Copy it on to a larger piece of paper, if you need to.

During this *remembering* phase, you may want to look back at your Memory Net, pages 198–199, and see what subjects come to mind as you look over all the notes you jotted down, there. Anything helpful, there? Jot it down in the table.

It is not, incidentally, worth agonizing over *which column* in the table you should list a particular subject. As long as it gets on the table, that's sufficient.

---

1. I am always asked, *"Can I list a subject I know nothing about, but* I know *I would like it?"* Sure, but then you've got to go learn all about that subject *before* you can embark on your new job or new career. If you're moving *slowly* into a new career or job, that's fine. But if you need to move *faster,* it's better by far to take the subjects you already like, and know something about. Reason: most of our *real* interests in life have been things we've liked to read magazine articles about, or converse about, or learn about, for quite some time now.

Subjects I Learned About in High School or College	Subjects I Learned About on the Job (Apprenticeship, Internship, Training, etc.)	Subjects I Learned About by Self-Study (Reading at Home, Correspondence Course, Video, TV, Audiotapes, Computer Programs)	Subjects I Learned About in a Workshop, Conference, Continuing Education, or Training Event	Subjects I Learned About on Vacation, or During Hobby Time

IF YOU JUST CAN'T REMEMBER,
TO SAVE YOUR LIFE

If you finish the table exercise, and are stymied at this point because it didn't work very well for you, then of course you will want to *supplement* the list that table produced, with some additions.

You would doubtless like a kind of dictionary list of *possible* subjects. Unfortunately, there is no list in the world that could possibly cover all the subjects that *you* might know something about. You will have to settle for **A Sampler**.

In using this list, the same admonition as set forth with the table above, applies here: "First, *remember. Evaluate* later." Go through the list and check off any subject that you know *anything* about. Do remember that the list is A Sampler. It's just a bunch of pegs on which to hang your memories. Be *sure* and jot down any other subjects you know something about, as they occur to you, which are not on this list.

Again, when you are all done, go back over the list for a second time, and cross off all the subjects you checked, that are *not* one of your favorites.

> ## A Sampler of Subjects
> ## You May Know Something About

General Fields[2]
- ☐ History
- ☐ Biology
- ☐ Physics
- ☐ Chemistry
- ☐ Geometry
- ☐ Astronomy
- ☐ Geography
- ☐ Knowledge of foreign countries
  (which one/s?)
- ☐ Spanish or some other language
  (which one/s?)
- ☐ Psychology
  - ☐ The way the brain works

The Arts
- ☐ Principles of art
- ☐ Cinema
- ☐ Musical knowledge and taste
- ☐ Drawing
- ☐ Graphic arts
- ☐ Art materials
- ☐ Music appreciation
- ☐ Photography
- ☐ Broadcasting
- ☐ Woodcuts, engravings, lithographs
- ☐ Paintings, drawings, silk screens
- ☐ How to make videos
- ☐ Music (what kinds?)
- ☐ Principles of recording
- ☐ Sociology
- ☐ Linguistics or languages
- ☐ Communication
  - ☐ Human nature's need for symbols
  - ☐ The use and meaning of words
  - ☐ Numbers or statistics
  - ☐ Instructional principles and techniques
  - ☐ Speed reading

2. If you want a much more detailed list of general fields, I refer you to pages 130–136 in another one of my books, entitled, *The Three Boxes of Life, and How To Get Out of Them: An introduction to life/work planning* (Ten Speed Press, 1981) -- available in your library, bookstore, or possibly on your own shelf (if you already own a copy).

How to Create Visuals
- ☐ Designs
- ☐ Blueprints
- ☐ Wall-charts
- ☐ Schematics

How To Produce
- ☐ Procedures
- ☐ Guidebooks
- ☐ Manuals
- ☐ Newsletters

Particular How-To's

- ☐ How to run a particular machine (which one/s?)
- ☐ How to drive an automobile
- ☐ How to sew
- ☐ Carpentry
- ☐ Plumbing
- ☐ Painting
- ☐ Electrical work
- ☐ Household repairs
- ☐ Typing or 'keyboarding'
- ☐ How to operate a computer
- ☐ How computers work
- ☐ Computer programming
- ☐ Knowledge of a particular program
- ☐ Design engineering
- ☐ Interior decorating
- ☐ Knowledge of antiques
- ☐ Knowledge of gardening
- ☐ Horticulture
- ☐ Car repairs
- ☐ How to play a musical instrument (which one/s?)
- ☐ Principles of comparison shopping

Kinds of Personal Problems People Have
That I Know Something About, and
Know How To Deal With

Economic/Planning Problems for Individuals
- [ ] Identifying and finding meaningful work
- [ ] Job-hunting, career-change, unemployment, being fired or laid off
- [ ] Work satisfaction
- [ ] Life/work planning
- [ ] Personal economics
  - [ ] Financial planning
  - [ ] Budgeting
- [ ] Financial planning and management
- [ ] How to do taxes

Educational Problems
- [ ] Illiteracy, educational needs
- [ ] Performance problems, appraisal

Health Problems
- [ ] Physical fitness
- [ ] Physical handicaps
- [ ] Principles of outdoor survival
- [ ] Weight control
- [ ] Low energy
- [ ] Sleep disorders
- [ ] Principles of behavioral modification
- [ ] Mental/emotional/psychosomatic illness
  - [ ] Depression
  - [ ] Psychiatric hospitalization
  - [ ] Stress
  - [ ] Various kinds of mental/emotional problems
- [ ] Holistic health
- [ ] Self-healing, psychic healing
- [ ] Nutritional problems
- [ ] Addictions
  - [ ] Drug problems
  - [ ] Alcoholism
  - [ ] Smoking
- [ ] Principles of preventative health care
- [ ] Dealing with hypertension
- [ ] Allergies
- [ ] Pain control
- [ ] Dealing with people in terminal illness

Relationship Problems
- ☐ Relationships
- ☐ Personal insight, therapy
- ☐ Sexual education, sexual problems
- ☐ Sexual dysfunction
- ☐ Marriage problems
- ☐ Pregnancy and childbirth
- ☐ Parenting
- ☐ Discipline problems, self-discipline
- ☐ Physical abuse, rape, sexual harassment
- ☐ Divorce
- ☐ Death and grief

Religious/Value Problems
- ☐ Spiritual principles
- ☐ Values identification
- ☐ The nature of religion or religions (which ones?)
- ☐ Philosophy of religion
- ☐ Philosophical problems
- ☐ Ethics
- ☐ Life after death
- ☐ Psychic phenomena

Kinds of Organizational Problems I Know Quite a Bit About and Know How to Deal With

With People
- ☐ Manpower requirements analysis and planning
- ☐ Personnel administration
- ☐ Recruiting
- ☐ Industry in-house training
- ☐ Principles of group dynamics
- ☐ The how-to of customer relations and service
- ☐ Performance specifications

With Finances
- ☐ Accounting
- ☐ Bookkeeping
- ☐ Financial records
- ☐ Fiscal analysis, controls, reductions, and programming
- ☐ Statistical analyses

With Organization Planning
- ☐ Principles of planning and management
- ☐ Systems analysis
- ☐ Data analysis studies
- ☐ Industrial applications
- ☐ Government contracts
- ☐ Merchandising
- ☐ Marketing/sales
- ☐ Packaging
- ☐ Distribution
- ☐ Policy development
- ☐ R & D program and project management
- ☐ How a volunteer organization works

When you are done checking off subjects on this list add the things you listed in your table exercise, so you have one big list. Time now to *evaluate*.

YOUR TOP TEN
FAVORITE SUBJECTS

Look at all the subjects on that one big list, now, and cross out *any* which you do **not** want to use in your next job or career. (Clue: you wouldn't want to work at a place where *this* was one of the languages you had to listen to, or use).

When you're finished crossing out things, study what's left. They should be your *favorites*. If the list is still too long (more than 20 items), go back over it and be more rigorous.

When that's done, you need to look at the 'survivors' on that list and, by guess and by gosh, circle your ten favorites. Don't sit and agonize about this. Just quickly circle the ten that your instincts tell you are your favorites -- never mind in what order (for the moment). Later, you can review, meditate, ponder, and agonize, if you wish.

When you are pretty well satisfied that you've got your top ten favorites, you will then need to prioritize them in *exact* order, using the Ten Item prioritizing grid on page 205, so that you end up with a list of your absolutely favorite subject/interest/ field in the number one position, your next favorite in the number two, etc.

It is always wise, when you are done, to review your list, and ask yourself, "Do I *really* want this subject to be one of the languages of my new career, or not?" Example: you may know how to play the trumpet, and this may have come up as number two or three on your prioritized list of favorite subjects. *But,* you know in your heart you don't *really* want to talk about, or deal with, trumpets all day. Or do you? Only you can say. Trumpet-playing could always be saved for your *hobby* or *avocation,* if you prize it, but don't want to use it at work.

PUTTING THEM ON THE FLOWER DIAGRAM

When you have your ten top favorite subjects/interests/fields it is time to put them on the diagram on the next page, called as you can see *My Favorite Kinds of Information.*

It is, again, part of the larger diagram, which we call *The Flower Diagram,* which is on page 210. This is another of the *petals* from that Flower.

Copy on to this *petal,* in the part called "Content," the list of your ten favorite fields of knowledge, in order. *(If you wish, you may of course copy this diagram on to a larger piece of paper, so that it is easier to read.)*

My Favorite
Kinds of Information

Kinds of
INFORMATION *I Like To*
Use My Skills With

FORM	CONTENT
e.g., "Do you prefer to work with information in the form of newspapers, magazines, books, computer output, reports, or pictures?" etc.	Among the fields of knowledge which you know something about, which ones are your favorites? And in what order of priority?
1.	1.
2.	2.
3.	3.
4.	4.
5.	5.
6.	6.
7.	7.
	8.
	9.
	10.

THE MATTER
OF FORM

On the left-hand side of that same *petal* diagram, you notice a column called "Form." Information, such as you listed on the right-hand side, comes in various *forms*. And we often care *a lot* about what form we use, at work. Some people, for example, like to read newspapers, but they don't like to read books. Some prefer information they get on their computer, from information they find in magazines or libraries.

So, it's often important to say what *form* you prefer when you work with whatever fields of knowledge you have chosen.

Here is a checklist, that may be helpful to you:

**I Prefer Information
That Interests Me
To Be in the Following Form(s):**
- ☐ Newspapers
- ☐ Magazines
- ☐ Books
- ☐ Computers
- ☐ Computer printouts
- ☐ Catalogs
- ☐ Handbooks
- ☐ Records, files
- ☐ Trade or professional literature
- ☐ Videotapes
- ☐ Audiotapes
- ☐ Conversation or interviews with others, in person or by phone
- ☐ Seminars, learning from trainers
- ☐ Courses, learning from teachers
- ☐ Surveys or polls
- ☐ Research projects, research and development projects, project reports
- ☐ Data analysis studies:

Add any other items that may occur to you; then take the *forms* you have checked above, prioritize them -- put them in their order of importance to you -- and enroll the top seven (or less) on the left-hand side.

Now you know the languages you would most like to listen to, speak, and deal with, at your workplace, in your next career or job. You know the *major* part of WHERE.

However, as you noticed, there are other *petals* on the *Flower* (page 210) that you haven't filled in, yet. These need now to be filled in, because they refer to the other factors -- besides your *favorite subjects* -- that determine **Where** you want to use your skills. We will now deal with each of these, in turn.

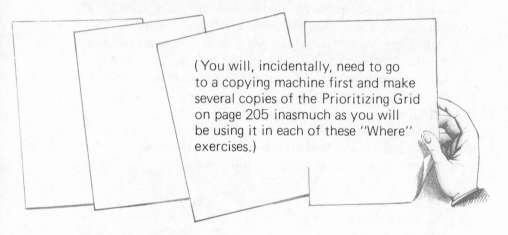

(You will, incidentally, need to go to a copying machine first and make several copies of the Prioritizing Grid on page 205 inasmuch as you will be using it in each of these "Where" exercises.)

YOUR FAVORITE THINGS
TO WORK WITH

Every job requires you to work with, or around, some kind of 'things.' Please check off one or more of your preferences in the following categories. *"I would prefer to work around, or with, the following kinds of THINGS:*

Growing Things
- ☐ Trees, bushes, landscaping stuff
- ☐ Flowers, plants
- ☐ Garden tools
- ☐ Crops
- ☐ Ploughs
- ☐ Threshing machines, reapers, harvesters

Materials
- ☐ Paper
- ☐ Woods, plywood, etc.
- ☐ Pottery, pewter
- ☐ Bronze, brass, or aluminum
- ☐ Textiles, cloth, felt, hides, synthetics

Clothing
- ☐ Sewing machines
- ☐ Patterns, safety pins, buttons, zippers
- ☐ Dyes
- ☐ Shoes
- ☐ Ski clothes, swimming suits

Shelter

- ☐ Tents
- ☐ Trailers
- ☐ Apartments, condos, houses
- ☐ Carpenter's tools
- ☐ Paints, wall coverings, carpeting
- ☐ Heating elements, furnaces, air-conditioners, fans
- ☐ Security devices, alarm systems, fire extinguishers, fire alarms
- ☐ Furniture
- ☐ Household items, furniture, kitchen items
- ☐ Washing machines, dryers
- ☐ Kitchen appliances, refrigerators, microwaves, ovens, dishwashers, compactors
- ☐ Cosmetics
- ☐ Tools, power tools

Food

- ☐ Meats
- ☐ Breads and other baked goods
- ☐ Health foods
- ☐ Vitamins
- ☐ Dairy equipment
- ☐ Winemaking equipment

Health Equipment or Materials

- ☐ Medicines, vaccines, thermometers
- ☐ Anesthetics
- ☐ Dental equipment
- ☐ X-ray machines
- ☐ False parts of the human body, hearing aids
- ☐ Spectacles, glasses, contact lenses
- ☐ Gym Equipment

Transportation

On Land
- ☐ Roads
- ☐ Bicycles, motorcycles, mopeds
- ☐ Automobiles
- ☐ Trains

In the Air
- ☐ Gliders
- ☐ Balloons
- ☐ Airplanes
- ☐ Parachutes

On the Water
- ☐ Rivers, streams, canals
- ☐ Lakes, oceans
- ☐ Boats, steamships, sailboats, canoes, kayaks

Amusement

- ☐ Amusement parks, game parks, aquatic parks
- ☐ Toys
- ☐ Cards, board games, checkers, chess, Monopoly, etc.
- ☐ Kites
- ☐ Musical instruments
    Specify:

Sports equipment
- ☐ Fishing rods, fishhooks, bait
- ☐ Skis, lodges

Manufactured Stuff

- ☐ Office supplies: pens, pencils, desks, tables
- ☐ Computers, typewriters
- ☐ Copying machines, fax machines, printers, printing presses
- ☐ Walkie-talkies, telephones, cellular phones, voice mail, answering machines
- ☐ Tools
- ☐ Clocks
- ☐ Telescopes
- ☐ Microscopes
- ☐ Electrical and electronics equipment
- ☐ Calculators
- ☐ Adding machines
- ☐ Cash registers
- ☐ Money
- ☐ Laser beams
- ☐ Educational materials: easels, projectors, flipcharts, etc.

When you have finished checking these off, circle your top ten favorites -- things you like to use your skills with, or like to have around you when you work, at your next job or career.

Once you have the top ten, you will then need to prioritize them in *exact* order, using the Ten Item prioritizing grid on page 205, so that you end up with a list where your absolutely favorite *thing* is in the number one position, your next favorite in the number two position, etc.

Then it is time to put them on the diagram on another one of the *petals* from *The Flower Diagram,* the one called *My Favorite Kinds of Things,* on the next page. (*If you wish, you may of course copy this diagram on to a larger piece of paper, so that it is easier to read.*)

My Favorite Kinds of Things

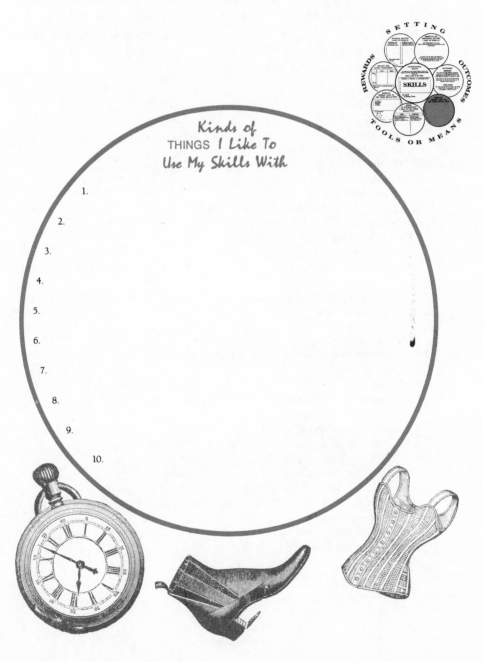

Kinds of
THINGS *I Like To
Use My Skills With*

1.
2.
3.
4.
5.
6.
7.
8.
9.
10.

YOUR FAVORITE PEOPLE
TO WORK WITH

Almost every job requires you to work with, or around, some kind of people. Please check off one or more of your descriptors in the following list. *"I would prefer to work around, or with, the following kinds of PEOPLE (as customers, clients, patients, students, target audience, and/or as co-workers, etc.)*

☐ Both sexes
☐ Men primarily
☐ Women primarily
☐ Individuals
☐ Groups, of eight or less
☐ Groups, larger than eight
☐ People who are easy to work with
☐ People who are difficult to work with
☐ All people regardless of age
☐ Babies
☐ School-age children
☐ Adolescents or young people
☐ College students
☐ Young adults
☐ People in their thirties
☐ The middle-aged
☐ The elderly
☐ The retired
☐ All people regardless of sexual orientation
☐ Heterosexuals
☐ Homosexuals
☐ All people regardless of economic background
☐ People who are well-off
☐ People who are poor
☐ People of a particular cultural background: *(specify)*
☐ People of a particular social background: *(specify)*
☐ People of a particular educational background: *(specify)*
☐ People of a particular philosophy or religious belief: *(specify)*
☐ Certain kinds of workers (blue-collar, white-collar, executives, or whatever): *(specify)*
☐ People in a particular place (the Armed Forces, prison, etc.): *(specify)*
☐ Any other kind you can think of:

Add any other *descriptors* that may occur to you. When you are finished circle your top ten favorites -- people you would like to use your skills with, or would like to have around you when you work, at your next job or career.

Drawing by Donald Reilly; © 1981 The New Yorker Magazine, Inc. Used by permission.

"I'm hoping to find something in a meaningful, humanist, outreach kind of bag, with flexible hours, non-sexist bosses, and fabulous fringes."

Once you have the top ten, you will then need to prioritize them in *exact* order, using the Ten Item prioritizing grid on page 205, so that you end up with a list where your absolutely favorite *people descriptor* is in the number one position, your next favorite in the number two position, etc.

Then it is time to put them on the diagram on another one of the *petals* from *The Flower Diagram,* the one called *My Favorite People,* on the next page. *(If you wish, you may of course copy this diagram on to a larger piece of paper, so that it is easier to read.)*

You may, incidentally, want to divide the descriptors between the two boxes you will find there: (1) *"As Clients, Customers, Students, or Other,"* and (2) *"As Co-workers."* But if this distinction is not meaningful to you, then just ignore it.

My Favorite People

Kinds of PEOPLE I Like To Use My Skills With

As Clients,
Customers,
Students, or
Other:

As Co-workers:

YOUR FAVORITE REWARDS

The next *petal* deals with the issue of *level* or *salary*. You probably know what is being asked here, but let me trace it out. *Level* is a matter of: do you want to be the boss or would you rather be a manager under the boss or would you rather be a supervisor under the manager or would you rather be someone just working in that department? Would you like to work all by yourself, or with a partner, or as a member of a team? Would you like to work relatively unsupervised, or do you enjoy having people tell you what tasks need to get done? Enroll your answers on the *petal* on the next page.

Salary is *usually* connected to *level*. The higher a salary you would like, *usually* the higher a level you must plan to work at. Answer as best you can the following statement: *"I would prefer to work for an organization that gives me the following . . .*

☐ Salary and level I would like to have, at a minimum:
☐ Salary and level I would like eventually to reach, if I can:

Enroll the answers on the *petal*, and then we swiftly move on:

My Favorite Rewards

Salary and Level I Want/Need

	LEVEL	
MAX		
MIN		

Other rewards I would like this job to give me:

YOUR FAVORITE OUTCOMES

Every job requires you to work toward some kind of *OUT-COME*. That's what we mean by 'work.' Otherwise, it's 'play.' Please check off one or more of the *outcomes* in the following list. *"I prefer work which is aimed toward the following outcome(s):*

☐ Work which brings more information/truth into the world.

☐ Work which brings more beauty into the world.

☐ Work which brings more justice, truth, and ethical behavior into the world.

☐ Work which produces or 'messages' information.

☐ Work which invents/produces/sells a product.

☐ Work which fixes something that is broken.

☐ Work which improves something or makes it better.

☐ Work which serves people.

☐ Work which serves or helps those who are in need.

☐ Work which combats some force/influence/pervasive trend.

☐ Work which has an impact, and attempts to cause change.

☐ Work which develops or builds something, where there was nothing.

☐ Work which begins a new business, or does some project from start to finish.

☐ Work where I will be in charge of whatever it is that I am doing, so that I get to be the decision-maker.

☐ Work which has a vision of what something could be, and helps that vision to come true.

Add any other *outcomes* that may occur to you. When you are finished, you then need to prioritize them in *exact* order, using the Ten Item prioritizing grid on page 205, so that you end up with a list where your absolutely favorite *outcome* is in the number one position, your next favorite in the number two position, etc.

Then it is time to put them on the diagram on another one of the *petals* from *The Flower Diagram,* the one called *My Favorite Outcomes,* on the next page. You should list them in the top section, called "Immediate." *(If you wish, you may of course copy this diagram on to a larger piece of paper, so that it is easier to read.)*

Once this is done, you will notice there is a sentence further down on that *petal,* asking about your 'central driving motivation.' This is a purely *optional* section, and requires a certain degree of self-knowledge. If it looks like fun, fill it out; if it doesn't, just skip over it. It is based on the idea that some *pleasure for the self* is often hidden in work we most enjoy -- *besides* pleasing God or honoring your true nature.

My Favorite Outcomes

Immediate

At the work I'd most love to do,
do I want to help produce a **product**
or do I want to help offer some **service** to people,
or do I want to help gather, manage or disseminate **information** to
people? Or all three? Or two? And what kind of product, service, or info?

And, what do I see as my central driving motivation in whatever job I take, or in whatever career I pursue?

Long-range

My long-range goals for my life -- the things I want to do, or the goals
I'd like to accomplish -- before I die, are:

For example, you might enjoy a particular kind of work **because it lets you**:

☐ Gain a response from people.
☐ Be in the spotlight, gain recognition, and be known.
☐ Excel and be the best -- at whatever it is you do.
☐ Master some technique, or field.
☐ Do something that no one has done before.
☐ Do something that everyone says couldn't be done.
☐ Allows you to go the second mile, in meeting people's needs.
☐ Make it into a higher echelon than you currently are, in terms of reputation, and/or prestige, and/or membership, and/or salary.[3]

Jot down whatever you think is true for you, and enroll it in the proper spot on that *petal*. It may save you from taking a job where you know, from the start, it will never let you have this motivation fulfilled.

Finally for this *petal,* you will notice at the very bottom it lists some long-range goals. You're on your own here (essay-type answer required), but looking over your previous answers on this *petal* may help. And, also, you may find the following exercise helpful.

YOUR BIOGRAPHY AS YOU WOULD LIKE IT TO READ, SOMEDAY

There are various ways to approach this. Some people sit down and write what they would like their imaginary obituary to say, after they die. Others find this approach too morbid for words, so they like to pretend that they someday get into *Who's Who;* and they write what they would like that entry to say about them. Others prefer to consider all their heroines or heroes, write what it is they like about them, and then circle those things which they would like to be true about themselves, after they reach retirement. You choose. Put a one- or two-sentence summary at the bottom of *My Favorite Outcomes petal,* under "Long-range." Now, you're done with that *petal.*

---

3. I am indebted to my friend, Arthur Miller, for suggesting many of these motivations. His pioneering work with respect to goals is enshrined in his book, *The Truth About You,* by Arthur F. Miller & Ralph T. Mattson; available from Ten Speed Press, Box 7123, Berkeley, CA 94707. My list, here, should not be understood as a representation or summary of Arthur's work; it is more like a rhapsody on his work.

YOUR FAVORITE
SPIRITUAL SETTING

What do you do with all the *stuff* left over from the previous exercise, that you *didn't* have room for, on the previous *petal?* Well, that brings us to our next-to-last *petal: My Favorite Spiritual or Emotional Setting.*

What you previously wrote about your heroes or heroines may have started you thinking about the general topic: "What life's all about -- at its best." The top part of this new *petal* asks you to say what you believe about life in general, and your life in particular. What are the important things in life, for you? What do you think is the purpose of our life here on earth? When you say, 'I want to be true to myself,' what do you mean by that? What parts of your self do you want to be true to? What do you want to remain constant, throughout your life? What values? What principles guide your conduct? What do you most prize, in the physical realm? What do you most prize, in the spiritual realm? You may wish to read the Epilogue at the end of this book, as a starting point. You may disagree with it emphatically, but then you will be perhaps better able to marshal your own thoughts and opinions on the various issues raised there. Or, you may agree with some things there, and again that will give you a starting point.

Write this however you want. Then summarize it, on this *petal.* In the bottom part of that same *petal,* put what values, etc. *must* be in any job where you are able to stay true to yourself.

My Favorite Spiritual or Emotional Setting

MY PHILOSOPHY OF LIFE.
What I believe about life in general,
and my life in particular
(key ideas here):

In order to do my best work,
these are the factors from my philosophy (above) that are especially important to me
to have at my work (or in my work):

My Favorite Physical Setting

GENERAL
Geographical Factors

The geographical area which would please me most, and therefore help me to do my most effective work, would have the following factors (e.g., warm dry summers, skiing in the winter, a good newspaper, etc.):

1.

2.

3.

4.

5.

6.

7.

The names of three places which fit these factors are:

1.

2.

3.

SPECIFIC
Working Conditions

At my place of work I could be happiest and do my most effective work, if I had the following working conditions (e.g., working indoors or out, not punching a time-clock, a boss who gave me free rein to do my work, having my own office, etc.):

1.

2.

3.

4.

5.

6.

7.

8.

9.

10.

YOUR FAVORITE
PHYSICAL SETTING

We come -- at last, as the sun is sinking slowly in the West, and the soft sounds of ukeleles are heard in the distance -- to the final *petal* on your *Flower Diagram* of your ideal job or career: *My Favorite Physical Setting.* The left side of this petal is for "Geographical Factors," and the work you need to do in order to fill that out, resides back in Chapter 7. You will certainly want to fill this part of this *petal* out, if you are thinking of moving but you don't know where. However, job-hunters in general have found this exercise immensely useful for focussing on *quality of life* factors that are important even if you *aren't* planning to move.

The other side of this petal deals, as you can see, with *Working Conditions.* This section, filled out, *may* not be useful to you when you are first trying to define your next job or career. But it sure does come in handy when you are weighing two different job-offers or job-possibilities, further down the line, believe me.

Furthermore, it may help a great deal during your job *search,* when you're trying to decide what kinds of places to choose as your *targets.*

You're pretty much on your own in defining your favorite working conditions, but here is a list to 'prime the pump' for you:

If I have a choice, I would prefer to work in the following kind of place:

- ☐ Outdoors
- ☐ Indoors
- ☐ A place with 5 or less employees
- ☐ A place with 20 or less employees
- ☐ A place with 100 or less employees
- ☐ A large corporation
- ☐ A place in a large city
- ☐ A place in the suburbs
- ☐ A place in the country
- ☐ In a particular part of this country (see Chapter 7)
- ☐ A profit-making firm
- ☐ A nonprofit firm or organization
- ☐ A service organization
- ☐ An old organization
- ☐ A new organization
- ☐ A place which is 'going and growing'
- ☐ An organization with lots of problems
- ☐ My own business (see Chapter 6)

You can add to this list by listing, on a separate sheet of paper, all the places you have ever worked, and what you *did not* like about that place (e.g., "too noisy," "too much supervision," etc.) Then, take the *opposite* of each of these factors, and *voila!* you have some more items to add to the list above.

When you've got all the items that occur to you, take the ones you have checked, or here added, circle the ten most important ones to you, and then prioritize them -- putting them in order of importance to you -- and enroll those top ten on the *petal* on page 251.

IN CONCLUSION

Now, you're done: you've got all eight *petals* of the *Flower Diagram* filled out. If you're in a 'cut and paste' mood, you might want to cut out all eight *petals* -- seven in this chapter, one in the previous chapter -- and paste them together on one large sheet.

Put it on a wall, or on the door of your refrigerator; and reflect on what kind of a job or career it might point *toward*. For some people, the *Flower*, at this point, doesn't do much. That's why we press on to our next chapter, where we put it all to use.

For other people looking at their *Flower* produces blinding insights: they *see* what job or career it points to. Just two warnings: first, don't prematurely close out *other* possibilities. Wait until you've done the work described in the next chapter.

And secondly, please *don't* say to yourself, at this point: "Well, I now see what it is that I would die to be able to do, but I *know* there is no job in the world like that, that *I* would be able to get."

You don't know any such thing. You need to do your (re)search first *(next chapter)*. Of course, it's possible that at the end of that search, you still may not be able to find *all* that you want, down to the last detail. But why not aim for it, and then settle for less *if and when* you find that you simply have to? Until then, you may be surprised at what you are able to turn up.

Of course, the *implementation* of your fondest vocational dream *may* have to be taken in *stages*. Let me illustrate what I mean. One man I know of, who had been a senior executive with a publishing company, found himself not enjoying retirement, after age 65. In fact, he was bored to death. He contacted a business acquaintance, who said apologetically, "We just don't have anything open that matches or requires your abilities; right now all we need is someone in our mail room." The 65-year-old executive said, "I'll take that job!" He did, and over the ensuing years steadily advanced once again, to just the job he wanted: as a senior executive, where he utilized all his prized skills, for some time. He retired as senior executive for the second time, at the age of 85.

It is amazing how often people do get their dreams, whether in stages or directly. The more you don't *cut* the dream down, because of what you *think* you know about *the real world,* the more likely you are to find what you are looking for.

Most people don't find their heart's desire, because they decide to pursue just half their dream – and consequently they hunt for it with only *half a heart.*

If you decide to pursue your whole dream, your best dream, the one you die to do, I guarantee you that you will hunt for it *with all your heart.* It is this *passion* which often is the difference between successful career-changers, and unsuccessful ones.

*Students spend four or more years
learning how to dig data out of the library
and other sources, but it rarely occurs
to them that they should also apply some of
the same new-found research skill to their
own benefit -- to looking up information
on companies, types of professions, sections
of the country that might interest them.*

Professor Albert Shapero
*The late William H. Davis Professor
of The American Free Enterprise System
at Ohio State University*

CHAPTER ELEVEN

The Systematic Approach To
The Job-Hunt and Career-Change:

PART III

How

Do You Identify At Least
Two Different Jobs
You'd Love to Do?

Chapter 11

What Career?

© Copyright, 1980, King Features Syndicate, Inc. Used by special permission.

"Same career, change of career, same career... change of..."

Now you have the flower diagram all completed.

(Well, of course in all likelihood you don't -- yet. You're still browsing through these chapters on career-change to see if it's *worth doing* all this work. But let's *pretend* you've got *the flower* diagram all done, and pasted together.)

What is it you have there? Well, it's a picture of *you* (sort of) and it's also a picture of *the ideal job or career* you're looking for. It's both, because you're looking for a job or career *that matches you.*

And now that you're holding the diagram in your hand, what comes next? Well, some of you *(about three in every hundred of those reading this book)* will have a big *Aha!* as you look at the flower diagram. A light bulb will go off, over your head, and you will say, "Now I see *exactly* what kind of career this points me to."

The rest of you -- most of you -- are staring at your flower diagram, and you haven't *a clue* as to what job or career it points to. Soooo, you're going to need some additional information, *of course.*

PEOPLE OR BOOKS?

And how do you find that information? You're hoping I'll tell you to go consult some books. Do some reading. You figure there must be some book you can take out of the library, that is going to spell it all out for you. *I wish!*

Unfortunately, the most dependable and up-to-date information on jobs and careers is *not* found by reading books. It's found by going and talking to people.

The reason for this is that last week's absolutely true certifiably guaranteed 100% accurate information about jobs and careers is, today, completely outdated. *Things are just moving too fast.* Books can't keep up. They're outdated before they're in print. So, if you want to identify a new career or job that *fits* you, it's mostly people you must go see -- with *some* reading on the side, to *supplement* what they tell you.

This idea -- that during this information-gathering part of your job-hunt or career-change you're going to have to actually go *talk to people* -- is very terrifying to some job-hunters, and career-changers. If that's true for you, just remember you're going to *have to* go talk to people at some point during your job-hunt or career-change. I'm referring to the interview where you're trying to get hired. Face to face, you will be then. Face to face with people. Whether you like it or not.

This task now before us -- of talking to people *in order to get information about jobs or careers* -- is not all that different. Talking to people is talking to people is talking to people.

PRACTICING

Since we have two different times when we need to *talk to people,* during the job-hunt, and some of us are anxious about that prospect, the late John Crystal[1] suggested you might as well throw in a third time of talking to people.

He suggested you first go out and talk to people about *any-*

Initial:	Pleasure P	Information I	Employment E
Kind of Interview	Practice Field Survey	Informational Interviewing or Researching	Employment Interview or Hiring Interview
Purpose	To Get Used to Talking with People to Enjoy It; To "Penetrate" Networks	To Find Out If You'd Like a Job, Before You Go Trying to Get It	To Get Hired for the Work You Have Decided You Would Most Like to Do
How You Go to the Interview	You Can Take Somebody with You	By Yourself or You Can Take Somebody with You	By Yourself
Who You Talk To	Anyone Who Shares Your Enthusiasm About a (for You) Non-Job-Related Subject	A Worker Who Is Doing the Actual Work You Are Thinking About Doing	An Employer Who Has the Power to Hire You for the Job You Have Decided You Would Most Like to Do
How Long a Time You Ask For	10 Minutes (and DON'T run over -- asking to see them at 11:50 may help keep you honest, since most employers have lunch appoint-ments at noon)	Ditto	
What You Ask Them	Any Curiosity You Have About Your Shared Interest or Enthusiasm	Any Questions You Have About This Job or This Kind of Work	You Tell Them What It Is You Like About Their Organization and What Kind of Work You Are Looking For.

© Copyright 1986 by D. Porot. Used by special permission. Not to be reproduced without permission in writing from D. Porot.

Initial:	Pleasure **P**	Information **I**	Employment **E**
What You Ask Them (*continued*)	If Nothing Occurs to You, Ask: 1. How did you start, with this hobby, interest, etc.? 2. What excites or interests you the most about it? 3. What do you find is the thing you like the least about it? 4. Who else do you know of who shares this interest, hobby or enthusiasm, or could tell me more about my curiosity? a. Can I go and see them? b. May I mention that it was you who suggested I see them? c. May I say that you recommended them? **Get their name and address**	If Nothing Occurs to You, Ask: 1. How did you get interested in this work and how did you get hired? 2. What excites or interests you the most about it? 3. What do you find is the thing you like the least about it? 4. Who else do you know of who does this kind of work, or similar work but with this difference: _____? 5. What kinds of challenges or problems do you have to deal with in this job? 6. What skills do you need in order to meet those challenges or problems? **Get their name and address**	You tell them the kinds of challenges you like to deal with. What skills you have to deal with those challenges. What experience you have had in dealing with those challenges in the past.
AFTERWARD: That Same Night	SEND A THANK YOU NOTE	SEND A THANK YOU NOTE	SEND A THANK YOU NOTE

thing just to get good at *talking to people*. He thought shy people particularly needed this. And so they do. Thousands of job-hunters and career-changers have followed his advice, over the past twenty-five years, and found it really helps. Indeed, people who have followed John's advice in this regard have had a success rate of 86% in finding a job -- and not just any job, but *the* job or new career that they were looking for.

Daniel Porot, the job-hunting expert in Europe, has put these three types of *talking to people* all together in a chart for the job-hunter or career-changer, called 'The PIE Method,' which has helped thousands of job-hunters and career-changers over in Europe. I reproduce that chart here, with his kind permission:[2]

Why is it called *'PIE'*? It's an acronym for $P + I + E$.

P? That's for the *warmup* phase. John Crystal named this warmup 'The Practice Field Survey.' Daniel Porot calls it **P** for *pleasure* -- that is, 'interviewing' for pleasure. Of course, it could equally well be **P** for *practice*.

I? That's when you're done with the warmup, and you're now taking your flower diagram and trying to figure out what career or job it points to, and what places have such jobs or careers. John Crystal called this 'informational interviewing.' Daniel Porot calls it **I** for *information* -- that is, 'interviewing' for information.

E? That's when you're done gathering information, and you have 'targeted' certain places that interest you *(whether or not they have a known vacancy)*, and, using a contact to introduce you, you're going there -- to each place -- to talk with the-person-who-has-the-power-to-hire-you, about being hired there. John Crystal called this 'the hiring interview.' Daniel Porot calls it **E** for *employment* -- that is, 'interviewing' for employment.

O.K., now let's see if we can get the hang of each phase, in turn.

---

1. John also was the inventor of WHAT, WHERE and HOW -- which I have used as the basic framework for Chapters 9, 10, and 11, here.

2. If you want further instructions about this whole process, I refer you to "The Practice Field Survey," pp. 187–196 in *Where Do I Go From Here With My Life?* by John Crystal and friend. Ten Speed Press, Box 7123, Berkeley, CA 94707.

The

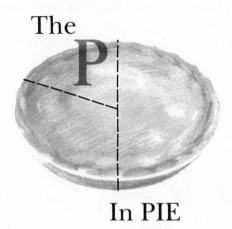

In PIE

The first thought that will occur to you, here, is *"Do I have to do this Practice Interviewing?"* Well, of course not, if you're not shy. Of course not, if the idea of going to talk to people doesn't faze you in the least. Of course not, if you're as good at listening as you are at talking, and you know how to ask for information you need.

This Practice was invented for people who don't like the idea of having to go talk with people. It's invented for people who are shy.[3] If this isn't *your* problem skip over this to the next section, beginning instead on page 269.

But let's suppose you *are* put off at the idea of going to talk to people about hiring, or about information you need. How do you use this Practice Interviewing to get comfortable about going out and talking to people *one-on-one?*

This is achieved first of all by having you choose a topic -- *any* topic, however silly or trivial -- that is a pleasure for you to talk about with your friends, or family. It should not be a topic that is connected to any present or future career that you are considering.

---

3. Job-hunters often imagine that books like this are written by very aggressive, *take charge* kind of people. Not true. I, for example, am painfully shy; always have been. Unless, of course, I'm talking about a subject *I love*. The same will be true for you.

If you want to do further reading about shyness, its nature and causes, the classic text is: Phillip G. Zimbardo, *Shyness, What It Is, What to Do About It.* Jove Publications, 757 Third Ave., New York, NY 10017. 1977.

Rather, the kinds of topics that work best, for this exercise, are:

• **a hobby** you *love,* such as skiing, bridge playing, exercise, computers, etc.

• **any leisure-time enthusiasm** of yours, such as a movie you just saw, that you liked a lot

• **a long-time curiosity**, such as how do they predict the weather, or what do policemen do

• **an aspect of the town or city you live in**, such as a new shopping mall that just opened

• **an issue** you feel strongly about, such as the homeless, AIDS sufferers, ecology, peace, health, etc.

There is only one condition about choosing a topic: it should be something you *love* to talk about with other people: movies, skiing, food, restaurants, summer travel, football, the area you live in, or whatever. A subject you know nothing about, but you feel a great deal of enthusiasm for it, is far preferable to something you know an awful lot about, but it puts you to sleep.

Enthusiasm

Throughout the job-hunt and career-change, the key to 'interviewing' is not found in memorizing a dozen rules about what you're supposed to say.

No, the key is just this one thing: now and always, be *sure* you are talking about something you feel *passionate about*.[4]

Enthusiasm is the key -- to *enjoying* 'interviewing,' and conducting *effective* interviews, at any level. What this exercise teaches us is that shyness always loses its power and its painful self-consciousness -- *if* and *when* you are talking about something *you love*.

For example, if you love gardens you will forget all about your shyness when you're talking to someone else about gardens and flowers. *"You ever been to Butchart Gardens?"*

If you love movies, you'll forget all about your shyness when you're talking to someone else about movies. *"I just hated that scene where they. . . ."*

If you love computers, then you will forget all about your shyness when you're talking to someone else about computers. *"Do you work on a Mac or an MS-DOS machine?"*

That's why it is important that it be your enthusiasms -- here, your hobbies -- later, your *favorite* skills and your *favorite* subjects -- that you are exploring and pursuing in these conversations with others.

WHO DO YOU TALK TO?
(OR WHOM)

As you see from the first part of Daniel's diagram of **P**, once you've chosen a topic, you need to go talk to someone who is as enthusiastic about this thing you love to talk about, as you are. *For best results with your later job-hunt, this should be someone you don't already know.* Otherwise, there are no rules.

How to find someone you don't already know? Use the Yellow Pages, ask around among your friends and family, *who do you*

---

4. This is what the late Joseph Campbell used to call 'your bliss.'

know that loves *to talk about this?* It's relatively easy to find the kind of person you're looking for.

You love to talk about skiing? *Try a ski-clothes store, or a skiing instructor.* You love to talk about writing? *Try a professor on a nearby college campus, who teaches English.* You love to talk about physical exercise? *Try a trainer, or someone who teaches physical therapy.*

Once you've identified someone you think shares your enthusiasm, you then go talk with them. You can do this with or without an appointment. It is often better during this **P**ractice 'interviewing' if your visit is spontaneous, rather than planned. (That's *not* true, later.) But you have to use your own intuition about each particular case.

HOW DO I GUIDE
THE CONVERSATION?

Once you are face to face with your *fellow enthusiast,* the first thing you must do is relieve their understandable anxiety. *Everyone* has had someone visit them who has stayed too long, who has worn out their welcome. If your *fellow enthusiast* is worried about you staying too long, they'll be so preoccupied with this, they won't *really* hear a word you are saying.

So, when you meet them, you ask for *ten minutes of their time, only.* Period. Stop. Exclamation point. And you watch your wristwatch *like a hawk,* to be sure you stay no longer. You *never* stay longer, unless they *beg* you to. And I mean, *beg, beg, beg.*[5]

Once they've agreed to give you ten minutes, you tell them why you're there -- that you're trying to get comfortable about talking with people, for information -- and you understand that you two share a mutual interest, which is. . . .

Then what? Well, a topic may have its own unique set of questions. For example, I love movies, so if I met someone who shared this interest, my first question would be, "What movies have you seen lately?" And so on. And so forth.

If it's a topic you love, and often talk about, you'll *know* what

---

5. A polite, "Oh do you have to go?" should be understood for what it is: politeness. Your response should be, "Yes, I promised to only take ten minutes of your time, and I want to keep to my word." This will almost always leave a *very* favorable impression behind you.

kinds of questions you begin with. The rules of this Practice Interview is that you may discuss anything and ask any questions which come to your mind, just as long as you're having *fun* talking to this person about the *enthusiasm* you have chosen.

But, if no such questions come to mind, no matter how hard you try, the following ones have proved to be good conversation starters for thousands of job-hunters and career-changers before you, no matter what their topic or interest.

So, look these over, memorize them *(or copy them on a little card that fits in the palm of your hand)*, and give them a try:

Addressed to the person you're doing the practice field survey with:

- How did you get involved with/become interested in this? (*"This"* is the hobby, curiosity, aspect, issue, or enthusiasm, that you are so interested in.)
- What do you like the most about it?
- What do you like the least about it?
- Who else would you suggest I go talk to that shares this interest?
- Can I use your name?
- May I tell them it was you who recommended that I talk with them?
- *Then, choosing one person off the list of several names they may have given you, you say,* Well, I think I will begin by going to talk to this person. Would you be willing to call ahead for me, so they will know who I am, when I go over there?

CAN I TAKE SOMEONE WITH ME?

During *this* Practice Interviewing, it's perfectly okay for you to take someone with you: your best friend, a fellow career-changer, your mother, whoever.

And if you're absolutely tongue-tied when you first go to see people, this *someone* should be someone who is more outgoing than you feel you are. And on the first few interviews, you can let them take the lead in the conversation, while you watch to see how they do it.

Once it is *your turn* to conduct the interview, it will by that time usually be easy for you to figure out what to talk about.

Alone or with someone, keep at this Practice Interviewing until you feel very much at ease in talking with people and asking them questions about things you are curious about.

In all of this, *fun* is the key. If you're having fun, you're doing it right. If you're not having fun, you need to keep at it, until you are. It may take your seeing four people. It may take ten. Or twenty. You'll know.

© Copyright 1989. Reprinted by permission of United Feature Syndicate, Inc.

SEND A THANK-YOU NOTE

After anyone has done you a favor, *at any time* during your job-hunt, you must *always* send them a thank-you note. Ideally it should be handwritten, but if your handwriting is the least bit difficult to read (ranging on up to indecipherable), by all means type it. It should be sent *the very next day* after you have visited someone. It can be just two or three sentences. Something like: *"I wanted to thank you for talking with me yesterday. It was very helpful to me. I much appreciated your taking the time out of your busy schedule, to do this. Best wishes to you,"* and then your signature. *Do* sign it, particularly if the thank-you note is typed. Typed letters without any signature seem to be multiplying like rabbits in the world of work, these days; it is usually perceived as making your letter *real* impersonal. You don't want to leave that impression.

The

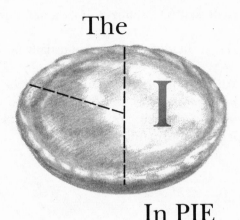

In PIE

When you feel comfortable doing Practice Interviewing, and it's easy and fun to talk to people about topics for which you feel enthusiasm, then you are ready to go on to informational interviewing, or the **I** in **P I E**.

Back to your Flower diagram. When you last looked at it, as you recall, you realized you needed more information about what job or career your Flower diagram points to. So, having gotten Practice Interviewing out of the way, you are now ready for the **I** phase: Informational interviewing. All the confidence you picked up during your Practice Interviewing, will now stand you in good stead, as you do your informational interviewing.

HOW TO DEVELOP
A STARTING POINT,
FOR YOUR
INFORMATIONAL INTERVIEWING

Before you go out to talk with anyone about your Flower Diagram, you want to summarize it a bit. Begin, here, by writing down your top skill here, and then your *three* favorite fields of knowledge, or fields of interest:

My top/favorite skill is: _____

My three favorite fields of interest/knowledge field / 'languages' are:

_____

As you will recall, skill(s) usually point toward a **job-title** or job-level.

Fields of interest or fields of knowledge usually point toward a **career field**.

Career fields can be *extremely* broad, like: *Agriculture,* or *Manufacturing,* or *Information industries,* or *Service industries.*[6] Which of these four do your favorite skill and knowledges *point to* -- as a starting point for your informational interviewing?

My answer: _____

---

6. While you're making up your mind, it is of historical interest to note that these large fields have changed dramatically in their dominance of the workplace, during this century, here in the U.S. and elsewhere. There was a time, around the turn of the century, when the majority of the work force -- that is, over 50% of all workers -- were employed in agriculture. Then, by mid-century, that had changed, and the majority of workers were employed in manufacturing. Today, that has changed again, and the majority of workers in this country are employed in careers which deal with information, and/or render services to people. Consequently, though many individuals still choose a career in manufacturing or even in agriculture, it is the services/information sector that is growing the most rapidly today, and therefore creating the most job opportunities. Hence, the common statement that the U.S. has become "The Information Society." From the point of view of the job-hunter, however, what the dominant economy is in this country at any one time, should never be the determining factor in choosing your career. If you want to be a blacksmith, you should be one, even if there *were* only three left in the country. (There's a blacksmith shop today right in the heart of San Francisco, for example.)

Career fields can also be more specific, like:

CAREER OR OCCUPATIONAL FAMILIES

1. Executive, Administrative, and Managerial Occupations
2. Engineers, Surveyors, and Architects
3. Natural Scientists and Mathematicians
4. Social Scientists, Social Workers, Religious Workers, and Lawyers
5. Teachers, Counselors, Librarians, and Archivists
6. Health Diagnosing and Treating Practitioners
7. Registered Nurses, Pharmacists, Dieticians, Therapists, and Physician Assistants
8. Health Technologists and Technicians
9. Writers, Artists, and Entertainers
10. Technologists and Technicians, Except Health
11. Marketing and Sales Occupations
12. Administrative Support Occupations, Including Clerical
13. Service Occupations
14. Agricultural, Forestry, and Fishing Occupations
15. Mechanics and Repairers
16. Construction and Extractive Occupations
17. Production Occupations
18. Transportation and Material Moving Occupations
19. Handlers, Equipment Cleaners, Helpers, and Laborers

Considering your favorite skill and knowledges, above, which of these nineteen broad fields are you most *attracted to* -- as a starting point for your informational interviewing?

My answer: _____

The 19 career fields can be broken down even further, in this fashion:

The World of Work:
A Sampler

	Job requirements									Work environment			Occupational characteristics				
	1. Leadership/persuasion	2. Helping/instructing others	3. Problem-solving/creativity	4. Initiative	5. Work as part of a team	6. Frequent public contact	7. Manual dexterity	8. Physical stamina	9. Hazardous	10. Outdoors	11. Confined	12. Geographically concentrated	13. Part-time	14. Earnings	15. Employment growth	16. Number of new jobs, 1984–95 (in thousands)	17. Entry requirements
Executive, Administrative, & Managerial Occupations																	
Managers & Administrators																	
Bank officers & managers	●	●	●	●	●	●			●					H	H	119	H
Health services managers	●	●	●	●	●	●								H	H	147	H
Hotel managers & assistants	●	●	●	●	●	●								(1)	H	21	M
School principals & assistant principals	●	●	●	●	●	●								H	L	12	H
Management Support Occupations																	
Accountants & auditors		●	●		●	●						●		H	H	307	H
Construction & building inspectors		●	●	●	●		●		●					M	L	4	M
Inspectors & compliance officers, except construction		●	●	●	●		●		●					H	L	10	M
Personnel, training & labor relations specialists	●	●	●	●	●									H	M	34	H
Purchasing agents	●		●		●									H	M	36	H
Underwriters			●											H	H	17	H
Wholesale & retail buyers	●	●	●	●	●									M	M	28	H
Engineers, Surveyors, & Architects																	
Architects			●	●	●	●	●							H	H	25	H
Surveyors	●			●		●	●		●					M	M	6	M
Engineers																	
Aerospace engineers			●	●	●							●		H	H	14	H
Chemical engineers			●	●	●									H	H	13	H
Civil engineers			●	●	●									H	H	46	H
Electrical & electronics engineers			●	●	●									H	H	206	H
Industrial engineers			●	●	●									H	H	37	H
Mechanical engineers			●	●	●									H	H	81	H
Metallurgical, ceramics & materials engineers			●	●	●									H	H	4	H
Mining engineers			●	●	●									H	L	(2)	H
Nuclear engineers			●	●	●									H	L	1	H
Petroleum engineers			●	●	●							●		H	M	4	H

1. Estimates not available.
2. Less than 500.

L = Lowest   M = Middle   H = Highest

From *Occupational Outlook Quarterly*, Vol. 30, No. 3   Fall 1986.

	Job requirements						Work environment			Occupational characteristics			
	1. Leadership/persuasion	2. Helping/instructing others	3. Problem-solving/creativity	4. Initiative	5. Work as part of a team	6. Frequent public contact	7. Manual dexterity	8. Physical stamina	9. Hazardous	10. Outdoors	11. Confined	12. Geographically concentrated	13. Part-time	14. Earnings	15. Employment growth	16. Number of new jobs, 1984-95 (in thousands)	17. Entry requirements
Natural Scientists & Mathematicians																
Computer & Mathematical Occupations																
Actuaries			●	●							●	●		H	H	4	H
Computer systems analysts	●	●	●	●	●							●		H	H	212	H
Mathematicians			●	●										H	M	4	H
Statisticians			●	●										H	M		H
Physical Scientists																
Chemists			●	●										H	L	9	H
Geologists & geophysicists			●	●	●					●		●		H	M	7	H
Meteorologists			●	●	●									H	M	1	H
Physicists & astronomers			●	●										H	L	2	H
Life Scientists																
Agricultural scientists			●	●										(1)	M	3	H
Biological scientists			●	●										H	M	10	H
Foresters & conservation scientists		●	●	●	●			●	●	●				H	L	2	H
Social Scientists, Social Workers, Religious Workers, & Lawyers																
Lawyers	●	●	●	●	●	●								H	H	174	H
Social Scientists & Urban Planners																
Economists			●	●										H	M	7	H
Psychologists		●	●	●		●								H	H	21	H
Sociologists			●	●		●								H	L	(2)	H
Urban & regional planners	●		●	●	●	●								H	L	2	H
Social & Recreation Workers																
Social workers	●	●	●	●	●	●								M	H	75	H
Recreation workers	●	●	●	●	●	●	●	●		●			●	L	H	26	M
Religious Workers																
Protestant ministers	●	●	●	●	●	●								L	(1)	(1)	H
Rabbis	●	●	●	●	●	●								H	(1)	(1)	H
Roman Catholic priests	●	●	●	●	●	●								L	(1)	(1)	H

1. Estimates not available.
2. Less than 500.

	Job requirements									Work environment			Occupational characteristics			
	1. Leadership/persuasion	2. Helping/instructing others	3. Problem-solving/creativity	4. Initiative	5. Work as part of a team	6. Frequent public contact	7. Manual dexterity	8. Physical stamina	9. Hazardous	10. Outdoors	11. Confined	12. Geographically concentrated	13. Part-time	14. Earnings	15. Employment growth	16. Number of new jobs, 1984-95 (in thousands)	17. Entry requirements
Teachers, Counselors, Librarians, & Archivists																	
Kindergarten & elementary school teachers	●	●	●	●	●	●	●	●	●					M	H	281	H
Secondary school teachers	●	●	●	●	●	●		●						M	L	48	H
Adult & vocational education teachers	●	●	●	●	●	●	●	●					●	M	M	48	H
College & university faculty	●	●	●	●	●	●		●					●	H	L	−77	H
Counselors	●	●	●	●	●	●								M	M	29	H
Librarians	●	●	●	●	●	●		●					●	M	L	16	H
Archivists & curators			●	●	●									M	L	1	H
Health Diagnosing & Treating Practitioners																	
Chiropractors	●	●	●	●	●	●	●							H	H	9	H
Dentists	●	●	●	●	●	●	●							H	H	39	H
Optometrists	●	●	●	●	●	●	●							H	H	8	H
Physicians	●	●	●	●	●	●	●					●		H	H	109	H
Podiatrists	●	●	●	●	●	●	●							H	H	4	H
Veterinarians	●	●	●	●	●	●	●	●	●					H	H	9	H
Registered Nurses, Pharmacists, Dietitians, Therapists, & Physician Assistants																	
Dietitians & nutritionists	●	●	●	●	●	●								M	H	12	H
Occupational therapists	●	●	●	●	●	●	●	●						(1)	H	8	H
Pharmacists	●	●	●	●	●	●	●					●		H	L	15	H
Physical therapists	●	●	●	●	●	●	●	●						M	H	25	H
Physician assistants	●	●	●	●	●	●	●							M	H	10	M
Recreational therapists	●	●	●	●	●	●	●	●		●				M	H	4	M
Registered nurses	●	●	●	●	●	●	●	●	●			●		M	H	452	M
Respiratory therapists	●	●	●	●	●	●	●							M	H	11	L
Speech pathologists & audiologists	●	●	●	●	●	●								M	M	8	H

1. Estimates not available.
2. Less than 500.

	1. Leadership/persuasion	2. Helping/instructing others	3. Problem-solving/creativity	4. Initiative	5. Work as part of a team	6. Frequent public contact	7. Manual dexterity	8. Physical stamina	9. Hazardous	10. Outdoors	11. Confined	12. Geographically concentrated	13. Part-time	14. Earnings	15. Employment growth	16. Number of new jobs, 1984-95 (in thousands)	17. Entry requirements
Health Technologists & Technicians																	
Clinical laboratory technologists & technicians		●		●		●					●			L	L	18	(3)
Dental hygienists		●		●	●	●	●						●	L	H	22	M
Dispensing opticians		●	●	●	●	●	●							M	H	10	M
Electrocardiograph technicians		●	●		●	●	●							(1)	M	3	M
Electroenceph. technologists & technicians		●	●		●	●	●							(1)	H	1	M
Emergency medical technicians	●	●	●		●	●	●	●	●	●				L	L	3	M
Licensed practical nurses		●			●	●	●	●					●	L	M	106	M
Medical record technicians					●							●		L	H	10	M
Radiologic technologists		●			●	●	●		●					L	H	27	M
Surgical technicians		●			●	●	●							L	M	5	M
Writers, Artists, & Entertainers																	
Communications Occupations																	
Public relations specialists	●		●	●	●	●								H	H	30	H
Radio & TV announcers & newscasters	●	●		●	●	●						●		L	M	6	H
Reporters & correspondents	●		●	●	●	●								(1)	M	13	H
Writers & editors	●		●	●	●							●	●	(1)	H	54	H
Visual Arts Occupations																	
Designers			●	●	●	●								H	H	46	H
Graphic & fine artists			●	●		●									H	60	M
Photographers & camera operators			●	●		●	●						●	M	H	29	M
Performing Arts Occupations																	
Actors, directors, & producers			●	●	●	●	●	●				●	●	L	H	11	M
Dancers & choreographers			●	●	●	●	●	●				●	●	L	H	2	M
Musicians			●	●	●	●	●					●	●	L	M	26	M
Technologists & Technicians Except Health																	
Engineering & Science Technicians																	
Drafters					●		●					●		M	M	39	M
Electrical & electronics technicians			●		●		●							M	H	202	M
Engineering technicians			●		●		●							M	H	90	M
Science technicians					●		●							M	M	40	M

1. Estimates not available.
2. Less than 500.
3. Vary, depending on job.

| | Job requirements | | | | | | | | | Work environment | | | | Occupational characteristics | | | |
	1. Leadership/persuasion	2. Helping/instructing others	3. Problem-solving/creativity	4. Initiative	5. Work as part of a team	6. Frequent public contact	7. Manual dexterity	8. Physical stamina	9. Hazardous	10. Outdoors	11. Confined	12. Geographically concentrated	13. Part-time	14. Earnings	15. Employment growth	16. Number of new jobs, 1984-95 (in thousands)	17. Entry requirements
Other Technicians																	
Air traffic controllers		•	•	•		•					•			H	L	(2)	H
Broadcast technicians			•		•	•					•			M	H	5	M
Computer programmers			•	•							•			H	H	245	H
Legal assistants			(3)		•	(3)								M	H	51	L
Library technicians		•			•	•	•					•		L	L	4	L
Tool programmers, numerical control		•				•		•						M	H	3	M
Marketing & Sales Occupations																	
Cashiers		•			•	•					•		•	L	H	566	L
Insurance sales workers	•	•	•	•	•								•	M	L	34	M
Manufacturers' sales workers	•	•	•	•	•									H	L	51	H
Real estate agents & brokers	•	•	•	•	•					•			•	M	M	52	M
Retail sales workers	•	•		•	•								•	L	M	583	L
Securities & financial services sales workers	•	•	•	•	•								•	H	H	32	H
Travel agents	•	•	•	•	•									(1)	H	32	M
Wholesale trade sales workers	•	•	•	•	•									M	H	369	M
Administrative Support Occupations, Including Clerical																	
Bank tellers					•	•					•		•	L	L	24	L
Bookkeepers & accounting clerks					•						•		•	L	L	118	L
Computer & peripheral equipment operators			•		•		•				•			L	H	143	M
Data entry keyers					•		•				•			L	L	10	L
Mail carriers						•	•	•		•				M	L	8	L
Postal clerks						•	•	•	•		•			M	L	−27	L
Receptionists & information clerks		•			•	•					•		•	L	M	83	L
Reservation & transportation ticket agents & travel clerks		•	•		•	•					•			M	L	7	L
Secretaries			•		•	•	•							L	L	268	L
Statistical clerks					•						•			L	L	−12	L
Stenographers			•		•	•	•							L	L	−96	L
Teacher aides	•	•			•	•	•						•	L	M	88	L
Telephone operators		•				•					•			L	M	89	L
Traffic, shipping, & receiving clerks			•	•	•									L	L	61	L
Typists						•					•		•	L	L	11	L

1. Estimates not available.
2. Less than 500.
3. Vary, depending on job.

	1. Leadership/persuasion	2. Helping/instructing others	3. Problem-solving/creativity	4. Initiative	5. Work as part of a team	6. Frequent public contact	7. Manual dexterity	8. Physical stamina	9. Hazardous	10. Outdoors	11. Confined	12. Geographically concentrated	13. Part-time	14. Earnings	15. Employment growth	16. Number of new jobs, 1984-95 (in thousands)	17. Entry requirements

Service Occupations

Protective Service Occupations

Occupation	1	2	3	4	5	6	7	8	9	10	11	12	13	Earnings	Empl. growth	New jobs	Entry req.
Correction officers	●	●		●		●	●		●					M	H	45	L
Firefighting occupations		●	●		●	●	●	●	●	●			●	M	M	48	L
Guards					●	●	●	●		●			●	L	H	188	L
Police & detectives	●	●	●	●	●	●	●							M	M	66	L

Food & Bev. Preparation & Serv. Occupations

Occupation	1	2	3	4	5	6	7	8	9	10	11	12	13	Earnings	Empl. growth	New jobs	Entry req.
Bartenders			●		●	●	●					●	●	L	H	112	M
Chefs & cooks except short order			●			●	●					●	●	L	H	210	M
Waiters & waitresses			●		●	●	●						●	L	H	424	L

Health Service Occupations

Occupation	1	2	3	4	5	6	7	8	9	10	11	12	13	Earnings	Empl. growth	New jobs	Entry req.
Dental assistants		●			●	●	●						●	L	H	48	L
Medical assistants		●			●	●	●		●					L	H	79	L
Nursing aides		●			●	●	●	●	●				●	L	H	348	L
Psychiatric aides		●			●	●		●	●					L	L	5	L

Cleaning Service Occupations

Occupation	1	2	3	4	5	6	7	8	9	10	11	12	13	Earnings	Empl. growth	New jobs	Entry req.
Janitors & cleaners								●					●	L	M	443	L

Personal Service Occupations

Occupation	1	2	3	4	5	6	7	8	9	10	11	12	13	Earnings	Empl. growth	New jobs	Entry req.
Barbers						●	●	●				●	●	L	L	4	M
Childcare workers	●	●		●		●		●					●	L	L	55	L
Cosmetologists & related workers						●	●	●	●			●	●	L	H	150	M
Flight attendants		●			●	●	●	●						M	H	13	L

Agricultural, Forestry, & Fishing Occupations

Occupation	1	2	3	4	5	6	7	8	9	10	11	12	13	Earnings	Empl. growth	New jobs	Entry req.
Farm operators & managers	●	●	●	●	●		●	●		●				M	L	-62	L

Mechanics & Repairers

Vehicle & Mobile Equip. Mechanics & Repairers

Occupation	1	2	3	4	5	6	7	8	9	10	11	12	13	Earnings	Empl. growth	New jobs	Entry req.
Aircraft mechanics & engine specialists			●		●		●	●	●	●		●		H	M	18	M
Automotive & motorcycle mechanics			●			●	●	●			●			M	H	185	M
Automotive body repairers			●				●	●	●		●			M	M	32	M
Diesel mechanics			●		●		●	●	●		●			M	H	48	M
Farm equipment mechanics			●				●	●	●	●				M	L	2	M
Mobile heavy equipment mechanics			●				●	●	●		●			M	M	12	M

	Job requirements									Work environment				Occupational characteristics			
	1. Leadership/persuasion	2. Helping/instructing others	3. Problem-solving/creativity	4. Initiative	5. Work as part of a team	6. Frequent public contact	7. Manual dexterity	8. Physical stamina	9. Hazardous	10. Outdoors	11. Confined	12. Geographically concentrated	13. Part-time	14. Earnings	15. Employment growth	16. Number of new jobs, 1984-95 (in thousands)	17. Entry requirements
Electrical & Electronic Equipment Repairers																	
Commercial & electronic equipment repairers		•	•		•	•								L	M	8	M
Communications equipment mechanics		•	•		•	•								M	L	3	M
Computer service technicians		•	•		•	•								M	H	28	M
Electronic home entertainment equip. repairers		•	•		•	•	•						•	M	M	7	M
Home appliance & power tool repairers		•	•		•	•								L	M	9	M
Line installers & cable splicers		•		•		•	•	•	•					M	M	24	L
Telephone installers & repairers		•		•	•	•	•	•						M	L	-19	L
Other Mechanics & Repairers																	
General maintenance mechanics		•				•		•						M	M	137	M
Heating, air-cond. & refrig. mechanics		•				•		•						M	M	29	M
Industrial machinery repairers		•				•	•	•						M	L	34	M
Millwrights		•				•		•						H	L	6	M
Musical instrument repairers & tuners						•								L	L	1	M
Office machine & cash register servicers		•	•	•		•								M	H	16	M
Vending machine servicers & repairers		•	•			•								(1)	M	5	M
Construction & Extractive Occupations																	
Construction Occupations																	
Bricklayers & stonemasons			•		•		•	•	•	•				M	M	15	M
Carpenters			•		•		•	•	•	•				M	M	101	M
Carpet installers			•	•	•		•	•						M	M	11	M
Concrete masons & terrazzo workers			•		•		•	•	•	•				M	M	17	M
Drywall workers & lathers			•		•		•	•		•				M	M	11	M
Electricians			•		•		•	•	•	•				H	M	88	M
Glaziers			•		•		•	•		•				M	H	8	M
Insulation workers			•		•		•	•		•				M	M	7	M
Painters & paperhangers			•		•		•	•	•	•				M	L	17	M
Plasterers			•		•		•	•		•		•		M	L	1	M
Plumbers & pipefitters			•	•	•		•	•	•	•				H	M	61	M
Roofers			•		•		•	•	•	•				L	M	16	M
Sheet-metal workers			•		•		•	•		•				M	M	16	M
Structural & reinforcing metal workers			•		•		•	•	•	•				H	M	16	M
Tilesetters			•		•		•	•						M	M	3	M
Extractive Occupations																	
Roustabouts			•		•		•	•	•	•		•		M	L	(2)	L

1. Estimates not available.
2. Less than 500.

	Job requirements									Work environment		Occupational characteristics				
	1. Leadership/persuasion	2. Helping/instructing others	3. Problem-solving/creativity	4. Initiative	5. Work as part of a team	6. Frequent public contact	7. Manual dexterity	8. Physical stamina	9. Hazardous	10. Outdoors	11. Confined	12. Geographically concentrated	13. Part-time	14. Earnings	15. Employment growth	16. Number of new jobs 1984-95 (in thousands)	17. Entry requirements
Production Occupations																	
Blue-collar worker supervisors	•	•	•	•		•		•						M	L	85	M
Precision Production Occupations																	
Boilermakers			•			•		•						M	L	4	M
Bookbinding workers		•			•	•	•	•			•			L	M	14	M
Butchers and meatcutters					•	•	•	•			•			L	L	-9	M
Compositors & typesetters						•	•	•			•			L	M	14	M
Dental laboratory technicians								•			•			L	M	10	M
Jewelers	•	•	•	•	•	•	•				•	•		L	L	3	M
Lithographic & photoengraving workers		•	•		•		•	•			•			H	M	13	M
Machinists			•			•	•	•			•			M	L	37	M
Photographic process workers						•					•			L	H	14	L
Shoe & leather workers & repairers		•			•	•	•							L	L	-8	M
Tool-and-die makers			•			•	•	•			•			H	L	16	M
Upholsterers						•	•				•			L	L	6	M
Plant & System Operators																	
Stationary engineers			•			•	•	•						M	L	4	M
Water & sewage treatment plant operators			•	•		•			•	•				L	M	10	M
Machine Operators, Tenders, & Setup Workers																	
Metalworking & plastic-working mach. operators						•	•	•			•	•		L		3	L
Numerical-control machine-tool operators			•			•	•	•			•			M	H	17	M
Printing press operators	•	•		•		•	•	•			•			M	M	26	M
Fabricators, Assemblers & Handwrkg. Occup.																	
Precision assemblers					•		•	•			•			L	M	66	L
Transportation equipment painters						•	•	•			•			M	M	9	M
Welders & cutters						•	•	•	•					M	M	41	M
Transportation & Material Moving Occupations																	
Aircraft pilots			•	•	•		•				•			H	H	18	M
Busdrivers				•		•	•	•			•		•	M	M	77	M
Construction machinery operators				•		•	•	•	•	•	•			M	M	32	M
Industrial truck & tractor operators				•		•	•				•			M	L	-46	M
Truckdrivers				•		•	•				•			M	M	428	M
Handlers, Equip. Cleaners, Helpers & Laborers																	
Construction trades helpers					•		•	•	•	•				L	L	27	L

Considering your favorite skill and knowledge, which of these almost 200 careers or jobs do you see yourself most *attracted to* -- as a starting point for your informational interviewing?[7]

My answer: _____

Career fields can be broken down *still* further, since within each job or career listed above you can choose particular work where you work primarily with *people* **or** primarily with *information/data* **or** primarily with *things*.

Let's take agriculture as an example. Within agriculture, you could be driving tractors and other farm machinery -- and thus working primarily with *things;* or you could be gathering statistics about crop growth for some state agency -- and thus working primarily with *information/data;* or you could be teaching agriculture in a college classroom, and thus working primarily with *people* and *ideas.*

---

7. As I have indicated, career-changers and job-hunters usually are not comfortable navigating their way around the *D.O.T.* or the other occupational resources so dear to the hearts of career counselors. But, just so you'll know what's *out there,* these are the traditional places where people look for further information about careers:

The *Dictionary of Occupational Titles (DOT), 4th ed.,* revised 1991. *In two volumes.* Supt. of Documents, U.S. Govt. Printing Office, Washington, DC 20402. A catalog of 12,741 occupations. It has an alphabetical index, by occupations. It is also available in an exact reprint from JIST Works, Inc., 720 North Park Ave., Indianapolis, IN 46202-3431. This is a very difficult, book. If you want to plumb its depths, I would recommend **strongly** that you *first* use Holland's Self-Directed Search, and thence *his* Dictionary *(both are explained more fully on pages 169ff.)* to tell you which occupations to go seeking in the DOT.

Occupational Outlook Handbook, 90–91. Bureau of Labor Statistics, available from Supt. of Documents, U.S. Govt. Printing Office, Washington, DC 20402. 225 occupations organized by interest and job title. This has also been published commercially under the title, *America's Top 300 Jobs,* by JIST Works, Inc., 720 N. Park Ave., Indianapolis, IN 46202-3431. 1990. The latter has some helpful indices and supplemental material.

Selected Characteristics of Occupations Defined in the Dictionary of Occupational Titles. U.S. Dept. of Labor, Employment and Training Admin., available from Supt. of Documents, U.S. Govt. Printing Office, Washington, DC 20402.

Job Selection Workbook, for use with Guide for Occupational Exploration. U.S. Employment Service, Employment and Training Admin., available from Supt. of Documents, U.S. Govt. Printing Office, Washington, DC 20402. 1979.

William E. Hopke, ed., *Encyclopedia of Careers and Vocational Guidance, 8th ed. 4 volumes.* Garrett Park Press, Box 190, Garrett Park, MD 20896. 1990.

There are also *numerous* books in most libraries, and certainly in most bookstores, on various groups of careers. You will find titles like Ten Speed Press's *Offbeat Careers: The Directory of Unusual Work,* career books on the health fields, etc., etc.

Almost all fields as well as career families offer you these three kinds of choices, though *of course* many jobs combine two or more of the three. Still, you do want to tell yourself what your *preference* is, and what you *primarily* want to be working with. Otherwise your job-hunt or career-change is going to leave you very frustrated, at the end.

In this matter, it is often your favorite skill that will give you the clue. If it *doesn't*, then go back and look at your total skills *petal*, on page 211. What do you think? Are those top eight weighted more toward working with *people*, or toward working with *information/data*, or toward working with *things*? And, no matter what that *petal* suggests, which do you prefer?

My answer: _____

Combining these answers you should end up with a statement somewhat like this.

Looking at all my answers here, I think the most important data for choosing my starting point for informational interviewing might be:

AN EXAMPLE

Let's see how a particular career-changer might have answered all the above. We'll take an actual career-changer. His answers were:

My top/favorite skill is: diagnosing, treating, or healing

My three top/favorite fields of knowledge are: psychiatry, plants, and carpentry.

Among the broad divisions of the job-market, I am most attracted to Service industries, because I want to serve people.

Among the 19 Career families, I am most attracted to (6) Health diagnosing and treating practitioners.

Among the almost 200 occupations, the ones that I would like to know more about are ones like psychiatric aide, or psychiatrist.

Looking at all my answers above, I feel my strongest lead is actually my fields of knowledge, that I have on my flower. It shows that I'm interested in the subjects of psychiatry, plants, and carpentry. At the moment, I don't want to let any of them go. I'd actually like to find out how to combine psychiatry and plants and carpentry in one career. That means I'll need to go talk to a psychiatrist, and a gardener, and a carpenter. I'm obviously going to have to discover a career that I've never even heard the name of, or if it doesn't exist, create it for myself.

Our job-hunter, in this example, has decided to mentally translate his fields of knowledge into persons with particular occupations, and then go talk to those persons. How does he decide which one to go interview first? Well, he asks himself which of these persons is most likely to have the largest *overview.* *(This is often, but not always, the same as asking: who took the longest to get their training?)* The particular answer here: the psychiatrist. He would then go see two or three psychiatrists -- say, the head of the psychiatry department at the nearest college or university, or those in private practice[8] and ask them: *Do you have any idea how to put these three subjects -- carpentry, plants, and psychiatry*

---

8. If there is no psychiatrist at any academic institution near you, then do all your research with private psychiatrists -- their names are in the phone book -- and ask to come see them for *a half session.* Pay them for their time, at the half-session rate, if there is no other way.

-- together into one job or career? And if you don't know, who do you think might? He would keep going until he found someone who had a bright idea about how you put this all together.

In this particular case *(as I said, this is from an actual career-changer's experience),* he was eventually told: "Yes, it can all be put together. There is a branch of psychiatry that uses plants to help heal people. That takes care of your interest in plants and psychiatry. As for your carpentry interests, I suppose you could employ that to build the planters for your plants."

WHAT DO YOU WANT TO LEARN FROM YOUR INFORMATIONAL INTERVIEWING?

When you go talk to people, you want them to give you ideas about what kinds of careers will use your skills and fields of knowledge/interest; but you also want them to give you some idea of what that work is like.

If they don't know -- say in the example above no one knew what it's like to be a psychiatrist working with plants, then you ask them for names of people who *do* that work, and then go talk to them -- for information only.

When you are face to face with workers who are doing the career you think you might like, you ask them *the same* four things we saw earlier, during our Practice Field Survey:

- How did you get into this work?
- What do you like the most about it?
- What do you like the least about it?
- And, where else could I find people who do this kind of work? *(You should always ask them for more than one name, so that if you run into a dead end at any point, you can easily go back and visit the other people they suggested.)*

In effect, what you are doing here, with your informational interviewing, is trying on jobs to see if they fit you.

It is exactly analogous to your going to a clothing store and trying on different suits (or dresses) that you see in their window. Why do you try them on? Well, the suits or dresses that look *terrific* in the window don't always look so hotsy-totsy when you see them on *you.* They don't hang quite right, etc., etc. Likewise, the careers that look so terrific in the books or in your

imagination don't always look so terrific when you see them up close, in all their true reality. What you're looking for, of course, is a career that looks terrific in the window, *and* on you.

If it becomes apparent to you, during any informational interview, that this career, occupation, or job definitely *doesn't* fit you, then the last question (above) is turned into a different kind of inquiry: "Do you have any ideas as to who I could go talk to about how I could use these -- here mentioning your skills and your fields of knowledge/interest -- in one career?

Then go visit the people they suggest.

If they can't think of anyone, ask them if they know who *might* know.

I do want to emphasize that it is workers you are going to see, during this 'I' (informational interviewing) phase of your job-hunt or career-change. You'll thus find out 'from the horse's mouth' whether these jobs or careers are as attractive up close, as they look from a distance.

"I LIKE THE WORK THEY DESCRIBE, BUT NOT HOW LONG THE PREPARATION TAKES"

In trying to find out more about a new field, or career, the workers will always tell you *what it takes* to get into that career. It will often turn out to be something like:

"In order to be hired for this job, you have to have a master's degree and ten years' experience at it."

But, if you aren't willing to go that long route, you will want *always* to search for the exception:

"Yes, but do you know of anyone in this field who got into it without that master's degree, and ten years' experience?
And where might I find him or her?
And if you don't know of any such person, who might know?"

One person's word as to what it takes to get into this career should rarely be taken as *gospel*. Believe me, there are exceptions to almost *every* rule, except where there are rigid examinations one must take, as in medicine or law. Yet, even here, you can get *close* to the profession *without* such exams, as in para-medical, or para-legal, work.

Sooner or later, as you interview one person after another, you'll begin to get some definite ideas about a career that is of interest to you. It uses your favorite skills. It employs your favorite fields of knowledge or fields of interest. You've interviewed people *actually doing that work*, and it all sounds fine. Just be sure that you get the names of at least *two* careers, or jobs, that you think you could be happy doing. Never, ever, put all your eggs in one basket. The secret of surviving out there in the jungle is *having alternatives*.

CUTTING DOWN THE TERRITORY

As workers tell you about their jobs or careers, they will incidentally volunteer information about the *kinds* of organizations, and the actual names of organizations that have such jobs -- including what's good or bad about the place where *they* work. This is important information for you. Jot it all down. Keep notes like it was part of your religion.

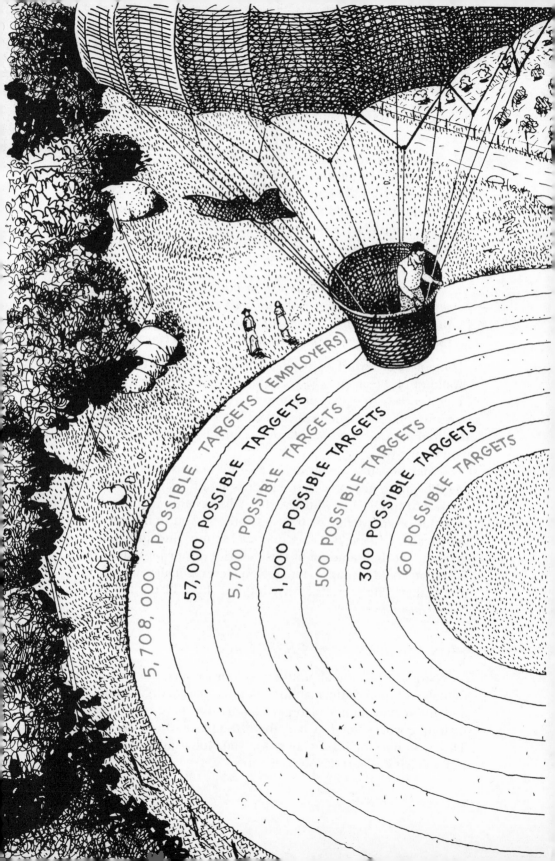

10 POSSIBLE TARGETS

YOUR SPIRITUAL VALUES

YOUR PREFERRED LEVEL AND SALARY

YOUR PREFERRED WORKING CONDITIONS YOU PREFER

THINGS, KINDS OF PEOPLE, AND INFORMATION

YOUR PREFERRED TASKS OR SKILLS

YOUR PREFERRED FIELD (OF KNOWLEDGE) OR CAREER FIELD

YOUR PREFERRED GEOGRAPHICAL LOCATION

You're liable, of course, to end up with too much information -- too many ideas of places which hire people in the career that interests you.

Hence you will want to **cut the territory down**, so that you have a manageable number of *'targets'* for your job-hunt.[9]

The Whole Job-Market

Let's take an example. Suppose you discovered that the career which interests you the most is *welding*. You want to be a welder. Well, that's a beginning. You've cut the 5,708,000 job-markets in the U.S., say, down to just those that hire welders.

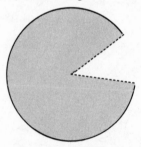

But the territory is still too large. There might be thousands of places that use welders. You can't go visit them all. So, you've got to cut the territory down, further.

Suppose that your geography *petal* said that you really want to live and work in, let us say, the San Jose area of California. That cuts the territory down further. You're looking for the names of organizations *in the San Jose area* which hire welders.

---

9. If you resist this idea of *cutting the territory down* -- if you feel you could be happy *anywhere* just as long as you were using your favorite skills -- then almost no organization in the country can be ruled out. In the U.S. currently there are 5,708,000 organizations, hence 5,708,000 job-markets, out there. (And a proportional number in other countries.) So if you aren't willing to cut the territory down, then you'll have to go visit them all. Good luck! We'll see you in about 43 years.

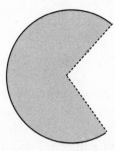

But, the territory is still too large. That could be 100, 200, 300 organizations which fit that description. So you look at your Flower Diagram, and you see that under working conditions you said you wanted to work for an organization with fifty or less employees. So now you're looking for the names of organizations having fifty or less employees which hire welders, in the San Jose area.

This territory may still be too large. So you look again at your Flower Diagram, and you see that on the Things *petal* you said you wanted to work for an organization which works with, or produces, *wheels*. So now what you're looking for are the names of organizations in the San Jose area, which produce wheels, and have fifty or less employees, and hire welders.

Using your Flower Diagram, you thus keep cutting the territory down, until the 'targets' of your job-hunt are no more than 20 places. That's a manageable number of places for you to approach about working there.

EXPANDING THE TERRITORY

Of course, sometimes your problem will be just the opposite. You've identified the career you would like, but you can't find enough places to 'target.'

If your informational interviewing doesn't turn up enough names of places where you could get hired in your new career, then you're going to have to consult some directories. If it's the name of large organizations that you're looking for, see the list at the beginning of Appendix B, in the back of this book. There are *many* directories of such large organizations. If it's the name of smaller organizations that you're looking for, consult the yellow pages of your phone book, under every related heading that you can think of. Also, see if the Chamber of Commerce publishes a business directory; often it will list not only small companies but also local divisions of larger companies, with names of department heads; and sometimes will even include the (SIC) industry codes. You won't likely lack for names, believe me -- unless it's a very small town you live in, in which case you'll need to cast your net a little wider, to include other places that are within commuting distance.

Another thing that's helpful, for expanding your list of *'target'* organizations, is to step back, take the larger view, and think out what *kinds* of place might employ a person with your skills and interests.

Let's take an example. Suppose in your new career you want to be a teacher. And you ask yourself: *what kinds of places hire teachers?* You might answer, *"just schools,"* -- and finding that schools in your geographical area have no openings, you might say, *"Well, there are no jobs for people in this career."*

But that is not true. There are countless other *kinds* of organizations and agencies out there, besides schools, which have a teaching arm, and therefore employ teachers. For example, corporate training and educational departments, workshop sponsors, foundations, private research firms, educational consultants, teachers' associations, professional and trade societies, military bases, state and local councils on higher education, fire and police training academies, and so on, and so forth.

'Kinds of places' also means places with different *hiring modes,* besides full-time hiring, such as:

• places that would employ you part-time (maybe you'll end up deciding to hold down two or even three part-time jobs, which altogether would add up to one full-time job, in order to give yourself more variety);

• places which you yourself would start up, if you want to be your own boss;

• places that are for profit;

• places that are nonprofit;

• places that take temporary workers, on assignment for one project at a time;

• places that take consultants, one project at a time;

• places that operate with volunteers, etc.

Your local town or city librarian can be a great help if you need to expand your territory for your job-hunt. So can people at universities or at businesses, who have an overview of the field or career that interests you.

FINDING OUT MORE
ABOUT YOUR 'TARGETS'

Once you've identified organizations *(plural, not singular)* by name, as your 'targets' for your job-hunt, you then try to think of every way in the world that you could find out more about those places, to see if you like them *before you go to see if you can get hired there.*

There are several ways you can do this.

• **What's In Print.** The organization itself may have stuff in print, about its business, purpose, etc. The CEO may have given talks, and the organization may have copies of those talks. Where? Well, the publicity office, or human relations office, are the places to check -- in larger organizations. The person that answers the phone is the person to check with, in small organizations. Libraries also may have files on the organization that interests you -- newspaper clippings, articles, etc. You never know; and it never hurts to ask. If it's a decent-sized organization you are interested in, one of the numerous directories mentioned at the beginning of Appendix B, in the back of this book, should serve you well.

• **People at the Organizations in Question, or at Similar Organizations.** You can go directly to organizations and ask questions about the place, but there are several *caveats.* First, you must make sure you're not asking them questions that are in print somewhere, which you could easily have read for yourself instead of bothering *them.* Secondly, you must make sure that you approach the people at that organization *whose business it is to give out information* -- receptionists, public relations people, 'the personnel office,' etc., *before* you ever approach other people higher up. Thirdly, you must make sure that you approach *subordinates* rather than the top person in the place, if the subordinates would know the answer to your questions. Bothering the boss there with some simple questions that someone else could have answered is job-hunting suicide.

Job-Hunters Who Are Tricksters

There is no honest, open-hearted *technique* that cannot be twisted by those with clever, devious hearts, into some kind of *trick*. This has happened with informational interviewing. *Some* job-hunters have thought, "Wouldn't this be a great *trick* to use so as to get in to see employers -- asking them for some of their time, claiming you need *information,* and then hitting them up for a job?"

In case *you,* even for a moment, are tempted to follow in their footsteps, let me gently inform you that employers universally detest this particular deception, and have usually thrown the liar/trickster out of their offices. One New York employer said to such a trickster: "You came to see me to ask for some information. And I gladly gave you my time. But now, it is apparent you really want a job here, and think you found a 'trick' that would get you in the door. Let me tell you something: on the basis of what I have just seen of your style of doing things, I wouldn't hire you if you were the last person on earth. I know this informational interviewing process well -- I've read *Parachute* -- but by turning it into a *trick,* you give the whole process a bad name, and make life difficult for every informational interviewer who comes after you." *Ouch!*

In this Age of Rudeness, Lies, and Manipulation, **you** will want, above all else, to be a beacon of integrity, truth, and kindness throughout your job-hunt or career-change. *That's* the kind of employee employers are *dying* to find. On the other hand, the quota for those who attempt to practice *deception* is already *more than* filled, in this fractured world.

• **Friends and Neighbors.** Another way to find out about a place is to ask *everybody* you know, if they know anyone who works there. And, if they do, you ask them if they could arrange for you and that person to get together, for coffee or tea. At that time, you tell them the place interests you, and you'd like to know more about it. (It helps if your mutual friend is sitting there with the two of you, so the purpose of this little chat won't be misconstrued.) This is the vastly preferred way to find out about a place. However, obviously you need a couple of additional alternatives up your sleeve, in case you run into a dead end here. The first alternative is *temporary agencies,* and the second is *volunteer work.*

• **Temporary Agencies.** Many job-hunters and career-changers have found that a useful way to explore organizations, alternatively, is to sign up with some temporary agency. As I remarked in Chapter 3, temporary agencies in the old days were solely for clerical workers and secretarial help. But the field has seen an explosion of services in recent years -- according to the Bureau of Labor Statistics, temporary or part-time workers now number over 35 million, and represent 29% of the total civilian labor force.

So, now there are temporary agencies *(at least in the larger cities)* for many different occupations. In your city you may find

temporary agencies for: accountants, industrial workers, assemblers, drivers, mechanics, construction people, engineering people, management/executives, nannies (for young and old), health care/dental/medical people, legal specialists, insurance specialists, sales/marketing people, underwriting professionals, financial services, and the like, as well as for the more obvious specialties: data processing, secretarial, and office services. See your local phone book, under 'Temporary Agencies.'

The advantage to you of temporary work is that if there is an agency which loans out people with your particular skills and expertise, you get a chance to visit a number of different employers over a period of several weeks, and see each one from the inside. Employers turn to these agencies in order to find: a) job-hunters who can work part-time for a limited number of days; and b) job-hunters who can work full-time for a limited number of days.

• Volunteer Work. This is a useful way to explore a place, if you have a long period of unemployment staring you in the face. You offer to do volunteer work at a place you're trying to find out more about. Because you offer your services *without pay* for a brief, limited period of time, it's relatively easy to talk them into letting you work there for a while. Thus you get a chance to know them from the inside. Not so coincidentally, if you decide you would really like to work there permanently, they've had a chance to see you in action, and when you are about to end your volunteer time there, *may* want to hire you permanently. I say *may*. Don't be mad if they simply say, "Thanks very much for helping us out." (That's what *normally* happens.) You've still learned a lot, that will stand you in good stead, in the future -- even with other organizations.

WHY SURVEY ORGANIZATIONS
AHEAD OF THE HIRING INTERVIEW?

Well, first of all, you want to know what their needs or problems or challenges are. What kind of work are they trying to achieve? What is keeping them from achieving their goals as much as they want to? How can your skills and knowledges help them? (You want, above all else, to be able to show them that you have something to offer, which they need.)

Secondly, you want to find out if you would enjoy working there. You want to take the measure of that organization or organizations. Everybody takes the measure of an organization, sooner or later. The problem with most job-hunters or career-changers is they take the measure of an organization *after* they are hired there.

In the U.S., for example, a survey of the Federal/State employment service found that 57% of those who found jobs through that service were not working at that job just 30 days later.

They were not working at that job just 30 days later, *because* they used the first ten or twenty days *on the job* to screen out the job.

By doing the exercises in this chapter, you are choosing a better way, by far. Essentially, you are *screening out* careers, jobs, places *before* you commit to them. How sensible! How smart!

SEND A THANK-YOU NOTE

As I said earlier in this chapter, after any one has done you a favor, *at any time* during your job-hunt, you must *always* send them a thank-you note. That applies, of course, to the people you see during this informational interviewing part of your job-hunt or career-change. It goes to *everyone* who helps you, or who talks with you. That means secretaries, receptionists, librarians, workers, or whoever.

Ask them, at the time you are face to face with them, for their calling card (if they have one), or ask them to write out their name and work-address, on a piece of paper, for you. You *don't* want to misspell their name. It is difficult to figure out how to spell people's names, these days, simply from the sound of it. What sounds like "Laura" may actually be "Lara." What sounds like "Smith" may actually be "Smythe," and so on. Get that name and address, but get it *right,* please. And write them the thank-you note that same night, or the very next day at the latest. *Timeliness* counts for a lot.

WHAT IF I GET OFFERED A JOB
ALONG THE WAY, WHILE I'M STILL
ONLY GATHERING INFORMATION

You probably won't. Let me remind you that during this information gathering, you are *not* talking primarily to employers. You're talking to workers.

Nonetheless, an occasional employer *may* stray across your path during all this informational interviewing. And that employer *may* be so impressed with the carefulness you're showing, in going about your career-change and job-search, that they want to hire you, on the spot. So, it's *possible* that you might get offered a job while you're still doing your information gathering. Not *likely,* but *possible.* And if that happens, what should you say?

Well, if you're desperate, you will of course say *yes.* I remember one wintertime when I had just gone through the knee of my last pair of pants, we were burning old pieces of furniture in our fireplace to stay warm, the legs on our bed had just broken, and we were eating spaghetti until it was coming out our ears. In such a situation, *of course* you say yes.

But if you're not *desperate,* if you have a little time to be more careful, then you respond to the job-offer in a way that will buy you some time. You tell them what you're doing: that the average job-hunter tries to screen a job *after* they take it. But you are doing what you are *sure* this employer would do if they were in your shoes: you are examining careers, fields, industries, jobs, organizations *before* you decide where you can do your best and most effective work.

And you tell them that since your informational interviewing isn't finished yet, it would be premature for you to accept their job offer, until you're *sure* that this is the place where you could be most effective, and do your best work.

But, you add: "Of course, I'm tickled pink that you would want me to be working here. And when I've finished my personal survey, I'll be glad to get back to you about this, as my preliminary impression is that this is the kind of place I'd like to work in, and the kind of people I'd like to work for, and the kind of people I'd like to work with."

In other words, *if you're not desperate yet,* you don't walk immediately through any opened doors; but neither do you allow
them to shut.

QUESTION ALL ASSUMPTIONS

As you conduct this informational interviewing, you should
keep in mind that there are people out there who will tell you
something that absolutely *isn't* so, with every conviction in their
being -- because they *think* it's true. Sincerity they have, one
hundred percent. Accuracy is something else again. You will
need to check and cross-check any information that people tell
you or that you read in books (even this one).

Throughout your informational interviewing, don't assume
anything ("But I just assumed that . . ."). Question *all* assumptions, no matter how many people tell you that 'this is the
way things are.'

Be careful. Be thorough. Be persistent. This is your life you're
working on, and your future. Make it glorious. Whatever it
takes, find out the name of your ideal career, your ideal occupation, your ideal job -- *or jobs.*

A SUMMARY FOR THOSE
WHO LIKE SUMMARIES

This has been a chapter filled with many ideas. Your head is swimming. You want to recall the central underlying theme in all of this. Okay, here it is:

*T*here is no limit to what you can find out about careers -- and places which hire for those careers -- if you go out and talk to people, rather than trying to do such research solely through books.

When you find careers and places that interest you, you research them ahead of time.

Whether an organization happens to have a vacancy, or happens to *want* you, is for the moment irrelevant. In this dance of life, called the job-hunt, you get first choice: you get to decide first of all whether or not *you* want *them*.

Only after you have decided that, is it appropriate to ask if they also want you.

You're a bunch of jackasses. You work your rear ends off in a trivial course that no one will ever care about again. You're not willing to spend time researching a company that you're interested in working for. Why don't you decide who you want to work for and go after them?

Professor Albert Shapero
The late William H. Davis Professor of The American Free Enterprise System at Ohio State University

CHAPTER TWELVE

Securing
The
Interview

You Must Identify
The Person Who Has
The Power To Hire You

Chapter 12

Okay, so you've found a place -- better yet, *places* -- where you'd *love* to work. But the person you'd have to see, in order to get hired there, is in an office with a ring of fire around it, three knights in full-armor guarding it, in a castle with fifty-foot walls, surrounded by a wide moat whose deep waters are filled with hungry alligators. And you want to know how to get in there for a job-interview. Right?

Well, it isn't as difficult as it might at first seem. There is a way:

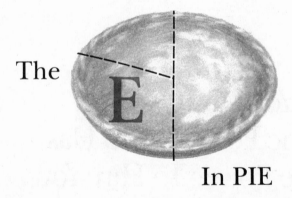

The **E** In PIE

E, as you recall if you read the previous chapter, stands for Interviewing for **E**mployment. Job-interviews are terrifying to a lot of people -- turning the knees to jelly, and causing the palms to sweat. There are two problems: one is even getting in to *see* the person–who–has–the–power–to–hire–you. That's a biggie. The other is persuading them to hire you, once they do agree to see you. That's even more difficult.

Interviewing. *Yuk!*

Frank and Ernest by Bob Thaves
© 1980 NEA, Inc. *Contra Costa Times*.
Used by special permission.

HOW TO BE
AN INTERVIEWING VETERAN

However, most of us make it more difficult for ourselves than it needs to be, because we wait until it's time for the job-interview, before we even think about *how do you do interviewing?* We're rusty. Out of practice. Out of shape. And so, we crash and burn right in front of the prospective employer we care the most about.

But -- as we saw in the previous chapter -- successful job-hunters and career-changers avoid this humiliation by only facing employers after they have been doing interviews *throughout their whole job-hunt.* They realize there are actually three types of *interviews* one must do, in the job-hunt. Early on, in your job-hunt, you tackle interviewing whose purpose is merely that of **P**ractice and pleasure; in the middle of your job-hunt, you tackle interviewing whose purpose is to dig up **I**nformation you need about careers, organizations, and employers; and then toward the end of your job-hunt, you approach *employers* for the first time, to see about **E**mployment, or getting hired there -- but by then you're *an interviewing veteran.* Voila! P–I–E is the key.

That's the way to tackle it. Most job-hunters, of course, don't.

If you would be wise beyond your years, my friend, go back and read *and do* Chapter 11. That's how you defang interviewing of all its terrors.

Then you are fully ready to tackle the two problems we are about to discuss: getting in to *see* the person–who–has–the–power–to–hire–you (which is the subject of *this* chapter). And persuading them to hire you, once they do agree to see you (which we deal with in the next).

Half Our 'Ills' In Life Are Self-Inflicted

This is a hard truth for me to write about, and hard for each of us to take to heart in our own lives.

However, here it is: when we have a problem, life often shows us the solution, but we duck it because it involves work, and we wait instead for magic -- which never comes. And so, the problem remains.

We like then to pretend to ourselves that some mysterious outside influence -- life, the labor market, the government, an uncaring society -- is doing this to us. But by refusing to adopt the solution life has shown us, it is actually we who are doing it to ourselves.

We are like prisoners in a cell where the jailor is gone and the door is open. But we still just sit there, claiming we are a prisoner still.

To apply this to our present problem: the P–I–E method will solve the terror of interviewing, on which our job-hunt depends. But most of us duck doing the P–I–E method because it involves work, and we hope instead for magic -- which never comes. And so, interviewing continues to oppress us.

THE FIRST CRUCIAL QUESTION: HOW LARGE IS THE ORGANIZATION?

All techniques or strategies for securing an interview fall into two groups, *depending* on whether the organization you are trying to approach is a relatively large organization, *or* is what we call 'a small organization' -- one which has twenty-five or less employees.

Most discussions of job-interviewing *assume* you are approaching a large organization -- you know, the ones where you need a floor-plan of the building, and an alphabetical directory of the staff. There *are* huge problems in approaching such giants for a job-interview, not the least of which is that generally speaking they are doing more layoffs than hiring, during these cost-cutting times.[1]

But then, there are the small organizations -- with 50 or less employees. In the U.S., for example, these total 80% of all private businesses. These small organizations, representing one-fourth of all workers in the private sector, are claimed by some to create two-thirds of all new jobs.[2]

In any event, small organizations are *much* easier to get into, believe me.

---

1. Like all generalizations, this one of course has a number of exceptions. In the U.S., Wal-Mart, Pepsico, U.P.S., Chrysler, Sara Lee, General Mills, Motorola, and Home Depot all added jobs -- in Wal-Mart's case, 182,000 -- between 1992 and 1994. Wal-Mart is now the second largest employer in the U.S. *(New York Times, 3/25/94.)*

2. This statistic, first popularized by David Birch of M.I.T., and 'bandied about' for years, has been widely debated, of late, by economists such as Nobel laureate Milton Friedman and Harvard economist James Medoff. The debate has been fueled, of late, due to a study conducted jointly by Steven J. Davis, a labor economist at the University of Chicago, John Haltiwanger at the University of Maryland, and Scott Schuh at the Federal Reserve. Their study is, however, of U.S. *manufacturing,* not of the economy as a whole. What these researchers discovered about manufacturing in the U.S. of A. is that small companies with 50 or fewer employees created *one-fifth* of all new manufacturing jobs. *(New York Times, 3/25/94.)* In the ongoing debate, criticism of small companies as 'a job engine' often concedes that small companies do create a lot of the new jobs in the *overall economy,* but adds that they don't necessarily last very long, and -- further -- "Small businesses are not the places you see *the best* jobs," as one economist put it. (The emphasis is mine.) 'Best jobs' means: jobs with high pay, high benefits, government-mandated health and safety regulations, and union representation. *(San Francisco Chronicle, 3/29/93.)*

> ### Target Small Organizations
>
> Were I myself looking for a job tomorrow, this is what I would do. After I had figured out, as in the previous chapter, what my ideal job looked like, and had collected a list of those workplaces that have such jobs, in my chosen geographical area, I would then circle the names and addresses of those which are *small* organizations (personally I would restrict my *first draft* to those with 25 or less employees) -- and then go after them, in the manner I will describe later in this chapter. However, since small organizations can sometimes be static or dying, I would look particularly for small organizations that are *established* or *growing.* And if *'organizations with 25 or less employees'* eventually didn't turn up enough *leads* for me, I would then broaden my search to *'organizations with 50 or less employees,'* and finally to *'organizations with 100 or less employees.'* But I would start *small.*[3]

With a small organization, there is no Personnel or Human Resources Department to screen you out.

With a small organization, you don't need to wait until there's a *known* vacancy, because they rarely advertise vacancies even when there is one. You just go there and ask if they need someone.

With a small organization, if it's growing, there is a greater likelihood that they will be willing to create a new position for you, *if they think you are too good to let you slip out of their grasp.*

With a small organization, there's no problem in identifying the person–who–has–the–power–to–hire–you. It's *the boss.* Everyone there knows who it is. They can point to their office door, easily.

With a small organization, you do not need to approach them through the mail; you can go in to see the boss. And if, by chance, he or she is well-protected from intruders, it is relatively

---

3. If you want further reading about this, see R. Linda Resnick's *A Big Splash in a Small Pond: Finding a Great Job in a Small Company* (written with Kerry Pechter). 1994. Fireside, Simon & Schuster Bldg., 1230 Avenue of the Americas, New York, NY 10020.

easy to figure out how to get around *that.* Contacts are the answer, as we shall see.

THE FOUR WAYS TO APPROACH
LARGE ORGANIZATIONS
FOR AN INTERVIEW

In securing job-interviews, it's the large organizations that are the problem -- the ones, as I mentioned above, where you need a floor-plan of the building, and an alphabetical directory of the staff. The ones where you can't even figure out *who* is the person–who–has–the–power–to–hire–you, much less get in to see them.

There is a way, as I will make clear.

It is the person–who–has–the–power–to–hire–you that you want to get in to see. But most job-hunters *don't* even *try* to find out *who* that person is.

Rather, they approach each large organization in what can only be described as a haphazard, scatter-shot fashion -- through one of four avenues. I will list these methods in order of *increasing* effectiveness, starting with the least effective method.[4]

1. *The **Most Ineffective** Way to Approach Large Organizations:* Going to some centralized place (such as a Job Fair) where employers come to hire people -- and getting an interview with the representative there. If you are a senior in college, the analog of this is a getting in to see a recruiter when -- and increasingly *if*-- they come to your campus.

This method *looks as though* it should have a 100% effectiveness rate in *getting a job-interview.* This is however an illusion, for two reasons.

First of all, there's no assurance that the large organization *you are particularly interested in* will even be there. If it's not there, the effectiveness of this particular approach to getting an interview with them is zero.

---

4. You will notice, of course, that some job-hunters use these approaches with small organizations, as well -- sad to say. It's so unnecessary.

Secondly, even assuming it is there, your concern is not merely to get an interview with just *anyone* in that organization. *That's* easy. You could swing by their personnel department and get *that*.

No, your concern as a job-hunter is to get an interview with one particular person: namely *(all together now)* the actual person–who–has–the–power–to–hire–you, for the job you want. In the case of centralized Job Fairs or recruiter visits to campuses, you will be talking (in most cases) only to a *representative* of the company -- who, if they like you, have no power except to *pass you on* to the person–who–has–the–power–to–hire–you. And if they don't like you, to turn you down. Flat.

In other words, that representative or recruiter has a function similar if not identical to that of the personnel department, and in many if not most cases they *are* from the personnel department.

Because of this, the effectiveness of this approach in getting you an interview with the actual person–who–has–the–power–to–hire–you at the organization of your choice is -- as I said -- *somewhere* between 8% and zero.

2. *The **Next Most Ineffective** Way to Approach Large Organizations* (Yes, that means 'next to the worst.'): Contacting the organization first of all through the mail, by sending them your resume or some covering letter, and hoping *they* will invite *you* in. This is based on the theory that your resume or covering letter will serve as a kind of job application, or function as a kind of extended calling-card -- that you *hope* will pique the employer's interest.

This is job-hunters' favorite way of approaching an organization for a job-interview. Never was faith so misplaced. True, when it works, it works well enough, but you *can* approach eight hundred organizations by mail (as millions of job-hunters have) and get not even one invitation to come in for an interview. Effectiveness rate in that case: zero.[5]

Taken overall, when used with a number of organizations, this approach turns out to have an effectiveness rate of 8% in getting an interview and subsequently a job.[6]

Wild Life, by John Kovalic, © 1989 Shetland Productions. Reprinted with Permission.

I covered the reason for this in Chapter 3, but if you skipped it or read it three months ago -- it is this: this 'mail approach' enables employers to screen you out *fast* without ever 'wasting their time' on an interview.

To be practical, if you're talking to some employer who is halfway across the country, you *may* need a resume. (Though oftentimes a long individual letter, summarizing the same stuff, is preferable -- since so many employers these days are highly allergic to resumes -- period -- and break out into a rash, if they even see one in their mail.) Or, if you're having a series of interviews with an employer in the same city as you are, you may want to *leave* a resume behind you, *after* the first interview.

The first rule (also the last rule) about preparing your resume or c.v. is that there is no such thing as a *right* format or

---

5. See *Resumes Don't Get Jobs: The Realities and Myths of Job Hunting,* by Bob Weinstein. McGraw Hill, Inc. 1221 Avenue of the Americas, New York, NY 10020. 1993. Naturally, I *love* the title of this book. But Bob, a journalist in this field, has written an entertaining and helpful book besides, about job-hunting in the '90s.

6. To help you, there are even organizations which will publish your resume *(along with a lot of other job-hunters')* in a small booklet, and circulate it to employers. Forty-Plus Clubs do this, through their *Executive Manpower Directory.* So do some of the State Job Service/Employment Development Departments *(California, for example, has such a system, called PROMATCH, with 23 offices, which does this for experienced professionals).* It sounds as if *it couldn't hurt,* but do remember (if this sounds appealing to you) that you're in that booklet with a *lot* of other people.

form for a resume or c.v. I used to have a hobby of collecting resumes that had actually gotten someone an interview and, ultimately, a job. Being somewhat mischievous, I delighted in showing them to employers whom I knew. Many of them didn't like the winning resume at all. "That resume will never get anyone a job," they would say. Then, I would tell them, "Sorry, you're wrong. It already has. What you are saying is that it wouldn't get them a job *with you.*"

The resume reproduced on the next page is a good example of what I mean. *(You did want an example of what I mean, didn't you?)* Jim Dyer, who had been in the Marines for twenty years, wanted a job as a salesman for heavy construction and mining equipment thousands of miles from where he was then living. He devised the resume you see, and had fifteen copies made. "I used," he said, "a grand total of seven before I got the job in the place I wanted!"[7]

Like the employer who hired him, I loved this resume. Yet, when I've shown it to other employers, they have criticized it for using a picture, for being too long (or too short), etc., etc. In other words, had Jim sent his resume to *them,* they wouldn't have been impressed enough to invite him in for an interview.

So, don't believe anyone who tells you there's one right format for a resume, or one style that's guaranteed to win. It's still a gamble, where you're hoping that the employer(s) you like will also like your resume. Generally speaking, the most endearing quality needed in it, besides completeness, neatness and clarity, is that *you* shine through it all. If you decide you *do* want or need a resume, you will want more guidance than this. A number of books are listed at the end of this chapter.

The next method I shall tell you about is six times as effective as this approaching an organization by mail.

---

7. Speaking of seven resumes, there is a Catch-22 situation about the number you send out. Every expert in the world will tell you that if you're going to send out resumes, send out as many as you possibly can. But, human nature being what it is, the more you send out, usually the higher your hopes get. Therefore, the more those hopes get dashed, when *even all those hundreds* don't get you a job. It's that old adage, 'The higher you go, the harder you fall.' Send out seven copies of your resume, you don't care if they don't work; send out 800, *you care.*

E.J. DYER   Street, City, Zip   Telephone No.

I SPEAK
THE LANGUAGE
OF
MEN
MACHINERY
AND
MANAGEMENT
...

OBJECTIVE: Sales of Heavy Equipment

QUALIFICATIONS   * Knowledge of heavy equipment, its use and maintenance.

                 * Ability to communicate with management and with men in the field.

                 * Ability to favorably introduce change in the form of new
                   equipment or new ideas... the ability to sell.

EXPERIENCE   * Maintained, shipped, budgeted and set allocation priorities for
                   85 pieces of heavy equipment as head of a 500-man organization
Men and   (1975-1977).
Machinery
                 * Constructed twelve field operation support complexes, employing
                   a 100-man crew and 19 pieces of heavy equipment (1965-1967).

                 * Jack-hammer operator, heavy construction (summers 1956-1957-1958).

Management   * Planned, negotiated and executed large scale equipment purchases
                   on a nation to nation level (1972-1974).

Sales   * Achieved field customer acceptance of two major new computer-
                   based systems:
                   - Equipment inventory control and repair parts expedite system
                     (1968-1971)
                   - Decision makers' training system (1977-1979).
                 * Proven leader ... repeatedly elected or appointed to senior posts.

EDUCATION   * B.A. Benedictine College, 1959. (Class President; Editor
                   Yearbook; "Who's Who in American Colleges").

                 * Naval War College, 1975. (Class President; Graduated "With
                   Highest Distinction").

                 * University of Maryland, 1973-1974. (Chinese Language).

                 * Middle Level Management Training Course, 1967-1968
                   (Class Standing: 1 of 97).

PERSONAL   * Family: Sharon and our sons Jim (11), Andy (8) and Matt (5)
                   desire to locate in a Mountain State by 1982, however, in
                   the interim will consider a position elsewhere in or outside
                   the United States ... Health: Excellent ... Birthdate: December
                   9, 1937 ... Completing Military Service with the rank of
                   Lieutenant Colonel, U.S. Marine Corps.

SUMMARY   A seeker of challenge ... experienced, proven and confident of
                 closing the sales for profit.

FRANK AND ERNEST · by Bob Thaves

© 1987 Newspaper Enterprise Association, Inc. Used by permission.

3. *The **Next** to '**Most Effective**' Way to Approach Large Organizations:* Going *face-to-face* at that organization, to seek a job -- though without any introductions or use of 'third-parties.' 47.7% of those job-hunters who use this approach, get an interview and job thereby.

This doesn't necessarily mean presenting yourself at an organization's personnel department. 85% of all organizations these days don't even have personnel departments *(or, as they prefer to be called now, Human Resources Departments),* so when you go face-to-face to 85% of all places, you simply talk to the receptionist in the front office.

But in the case of those 15% which *do* have personnel offices or departments -- and that includes *all* really large organizations -- when you go face-to-face it is with the personnel office that you will be speaking, if you have no 'third-party' introduction.

Coming in 'cold' this way, the receptionist or personnel department will probably ask you to fill out a job application. Job applications are application forms which have such simple questions as: Name, Address, Age, Places of Previous Employment, etc. Such applications vary greatly in their complexity, from ones used by fast-food chains, to those used by, say, engineering firms. If you've never seen one in your life, and you plan to approach organizations this way, you should familiarize yourself with an application form ahead of time. One way to do this without jeopardizing your job chances, is to go to visit some fast-food place or any large organization that has a personnel department, and simply *ask* for a job application, then immediately go back out the front door. Take the form home with you, where you can study it, and take a stab at filling it out, just for practice. Then throw it in the waste basket, after you've learned what you need to know. Now you know what an application form looks like, and how to fill it out. I hope you never need to.

Why is the effectiveness rate of this approach only 47.7%? The reason is that receptionists' or personnel departments' primary function, vis-a-vis job-hunters, is either to screen you *out*, or -- if they like you -- to pass you on to some person 'upstairs' -- namely, the person–who–has–the–power–to–hire–you. In over half the cases, you *do* get screened out. No personnel employee wants some *upstairs* executive screaming, "You're sending me too many people." Therefore, Personnel tends to live by the motto: *"When in doubt, screen them out."*

The last method of approach I am about to describe has almost *twice* the effectiveness rate of this method. *However,* it should be noted that in their pioneering study of the job-hunt some years ago, *The Job Hunt: Job-Seeking Behavior of Unemployed Workers in a Local Economy,* Harvey Belitsky and Harold A. Sheppard discovered that going face-to-face at a workplace, without introduction or *leads,* was *the* most effective job-hunting method if you were a blue-collar worker. Blue-collar workers take note.

4. *The **Most Effective** Way to Approach Large Organizations:* Going face-to-face at that organization, to seek a job -- after you *first* use your personal acquaintances or contacts to find out *who* at that organization has the power to hire you for the position you have in mind, and after you use your contacts to help you secure an appointment there, with that person–who–has–the–power–to–hire–you. When used with a number of organizations, and not just one, this method has an 86% effectiveness rate, for getting an interview and, subsequently, a job. (I shall say more about this, in a minute.)

Okay, now you've seen the four ways to approach the large organization of your choice for a job-interview.

You get to choose: which approach do you want to use: one

that gets you a job-interview with the organization of your choice:

- ☐ Zero percent of the time
- ☐ 8% of the time
- ☐ 47.7% of the time
- ☐ 86% of the time

It's your *call*. Personally, I vote for the 86% approach. So, let's examine it in more detail.

It begins of course with the assumption that you are going to approach directly the person–who–has–the–power–to–hire–you. Small problem:

HOW DO I FIND OUT
WHO HAS THE POWER
TO HIRE ME?

Hey, in a small organization with 50 or less employees, as I said earlier, this is an easy problem. Calling the place and asking for the name of the boss, should do it. It's what we call *The One Minute Research Project.*

But if the place where you are dying to work is a much larger organization, then the answer is: "Through the research you already learned how to do (in Chapter 11), and by asking every *contact* you have."

Since this subject of *contacts* is widely misunderstood by job-hunters, let's be very specific, here.

Every person you know, is a contact.

Every member of your family.

Every friend of yours.

Every person in your address book.

Every person on your Christmas-card list.

Every merchant or salesperson you ever deal with.

Every person who comes to your apartment or house to do any kind of repairs or maintenance work.

Every check-out clerk you know.

Every gas station attendant you know.

Every leisure partner you have, as for walking, exercising, swimming, or whatever.

Every doctor, or medical professional you know.

Every professor, teacher, etc. you once knew or maybe still know how to get a hold of.

Every clergyperson, rabbi, or religious leader you know.

Every person in your church, synagogue, mosque, or religious assembly.

Everyone you know in Rotary, Kiwanis, Lions, or other service organizations.

Every person you are newly introduced to.

Every person you meet, stumble across, or blunder into, during your job-hunt, whose name, address, and phone number you have the grace to ask for. (*Always* have the grace to ask for it.)

Got the picture?

CULTIVATING NEW CONTACTS

Some job-hunters cultivate new contacts wherever they go, during their time of unemployment. For example, if they go to hear a speaker on some subject that interests them, they make it a point to join the crowd that gathers 'round the speaker at the end of the talk, and -- with notepad poised -- ask such questions as: "Is there anything special that people with my expertise can do?" And here they mention their *generalized* job-title: computer scientist, health professional, chemist, writer, or whatever. Very useful information has thus been turned up. You can also ask if you can contact the speaker for further information -- "and at what address?"

Conventions, likewise, afford rich opportunities to make contacts. Says one college graduate: "I snuck into the Cable Advertisers Convention at the Waldorf in N.Y.C. That's how I got my job."

Another way people have cultivated contacts, is to leave a message on their telephone answering machine which tells everyone who calls, what information they are looking for. One job-hunter used the following message: "This is the recently laid off John Smith. I'm not home right now because I'm out looking for a good job as a computer trouble-shooter in the telecommunications field; if you have any leads or just want to leave a message, please leave it after the tone."

You may also cultivate contacts by studying the *things* that you like to work with, and then writing to the manufacturer of that *thing* to ask them for a list of organizations in your geographical area which use that *thing*. For example, if you like to work on a particular machine, you would write to the manufacturer of that machine, and ask for names of organizations in your geographical area which use that machine. Some manufacturers will not be at all responsive to such an inquiry; but others graciously will, and and thus you may gain some very helpful leads.

GET OUT THE FILE CARDS

Because your memory is going to be overloaded during your job-hunt or career-change, it is useful, as you begin this process, to put each of the above names on a 3 × 5 card, with addresses, phone numbers, and anything about where they work or who they know that may be of use at a later date. Go back over those cards frequently.

Yes, that does add up to *a lot* of file cards. You've got *a lot* of contacts. But that's the whole point.

You may need *every one* of them.

Whenever a job-hunter writes me and tells me they've run into a brick wall, as far as finding out names of organizations or names of the person–who–has–the–power–to–hire is concerned, the problem *always* turns out to be: they aren't making sufficient use of their contacts.

The more people you know, the more people you meet, the more people you talk to, the more people you enlist as part of your own personal job-hunting network, the better your job-finding success is likely to be.

It takes about eighty pairs of eyes, and ears, to help find the career, the workplace, the job that you are looking for.

Your contacts are those eyes and ears.

They are what will help you get the ideal job you are looking for.

HOW DO YOU USE
YOUR CONTACTS?

Well, let's say it is a mythical organization called *Mythical Corporation* that interests you.

You know the kind of job you'd like to get there, but first you want to find out the name of the person–who–has–the–power–to–hire–you there. What do you do?

If it's a large organization, you go to your local public library, and search the directories there that I listed at the beginning of Appendix B *("Sampler of Information Sources")*. Hopefully that search will yield the name of the person you want.

If it doesn't, which will particularly be the case with smaller organizations, *then you turn to your contacts.*

You approach as many people as necessary, among all those you know, and you ask each of them, "Do you know anyone who works, or used to work, at *Mythical Corporation?*"

You ask that question again and again of *everyone* who is on your file cards, until you find someone who says, *"Yes, I do."*

Then you ask them:

• "What is the name of the person you know who works, or used to work, at *Mythical Corporation?* Do you have their phone number and/or address?"

• "Do you think it would be worth my while to go see them?"

• "May I tell them it was you who recommended that I talk with them?"

• "Would you be willing to call ahead, to set up an appointment for me, and tell them who I am?"

You may then want to conduct the appointment over the phone, at an agreed-upon time, or you may want to go see them face-to-face, away from their worksite.

If you do go see them, try *never* to travel across town so as to arrive there just on time. This makes no allowance for the normal unpredictable things that happen to delay us all, when we least expect it.

No, you always leave for the appointment with about *double the time* you think it will take to get there, which means you will usually arrive at the site ahead of time. Then you go get a cup of coffee nearby, or you park down the block if you need to, until it's actually time for the appointment. Then you go in the front door right on time.

(When a reporter arrived late, once, for an appointment with a very famous person, that person replied, "How dare you keep me waiting? Are you that stupid?" You may wince at the put-down, *but* that's how a lot of people *feel* about people who are late for appointments, even if they would *never* say it, or at any rate not so strongly. You *don't* want anyone thinking that about *you* -- and especially not, when you are coming to them to ask for their help.)

After the usual polite chit-chat, you ask them the question you are dying to know. Because they are *inside* the organization that interests you, they are usually able to give you the exact answer to your question: "Who would have the power to hire me here, for this kind of position *(which you then describe)*?"

Then you further ask them what they can tell you about that person's job, that person's interests, and anything about their style of interviewing.

You also ask them about the organization, in general, for any information that they might think useful for you to know.

Finally, you ask them if they could help you get an appointment with that person.

Then you thank them, and leave; and you *never never* let the day end, without sitting down to write them a thank-you note. *Always* do it. *Never* forget to.

GETTING IN

If the contact you talked to, doesn't know the person–who–has–the–power–to–hire well enough to get you an interview, then you go back to your other contacts -- now armed with the name of the person you are trying to get in to see -- and pose a new question. Approaching as many of your contacts as necessary, you ask each of them, "Do you know Ms. or Mr. See, at *Mythical Corporation* or do you know someone who does?"

You ask that question again and again of *everyone* who is on your file cards, until you find someone who says, "*Yes, I do.*"

Then of course, over the phone or -- better -- in person, you ask them the same familiar questions:

• "What can you tell me about him -- or her?"

• "Given the kind of job I am looking for *(which you here describe)*, do you think it would be worth my while to go see them?"

• "May I tell them it was you who recommended that I talk with them?"

• "Do you have their phone number and/or address?"

• "Would you be willing to call ahead, to set up an appointment for me, and tell them who I am?"

Getting in to see someone, even for the purpose of a job-interview, is not that difficult. Everyone has friends, including this person–who–has–the–power–to–hire–you. You are simply approaching them through their friends. And you are doing this, not as one who is coming to ask a favor. You are doing it as one who is coming to offer a gift.

A gift? Yes, because while *you* are bemoaning the difficulty of getting in to see an employer of your choice -- for a job-interview -- employers are having an equally difficult time getting interviews with the person *they* are looking for: namely, you.

I cannot tell you the number of employers I know who can't figure out how to find the right employee. It is absolutely mind-boggling, particularly in these hard times when job-hunters would seem to be gathered on every street corner.

You're having trouble finding the employer. The employer is having trouble finding you. *What a great country!*

However, if you now present yourself directly to the person–who–has–the–power–to–hire–you, you are not only answering your own prayers. You are hopefully answering the employer's, as well. You are *just* what the employer is looking for, but didn't know how to find, if . . .

if you took the trouble to do Chapters 9, 10, and 11, and

if you took the trouble to figure out what your favorite and best skills are, and

if you took the trouble to figure out what your favorite and best subjects or *languages* are, and

if you took the trouble to figure out what places *might* need such skills and such *languages*, and

if you researched the place with the intent of finding out what their tasks and problems are, and

if you took the trouble to figure out who there has the power to hire you.

Of course, you don't for sure *know* they need you; that remains for the job-interview to uncover. But at least, by this thorough preparation, you have *increased* the chances that you are at the right place -- whether they have an announced vacancy or not. And, if you are, you are not imposing on this employer. You are coming not as 'job-beggar,' but as 'resource person.' You are rescuing him or her, believe me.

CONCLUSION

I close this chapter with my favorite (true) story about approaching an organization. This concerns a job-hunter in Virginia. He decided he wanted to work for a particular health-care organization in that State, and not knowing any better, he approached them by visiting their Personnel department. After dutifully filling out a job application, and talking to someone there in that department, he was told there were no jobs available. Stop. Period. End of story.

Approximately three months later he learned about this technique of approaching your favorite organization by using contacts. He did the kind of work described above, and succeeded in getting an interview with the person–who–had–the–power–to–hire–him for the position he was interested in. The two of them hit it off, immediately. The appointment went swimmingly.

"You're hired," said the person–who–had–the–power–to–hire–him. "I'll call Personnel and tell them you're hired, and that you'll be down to fill out the necessary stuff."

Our job-hunter never once mentioned that he had previously approached that same organization through that same Personnel department, and been turned down.

Here is a *sampler,* only, of the hundreds of resume books that are out there:

Richard Lathrop, *Who's Hiring Who?* 12th ed. 1989. Ten Speed Press, Box 7123, Berkeley, CA 94707. This is used more often by our readers than any other book, except *Parachute.* He describes and recommends "a qualifications brief" -- an idea akin to what John Crystal used to propose -- that in approaching an employer you should think of offering him or her a written proposal of what you *will* do in the future, rather than "a resume" of what you did do in the past.

David Swanson, *The Resume Solution; How To Write (and Use) A Resume That Gets Results.* 1991. JIST Works, Inc., 720 North Park Ave., Indianapolis, IN 46202-3431. This is a relatively new book on resumes, with tips not to be found in other books. It is very popular. (Dave has been on my staff at my workshops since 1978.)

Yana Parker, *The Damn Good Resume Guide.* New edition. Ten Speed Press, Box 7123, Berkeley, CA 94707. 1989. Describes how to write a functional resume. Employers' comments upon *resumes which actually got people jobs,* are especially helpful. The other most popular resume book (according to our mail). Yana's other resume resources are:

The Resume Catalog: 200 Damn Good Examples. 1988. Ten Speed Press, Box 7123, Berkeley, CA 94707.

Resume Roundup, Volume 1: "Blue Collar" Resumes. 1994. Some examples of resumes written for construction and the trades, automotive and heavy equipment, warehouse, manufacturing, electronics, services, food and hospitality. Available from Damn Good Resume Service, P.O. Box 3289, Berkeley, CA 94703.

Damn Good Self-Teaching Resume Templates. 1991. This is a computer disk, and manual, for both MAC and DOS computers. Available from Damn Good Resume Service.

Tom Jackson, *The Perfect Resume.* 1981. Anchor Press/Doubleday, Garden City, NY 11530. This is Tom's best-selling book, and with good reason.

William S. Frank, *200 Letters for Job Hunters,* rev. ed. 1993. Ten Speed Press, Box 7123, Berkeley, CA 94707.

Robert Hochheiser, *Throw Away Your Resume* (2nd ed.). 1982. Barron's Educational Series, Inc., 250 Wireless Boulevard, Hauppauge, NY 11788. Well, of course I like the title, even if he doesn't fully mean it, as the body of the book makes clear. Nonetheless, he has some interesting perspectives if you are going to present yourself in writing to an employer.

J.I. Biegeleisen, *Job Resumes.* 1991. Perigee Books, The Putnam Publishing Group, 200 Madison Ave., New York, NY 10016. The author has been writing resume books since 1969 at least. This is revised and updated.

Peggy Schmidt, *The 90 Minute Resume.* Peterson's Guides, P.O. Box 2123, Princeton, NJ 08543. 1990. Contains interesting sections, such as "How to Make an Ordinary Job Sound Important."

Carl McDaniels, *Developing a Professional Vita or Resume,* rev. ed. 1990. Garrett Park Press, Box 190, Garrett Park, MD 20896. Especially for candidates for academic positions.

Tom Washington, *Resume Power: Selling Yourself on Paper,* rev. ed. 1990. Mount Vernon Press, 1750 112th N.E. C-244, Bellevue, WA 98004.

Ronald L. Krannich and William J. Banis, *High Impact Resumes & Letters.* 5th ed., 1992, Impact Publications, 9104-N Manassas Drive, Manassas Park, VA 22111.

Marci Mahoney, *Strategic Resumes: Writing for Results.* 1992. Crisp Publications, Inc., 1200 Hamilton Ct., Menlo Park CA 94025-1427.

Di Inchley, *Résumés for Results: A Complete Guide to Preparing Resumes and Written Applications.* 1992. The Business Library, Information Australia, A.C.N. 006 042 173, 45 Flinders Lane, Melbourne, VIC 3000, Australia. A book on resumes for Australian readers.

We note there are a number of books out there devoted to cover letters, either to go with a resume or by themselves instead of a resume. These include:

Ronald L. Krannich and Caryl Rae, *Dynamite Cover Letters.* 1992, Impact Publications, 9104-N Manassas Drive, Manassas Park, VA 22111.

If the above sampling is not enough for you, see your local bookstore. It should also be noted that there are a number of software packages out there, to help job-hunters prepare a resume. Some of these are listed on page 408.

The Inquiring Reporter
asked the young woman why
she wanted to be a mortician.
"Because," she said, "I enjoy
working with people."
  The San Francisco Chronicle

CHAPTER THIRTEEN

Conducting
The
Interview

You Must Show The Person
Who Has The Power To Hire You
How Your Skills Can Help Them
With Their Problems

THE TEN GREATEST MISTAKES MADE IN JOB INTERVIEWS

Whereby Your Chances of Finding a Job Are Greatly Decreased

I. Going after large organizations only (such as the Fortune 500).

II. Hunting all by yourself for places to visit, using ads and resumes.

III. Doing no homework on an organization before going there.

IV. Allowing the Personnel Department (or Human Resources) to interview you -- *their primary function is to screen you OUT*.

V. Setting no time limit when you make the appointment with an organization.

VI. Letting your resume be used as the agenda for the job interview.

VII. Talking primarily about yourself, and what benefit the job will be for you.

VIII. When answering a question of theirs, talking anywhere from 2 to 15 minutes, at a time.

IX. Basically approaching them as if you were a job-beggar, hoping they will offer you a job, however humble.

X. Not sending a thank-you note right after the interview.

THE TEN COMMANDMENTS FOR JOB INTERVIEWS

Whereby Your Chances of Finding a Job Are Vastly Increased

I. **Go after small organizations, with twenty or less employees, since they create 2/3 of all new jobs.**

II. **Hunt for interviews using the aid of friends and acquaintances, because a job-hunt requires fifty eyes and ears.**

III. **Do thorough homework on an organization before going there, using Informational Interviews plus the library.**

IV. **At any organization, identify who has the power to hire you there, for the position you want, and use your friends and acquaintances' contacts, to get in to see that person.**

V. **Ask for just 20 minutes of their time, when asking for the appointment; and keep to your word.**

VI. **Go to the interview with your own agenda, your own questions and curiosities about whether or not this job fits you.**

VII. **Talk about yourself only if what you say offers some benefit to that organization, and their 'problems.'**

VIII. **When answering a question of theirs, talk only between 20 seconds and 2 minutes, at any one time.**

IX. **Basically approach them as if you were a resource person, able to produce better work for that organization than any predecessor.**

X. **Always write a thank-you note the same evening of the interview, and mail it at the latest by the next morning.**

Chapter 13

IS THIS ANY WAY
TO RUN A BUSINESS?

To begin with, the job-interview is not a very reliable way to choose an employee. In a survey conducted among a dozen top United Kingdom employers,[1] it was discovered that the chances of an employer finding a good employee through the hiring interview was only *3% better* than if they had picked a name out of a hat. In a further ironic finding, it was discovered that if the interview were conducted by someone who would be working directly with the candidate, the success rate dropped to *2% below* that of picking a name out of a hat. And if the interview were conducted by a personnel expert, the success rate dropped to *10% below* that of picking a name out of a hat.

No, I don't know how they came up with these figures. But they strike me as totally consistent with what I know of the world of hiring. I have watched so-called personnel experts make wretchedly bad choices about hiring for their own office, and when they would morosely confess this some months later, over lunch, I would puzzle out loud, "If you don't even know how to hire well, yourselves, how do you keep a straight face when you're called in as consultant to another organization?" And they would ruefully reply, "We treat it *as though it were* a science."

Let me tell you, folks, the job-interview is *not* a science. It is a very very hazy art, and done badly by most of its employer-practitioners, in spite of their best intentions and goodwill.

Moreover, it requires you as job-hunter to *compete* with others, and show the employer why you are *better* than the other people competing for the same job. Many job-hunters *hate* this aspect of job-interviewing.

I once met an eighty-year-old woman who was telling me about a different culture altogether. Back in the early '30s, she said, there was a small mine up in the hills above the town where she lived. One day, the news in the town was that the mine was hiring, at a little shack up in the hills. The men in the town, many of whom were out of work, lined up early outside the hiring shack, to try to get those jobs. The men were called in, one at a time. Her father was in the line, she said, and while waiting, he struck up a conversation with the man in the line behind him. That conversation was interrupted when it was her father's turn to go into the shack. The man who was hiring there, said to him, "Man, you're lucky. This is the last job I have to give out, today." "Well, in that case," replied her father, "give it to the next man out there. He has five children depending on him to feed them, while I have only three. I'll find another job, I'm sure."

This nobility of spirit was not *universal* in that Age. But that it existed at all, compared to the current popular *rule* of life -- *every man for himself,* or *every woman for herself* seems stirring and inspiring. This cut-throat competition of our Day, stepping over

---

1. Reported in the *Financial Times Career Guide 1989* in the United Kingdom.

the bodies of others in order to get to the top, is obscene. The job-interview process throughout the world, *contributes* mightily to this continuing fragmentation of the human family.

Nonetheless, if you would work for another, this job-interview process -- competitive and unscientific though it may be -- is your *only* doorway to getting a job. So, you're going to have to participate in the whole dumb and Neanderthal ritual, no matter how much it offends your simple common sense.

If you simply can't stand the idea, and would pay *millions* to avoid it, then you will want to look at the various strategies described in Chapter 6: *New Ways to Work*.

THE ELEVEN MOST IMPORTANT TRUTHS ABOUT A JOB-INTERVIEW

You want to prepare, of course, for the interview -- do a little planning ahead of time, don't you? *How much time do you have?* I ask, because whole books have been written about the job-interview, so obviously there's a lot that can be said.[2]

If you don't have the time, or inclination, to do all that reading, perhaps I can condense it for you. Over the years it has seemed to me that there are eleven really important, basic truths about interviewing, which stand out above all the rest. I list those eleven -- with titles -- on the file cards which follow, along with some brief commentary of mine:

BEFORE THE INTERVIEW: PRACTICE

1. Before you go on job-interviews, be sure to practice the PIE process first (see pages 260–269) until you are so used to talking with people about mutual interests, that interviewing has lost all of its terrors for you.

If you have several organizations to interview at, you should probably save the interview you care the most about until last, so you can make all your mistakes at the interviews you don't care about as much.

The manner in which you do your interviews -- and the manner in which you would do the job you are seeking -- are not assumed by most employers to be two unrelated subjects, but one and the same. A slipshod half-hearted interview is taken as a warning that you might do a

slipshod half-hearted job, were they foolish enough to hire you. Therefore, prepare thoroughly for each interview; know a lot about the place, before you walk in.

2. Martin John Yate, *Knock 'Em Dead with Great Answers to Tough Interview Questions*. Bob Adams, Inc., 260 Center St., Holbrook, MA 02343. 1992.

H. Anthony Medley, *Sweaty Palms: The Neglected Art of Being Interviewed*. Ten Speed Press, Box 7123, Berkeley, CA 94707. 1992, revised.

David Krause, *Get The Best Jobs in DP: The Computer Professional's Technical Interview Guide*. Mind Management, 9815 239th Pl. SW, Edmonds, WA 98020. 1989. How to survive interviews that are essentially tests of your technical expertise.

Phillip G. Zimbardo, *Shyness, What It Is, What to Do About It*. Addison-Wesley, Route 128, Reading, MA 08167. 1977.

David Bowman and Ronald Kweskin, *Q: How Do I Find The Right Job? A: Read This Book*. John Wiley & Sons, Inc., Professional and Trade Division, 605 Third Ave., New York, NY 10158-0012. 1990.

John Caple, *The Ultimate Interview*. Doubleday, 1540 Broadway, New York, NY 10036. 1991.

THE INTERVIEW IS A TWO WAY STREET

2. Your natural question to yourself, as you approach any job-interview, will be, "How do I convince this employer to hire me?" Wrong question. It implies that you have already made up your mind that this would be a grand person to work for, so all that remains is for you to sell yourself. That is rarely the case. In most cases, you don't know enough yet, to say that -- despite all your research. You have to use the job-interview as a chance to gather further information about this organization, and this boss, before you can decide, "Do I really want to work here?" That's the nature of the job-interview: each of you has to gather information, and if you both like what you see, then each has to 'sell' the other on the idea of working there.

If you understand *this* about an interview, you will be ahead of 98% of all other job-hunters -- who all too often go to the job-interview as a lamb goes to the slaughter, or as a criminal goes on trial before a judge.

You *are* on trial, of course, in the employer's eyes. *But,* so is that employer and that organization, in *your* eyes. This is what makes the job interview tolerable or sometimes *borderline* enjoyable: you are studying everything about this employer, at the same time that they are studying everything about you.

Two people, both sizing each other up. You know what that reminds you of. Dating. Well, the job interview is every bit like 'the dating game.' Both of you have to like each other, before you can even discuss the question of *'going steady,'* i.e., a job.

The importance of your actively weighing this organization and this job, *during* the job-interview, cannot be overstated. As we discussed in Chapter 11, the tradition in the U.S., and throughout the world for that matter, is to find a job, take it, and *then* try to figure out after you're in it whether it is a good job or not.

You're going against that tradition, as any sensible job-hunter or career-changer should, by using the job-interview to screen the organization *before you go to work there.*

The employer will thank you, you will thank you, your Mother will thank you.

WHAT THE EMPLOYER IS TRYING TO FIND OUT

3. Beneath the dozens of Possible Questions that employers may ask in a job-interview, there are really only five basic ones:

1. "Why are you here?" They mean by this, why did you pick out our organization to seek a job at?

2. "What can you do for us?" They mean by this, what are your skills and your fields of knowledge?

3. "What kind of person are you?" They mean by this, do you have a personality that they will enjoy working with, or not? Do you get along with people? What are your values?

4. Assuming you can do the job, "what distinguishes you from nineteen other people who can do the same thing?"

5. "Can we afford you?" They mean by that, if they decide they want you, what will it take to get you, and are they willing and able to pay that amount?

Books on interviewing, of which there are many, often publish lists of up to eighty-nine questions that an employer may ask you. They list things like:

- Tell me about yourself.
- Why are you applying for this job?
- What do you know about this job or company?
- How would you describe yourself?
- What are your major strengths?
- What is your greatest weakness?
- What type of work do you like to do best?
- What are your interests outside of work?
- What accomplishment gave you the greatest satisfaction?
- What was your worst mistake?
- Why did you leave your last job?
- Why were you fired (if you were)?
- How does your education or experience relate to this job?
- Where do you see yourself five years from now?
- What are your goals in life?
- How much did you make at your last job?

But they all boil down, in essence, to the five basic questions on the file card above. And this is the case, even if the interview begins and ends with these five questions never once being uttered aloud. They're still there, beneath the surface of the conversation, all the time.

The good news is that since there are really only five questions, there are really only five answers you need to know. But, you had *better* know those five answers. Of course, if you did your homework (Chapters 9, 10, and 11) you will. If you didn't, you won't, sad to say. Period. End of story.

WHAT YOU ARE
TRYING TO FIND OUT

4. The most basic thing you are trying to figure out, as described above, is do you want to work there? (The answer is not necessarily Yes.)

If you have any kind of a real or imagined handicap -- age, inexperience, physical or mental disability, ethnic background, etc. -- you are also trying to find out which kind of employer you are talking to:

a) Those who are bothered by your handicap; OR

b) Those who are not bothered by your handicap

If you discover you are talking to one who is bothered, you want to thank them for their time and quickly excuse yourself. If you discover this employer isn't bothered by your handicap, then you want to continue the discussion.

Every job-hunter or career-changer in the world is handicapped -- so far as the job-hunt is concerned. If you doubt this, sit down and think for a moment. There are, let us say, 13,000 truly different skills that human beings possess. The average job-hunter has 700 skills.[3] That's a lot, but it still means that there are 12,300 things each of us *can't* do. Believe me, we're *all* handicapped. The only question is: what is your handicap, and how much does it show?

Typical job-hunting handicaps are: I have held too many jobs before; I am overqualified; I am too inexperienced; I am too old; I am too shy; I've only worked for large organizations; I've only worked for small organizations; I've only worked for volunteer organizations; I've only worked at home; I'm a woman; I am gay; I belong to an ethnic minority; I'm a recent immigrant; I am too much of a generalist; I am too much of a specialist; I have a police or prison record; I have a psychiatric

---

3. I discovered this at my annual two-week workshops years ago, when we asked each participant to do their own unaided skill analysis, and then put each skill on a separate filecard. Typically, they ended up with 700 cards.

history; I didn't get good enough grades in school; I have a physical or mental disability; I have a chronic illness; I have AIDS, etc.[4]

Our job-hunting handicaps always lead us to say something like *'Employers' won't hire me*. However, there's no such thing as just *'Employers,'* because (all together, now):

There are two kinds of employers *out there*:
● those who *will* be put off by your job-hunting handicaps, and therefore *won't* hire you;
AND
●those who will *not* be put off by your job-hunting handicaps, and therefore *will* hire you, if you are qualified for the job.

You are only looking for the second kind of employer, who is *not* put off by your job-hunting handicap, and therefore will hire you if you can do the job. The first kind of employer is of no interest to you, *except as they may give you leads to the second* -- and you must not allow yourself to become discouraged because you are running into a lot of *them,* and they are all rejecting you.

To take a 'worst case' scenario, if out of 100 employers, 90 would be bothered by your job-hunting handicap or history, but 10 wouldn't care about it in the slightest -- so long as you can do the work well -- your task is to make your way as quickly as you can through the 90, and find those other 10. They are the only ones you want to work for, anyway. You wouldn't *really* want to work for those who are prejudiced against you, now would you? We all want to work for an employer who's rootin' for us to succeed, not one who's just waiting for us to fall flat on our face.

In reading all this, I'm sure you think *you've* got the one handicap that *all* employers would find bothersome. For example, that you're over 60 years old, and 'employers' wouldn't want someone that old. Okay, let's all repeat it anew:

4. For those with evident disabilities, I refer you to a companion booklet to *Parachute* entitled, *Job-Hunting Tips For The So-Called Handicapped or People Who Have Disabilities*, Ten Speed Press, Box 7123, Berkeley CA 94707. 1991. To save yourself some money, see if your library has it, first.

> "All employers divide into two groups:
> • those who would be put off by your age,
> AND
> • those who would not be put off by your age, so long as
> you are qualified for the job.
> Your job is to find the second kind of employer, and not
> pay any attention to the first, except as they may give you
> *leads* to the second."

And so it goes. So, it always goes.[5]

---

5. Remember the story of one 66-year-old man, at the end of Chapter 7.

WHAT THE EMPLOYER DOES DURING INTERVIEW

5. The employer observes everything about you, and also asks questions. Most of those questions are about your past. But their intent is to find something in your past, that will predict the future -- because, in the end, all any employer can really be interested in is the future. You need to pay attention to the time frame of the employer's questions. For example, "Where did you go to high school?" is in the past. If the questions' time frame stays stuck in the past, you are not likely to be hired. As the employer's questions move, in their time frame, from being preoccupied with the distant past, to the near past, to the present, and then to the future, this is very favorable for you. It means they're thinking seriously about hiring you.

Distant past: *"Where did you grow up?"*
Near past: *"Tell me about your last job."*
Present: *"What kind of a job are you looking for?"*
Future: *"If you were offered this job, where would you see yourself five years from now?"*

I will have more to say about the employer's questions, at the end of this chapter.

Now -- just as you are studying the employer during the job-interview, so the employer is studying you. It is likely that *nothing* will escape the scrutiny of that person on the other side of the desk. And I mean: your haircut or hairdo; your manner of dress; your posture; your use of your hands; your body odor or perfume; your breath (good or bad); your fingernails (dirty or clean, clipped or not); the sound of your voice; the way in which you do or don't interrupt; the hesitant or assured manner in which you ask your questions or give your answers; your values as evidenced by the things which impress you or don't impress

you in the office, in your history, and so on; the carefulness with
which you did or didn't research this company before you came
in; the thoroughness with which you know your own skills and
strengths; your awareness of what you are willing to sacrifice in
order to get this job *and* what you are *not* willing to sacrifice in
order to get this job; your enthusiasm for your work; and blah,
blah, blah. We can also throw in whether or not you smoke *(in a
race between two equally qualified people, the nonsmoker will win out
over the smoker 94% of the time, according to a study done by a
professor of business at Seattle University);* whether, if at lunch, you
order a drink or not (don't); whether you show courtesy to the
receptionist, secretary, waiter or waitress, or not (do); and so
forth. *Everything* is grist for the mill, as the employer tries to
divine "what kind of person is this?"

What the employer will typically use to screen you *out*, are:

- any signs of dishonesty or lying;
- any signs of irresponsibility or tendency to goof off;
- any sign of arrogance or excessive aggressiveness;
- any sign of tardiness or failure to keep appointments and
  commitments on time, including the job-interview;
- any sign of not following instructions or obeying rules;
- any sign of constant complaining or blaming things on
  others;
- any sign of laziness or lack of motivation;
- any sign of a lack of enthusiasm for this organization and
  what it is trying to do;
- any sign of instability, inappropriate response, and the
  like.

Since the employer would probably end up having to fire
anyone with these personality traits, the employer would like to
find these things out *now*.

Beyond these tangibles, there are the intangibles of *making a good impression*. Study after study has confirmed that if you are a male, you will make a better impression if:

- your hair or beard are neatly trimmed;
- you have obviously freshly bathed, used a deodorant and mouthwash, and have clean fingernails;
- you have freshly laundered clothes on, and a suit rather than a sports outfit, and sit without slouching;
- your breath does not dispense gallons of garlic, onion, stale tobacco, or strong drink, into the enclosed office air;
- your shoes are neatly polished, and your pants have a sharp crease;
- you are not wafting tons of after-shave cologne fifteen feet ahead of you.

And, if you are a female, you will make a better impression if:

- your hair is newly 'permed' or 'coiffed';
- you have obviously freshly bathed, used a deodorant and mouthwash, and have clean or nicely manicured finger nails;
- you wear a bra, freshly cleaned clothes, a suit or sophisti-cated-looking dress, and sit without slouching;
- your breath does not dispense gallons of garlic, onion, stale tobacco, or strong drink, into the enclosed office air;
- you wear shoes rather than sandals;
- you are not wafting tons of perfume fifteen feet ahead of you.

Now please, dear friend, do not send me mail telling me how asinine you think some of these 'requirements' are. I already *know* that. I'm only reporting what study after study has revealed about why you get hired -- or *don't* get hired. There are of course employers who care about none of these things, and will hire you if you can do the job. Period. Do remember, however, that where you have to work with other people, these things will often be given a lot of weight. This employer already has other employees; you must, at least generally, 'fit in.'

If you don't want to 'fit in,' then you might want to consider forming your own (one-person) business (see Chapter 6). Then

-- particularly if it is a mail-order business -- you can dress or conduct yourself as you please, and no one will notice.

If, however, you want to work for someone else, all the above factors are likely to count.

WHAT YOU MUST DO DURING THE INTERVIEW

6. You are trying to find out the answers to five questions. Though they will rarely ever be said out loud, you must keep them in your head throughout the interview:

1. What does this job involve?

2. Do my skills truly match this job?

3. Are you the kind of people I would like to work with?

4. If we do match, can I persuade you that there is something unique about me, that makes me different from nineteen other people who can do the same thing I can do?

5. Can I persuade you to hire me, and at the salary I need or want?

If you did the homework in Chapters 9, 10, 11, and 12 in this book, you might begin your part of the job-interview by reporting to them just exactly how you've been conducting your job-hunt, and what impressed you so much about *their* organization during your research, that you decided to come in and talk to them about a job. Then you can devote your attention, during the remainder of the interview, to exploring the five questions on the file card above.

If you're not there about a job that already exists, but rather, you want them to *create* a job for you, then your five questions get changed into four statements:

1. What you like about this organization.

2. What sorts of **needs** you find intriguing in this field and in this organization (don't ever use the word *"problems,"* as most employers prefer synonyms, such as *'needs'* unless you hear the word *'problems'* coming out of their mouth, first).

3. What skills seem to you to be needed in order to meet such needs.

4. Evidence from your past experience that demonstrates you have the very skills in question, and that you perform them in the manner or style you claim.

5. What is unique about the way *you* perform those skills. This is something you must devote some thought to, ahead of time. For example, if you analyze problems, how do you do that? *Painstakingly? Intuitively, in a flash? By consulting with greater authorities in the field?* You see the point. You are trying to put your finger on the 'style' or 'manner' in which you do your work, that is distinctive and hopefully appealing, to this employer.

Every prospective employer wants to know what makes you different from nineteen other people who can do the same kind of work as you do. You have to know what that is. And then demonstrate it, during the interview.

IT'S WHAT I'VE ALWAYS HEARD.. TIMING IS EVERYTHING..

PEANUTS reprinted by permission of UFS, Inc.

**YOU AS
TIMEKEEPER**

7. You want to come across as someone who knows the value of Time. For example, when you ask for an appointment with an employer, ask for twenty minutes only, of their time, and don't stay one minute longer, unless the employer begs you to. Watch your watch like a hawk. Tell them you like to honor agreements. That will almost always make a big impression.

You want to come across as someone who doesn't hog the Time. Whenever you are interviewing with an employer, talk one-half the time only, and let the employer talk the other half of the time. When the employer asks you a question, don't 'hold forth' for longer than two minutes, at any one time.

You want to come across as someone who values Timing, also. For example, the timing of salary negotiation should be the very last thing you two ever discuss, and only after they have definitely said they want you. Observe that timing, rigorously.

There are reasons for the above advice. For example, studies[6] have revealed that generally speaking the people who get hired are those who mix speaking and listening fifty-fifty in the interview. That is, half the time they spend letting the employer do the talking, half the time in the interview the job-hunter does the talking. People who didn't follow that mix, were the ones who didn't get hired, according to the study. I think the *reason* why this is so, is that if you talk too much about yourself, you come across as one who would ignore the needs of the organization; while if you talk too little, you come across as trying to hide something about your background.

6. This one done by a researcher at Massachusetts Institute of Technology.

Again, studies[7] have revealed that when it is your turn to speak, you should not speak any longer than two minutes at a time, if you want to make the best impression. In fact, a good answer to an employer's question sometimes only takes twenty seconds to give. This is useful information for you to know, in conducting a successful interview -- as you certainly want to do.

With regard to *Timing,* observe it rigorously, even if the employer doesn't. He or she may ask you *early on,* "What kind of a salary are you looking for?" You need to resist the question *at that time,* and gently insist that until *they* have said "We want you," and *you* have decided, "I want them," all discussion of salary is highly inappropriate. This is explained further, in the next chapter.

YOU AS PROBLEM-SOLVER

8. You want to come across as focussed on what you can do for the employer, rather than on what the employer can do for you. You want the employer to see you as a Resource Person, rather than as a 'job-beggar,' to quote Daniel Porot. The major issue is not merely what skills you have, but also how you use them. You want to come across as a Problem-Solver there at work, rather than as one who simply 'keeps busy.' If you don't know what kind of problems, think of what a bad employee would do, in your position (come in late, take too much time off, not care about what the employer wants, etc.). Emphasize how much you do the opposite. You want them to know you will increase the organization's effectiveness, and (where applicable) their profits.

---

7. This one conducted by my colleague, Daniel Porot, in Geneva, Switzerland.

Every organization has two main topics for its continuing day-by-day preoccupation: the problems they are facing, and what the solutions might be.

The main thing the employer is trying to figure out during the job-interview, is -- if they hire you -- will you be part of the solution there, or just another part of their problems.

You will be part of the solution if you come to them as A Resource Person. And the secret of coming to them as A Resource Person is that you have previously tackled Chapters 9, 10, and 11 in this book, systematically and methodically, prior to the job-interview. The three questions there -- WHAT, WHERE, and HOW -- when thoughtfully and diligently answered, will identify you immediately as more than just a job-beggar.

During the course of the interview, you need to make it clear that you are there to see this employer, in order to make an oral proposal, followed hopefully by a written proposal, of what *you can do for them,* to help them with *their* problems. You will see immediately what a switch this is from the way most job-hunters approach an employer! *("How much do you pay, and how much time off will I have?")* Will he or she be glad to see you, with this different emphasis? In most cases, you bet they will. They *want* a resource person, and a problem-solver.

Toward this end, you need to find out as much about that organization as you possibly can, before you ever go in for an interview. Lay your hands on everything you can, that is in print about them. If this is a large organization, read as many of their brochures, annual reports, addresses of the chairman or boss -- whatever -- as you can. If they have a personnel or human relations department, or a public relations department, that's where you'll find that stuff. Also, go to your local library and ask the librarian or reference librarian to see every clipping they may have about that organization.

If it is a small organization, you can still find out if there is anything in print about their work or what they do. *(Even places that only have two employees often have something in print about what the organization is trying to achieve. Also, some local daily or weekly paper may have run an article about them.)* Be sure and talk to everybody you know, to find out anything they may know, about this organization.

This is not a matter of prying into their private life. It is a matter of knowing their history, so that you can understand their purposes and goals. Moreover, all organizations, be they large or small, profit or nonprofit, love to be loved. If you have gone to all this trouble, to learn so much about them -- before you ever walk in their doors, they will be impressed, believe me.

Most job-hunters never go to this trouble. They walk in knowing little or nothing about the organization. This drives employers *nuts*. One time, the first question an IBM college recruiter asked a graduating senior was, "What do the initials IBM stand for?" The senior didn't know, and the interview was over. Another time, an employer said to me, "I'm so tired of job-hunters who come in, and ask, "Uh, what do you do here?" that the next time someone walks in who already knows something about us, I'm going to hire him or her, on the spot."

Thus, if *you* come in, and have done your homework on the organization, this immediately makes you stand out from other job-hunters, and dramatically increases your chances of getting a job there. How much information should you gather? Well, in a nutshell, more than you are going to need -- at least during the hiring interview. The depth of your research will pay off in the quiet sense of knowledgeability that you exude.

YOU AS PROOF-GIVER

9. The most important thing during the interview, regarding your skills, is that you not merely claim you have certain skills, but prove you have them. You must set yourself apart from other job-hunters by being a Proof-giver, not merely a Claimer. Often you do this by the way in which you conduct the interview.

If, for example, you say you are very thorough in all you do, but you haven't researched the organization you are presently interviewing at, your actions will contradict your claims.

If you are an artist, craftsperson, or other person who produces something, try to think of some way to show the employer what you are capable of doing -- through pictures, samples of things you have made or produced, videotape, or whatever -- during the interview.

YOU AS
COURTEOUS AND KIND

10. Be courteous at all times. Employers are a fraternity. Or a sorority. The task of hiring makes them feel like they are members of the same tribe. During the interview, you want to be observed as one who has courtesy toward all members of that tribe, i.e., all employers. Don't ever bad-mouth a previous employer. Say something nice, or else keep quiet about them. You will immediately stand out from other job-hunters, because of your graciousness.

And, be courteous to this employer, even if they are obviously not going to hire you. During the following week, or two, they may be having lunch with another

employer, who says, "I'm looking for someone. Do you know of anybody?" If you were well-remembered for your courtesy, the employer who turned you down, may submit your name to this new employer.

YOU AS THANKS-GIVER

11. Every evening, after a job-interview, you must take time to sit down and write (with pen or typewriter) a brief thank-you note to each person you saw that day. That means, not only employers, but also their secretaries, receptionists, or anyone else who gave you a friendly welcome or a helping hand. (Be sure and ask for their names, or cards, while you are still there visiting that organization.) Don't make the note just a perfunctory 'Thanks very much for your time.' Add something individual about the way they treated you. Use the note to mention anything you forgot to mention while there, and -- with employers -- to underline the main points you want them to remember about you. Mail the note promptly the very next morning, or even that night.

A job-hunter presented herself for a job-interview as public relations officer for a major-league baseball team. That evening, she wrote and mailed a thank-you note. She was eventually hired for the job, and when she asked why, they told her that they had decided to hire her because, out of thirty-five applicants, she was the only one who had written a thank-you note, after the interview.

Every expert on interviewing knows two things: (1) Thank-you notes *must* be sent after *every* interview, by every job-hunter; and (2) Most job-hunters ignore this advice. Indeed, it is safe to say that it is the most overlooked step in the entire job-hunting process.

If you want to stand out from the others applying for the same job, send thank-you notes -- to *everyone* you meet there, that day. If you need any additional encouragements *(besides the fact that it may get you the job),* here are six additional reasons for sending a thank-you note -- particularly to the employer who interviewed you:

First, you are presenting yourself as one who has good skills with people. Your actions with respect to the job-interview must back this claim up. Sending a thank-you note does that. You *are* good with people; you remember to thank them.

Secondly, it helps the employer to remember you.

Thirdly, if a committee is involved in the hiring process, the one man or woman who interviewed you has something to show the committee.

Fourth, if the interview went rather well, and you are hopeful of being invited back, the thank-you letter can reiterate your interest in further talks.

Fifth, the thank-you note gives you an opportunity to correct any wrong impression you left behind you. You can add anything you forgot to tell them, that you want them to know. And from among all the things you two discussed, you can underline the main two or three points that you want to stand out in their minds.

Lastly, if the interview did not go well, and you lost all interest in working there, they may still hear of other openings, elsewhere, that might be of interest to you. In the thank-you note, you can mention this, and ask them to keep you in mind. Thus you may gain additional leads.

Should you include a resume with your thank-you note to the employer who interviewed you? Some experts will advise you to. Under the third canon above, it gives your interviewer something additional to show the other members of the hiring committee, if there is such.

However, infinitely preferred to a resume is a piece of paper that is, in essence, a *brief* written proposal *(one or two pages at most)* as to what it is you would like to be able to do at that organization, and what you hope you could accomplish for them.

As evidence of your ability to do that, you should cite relevant past accomplishments of yours, taking care in each case to cite:

a) what the problem was

b) what especial obstacle (timewise, or otherwise) you had to overcome

c) what means you used to overcome the obstacle, and solve the problem

d) what the results were, of your actions, stated as concretely as possible in terms of things accomplished, money saved, money earned, etc.

The virtue of such a written proposal is that it looks forward rather than (as the resume does) backward. And it puts into writing the essence of the hiring interview: you are not asking them merely to do something for you. More importantly, you are offering to do something for them.

CONCLUSION:
FEAR AND THE INTERVIEW

If the employment interview were simply two people, job-hunter and employer, trying to get answers to natural questions, the interview would be a snap. Unfortunately, this simple exchange is corrupted by the fact that both individuals sitting there are filled with a number of fears and anxieties, which they don't feel free to discuss openly. Yes, I said, *both of you.* You know *you* are sitting there with sweaty palms, but you will probably assume that the employer is sitting there enjoying this whole masochistic process. That is sometimes, but rarely, true.

The employer is a human being just like you are. He or she may *never* have been hired to do *this*. *This* just got thrown in with all their other duties. And they may *know* they're not very good at it.

So, let's briefly catalog some of the employer's typical fears. You are sitting there. The employer is sitting there. This is what they are afraid of, as the job-interview begins:

a. That You Won't Be Able to Do the Job: That You Lack the Necessary Skills or Experience

b. That If Hired, You Won't Put In a Full Working Day

c. That If Hired, You'll Be Frequently "Out Sick," or Otherwise Absent Whole Days

d. That If Hired, You'll Only Stay Around for a Few Weeks or At Most a Few Months

e. That It Will Take You Too Long to Master the Job, and Thus Too Long Before You're Profitable to That Organization

f. That You Won't Get Along with the Other Workers There, or That You Will Develop a Personality Conflict with the Boss Himself (or Herself)

g. That You Will Do Only the Minimum That You Can Get Away With, Rather Than the Maximum That You Are Capable Of

h. That You Will Always Have to Be Told What to Do Next, Rather Than Displaying Initiative; That You Will Always Be in a Responding Rather Than an Initiating Mode (and Mood)

i. That You Will Have a Work-Disrupting Character Flaw, and Turn Out to Be: Dishonest, Totally Irresponsible, a Spreader of Dissention at Work, Lazy, an Embezzler, a Gossip, a Sexual Harasser, a Drug-User or Substance Abuser, a Drunk, a Liar, Incompetent -- In a Word: Bad News

j. *(If This Is a Large Organization, and Your Would-Be Boss Is Not the Top Person)* That You Will Bring Discredit upon Them, and upon His or Her Department/Section/Division, etc., for Ever Hiring You in the First Place -- Making Them Lose Face, and Possibly Costing Your Would-Be Boss a Raise or Promotion

k. That You Will Cost A Lot of Money, if They Make A Mistake in Hiring

Incidentally, the cost of the interviewing time, plus the cost of relocation, moving, etc., added up *(as recently as 1988)* to an average cost of $6,076 for each new professional or managerial employee hired, according to the Employment Management Association. Therefore, that is also the minimum cost of a mistake. No wonder the employer is sweating.

Now, how are they going to find out the answers to these fears? Well, in the old days, an employer might have gotten useful information *outside* the job-interview, by obtaining references from your previous employers. No more. In the past decade, as job-hunters have started filing lawsuits left and right, alleging 'unlawful discharge,' or 'being deprived of an ability to make a living,' about half of all Previous Employers have adopted the policy of refusing to volunteer any information about Past Employees, except name, rank and serial number -- i.e., the person's job-title and dates of employment.

The interviewer is therefore completely on his own -- or her own -- in trying to figure out whether or not to hire you. The hiring interview is *everything*.

The most important thing for you to keep in mind during the interview, as I mentioned on an earlier file card, is that no employer cares about your past. The only thing any employer can possibly care about is your future. Therefore, the more a question *appears* to be about your past, the more certain you may be that some Fear is behind it. And that Fear is about your future -- i.e., what will you be like, *after* the employer decides to hire you, *if* they decide to hire you.

It will help you greatly in the interview if you simply remind yourself, "This guy is afraid," or "This woman is afraid." It will also help you if you can sense *what* fear lies beneath each question that employer asks you -- so that you can tacitly answer the fear, and not just the surface question.

Here are some *examples:*

Employer's Question	The Fear Behind The Question	The Point You Try to Get Across	Phrases You Might Use To Get This Across
"Tell me about yourself"	The employer is afraid he/she isn't going to conduct a very good interview, by failing to ask the right questions. Or is afraid there is something wrong with you, and is hoping you will blurt it out.	You are a good employee, as you have proved in the past at your other jobs. (Give the briefest history of who you are, where born, raised, interests, hobbies, and kind of work you have enjoyed the most to date.) *Keep it to two minutes, max.*	In describing your past work history, use any *honest* phrases you can about your work history, that are self-complimentary: "Hard worker" "Came in early, left late" "Always did more than was expected of me" etc.
"What kind of work are you looking for?"	The employer is afraid that you are looking for a different job than that which the employer is trying to fill. e.g., he/she wants a secretary, but you want to be an office manager, etc.	You are looking for precisely the kind of work the employer is offering (but don't say that, if it isn't true). Repeat back to the employer, in your own words, what he/she has said about the job, and emphasize the skills you have to do *that*.	If the employer hasn't described the job at all, say, "I'd be happy to answer that, but first I need to understand exactly what kind of work this job involves." *Then* answer, as at left.
"Have you ever done this kind of work before?"	The employer is afraid you don't possess the necessary skills and experience to do this job.	You have skills that are transferable, from whatever you used to do; and you did it well.	"I pick up stuff very quickly." "I have quickly mastered any job I have ever done."

Employer's Question	The Fear Behind The Question	The Point You Try to Get Across	Phrases You Might Use To Get This Across
"Why did you leave your last job?" *-- or* "How did you get along with your former boss and co-workers?"	The employer is afraid you don't get along well with people, especially bosses, and is just waiting for you to 'bad-mouth' your previous boss or co-workers, as proof of that.	Say whatever positive things you possibly can about your former boss and co-workers *(without telling lies).* Emphasize you usually get along very well with people -- and then let your gracious attitude toward your previous boss(es) and co-workers prove it, right before this employer's very eyes (and ears).	If you left voluntarily: *"My boss and I* both felt I would be happier and more effective in a job where (here describe your strong points, such as) I would have more room to use my initiative and creativity." If you alone were fired: "Usually, I get along well with everyone, but in this particular case the boss and I just didn't get along with each other. Difficult to say why." *You don't need to say any more than that.* If you were laid off and your job wasn't filled after you left: "My *job* was terminated."
"How is your health?" *-- or* "How much were you absent from work during your last job?"	The employer is afraid you will be absent from work a lot, if they hire you.	You will not be absent. If you have a health problem, you want to emphasize that it is one which will not keep you from being at work, daily. Your productivity, compared to other workers', is excellent.	If you were *not* absent a lot at your last job: "I believe it's an employee's job to show up every work day. Period." If you *were* absent a lot, say why, and stress that it was due to a difficulty that is now *past.*

Employer's Question	The Fear Behind The Question	The Point You Try to Get Across	Phrases You Might Use To Get This Across
"Can you explain why you've been out of work so long?" -- or "Can you tell me why there are these gaps in your work history?" *(usually said after studying your resume)*	The employer is afraid that you are the kind of person who quits a job the minute he/she doesn't like something at it; in other words, that you have no 'stick-to-it-iveness.'	You love to work, and you regard times when things aren't going well as challenges, which you enjoy learning how to conquer.	"During the gaps in my work record, I was studying/doing volunteer work/doing some hard thinking about my mission in life/finding redirection." (Choose one)
"Wouldn't this job represent a step down for you?" -- or "I think this job would be way beneath your talents and experience." -- or "Don't you think you would be underemployed if you took this job?"	The employer is afraid you could command a bigger salary, somewhere else, and will therefore leave him/her as soon as something better turns up.	You will stick with this job so long as you and the employer agree this is where you should be.	"This job isn't a step down for me. It's a step up -- from welfare." "We have mutual fears: every employer is afraid a good employee will leave too soon, and every employee is afraid the employer might fire him/her, for no good reason." "I like to work, and I give my best to every job I've ever had."
And, lastly "Tell me, what is your greatest weakness?"	The employer is afraid you have some character flaw, and hopes you will now rashly blurt it out, or confess it.	You have limitations just like anyone else, but you work constantly to improve yourself and be a more and more effective worker.	Mention a weakness and then stress its positive aspect. e.g., "I don't like to be oversupervised, because I have a great deal of initiative, and I like to anticipate problems before they even arise."

*It has long been an axiom of mine
that the little things
are infinitely the most important.*

Sir Arthur Conan Doyle

God is in the details.

Mies van der Rohe

CHAPTER FOURTEEN

Salary Negotiation

© Copyright, 1980. Universal Press Syndicate.
All rights reserved. Used by special permission.

Chapter 14

FRANK & ERNEST reprinted by permission of NEA, Inc.

The New Poverty

Because of the new 'belt-tightening' that is going on at workplaces throughout the world during these times, it is becoming harder and harder to find a salary which will pay you what you got *in the old days*-- five years ago. Consequently, more and more people are being forced to live minimally, and do their own belt-tightening.

In the U.S., for example, there are now 33.6 million people below the poverty line. Two million of these joined the rest just during the year 1990, due to their declining income. (In the U.S. currently, you are considered to be below the poverty line if you are a family of four and are making less than $13,921 annually.) Support for those living below the poverty line is decreasing in the U.S., from both the Federal and State governments, due to the fact that these governments themselves are in dire financial straits. As of 1991, 40 States had cut or frozen benefits to families with children.

Nearly one out of every five workers in the U.S. is currently working part-time, many of them involuntarily -- they'd like to find full-time work, if they could. (The average work-week in the U.S. is now only 34.7 hours.)

Part-timers, on average, earn only 60% as much, per hour, as full-time workers, and are also less likely to have medical or pension benefits.

MEANWHILE, BACK AT
THE RANCH

While you are writing out your thank-you note, the employer you saw that day is very likely reflecting on the whole day's interviews -- mentally sifting through all the candidates they saw, trying to decide who stands out, so far. And -- if that includes you -- weighing whether to invite you back, for a second round of interviews. There usually *is* a second round. And, often, a third, and fourth. You, of course, want to be in that second round, and you are wondering how many days you should give them, before you contact them again.

It helps a lot if you established some kind of understanding about all of this, at the end of your *first* interview, by asking three questions: *"When may I expect to hear from you?"* (Wait for their answer.) *"What would be the latest I can expect to hear from you?"* (Wait for their answer.) *"May I contact you after that date, if for any reason you haven't gotten back to me by that time?"* (Wait for their answer.) Then, after you leave, keep this covenant, and don't contact them except with the mandatory thank-you note, until after the *latest* deadline agreed upon.

If they forget about you, and you do have to contact them after the agreed-upon date, and if they tell you things are still up in the air, you ask the same three questions all over again. And so on, and so forth.

Incidentally, it is entirely appropriate for you to insert a thank-you note into the running stream, after *each* interview or telephone contact. That will help them remember you.

WHEN EMPLOYERS NEVER
INVITE YOU BACK

There are many job-hunters who have no difficulty in getting a first interview at various places, but they *never* get invited back for a second interview, and hence never get a job. If this is happening to you, there may be something wrong with the way you are coming across during interviews. Unfortunately, employers will hardly ever tell you this. You will never hear them say something like, "You're too cocky and arrogant during the interview." You will always be left completely in the dark as to what it is you're doing wrong.

One way around this deadly silence, is to ask for *generalized* feedback, from some friendly employer you saw back a while ago. You can try phoning them, reminding them of who you are, and then asking the following question -- deliberately kept generalized, vague, unrelated just to *that* place, and above all, *future-directed:* "You know, I've been on several interviews at several different places now, where I've gotten turned down. From what you've seen, is there something about me in an interview, that is causing me not to get hired at those places? If so, I'd really appreciate your giving me some pointers so I can do better in my future job-interviews."

Most of the time they'll *still* duck saying anything hurtful or helpful. (Said an old veteran to me once, "I used to think it was my duty to hit everyone with the truth. Now I only give it to those who can use it.") *Occasionally* you will run into an employer who is willing to risk giving you the truth, because they think you know how to use it.

In the absence of any help from employers, you might want to get a good business friend of yours to role-play a mock job-interview with you, in case they see something glaringly wrong with how you're 'coming across.' If from either friend or employer-on-the-phone, you do get feedback, no matter how painful it is, thank them from the bottom of your heart. Their advice, seriously heeded, can bring about just the changes in your interviewing strategy that you most need.

WHEN EMPLOYERS DO
INVITE YOU BACK

But, assuming things went favorably in the first interview, you *will* be invited back for another interview, *or interviews* at that place -- either with the person you saw before, and/or with a committee. Eventually, after the second, third, or fourth interview, if *you* like them and *they* increasingly like you, a job offer *will* be made.

Then, and only then, it is time to deal with the question that is inevitably on any employer's mind, as we saw in Chapter 13: *how much is this person going to cost me?* And the question that is on *your* mind: *how much does this job pay?*

It's time for salary negotiation.

Salary negotiation would never happen if *every* employer in *every* job-interview were to mention, right from the start, the top figure they are willing to pay for that position. *Some* employers do. And that's the end of any salary negotiation. But, of course, most of them don't. Hoping they'll be able to get you for less, they start *lower* than they're ultimately willing to go. This creates *a range*. And that range is what salary negotiation is all about.

For example, if the employer wants to hire somebody for no more than $12 an hour, they may start *the bidding* at $8 an hour. In which case, the range runs from $8 to $12 an hour. Or if they want to pay no more than $14 an hour, they may start the bidding at $11 an hour. In which case the range runs from $11 to $14 an hour.

If a range *is* involved, then you have every right to try to negotiate a higher salary *within that range*. The employer's goal, is to save money, if possible. Your goal is to bring home to your family, partner, or your own household, the best salary that you can, for the work you will be doing. Nothing's wrong with the goals of either of you. But it does mean that, where the employer starts lower, salary negotiation is proper, and expected.

U.S. Statistics about Salaries

Of the 12 million new jobs created in the last decade, more than half pay less than $7,000 a year.[1]

The median hourly wage in the U.S. in 1992 was $10.50 per hour.[2] High school graduates earn, on average, $10.72 per hour. College graduates earned, on average, $16.69 an hour. These figures did not include 'perks,' such as health-care, retirement funds, etc., which often add about 28% to the total wage.

The median *individual* income for all full-time workers in the U.S. in 1992 was $22,672. The median individual income for production or nonsupervisory workers was $18,946.

The median *family* income was $35,225.[3] (Again, *median* means as many families earned above that figure as below it.)

People making $18,500–$74,000 per year currently are defined as middle-income families.

Pay raises in 1994 were running around 3.5%.

---

1. Time, 12/17/90.
2. This figure is as of May, 1992, and it is for production or nonsupervisory workers on non-farm payrolls.
3. *The (Bend, Oregon) Bulletin,* p. B-1. This figure was for the most recent year available (1990).

THE FIVE KEYS TO SALARY NEGOTIATION

There are five basic keys to successful salary negotiation during a job-interview. They are:

1. *Never* discuss salary until the end of the interviewing process, when they have definitely said they want you.

2. *Never* be the first one to mention a salary figure.

3. Before you go to the interview, do homework on how much you need.

4. During the interview, try to determine whether the salary being offered is fixed or contains room for negotiation.

5. Before you go in, do research on salaries for your field and that organization.

The rest of this chapter is devoted to a discussion of these five keys.

---

1. If you can avoid it, never discuss salary until the end of the interviewing process, after they have definitely said they want you.

You will, of course, envision immediately some exception to this rule. You are face to face with an employer, and they *demand* to know what salary you are looking for, within the first two minutes that you're in the room. You have an excellent response prepared for this very eventuality: "I'll gladly come to that, but could you first help me to understand what this job involves?" But it doesn't work. The employer with rising voice says, "Come, come, don't play games with me. I want to know what salary you're looking for." You have a response prepared for *this* eventuality, too. You answer in terms of a *range,* but this employer insists on a single figure. "How much per hour?" they bark.

In today's market, this is increasingly where many interviews start, and this is increasingly where many interviews end. That's because many employers are making the salary their major criterion for deciding who to hire, and who not to hire. If you try putting it off, *you're outta there*. If you give the wrong answer, *you're outta there*. You can't win.[4]

It's an old game, played with new determination by employers these days, called *"among a bunch of equally qualified candidates, the one who is willing to work for the lowest salary wins."*

Salary negotiation, with them, is non-existent. If you run into this situation, and you want that job badly enough, you have no choice but to capitulate. Ask what they are offering, and take it from there.

However, this *worse case scenario* is not *always* the way things go, by any means. In lots and lots of interviews, these days, salary is still negotiable *if* you save the discussion to the very end of the interviewing process. That's why most experts on salary negotiation will tell you:

When To Discuss Salary

Not until all of the following conditions have been fulfilled --

• Not until they've gotten to know you, at your best, so they can see how you stand out above the other applicants.
• Not until you've gotten to know them, as completely as you can, so you can tell when they're being firm, or when they're flexible.
• Not until you've found out exactly what the job entails.
• Not until they've had a chance to find out how well you match the job-requirements.
• Not until you're in the final interview at that place, for that job.
• Not until you've decided, "I'd really like to work here."
• Not until they've said, "We want you."
• Not until they've said, "We've *got* to have you."

-- should you get into salary discussion with this employer.

If you'd prefer this to be put in the form of a diagram, here it is:[5]

---

4. One job-hunter said his interviews *always* began with the salary question, and no matter what he answered, that ended the interview. Turned out, this job-hunter was doing all the interviewing *over the phone*. That was the problem. Once he went *face-to-face*, salary was no longer the first thing discussed in the interview.

5. Reprinted, by permission of the publisher, from *Ready, Aim, You're Hired*, by Paul Hellman, © 1986 Paul Hellman. Published by AMACOM, a division of American Management Association, New York. All rights reserved.

Reprinted, by permission of the publisher, from *Ready, Aim, You're Hired,* by Paul Hellman, © 1986 Paul Hellman. Published by AMACOM, a division of American Management Association, New York. All rights reserved.

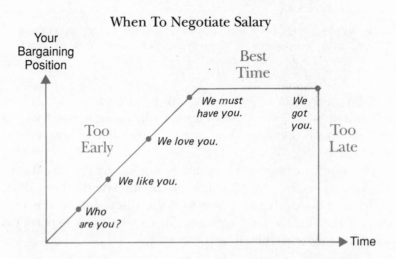

When To Negotiate Salary

Your Bargaining Position — Best Time

Too Early — We must have you. — We got you. — Too Late

We love you.

We like you.

Who are you?

Time

Why is it to your advantage to delay salary discussion? Because, if you really *shine* during the job-interview, they may -- at the end -- mention a higher salary than they originally had in mind, just because they're determined to have you.

If the employer raises the salary question earlier, but seems like a kindly man or woman, your best reply might be: "Until you've decided you definitely want me, and I've decided I definitely could help you with your tasks here, I feel any discussion of salary is premature."

---

2. If you can help it, try not to be the first one to mention a salary figure.

Where you are in an interview where salary negotiation has been kept *off stage* for much of the interview, when it does come *on stage* you want the employer to be the first one to mention *a figure,* if you can manage that.

The reason for this is that the employer wants to pay the least they can, while on the other hand you want them to pay the most they can, *within their range.* So, it's going to be a kind of verbal arm-wrestling. And, never mind the reason why, what has been observed over the years is that in this contest *whoever mentions a salary figure first, generally loses at the last.*

Inexperienced employer/interviewers don't know this. Experienced ones do; that's why they will *always* toss the ball to you, with the innocent-sounding question, "What kind of salary are you looking for?" *Well, how kind of them to ask what you want* -- you may be thinking. No, no, no. Kindness isn't the point. They are hoping *you* will be the first to mention a figure, because they know this obscure rule well, that *whoever mentions a salary figure first, generally loses at the last.*

So of course, you will *always* want to respond, if you can: "Well, you created this position, so you must have some figure in mind, and I'd be interested in knowing what that is."

---

3. Before you go to the interview, do homework on how much you need.

When you are in an interview where salary discussion is saved to the end, salary negotiation is possible. *But,* you cannot possibly do salary negotiation unless you know what is *the floor,* below which you simply cannot afford to go. And this is particularly important in these troubled times, since many employers have *a fixed ceiling* above which they simply cannot afford to go. When you're in the middle of salary negotiation, you've *got* to know instantly if *their* ceiling turns out to be beneath *your* floor.

That means knowing, beforehand, just how much it is you need to make, at a minimum. You can determine this in one of two ways: a) take a wild guess -- and risk finding out after you take the job that it's simply impossible for you to live on that salary *(the favorite strategy in this country, and most others);* or, b) make out a detailed outline of your estimated expenses *now,* listing what you need *monthly* in the following categories:[6]

---

6. If this kind of financial figuring is not your cup of tea, find a buddy, friend, relative, family member, or *anyone,* who can help you do this. If you don't know anyone who could do this, go to your local church, synagogue, religious centre, social club, gym, or wherever you hang out, and ask the leader or manager there, to help you find someone. If there's a bulletin board, put up a notice on the bulletin board.

Housing
    Rent or mortgage payments ....$_____
    Electricity/gas ....$_____
    Water ....$_____
    Telephone ....$_____
    Garbage removal ....$_____
    Cleaning, maintenance, repairs[7] ....$_____
Food
    What you spend at the supermarket
    and/or meat market, etc. ....$_____
    Eating out ....$_____
Clothing
    Purchase of new or used clothing ....$_____
    Cleaning, drycleaning, laundry ....$_____
Automobile/transportation[8]
    Car payments ....$_____
    Gas ....$_____
    Repairs ....$_____
    Public transportation *(bus, train, plane)* ....$_____
Insurance
    Car ....$_____
    Medical or health-care ....$_____
    House and personal possessions ....$_____
    Life ....$_____
Medical expenses
    Doctors' visits ....$_____
    Prescriptions ....$_____
    Fitness costs ....$_____
Support for other family members
    Child-care costs *(if you have children)* ....$_____
    Child-support *(if you're paying that)* ....$_____
    Support for your parents *(if you're helping out)* $_____
Charity giving/tithe *(to help others)* ....$_____
School/learning
    Children's costs *(if you have children in school)* ..$_____
    Your learning costs *(adult education, job-*
    hunting classes, etc.) ....$_____
Pet care *(if you have pets)* ....$_____

Bills and debts *(Usual monthly payments)*
    Credit cards ....$_____
    Local stores ....$_____
    Other obligations you pay off monthly ....$_____
Taxes
    Federal[9] *(next April's due, divided by months*
    remaining until then) ....$_____
    State *(likewise)* ....$_____
    Local/property *(next amount due, divided by*
    months remaining until then) ....$_____
    Tax-help *(if you ever use an accountant, pay*
    a friend to help you with taxes, etc.) ....$_____
Amusement/discretionary spending
    Movies, video rentals, etc.................................$_____
    Other kinds of entertainment.........................$_____
    Reading, newspapers, magazines, books ....$_____
    Gifts *(birthday, Christmas, etc.)* ....$_____

Total Amount You Need Each Month ....$_____

Parenthetically, you may want to prepare two different versions of the above budget: one with the expenses you'd ideally *like* to make, and the other a minimum budget, which will give you what you are looking for, here: the floor, below which you simply cannot afford to go.

---

7. If you have extra household expenses, such as a security system for example, be sure and include the quarterly (or whatever) expenses here, divided by three.

8. Your checkbook stubs will tell you a lot of this stuff. But you may be vague about your cash or credit card expenditures. For example, you may not know how much you spend at the supermarket, or how much you spend on gas, etc. But there is a simple way to find out. Just carry a little notepad and pen around with you for two weeks or more, and jot down *everything* you pay cash *(or use credit cards)* for -- *on the spot, right after you pay it.* At the end of those two weeks, you'll be able to take that notepad and make a realistic guess of what should be put down in these categories that now puzzle you. *(Multiply the two-weeks figure by two, and you'll have the monthly figure.)*

9. Incidentally, looking ahead to next April 15th, be sure and check with your local IRS office or a reputable accountant to find out if you can deduct the expenses of your job-hunt on your Federal (and State) income tax returns. At this writing, some job-hunters can, if -- big IF -- this is not your first job that you're looking for, if you haven't been unemployed too long, and if you aren't making a career-change. Do go find out what the latest "if"s are. If IRS tells you you are eligible, keep careful receipts of everything related to your job-hunt, as you go along: telephone calls, stationery, printing, postage, travel, etc.

> ## 4. Try to determine whether the salary being offered is fixed or contains room for negotiation.

Salary negotiation has become infinitely more complicated these days because so many companies are seeking to cut costs, beginning with the salaries they pay. Many employers have fired or laid off experienced workers who have given years to the company, and they have done so for one reason and one reason only: those experienced, dedicated employees now cost too much. They can be replaced by new workers who may not have the experience, and may make a lot of mistakes. But these new employees have one sterling virtue: they cost *half* of what the previous employees cost.

Even among the new candidates, cost is often *the deciding factor*. This is particularly true if applicants for this position are 'a dime a dozen,' and you are viewed by the employer as *only one among many*.

But, as I said earlier, salary negotiation is still possible even in the belt-tightening times, anytime the employer does not open their discussion of salary by naming the top figure they have in mind, but starts instead with a lower figure.

Okay, so here is our $64,000 question: how can you tell whether the figure the employer first offers you is only their *starting bid*, or is their *final final offer*? The answer is: by doing some research first.

> ## 5. Before you go in, do research on salaries for your field and that organization.

You, of course, want to know if it's *really necessary* to do this kind of research. Trust me, salary research pays off *handsomely*.

Let's say it takes you from one to three days to run down this sort of information on the three or four organizations that interest you the most. And let us say that because you've done this research, when you finally go in for the job-interview you are able to ask for and obtain a salary that is $4,000 a year higher in range, than you would otherwise have gotten. In just the next three years, you will be earning $12,000 extra, because of your salary research. *Not bad pay, for one to three days' work!* And it can be even more.

If it is true that *information* is the key to a successful job-hunt and to successful salary-negotiation, it is equally true that there is a financial penalty exacted from those who are too lazy, or in too much of a hurry, to go gather that information.

If you want to find out what the salary is for the kind of job you are being considered for, there is a simple rule: abandon books, and go talk to people. Preferably to people who are in the same job *at another company or organization.* Or, go talk to people at the nearby university or college who *train* such people: whatever the department is, where people get trained for this kind of job. These teachers will usually know what their graduates are getting.

Use books only as a *second,* or *last,* resort. I have listed in the footnote below a sampling of the kind of information you can dig up at your local library, using the resources listed in Appendix B and elsewhere.[10] This is for the U.S. Other countries should have similar resources. Ask your local librarian.

---

10. Some books or journals will give yearly figures; others will give hourly. The yearly figures are roughly convertible to hourly wages, and vice versa. Assume a 40 hour week, and a 50 week year, which is less than some people work, and more than others -- but close enough. Take *however many* thousands the yearly figure is, and divide the number of thousands by two; that will give you the *approximate* hourly wage. Thus, with $30,000 a year, you take the 30, divide by two, and you find it equals (approximately) $15 an hour. Or, to reverse, take the hourly figure, multiply it by two, and add three zeroes. Now, where do you look? In the U.S., the places to look for your information include the Department of Labor's monthly *Employment and Earnings,* ("Household Data, Annual Averages, Median weekly earnings of full-time wage and salary workers by detailed occupation and sex") -- plus its annual *Supplement to Employment and Earnings; Area Wage Surveys* (covers office, professional, technical, maintenance, custodial, and material movement jobs in major metropolitan areas), and individual area bulletins which are available separately, and cover mainly production and nonsupervisory workers. Order from the Bureau of Labor Statistics, Publications Sales Center, P.O. Box 2145, Chicago IL 60690. Areas covered include Alexandria–Leesville, Virginia, Ashville, North Carolina, Atlanta, Beaumont–Port Arthur and Lake Charles, Texas, Cedar Rapids, Iowa, Houston, Huntsville, Logansport–Peru, Indiana, Milwaukee, Minneapolis–St. Paul, Monmouth-Ocean, New Jersey, Newark, New Jersey, Norfolk–Virginia Beach–Newport News, Virginia, Northern New York, Northwestern Florida,

Apropos of talking to people, in order to get this information, let's look at some examples:

> First Example: *Working at your first entry-level job, say at
> a fast-food place.*

You may not need to do any salary research. They pay what
they pay. You can walk in, ask for a job application, and interview with the manager. He or she will usually tell you the pay,
outright. It's usually *inflexible*. But at least you'll find it easy to
discover what the pay is. (Incidentally, filling out an application,
or having an interview there, doesn't commit you to take the

Oakland, California, Pittsburgh, Portsmouth–Chillicothe–Gallipolis, Ohio, Raleigh–
Durham, North Carolina, St. Louis, San Francisco, San Jose, California, Washington
DC–Maryland.

11. Daniel Porot, in Europe, suggests that if you and an employer really hit it off, and
you're *dying* to work there, but they cannot afford the salary you need, consider
offering them part of your time. If you need, and believe you deserve, say $25,000, but
they can only afford $15,000, you might consider offering them three days a week of
your time for that $15,000 (15/25 = 3/5). This leaves you free to take other work those
other two days.

12. In any good-sized organization, you will often be amazed at how little attention
your superiors pay to your noteworthy accomplishments, and how little they are aware
at the end of the year that you really are *entitled* to a raise. Noteworthy your accomplishments may be, but no one is taking notes . . . unless *you* do.

job -- but you probably already know that. You can always decline an offer from *any place*. That's what makes this approach
harmless.)

> Second Example: *Working at a place where you can't*
> *discover what the pay is, say at a construction company.*

If that construction company where you would *hope* to get a
job is difficult to research, go visit a *different* construction company in the same town -- one that isn't of much interest to you --
and ask what they make *there*. Or, if you don't know who to talk
to there, fill out one of their applications, and talk to the hiring
person about what kinds of jobs they have (or might have in the
future), at which time prospective wages is a legitimate subject
of discussion. Then, having done this research on a place you
don't care about, go back to the place that *really* interests you,
and apply. You still don't know *exactly* what they pay, but you do
know what their competitor pays -- which will usually be *close*.

> Third Example: *Working in a one-person office, say as*
> *a secretary.*

Here you can often find useful salary information by perusing the *Help Wanted* ads in the local paper for a week or two.
Most of the ads probably won't mention a salary figure, but a
few *may*. Among those that do, note what the lowest salary
offering is, and what the highest is, and see if the ad reveals
some reasons for the difference. It's interesting how much you
can learn about salaries, with this approach. I know, because I
was a secretary myself, once upon a time.

Another way to do salary research is to find a *Temporary Work*
Agency that places secretaries, and let yourself be farmed out to
various offices: the more, the merrier. It's relatively easy to do
salary research when you're *inside* the place. (Study what that
place pays *the agency*, not what the agency pays you.) If it's an
office where the other workers *like* you, you'll be able to ask
questions about a lot of things, including salary. It's like *summer-*
time, where the research is easy.

AT HOME
ON THE RANGE

Before you finish your research, before you go in there for
your first or final interview, you want more than just one figure.
You want *a range*. In any organization which has more than five
employees, that range is relatively easy to figure out. It will be
less than what the person *who would be above you* makes, and
more than what the person *who would be below you* makes.

If The Person Who Would Be Below You Makes	And The Person Who Would Be Above You Makes	The Range For Your Job Would Be
$22,000	$27,000	$23,000 – $26,000
$10,000	$13,500	$10,500 – $12,500
$ 6,240	$ 7,800	$ 6,400 – $ 7,600

One teensy-tiny little problem: *how* do you find out the salary
of those who would be above and below you? Well, first you have
to find out their *names* or the names of their *positions*. If it is a
small organization you are going after -- one with twenty or less
employees -- finding this information out should be *duck soup*.
Any employee who works there is likely to know the answer, and
you can usually get in touch with one of those employees, or
even an ex-employee, through your contacts. Since two-thirds of
all new jobs are created by companies of that size, that's the size
organization you are likely to be researching, anyway.

If you are going after a larger organization, then you have
our familiar life-preserver to fall back on, namely, every contact
you have (family, friend, relative, business, or church acquaintance) who might know the company, and therefore, the information you seek. You are looking for Someone Who Knows
Someone who either is working, or has worked, at the particular
place or places that interest you, who therefore has or can get
this information for you.

If you absolutely run into a blank wall on a particular organization (everyone who works there is pledged to secrecy, and
they have shipped all their ex-employees to Siberia), then seek

out information on their nearest *competitor* in the same geographic area. *For example,* let us say you were researching Bank X, and they were proving to be inscrutable about what they pay their managers. You would then try Bank Y as your research base, to see if the information were easier to come by, there. And if it were, you would then assume the two were similar in their pay scales, and that what you learned about Bank Y was applicable also to Bank X.

GETTING THE HIGHEST SALARY

With this research in your hip pocket, when you are in the actual job-interview, and the employer mentions the figure *they* have in mind, you are then ready to respond: "I understand of course the constraints under which all organizations are operating in the '90s, but I believe my productivity is such that it would *justify* a salary in the range of . . ." -- *and here you mention a figure near the top of their range.*

It will help a lot if during this discussion, you are prepared to show in what ways you will *make money* or in what ways you will *save money* for that organization, such as will justify the higher salary you are seeking. Hopefully, this will succeed in getting you the salary you want.[11]

During your salary negotiation, do not forget to pay attention to so-called fringe benefits. 'Fringes' such as life insurance, health benefits or health plans, vacation or holiday plans, and retirement programs typically add another 28% to many workers' salaries. That is to say, if an employee receives $800 salary per month, the fringe benefits are worth another $200 per month. You should therefore remember to ask what benefits are offered, and negotiate if necessary for the benefits you want. Thinking this out ahead of time, of course, makes your negotiating easier, by far. You can prepare the ground during your salary negotiation, by saying: *"If I accomplish this job to your satisfaction, as I fully expect to -- and more -- when could I expect to be in line for a raise?"*

Once all salary negotiation is concluded to your satisfaction, do remember to ask to have it summed up in a letter of agreement -- or employment contract -- that they give to you. It may be you cannot get it in writing, but do try! The Road to Hell is paved with oral promises that went unwritten, and -- later -- unfulfilled.

Many executives unfortunately 'forget' what they told you during the job-interview, or even deny they ever said such a thing.

Also, many executives leave the company for another position and place, and their successor or the top boss may disown any *unwritten* promises: *"I don't know what caused them to say that to you, but they clearly exceeded their authority, and of course we can't be held to that."*

Plan to keep track of your accomplishments at this new job, on a weekly basis -- jotting them down, every weekend, in your own private diary. Career experts, such as Bernard Haldane, recommend you do this without fail. You can then summarize these accomplishments annually on a one-page sheet, for your boss's eyes, when raise or promotion is a legitimate subject for you to bring up.[12]

SUMMARY

Job-hunting always involves luck, to some degree. But with a little bit of luck, the techniques described in these chapters should work for you, even as they have worked for so many thousands before you.

Assuming they do, when you are in that next job -- hopefully your *ideal job* -- you will know the truth of something Dick Lathrop first said over twenty years ago, in his book *Who's Hiring Who:*

here may be others who applied there who could have done the job better than you. But it is true today, and it will ever be true: the person who gets hired is not necessarily the one who can do that job best; but, the one **who knows the most about how to get hired.**

The Pink Pages

Two are better than one;
　　　for if they fall,
the one will lift up his fellow;

but woe to him that is alone when he falleth,
and hath not another to lift him up.

　　　　　　Ecclesiastes

Appendix A

When Books Are Not Enough
and
You Want A Live Person
To Help You:

Career Counselors
and
Other Resources

HOW TO CHOOSE A CAREER COUNSELOR,

LOOK BEFORE YOU LEAP:

There are two basic types of career counselors.

One type's *primary* expertise is in the area called 'career development' or 'career assessment.' They help people figure out what they want to do with their lives, by way of career choice, etc. They *may* know very little about the actual job-hunting process.

The other type almost always also know something about 'career development' or 'career assessment,' but their *primary* expertise is in the job-search process.

Some of these follow the *traditional* approach: resumes and interviewing, as described in Chapters 3 and 13 in this book. If you have already given up on that traditional approach, then this is not the counselor for you.

Others follow the *creative* process of job-hunting, described in Chapters 9, 10, 11, and 12, as well as 4, in this book. This is the one you want.

All counselors, of either type, divide into a) sincere and good at what they do; or b) sincere and inept; or c) wolves in sheep's clothing, ready to take you to the cleaners (or to the shearing).

No one has a list of counselors who are sincere and *good* at what they do, either in this country or in any other part of the world.

IF YOU DECIDE YOU NEED ONE

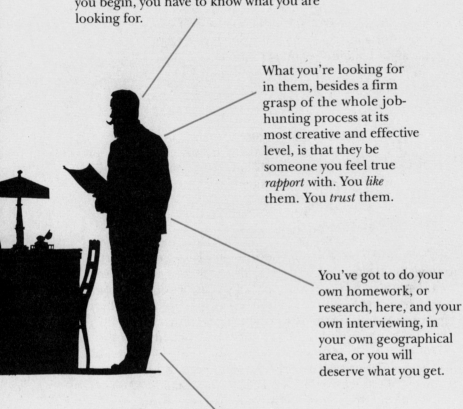

You have to go find them yourself. You *can* do it. But it's going to take some work. And before you begin, you have to know what you are looking for.

What you're looking for in them, besides a firm grasp of the whole job-hunting process at its most creative and effective level, is that they be someone you feel true *rapport* with. You *like* them. You *trust* them.

You've got to do your own homework, or research, here, and your own interviewing, in your own geographical area, or you will deserve what you get.

No one but you knows whether or not you're going to get along with a particular career counselor. Maybe he's a wonderful man, but unhappily he reminds you of your Uncle Harry. You've always **hated** your Uncle Harry. No one knows that, but you. Or maybe the counselor is a wonderful woman, but unhappily . . . *well, you get the point.*

No one can do this research for you. Because the real question is not "Who is best?" but "Who is best **for you**?" Those last two words demand that it be you who 'makes the call.'

Now, what do you want? First of all, you want <u>names</u>.

You want to find the names of at least three career counselors in your community.

Where do you find names?

First, from your friends: ask if any of them have ever used a career counselor. And if so, what is that counselor's name; and what did they think of them.

Secondly, from the *Sampler* toward the rear of this Appendix. See if there are any names near you. They may know how you find out the other names in your community.

Try also your telephone book's local Yellow Pages, under such headings as: *Aptitude and Employment Testing, Career and Vocational Counseling, Personnel Consultants,* and (if you are a woman) *Women's Organizations and Services.* You will discover that even the Yellow Pages can't keep up with the additional groups that spring up daily, weekly, and monthly -- including job clubs and other group activities, but many of these (in the U.S.A., at least) *are* listed in the *National Business Employment Weekly,* on its pages called "Calendar of Career Events." Available on newsstands, $3.95 per issue; or, order an issue directly from: National Business Employment Weekly, 420 Lexington Ave., New York, NY 10170. 212-808-6792, or 800-JOB HUNT.

Then you want <u>talk</u>.

You want to go talk with all three of them, and decide which of the three (if any) you want to hook up with.

You're going to be doing comparison shopping.

You <u>visit</u> in person each of the three places you have chosen.
Don't try to do this over the telephone, *please!* There is so much
more you can tell, when you're looking the person straight in
the eyes.

When face-to-face, you ask *each* of the three
places the same questions. Keep a little
pad or notebook with you that looks like
this form below.

MY SEARCH FOR A GOOD CAREER COUNSELOR			
Questions I Will Ask Them	Answer from counselor #1	Answer from counselor #2	Answer from counselor #3
1. What is your program?			
2. Who will be doing it? And how long have you been doing it?			
3. What is your success rate?			
4. What is the cost of your services?			
5. Is there a contract?			

Remember, you don't have to choose any of the three counselors,
if you didn't really care for any of them. If that is the case, then
choose three new counselors, dust off the notebook, and go out
again. It may take a few more hours to find what you want. But the
wallet, the purse, the job-hunt, the life, you save will be your own.

Back home now, after visiting the three places you chose for your comparison shopping, you have to decide: a) whether you want none of the three, or b) one of the three (and if so, which one). Look over your notes on all three places. Compare those places. The simple fact is: there is no definitive way for you to determine a career counselor's expertise. It's something you'll have to smell out, as you go along. But here are some clues:

BAD ANSWERS

If they asked you to bring in your partner or spouse with you,
(5 bad points)
This is a well-known tactic of some of the slickest salespeople in the world, who want your spouse or partner there so they can manipulate one or the other or both of you to reach a decision on the spot, while they have you in their 'grasp.'

If they give you the feeling that everything will be done for you, by them (including interpretation of tests, and decision making about what this means you should do, or where you should do it) -- rather than you having to do all the work, with their basically assuming the role of coach,
(15 bad points)
You want to learn how to do this for yourself; you're going to be job-hunting again, you know.

If they say they are not the person who will be doing the program with you, but deny you any chance to meet the counselor you would be working with,
(75 bad points)
You're talking to a salesperson. Avoid any firm that has a salesperson.

If you do get a chance to meet the counselor, but you don't like the counselor as a person,
(150 bad points)
I don't care what their expertise is, if you don't like them, you're going to have a rough time getting what you want. I guarantee it. Rapport is everything.

If you ask how long the counselor has been doing this, and they get huffy or give a double-barreled answer, such as: "I've had eighteen years' experience in the business and career counseling world,"
(20 bad points)
What that may mean is: seventeen and a half years as a fertilizer salesman, and one-half year doing career counseling. Persist. "How long have you been with this firm, and how long have you been doing formal career counseling, as you are here?" You might be interested to know that some executive or career counseling firms hire yesterday's clients as today's new staff. Such new staff are sometimes given training only after they're "on-the-job." They are practicing on you.

If they try to answer the question of their experience by pointing to their degrees or credentials,
(3 bad points)
Degrees or credentials tell you they've passed certain tests of their qualifications, but often these tests bear more on their expertise at career assessment than on their knowledge of creative job-hunting.

If, when you ask about their success rate, they say they have never had a client that failed to find a job, no matter what,
(15 bad points)
They're lying. I have studied career counseling programs for over twenty years, have attended many, have studied records at State and Federal offices, and I have hardly ever seen a program that placed more than 86% of their clients, tops, in their best years. And it goes downhill from there. A prominent executive counseling firm was reported by the Attorney General's Office of New York State to have placed only 38 out of 550 clients (a 93% failure rate).[1] If they make it clear that they have had a good success rate, but if you fail to work hard at the whole process, then there is no guarantee you are going to find a job, give them three stars.

If you ask what is the cost of their services, and they reply that it is a lump sum that must all be paid "up front" before you start or shortly after you start, either all at once or in installments,
(100 bad points)
For twenty-five years I've tried to avoid saying this, but I have grown weary of the tears of job-hunters who 'got taken.' So now I say it without reservation: if the firm charges a lump sum for their services, rather than allowing you to simply pay for each hour as you go, go elsewhere. Every insincere and inept counselor or firm charges a lump sum. So, of course, do a few sincere and good counselors and firms. Trouble is: you won't know which kind you've signed up with, until they've got all your money. The risk is too great, the cost is too high. If you really like to gamble that much, go to Las Vegas. They give better odds.

---

1. For further details, go to your local library and look up "Career Counselors: Will They Lead You Down The Primrose Path?" by Lee Guthrie, in the December 1981 issue of *Savvy Magazine*, pp. 60ff.

If they ask you to sign a contract,
(1000 bad points)

With insincere and inept firms or counselors, there is always a written contract. And you must sign it, before they will help you. (Often, your partner or spouse will be asked to sign it, too.) The fee normally ranges from $1000 on up to $10,000 or more.

You may think the purpose of that firm's contract is that they are promising you something, that they can be held to. Uh-uh! More often, the main purpose of the contract is to get you to promise them something. Like, your money. Don't . . . do . . . it.

You will sometimes be told that, "Of course, you can get your money back, or a portion of it, at any time, should you be dissatisfied with the career counselor's services." Nine times out of ten, however, you are told this verbally, and it is not in the written contract. Verbal promises, without witnesses, are difficult if not impossible for you to later try to enforce. The written contract is binding.

Sometimes the written contract will claim to provide for a partial refund, at any time, until you reach a cut-off date in the program, which the contract specifies. Unfortunately, many crafty fraudulent firms bend over backwards to be extra nice, extra available, and extra helpful to you until that cut-off point is reached. So, when the cut-off point for getting a refund has been reached, you let it pass because you are very satisfied with their past services, and believe there will be many more weeks of the same. Only, there aren't. At fraudulent firms, once the cut-off point is passed, the career counselor becomes virtually impossible for you to get ahold of. Call after call will not be returned. You will say to yourself "What happened?" Well, what happened, my friend, is that you paid up in full, they have all the money they're ever going to get out of you, and now they don't want to give you any more time.

You may think I am exaggerating: I mean, can there possibly be such mean men and women, who would prey on job-hunters, when they're down and out. Yes, ma'am, and yes, sir, there are. That's why you have to do this preliminary research so thoroughly.

I quote from the late Robert Wegmann, former director of the UHCL Center for Labor Market Studies: "One high-charging career counseling firm went bankrupt a few years ago. They left many of their materials behind in their former office. A box of what they abandoned has come into my possession. Going through the contents of the box has been fascinating.

"Particularly interesting are several scripts used to train their salespeople. The goal of the sales pitch is to convince the unemployed (or unhappily employed) person that he or she can't find a good job alone, but can do it with professional help. Hiring us, they argue, is just like hiring a lawyer. . . .

"Then, at the end of the pitch, comes the 'takeaway.' The firm may not accept your money, you are warned! There will have to be a review board meeting at which your application is considered. Only a minority of applicants are accepted. The firm only wants the right kind of clients.

"That's the pitch. But the rest of the documents tell a very different story. In fact, the firm is running a series of sales contests with all the 'professionalism' of a used car lot. . . .

"These salespeople were paid on commission. The higher the sales the higher the percentage of the customer's fee they got to keep.

"There are sales contests. The winner receives a handsome green Master's jacket. Each monthly winner qualifies for a Grand Master's Tournament, with large prizes. . . .

"So take this one piece of advice. . . . If someone offers to help you find a great job as long as you'll pay several thousand dollars in advance, do as follows:

"A. Find door

"B. Walk out same

"C. Do not return."

Over the last twenty years, I have had to listen to grown men and women cry over the telephone, all because they signed a contract. Most often they were executives, or senior managers, who never had to go job-hunting before, and unknowingly signed up with some executive counseling firm that was fraudulent, or at least on the edge of legality.

If you want to avoid their tears in your own job-search, don't sign anything -- ever.[2]

---

2. If you are **dying** to know more, and your local library has back files of magazines and newspapers (on microfiche, or otherwise) there was a period when bad firms and counselors came under heavy fire (1978–1982) and you can look up some of the articles of that period, as well as those articles which have appeared more recently, to wit:

"A Consumer Guide to Retail Job-Hunting Services," Special Report, reprinted from the *National Business Employment Weekly;* available from National Business Employment Weekly Reprint Service, P.O. Box 300, Princeton, NJ 08543-0300. 1-800-730-1111. $8. by mail; $12.95 by fax. A *very* thorough series of articles on the industry, and its frauds, which names *names,* and gives the addresses of Consumer protection agencies in each state, to whom you may complain. **Required reading** for anyone who wants to avoid getting 'burned.'

" 'Employment counselors' costly, target of gripes," *The Arizona Republic,* 10/8/89.

"Career-Counseling Industry Accused of Misrepresentation," *New York Times,* 9/30/82.

"Consumer Law: Career Counselors and Employment Agencies" by Reed Brody, *New York Law Journal,* Feb. 26, 1982, p. 1. Reed was Assistant Attorney General of the State of New York, and more recently Deputy Chief of the Labor Bureau within that State's Department of Law; in this capacity he became the leading legal expert in the country, on career counseling malpractices, though unfortunately (for us) he now works overseas in Europe, in another profession.

"Career Counselors: Will They Lead You Down the Primrose Path?" by Lee Guthrie, *Savvy Magazine,* 12/81, p. 60ff.

"Franklin Career Search Is Accused of Fraud In New York State Suit," *Wall Street Journal,* 1/29/81, p. 50.

"Job Counseling Firms Under Fire For Promising Much, Giving Little," *Wall Street Journal,* 1/27/81, p. 33.

> *Of course,* you're tempted to skip over all this research. "Well, I'll just call up one place, and if I like the sound of them, I'll sign up. I'm a pretty good judge of character." *Right.* I hear many a sad tale from people who adopted that attitude, and then found out too late that they had been *taken.* My reply usually is, "I'm sorry indeed to hear that you had a very disappointing experience; that is very unfortunate, I know, I've been through it myself. But -- as the Scots would say -- 'Ya dinna do your homework.'"[3] Often you could easily have discovered whether a particular counselor was competent or not, before you ever gave them any of your money, simply by asking the right questions during the research I'm pleading with you to take seriously.

GOOD ANSWERS

Fortunately there are career counselors who charge by the hour. With them, there is no written contract. You sign nothing. You pay only for each hour as you use it, according to their set rate. Each time you keep an appointment, you pay them at the end of that hour for their help, according to that rate. Period. Finis. You never owe them any money. You can stop seeing them at any time, if you feel you are not getting the help you wish.

What will they charge? You will find, these days, that the best career counselors (and some of the worst, too) will charge you whatever a really good therapist or marriage counselor charges per hour, in your geographical area. Currently, in large metropolitan areas, that runs around $100 an hour, sometimes more. In suburbia or rural areas, it may be much less.

That fee is for individual time with the career counselor. If you can't afford that fee, ask whether they also run groups. If they do, the fee will be much less. And, in one of those delightful ironies of life, since you get a chance to listen to problems which other job-hunters in your group are having, the group will often give you more help than an individual session would. Not always; but often. It's always ironic when *cheaper* and *more helpful* go hand in hand.

If the career counselor in question does offer groups, there should (again) never be a contract. The charge should be payable at the end of each session, and you should be able to drop out at any time, without further cost, if you decide you are not getting the help you want.

---

3. If you are reading this too late, did pay some firm's fee all in advance, and feel you were ripped off, you will want to know about Mr. Stuart Alan Rado. Mr. Rado is a former victim of one of the career counseling agencies, and ever since he has been waging a sort of "one-man crusade" against career counseling firms which take advantage of the job-hunter. Send Mr. Rado your story, together with a self-addressed stamped envelope, and he will send you a one-page sheet of some actions you can take. It may not get your money back, but at least you'll feel better for having done *something.* His address is: 1500 23rd St., Sunset Island #3, Miami Beach, FL 33140. 305-532-2607.

There are, incidentally, some career counselors who run free (or almost free) job-hunting workshops through local churches, synagogues, chambers of commerce, community colleges, adult education programs, and the like, as their community service, or pro bonum work (as it is technically called). I have had reports of such workshops from a number of places in the U.S. and Canada. They surely exist in other parts of the world as well. If money is a big problem for you, in getting help with your job-hunt, ask around to see if such workshops as these exist in your community. Your chamber of commerce will likely know, or your church or synagogue.

A Sampler

This is not a complete directory of anything. It is exactly what its name implies: a **Sampler.** Were I to list all the career counselors *out there*, we would end up with an encyclopedia. Some states, in fact, have *encyclopedic* lists of counselors and businesses, in various books or directories, and your local bookstore or library should have these, in their *Job-Hunting Section,* under such titles as "How to Get A Job in . . ." or "Job-Hunting in . . ."

Most of the places listed in this **Sampler** are listed at their own request, simply as places for you to begin your investigation with -- nothing more.

Many truly *helpful* places are *not* listed here. If you discover such a place, which is very good at helping people with *Parachute* and creative job-hunting or career-change, do send us the pertinent information. We will ask them, as we do all the listings here, a few intelligent questions and if they sound okay, we will add that place to next year's edition.

We do ask a few questions because our readers want counselors and places which claim some expertise in helping them finish their job-hunt, *using this book.* So, if they've never even heard of *Parachute,* we don't list them. On the other hand, we can't measure a place's expertise at this long distance, no matter how many questions we ask.

Even if listed here, you must do your own sharp questioning before you decide to go with anyone. If you don't take time to research two or three places, before choosing a counselor, you will deserve whatever you get (or, more to the point, *don't* get). So, please, *do your research.* The purse or wallet you save, will be your own.

Yearly readers of this book will notice that we do remove people from this Sampler, over time. Specifically, we remove (without further notice or comment):

Places which have disconnected their telephone, or otherwise suggest that they have gone out of business.

Places which have moved, and don't bother to send us their new address; we have not the staff to try to track them down.

Places which our readers lodge complaints against, with us, as being either unhelpful or obnoxious. The complaints may be falsified, but we can't take that chance.

Places which change their personnel, and the new person has never even heard of *Parachute*, or creative job-search techniques.

Places which misuse their listing here, claiming in their brochures, ads, or interviews, that they have some kind of 'Parachute Seal of Approval,' -- that we feature them in *Parachute*, or recommend them or endorse them. This is a big 'no-no.' A listing here is no more of a recommendation than is a listing in the phone book.

College services that we discover (belatedly) serve only 'Their Own.'

Counseling firms which employ salespeople as the initial 'in-take' person that a job-hunter meets.

If you discover that any of the places listed in this Sampler falls into any of the above categories, you would be doing a great service to our other readers by dropping us a line and telling us so. (P.O. Box 379, Walnut Creek, CA 94597.)

The listings which follow are alphabetical within each state, except that counselors listed by their name are in alphabetical order according to their *last* name. To make this clear, only their last name is in **bold** type.

What do the letters after their name mean? Well, B.A., M.A., and Ph.D. you know. However, don't assume that degree is in career counseling. Ask. N.C.C. means "Nationally certified counselor." There are about 20,000 such in the U.S. This can mean *general counseling expertise*, not necessarily career counseling. On the other hand, N.C.C.C. does mean "Nationally certified career counselor." There are currently about 850 in the U.S. Other initials, such as L.P.C. -- "Licensed professional counselor" -- and the like, often refer to State licensing. There are a number of States, now, that have some sort of regulation of career counselors. In some States it is mandatory, in others it is optional. But, *mostly*, this field is unregulated.

Sharp-eyed readers (and professional proofreaders) will note that there is no uniform *form* to the degrees, or to the addresses below (sometimes, for example, you will see *Avenue*, sometimes *Ave.*). This is because we have tried to list their degrees and addresses the way *they* want them to be listed, rather than imposing one uniform style upon all.

Incidentally, the places listed offer a variety of services, which we have not space to list: for example, some offer group career counseling, some offer testing, some offer access to job-banks, etc.

Generally speaking, these places counsel *anybody*. A few, however, take only women as clients, or have other restrictions unknown to us. So you must ask if they will take you. If they aren't able to help you, your phone call wasn't wasted, *so long as* you then go on to ask them "who else in the area can you tell me about, who helps with job-search, and are there any (among them) that you think are particularly effective?"

If you are looking for places which specialize in doing career counseling from a religious point of view, these are listed separately at the end of The Epilogue, "How To Find Your Mission in Life," on page 464. However, many of the counselors listed below also are people of faith.

ALABAMA

Enterprise State Junior College, P.O. Box 1300, Enterprise, AL 36331. 205-347-2623 or 393-ESJC. Nancy Smith, Director of Guidance Services.

Interchange, 2 Perimeter Park S., Suite 200W, Birmingham, AL 35243. 205-324-5030. Michael Tate, Vice-President.

Joseph G. **Law**, Jr., Ed.D., L.P.C., 900 Western America Circle, Suite 501, Executive Center 1, Mobile, AL 36609. 205-341-0600.

ALASKA

Career Transitions, 2221 East Northern Lights Boulevard, Suite 207, Anchorage, AL 99508. 907-278-7350. Deeta Lonergan, Director.

ARIZONA

College PLUS Career Connections, 4540 S. Rural Rd., #P-8, Tempe, AZ 85282. 602-730-5246. Dr. Warren D. Robb, Director.

Debra Davenport Associates, 6619 N. Scottsdale, Scottsdale, AZ 85250. 602-391-2802. Debra Davenport, M.A., L.C.C.

NewStart Career Counseling Services, 3080 N. Civic Center Plaza, Scottsdale, AZ 85251. 602-947-3311. Sheila Iosty.

Southwest Institute of Life Management, 11122 E. Gunshot Circle, Tucson, AZ 85749. 602-749-2290. Theodore Donald Risch, Director.

Tucson/Pima County Job Club, 110 E. Pennington, Lower Level, Tucson, AZ 85701. 602-884-8280. *(Their mailing address, should you need it, is 2510 North Winstel Boulevard, #184, Tucson, AZ 85716-2350.)* Stuart R. Thomas, President/Founder.

ARKANSAS

Donald **McKinney**, Ed.D., Career Counselor, Rt. 1, Box 351-A, DeQueen, AR 71832. 501-642-5628.

CALIFORNIA

Alumnae Resources, 120 Montgomery St., Suite 1080, San Francisco, CA 94104. 415-274-4700.

Judy Kaplan **Baron Associates**, 6046 Cornerstone Ct. West, Suite 208, San Diego, CA 92121. 619-558-7400. Judy Kaplan Baron, Director.

Astrid **Berg**, M.S., Career and Life Planning, P.O. Box 1686, Capitola, CA 95010. 408-462-4626.

Dwayne **Berrett**, M.A., Center for Counseling and Therapy, 6245 N. Fresno St., Ste. 106, Fresno, CA 93710. 209-431-5893.

Beverly **Brown**, M.A., N.C.C.C., N.C.C. 809 So. Bundy Drive, #105, Los Angeles, CA 90049. 310-447-7093.

Career Action Center, 445 Sherman Ave., Palo Alto, CA 94306. 415-324-1710. Betsy Collard, Program Director, Linda Surrell, Manager, Counseling Services. *One of the largest career centers in the country, with a very impressive number of job listings (81,000) and other resources, including individual counseling, workshops, books, videos, etc.*

Career and Personal Development Institute, 690 Market St., Suite 402, San Francisco, CA 94104. 415-982-2636. Bob Chope.

Career Decisions, 760 Market St., Suite 962, San Francisco CA 94102-2304. 415-296-7373. Mark Pope, Ed.D., NCC, NCCC.

Career Development Center, John F. Kennedy University, 1250 Arroyo Way, Walnut Creek, CA 94596. 510-295-0610. Susan Geifman, Director. *Open to the public.*

Career Development Life Planning, 3585 Maple St., Suite 237, Ventura, CA 93003. 805-656-6220. Norma Zuber, N.C.C.C., M.S.C., & Associates.

Career Dimensions, Box 7402, Stockton, CA 95267. 209-473-8255. Fran Abbott.

Career Directions, 215 Witham Road, Encinitas CA 92024. 619-436-3994. Virginia Byrd, M.Ed., Career Consultant.

Career Planning Center/Business Action Center, 1623 S. La Cienega Blvd., Los Angeles, CA 90035. 310-273-6633.

Career Strategy Associates, 1100 Quail Street, Suite 201, Newport Beach, CA 92660. 714-252-0515. Betty Fisher.

The **Center for Life & Career Development**, 655 University Ave., Suite 127, Sacramento, CA 95825. 916-646-3414. Dr. Fran A. Epstein.

The **Center for Life and Work Planning**, 1133 Second St., Encinitas, CA 92024. 619-943-0747. Mary C. McIsaac, Executive Director.

Stephen **Cheney-Rice**, M.S., 2113 Westboro Ave., Alhambra, CA 91803-3720. 818-281-6066 or 213-740-9112.

Constructive Leisure, Patsy B. Edwards, 511 N. La Cienega Blvd., Los Angeles, CA 90048. 310-652-7389.

Consultants in Career Development, 2017 Palo Verde Ave., Suite 201B, Long Beach, CA 90815. 310-598-6412. Dean Porter and Mary Claire Gildon.

Criket Consultants, 502 Natoma St., P.O. Box 6191, Folsom, CA 95763-6191. 916-985-3211.

Cypress College, Career Planning Center, 9200 Valley View St., Cypress, CA 90630. 714-826-2220, Ext. 120.

Margaret L. **Eadie**, M.A., A.M.Ed., WHAT NEXT Education and Career Consultant, 1000 Sage Pl., Pacific Grove, CA 93050. 408-373-7400.

Experience Unlimited Job Club. There are 35 Experience Unlimited Clubs in California, found at the Employment Development Department in the following locations: Anaheim, Corona, El Cajon, Escondido, Fremont, Fresno, Hemet, Hollywood, Lancaster, Monterey, North Hollywood, Oakland, Ontario, Pasadena, Pleasant Hill, Redlands, Ridgecrest, Riverside, Sacramento (Midtown and South), San Bernardino, San Diego (also East and South), San Francisco, San Mateo, San Rafael, Santa Ana, Santa Cruz, Santa Maria, Simi Valley, Sunnyvale, Torrance, Victorville, and West Covina. Contact the club nearest to you through your local Employment Development Department (E.D.D.).

Mary Alice **Floyd**, M.A., N.C.C., Career Counselor/Consultant, Career Life Transitions. 3233 Lucinda Lane, Santa Barbara, CA 93105. 805-687-5462.

Futures . . ., 103 Calvin Place, Santa Cruz, CA 95060. 408-425-0332. Joseph Reimuller.

Marvin F. **Galper**, Ph.D., 3939 Third Ave., Suite 204, San Diego, CA 92103. 619-295-4450.

Judith **Grutter**, M.S., Career Development Counselor/Consultant, 130 S. Euclid Ave., Suite #5, Pasadena, CA 91101. 818-795-3883. Office also at South Lake Tahoe: Post Office Box 7855, South Lake Tahoe, CA 96158. 916-541-8587.

Life's Decisions, 1917 Lowland Ct., Carmichael CA 95608. 916-486-0677. Joan E. Belshin, M.S., N.C.C.C.

Susan W. **Miller**, M.A., 6363 Wilshire Blvd., Suite 210, Los Angeles CA 90048. 213-651-5514.

Sacramento Women's Center, Women's Employment Services and Training (WEST) for income-eligible women, 1924 "T" St., Sacramento, CA 95814. 916-736-6942.

Saddleback College, Counseling Services and Special Programs, 28000 Marguerite Pkwy., Mission Viejo, CA 92692. 714-582-4571. Jan Fritsen, Counselor.

George H. **Schofield**, 1529 Hearst Ave., Berkeley, CA 94703. 510-704-9406.

Stoodley & Associates, 1434 Willowmont Ave., San Jose, CA 95118. 408-448-3691. Martha Stoodley, M.S., M.F.C.C., President.

Transitions Counseling Center, 171 N. Van Ness, Fresno, CA 93701. 209-233-7250. Margot E. Tepperman, L.C.S.W.

Turning Point Career Center, University YWCA, 2600 Bancroft Way, Berkeley, CA 94704. 510-848-6370. Winnie Froehlich, M.S., Director.

Caroline **Voorsanger**, Career Counselor for Women, 1650 Jackson St., #608, San Francisco, CA 94115. 415-567-0890.

Patti **Wilson**, P.O. Box 35633, Los Gatos, CA 95030. 408-354-1964.

Women at Work, 50 N. Hill Ave., Pasadena, CA 91106. 818-796-6870.

COLORADO

Samuel **Kirk and Associates**, Central Office, 1418 S. Race, Denver, CO 80210. 303-722-0717.

Patricia **O'Keefe**, M.A., 350 Cook St., Denver, CO 80206. 303-393-8747.

Resource Center, Arapahoe Community College, 2500 West College Dr., P.O. Box 9002, Littleton, CO 80160-9002. 303-797-5805.

Women's Resource Agency, 1018 N. Weber, Colorado Springs, CO 80903. 719-471-3170.

CONNECTICUT

Accord Career Services, The Exchange, Suite 305, 270 Farmington Ave., Farmington, CT 06032. 203-674-9654. Tod Gerardo, M.S., President and Director.

Associated Counseling Professionals, Career Development Division, 415 Silas Deane Hwy., Suite 224, Wethersfield, CT 06109-2119. 203-296-5523 or toll-free in CT, 1-800-654-4320. John H. Wiedenheft, M.A., Clinical Director.

Career Choices/RFP Associates, 141 Durham Rd., Suite 24, Madison, CT 06443. 203-245-4123.

Career Services Inc., 94 Rambling Rd., Vernon, CT 06066. 203-871-7832. Jim Cohen, Ph.D., C.R.C.

Fairfield Adult Career & Educational Services, Fairfield University, Dolan House, Fairfield, CT 06430. 203-254-4110.

Ilise Gold Life Management, L.L.C., P.O. Box 2514, 56 Post Rd. W., Westport, CT 06880. 203-454-3745.

People Management, Inc., This used to be headquartered in Connecticut; it is now in *Washington State*. Look there for its current listing.

The Offerjost-Westcott Group, 263 Main St., Old Saybrook, CT 06475. 203-388-6094. Russ Westcott.

Vocational and Academic Counseling for Adults (VOCA), 115 Berrian Rd., Stamford, CT 06905. 203-322-8353. Ruth A. Polster.

DELAWARE

YWCA of New Castle County, Women's Center for Economic Options, 233 King St., Wilmington, DE 19801. 302-658-7161.

DISTRICT OF COLUMBIA

Community Vocational Counseling Service, The George Washington University Counseling Center, 718 21st St. NW, Washington, DC 20052. 202-994-4860. Robert J. Wilson, M.S., Asst. Director for Educational Services.

George Washington University, Center for Career Education, 2020 K Street, Washington, DC 20052. 202-994-5299. Abigail Pereira, Director.

Horizons Unlimited Inc., 1133 15th St. N.W., Suite 1200, Washington, DC 20005. 202-296-7224. Marilyn Goldman, NCCC.

FLORIDA

The **Career and Personal Counseling Center**, Eckerd College, 4200 54th Ave. South, St. Petersburg, FL 33711. 813-864-8356. John R. Sims.

Career Consultants of America, Inc., 2701 W. Busch Blvd., Suite 111, Tampa, FL 33618. 813-933-4088. Michael Shahnasarian, Ph.D., Executive Director.

Career Moves, Inc., 5300 North Federal Highway, Fort Lauderdale, FL 33308. 305-772-6857. Mary Jane Ward, M.Ed., NCC, NCCC.

Center for Career Decisions, 980 N. Federal Hwy., Suite 203, Boca Raton, FL 33432. 407-394-3399. Linda Friedman, M.A., N.C.C., N.C.C.C., Director.

The Women's Center, Valencia Community College, 1010 N. Orlando Ave., Winter Park, FL 32789. 407-628-1976.

Centre for Women, 305 S. Hyde Park Ave., Tampa, FL 33606. 813-251-8437. Stacy Clark, Employment Counselor.

Chabon & Associates, 1665 Palm Beach Lakes Blvd., Suite 402, West Palm Beach, FL 33401. 407-640-8443. Toby G. Chabon, M.Ed., N.C.C., President.

The Challenge: Program for Displaced Homemakers, Florida Community College at Jacksonville, 101 W. State St., Jacksonville, FL 32202. 904-633-8316. Rita Patrick, Project Coordinator.

Colonial Clinic, 1155 South Semoran Boulevard, Suite 1139, Building 3, Winter Park, FL 32792. 407-657-8488. Neal A. Carter, Ph.D., Career/Life Specialist.

Crossroads, Palm Beach Community College, 4200 Congress Ave., Lake Worth, FL 33461-4796. 407-433-5995. Pat Jablonski, Program Manager.

Larry **Harmon**, Ph.D., Career Counseling Center, Inc., 2000 South Dixie Highway, Suite 103, Miami, FL 33133. 305-858-8557.

Ellen O. **Jonassen**, Ph.D., 10785 Ulmerton Rd., Largo, FL 34648. 813-581-8526.

Life Designs, Inc., 7860 SW 55th Ave. #A, South Miami, FL 33143. 305-665-3212. Dulce Muccio and Deborah Tyson, co-founders.

New Beginnings, Polk Community College, Station 71, 999 Avenue H, NE, Winter Haven, FL 33881-4299 (Lakeland Campus). 813-297-1029.

Resource Center for Women, formerly FACE Learning Center, Inc., 12945 Seminole Blvd., Bldg. II, Suite 6, Largo, FL 34648. 813-585-8155 or 586-1110.

WINGS Program, Broward Community College, 1000 Coconut Creek Blvd., Coconut Creek, FL 33066. 305-973-2398.

GEORGIA

Emmette H. **Albea**, Jr., M.S., LPC, NCCC, 2706 Melrose Drive, Valdosta, GA 31602. 912-241-0908.

D & B Consulting, 2221 Peachtree Road, NE, Suite D-421, Atlanta, GA 30309. 404-874-9379. Deborah R. Brown, MSM, MSW, Career Consultant.

Jewish Vocational Service, 1100 Spring St., Suite 700, Atlanta, GA 30309. 404-876-5872. Anna Blau, Acting Executive Director.

The **Mulling Group**, 990 Hammond Drive, Suite 900, Atlanta, GA 30328. 404-395-3131. Harvey Brickley, Consultant.

St. Jude's Job Network, St. Jude's Catholic Church, 7171 Glenridge Dr., Sandy Springs, GA 30328. 404-393-4578.

Mark **Satterfield**, 5262 Walker Rd., Stone Mountain, GA 30088. 404-469-3462.

HAWAII

No listings.

ILLINOIS

Career Path, 3033 Ogden Ave., Suite 203, Lisle, IL 60532. 708-369-3390. Donna Sandberg, M.A., Owner/Counselor.

Career Workshops, 5431 W. Roscoe St., Chicago, IL 60641. 312-282-6859. Patricia Dietze.

Jean **Davis**, Adult Career Transitions, 1405 Elmwood Ave., Evanston, IL 60201. 708-492-1002.

Barbara Kabcenell **Grauer**, M.A., N.C.C., 1370 Sheridan Road, Highland Park, IL 60035. 708-432-4479.

Grimard Wilson Consulting, 111 N. Wabash Ave., Suite 1006, Chicago, IL 60602. 312-201-1142. Diane Grimard **Wilson**, M.A.

Harper College Career Transition Center, Building A, Room 124, Palatine, IL 60067. 708-459-8233. Mary Ann Jirak, Coordinator.

David P. **Helfand**, Ed.D., N.C.C.C., 250 Ridge, Evanston, IL 60202. 708-328-2787.

Lansky Career Consultants, 500 N. Michigan Ave., Suite 430, Chicago, IL 60611. 312-494-0022. Judi Lansky, President.

Midwest Women's Center, 828 S. Wabash, Suite 200, Chicago, IL 60605. 312-922-8530.

Moraine Valley Community College, Job Placement Center, 10900 S. 88th Ave., Palos Hills, IL 60465. 708-974-5737.

Right Livelyhood$, 23 W. 402 Green Briar Drive, Naperville, IL 60540. 708-369-9066, Marti Beddoe, Career/Life Counselor, or 312-281-7274, Peter LeBrun.

Jane **Shuman**, Career Management Consultant, 1S 283 Danby, Villa Park, IL 60181. 708-916-7754.

Widmer & Associates, 1510 W. Sunnyview Dr., Peoria, IL 61614. 309-691-3312. Mary F. Widmer, President.

INDIANA

Career Consultants, 107 N. Pennsylvania St., Suite 400, Indianapolis, IN 46204. 317-639-5601. Al Milburn, Career Management Consultant.

Sally **Jones**, Program Coordinator/Developer, Indiana University, School of Continuing Studies, Owen Hall, Room 202, Bloomington IN 47405. 812-855-4991.

KCDM Associates, 10401 N. Meridian St., Suite 300, Indianapolis, IN 46290. 317-581-6230. Mike Kenney.

John D. **King & Associates**, Career Counseling and Consulting, 205 N. College, Suite 614, Bloomington, IN 47404. 812-332-3888.

William R. **Lesch**, M.S., Career & Life Planning, Health Associates, 9240 N. Meridian St., Suite 292, Indianapolis, IN 46260. 317-844-7489.

IOWA

Rosanne **Beers**, Beers Consulting, 5505 Boulder Dr., West Des Moines, Iowa 50266. 515-225-1245.

Jill **Sudak-Allison**, 3219 SE 19th Court, Des Moines, IA 50320. 515-282-5040.

University of Iowa, Center for Career Development and Cooperative Education, 315 Calvin Hall, Iowa City, IA 52242. 319-335-3201.

Suzanne **Zilber**, 801 Crystal St., Ames, IA 50010. 515-232-9379.

KANSAS

Leigh **Branham**, Right Associates, 6201 College Blvd., Suite 360, Overland Park, KS 66211. 913-451-1100.

KENTUCKY

OI/Ronniger, Career Consultants, The Summit II, 4360 Brownsboro Rd., Louisville, KY 40207. 502-894-9400. Phillip Ronniger.

LOUISIANA

Career Planning and Assessment Center, Metropolitan College, University of New Orleans, New Orleans, LA 70148. 504-286-7100.

MAINE

Career Perspectives, 75 Pearl Street, Suite 204, Portland, ME 04101. 207-775-4487. Deborah L. Gallant.

Heart at Work, 78 Main St., Yarmouth, ME 04096. 207-846-0644. Barbara Sirois Babkirk, M.Ed., N.C.C., L.C.P.C., Licensed Counselor and Consultant.

Women's Worth Career Counseling, 18 Woodland Rd., Gorham, ME 04038. 207-892-0000. Jacqueline Murphy, Counselor.

MARYLAND

Careerscope, Inc., One Mall North, Suite 216, 1025 Governor Warfield Pkwy., Columbia, MD 21044. 410-992-5042 or 301-596-1866. Constantine Bitsas, Executive Director.

Career Transition Services, 3126 Berkshire Rd., Baltimore MD 21214-3404. 410-444-5857. Michael Bryant.

College of Notre Dame of Maryland, Continuing Education Center, 4701 N. Charles St., Baltimore, MD 21210. 410-532-5303.

Goucher College, Goucher Center for Continuing Studies, 1021 Dulaney Valley Rd., Baltimore, MD 21204. 410-337-6200. Carole B. Ellin, Career/Job-Search Counselor.

Maryland New Directions, Inc., 2220 N. Charles St., Baltimore, MD 21218. 410-235-8800. Rose Marie Coughlin, Director.

Prince George's Community College, Career Assessment and Planning Center, 301 Largo Rd., Largo, MD 20772. 301-322-0886. Margaret Taibi, Ph.D., Director.

TransitionWorks, 7812 Mary Cassatt Drive, Potomac, MD 20854. Stephanie Kay, M.A., A.G.S., Principal, 301-983-1128. Nancy K. Schlossberg, ED.D., Principal, 202-298-6973.

MASSACHUSETTS

Affordable Counseling, 29 Leicester St., Brighton, MA 02135. 617-783-1717. Carl Schneider. Carl also provides low-cost individual and group psychotherapy for job-hunters who have conflicts that interfere with their job-hunt.

Career Link, Career Information Center, Frederic C. Adams Public Library, 33 Summer St., Kingston, MA 02364. 617-585-0517. Free videos, audiocassettes, and books on job search, plus computerized career guidance (SIGI), public access computer, and workshops. Kathleen Glynn.

Career Management Consultants, Thirty Park Ave., Worcester, MA 01605. 508-853-8669. Patricia M. Stepanski, President.

Career Resource Center, Worcester YWCA, 1 Salem Square, Worcester, MA 01608. 508-791-3181.

Center for Career Development & Ministry, 70 Chase St., Newton Center, MA 02159. 617-969-7750. Stephen Ott, Director.

Center for Careers, Jewish Vocational Service, 105 Chauncy St., 6th Fl., Boston, MA 02111. 617-451-8147. Lee Ann Bennett, Coordinator, Core Services.

Jewish Vocational Service, Mature Worker Programs, 333 Nahanton St., Newton, MA 02159. 617-965-7940.

Wynne W. **Miller**, 785 Centre St., Newton, MA 02158-2599. 617-527-4848.

Linkage, Inc., 110 Hartwell Ave., Lexington MA 02173. 617-862-4030. David J. Giber, Ph.D.

Murray Associates, P.O. Box 312, Westwood, MA 02090. 617-329-1287. Robert Murray, Ed.D., Licensed Psychologist.

Neville Associates, Inc., 10 Tower Office Park, Suite 416, Woburn, MA 01801. 617-938-7870. Dr. Joseph Neville, Career Development Consultant.

Radcliffe Career Services (open to the general public), 77 Brattle St., Cambridge MA 02138. 617-495-8631.

Suit Yourself International, Inc., 115 Shade St., Lexington, MA 02173-7724. 617-862-6006. Debra Spencer, President.

Women's Educational & Industrial Union, Career Services, 356 Boylston St., Boston, MA 02116. 617-536-5657.

MICHIGAN

New Options: Counseling for Women in Transition, 2311 E. Stadium, Suite B-2, Ann Arbor, MI 48104. 313-973-0003. Phyllis Perry, M.S.W.

Lansing Community College, 2020 Career and Employment Development Services, PO Box 40010, Lansing, MI 48901-7210. 517-483-1221 or 483-1172. James C. Osborn, Ph.D., L.P.C., Director, Career and Employment Services.

Oakland University, Continuum Center for Adult Counseling and Leadership Training, Rochester, MI 48309. 313-370-3033.

University of Michigan, Center for the Education of Women, 330 East Liberty, Ann Arbor, MI 48104. 313-998-7080.

Women's Resource Center, 252 State St. SE, Grand Rapids, MI 49503. 616-458-5443.

MINNESOTA

Richard E. **Andrea**, Ph.D., Titan Office Park, Suite 202A, 1399 Geneva Ave., Oakdale, MN 55119. 612-738-6600.

Associated Career Services, 3550 Lexington Ave. N., Suite 120, Shoreview, MN 55126. 612-787-0501.

Career Dynamics, Inc., 8400 Normandale Lake Blvd., Suite 1220, Bloomington, MN 55437. 612-921-2378. Joan Strewler, Psychologist.

Human Dynamics, 3036 Ontario Rd., Little Canada, MN 55117. 612-484-8299. Greg J. Cylkowski, M.A., founder.

Stanley J. **Sizen**, Vocational Services, P.O. Box 363, Anoka, MN 55303. 612-441-8053.

Working Opportunities for Women, 2700 University Ave., #120, St. Paul, MN 55114. 612-647-9961.

MISSISSIPPI

Mississippi State University, Career Services Center, P.O. Box P, Colvard Union, Suite 316, Mississippi State, MS 39762-5515. 601-325-3344.

Mississippi Gulf Coast Community College, Jackson County Campus, Career Development Center, P.O. Box 100, Gautier, MS 39553. 601-497-9602. Rebecca Williams, Manager.

MISSOURI

Career Center, Community Career Services, 110 Noyes Hall, University of Missouri, Columbia, MO 65211. 314-882-6803.

Women's Center, University of Missouri–Kansas City, 5100 Rockhill Rd., 104 Scofield Hall, Kansas City, MO 64110. 816-235-1638.

MONTANA

No listings.

NEBRASKA

Career Management Services, 5000 Central Park Dr., Suite 204, Lincoln, NE 68504. 402-466-8427. Vaughn L. Carter, President.

Olson Counseling Services, 8720 Frederick, Suite 105, Omaha, NE 68128. 402-390-2342. Gail A. Olson, P.A.C.

Student Success Center, Central Community College, Hastings Campus, Hastings, NE 68902. 402-461-2424.

NEVADA

No listings.

NEW HAMPSHIRE

Individual Employment Services, 90-A Sixth St., P.O. 917, Dover, NH 03820. 603-742-5616. James Otis, Employment Counselor.

NEW JERSEY

Adult Advisory Service, Kean College of New Jersey, Administration Bldg., Union, NJ 07083. 908-527-2210.

Adult Resource Center, 100 Horseneck Road, Montville, NJ 07045. 201-335-6910.

Arista Concepts Career Development Service, P.O. Box 2436, Princeton, NJ 08540. 609-921-0308. Kera Greene, M.Ed.

Behavior Dynamics Associates, Inc., 34 Cambridge Terrace, Springfield, NJ 07081. 201-912-0136. Roy Hirschfeld.

Career Options Center, YWCA Tribute to Women and Industry (TWIN) Program, 232 E. Front St., Plainfield, NJ 07060. 908-756-3836, or 908-273-4242. Janet M. Korba, Program Director.

Loree **Collins**, 3 Beechwood Rd., Summit, NJ 07901. 908-273-9219.

Douglass College, Douglass Advisory Services for Women, Rutgers Women's Center, 132 George St., New Brunswick, NJ 08903. 908-932-9603.

Sandra **Grundfest**, Ed.D., Princeton Professional Park, 601 Ewing St., Suite C-1, Princeton, NJ 08540. 609-921-8401. Also at 11 Clyde Rd., Suite 103, Somerset, NJ 08873. 908-873-1212.

Job Seekers of Montclair, St. Luke's Episcopal Church, 73 S. Fortune, Montclair NJ. 201-783-3442. Meets Thursdays 7:30–9:30 p.m.

Lester **Minsuk & Associates**, 29 Exeter Rd., East Windsor, NJ 08520. 609-448-4600.

W.L. **Nikel & Associates**, Career Development and Outplacement, 28 Harper Terrace, Cedar Grove, NJ 07009. 201-239-7460. William L. Nikel, M.B.A., Founder.

The **Professional Roster**, 171 Broadmead, Princeton, NJ 08540. 609-921-9561.

NEW MEXICO

Young Women's Christian Association, YWCA Career Services Center, 7201 Paseo Del Norte NE, Albuquerque, NM 87113. 505-822-9922.

NEW YORK

Alan B. **Bernstein** CSW, PC, 122 East 82nd St., N.Y., NY 10028. 212-288-4881.

Career Agenda, Inc., 560 West 43rd St.,, New York, NY 10036. 212-595-9226 or 268-0564. Carol Allen, President.

Career Development Center, Long Island University, C.W. Post Campus, Brookville, NY 11548. 516-299-2251. Pamela Lennox, Ph.D., Director.

Career Development Services, 14 Franklin St., Temple Bldg., Suite 1200, Rochester, NY 14604. 716-325-2274.

The John C. **Crystal Center,** 152 Madison Ave., 23rd Fl., New York, NY 10016. 212-889-8500 or 1-800-333-9003. Nella G. Barkley, President. *(John died in 1988; Nella was his business partner, for many years preceding his death, and now carries on his work. The Center also has offices in Chicago and Los Angeles, run under the aegis of The Crystal-Barkley Corporation. The 800 number above will work for reaching all three centers.)*

Susan **Hadley,** Career and Life/Work Planning Consultant, 59 Jefferson St., Nyack, NY 10960. 914-353-0579.

Hofstra University, Career Counseling Center, Room 120, Saltzman Community Center, 131 Hofstra, Hempstead, NY 11550. 516-463-6788.

Kingsborough Community College, Office of Career Counseling and Placement, 2001 Oriental Blvd., Rm. C102, Brooklyn, NY 11235. 718-368-5115.

Irene **Komor,** M.Ed., N.C.C., Career Counselor, 125 Muriel St., Ithaca, NY 14850. 607-257-9462.

Janice **La Rouche** Assoc., 333 Central Park W., New York, NY 10025. 212-663-0970.

Livelyhood Job Search Center, 301 Madison Ave., 3rd Floor, New York, NY 10017. 212-687-2411. John Aigner, Director.

New Options, 960 Park Ave., New York, NY 10028. 212-535-1444.

Orange County Community College, Counseling Center, 115 South St., Middletown, NY 10940. 914-341-4070.

Celia **Paul Associates,** 1776 Broadway, Suite 1806, New York, NY 10019. 212-397-1020.

Leslie B. **Prager,** M.A., The Prager-Bernstein Group, 441 Lexington Avenue, Suite 1404, New York, NY 10017. 212-697-0645.

Personnel Sciences Center, Inc., 276 Fifth Ave., Suite 704, New York, NY 10001. 212-683-3008. Dr. Jeffrey A. Goldberg.

Schenectady Public Library, Job Information Center, 99 Clinton St., Schenectady, NY. Has weekly listings, including job search listings of companies nationwide.

L. Michelle **Tullier,** Ph.D., Career Counselor. Virginia J. Bush & Associates, 444 E. 86th St., New York, NY 10028. 212-772-3244.

WIN Workshops (Women in Networking), Emily Koltnow, 1120 Avenue of the Americas, Fourth Floor, New York, NY 10036. 212-333-8788.

NORTH CAROLINA

Career Consulting Associates of Raleigh, P.O. Box 17653, Raleigh, NC 27619. 919-782-3252. Susan W. Simonds, President.

Career, Educational, Psychological Evaluations, 2915 Providence Rd., Suite 300, Charlotte, NC 28211. 704-362-1942.

Career Management Center, 3203 Woman's Club Drive, Suite 100, Raleigh, NC 27612. 919-787-1222, ext. 109. Temple G. Porter, Director.

Sally **Kochendofer,** Ph.D., P.O. Box 1180, Cornelius, NC 28031. 704-892-4976.

Diane E. **Lambeth,** M.S.W., Career Consultant. P.O. Box 18945, Raleigh, NC 27619. 919-571-7423.

Joyce **Richman & Associates, Ltd.,** 2911 Shady Lawn Dr., Greensboro, NC 27408. 910-288-1799.

Bonnie M. **Truax,** Ed.D., N.C.C.C., Career/ Life Planning and Relocation Services, 2102 N. Elm St., Suite K1, Greensboro, NC 27408. 910-271-2050. *Free support group.*

Women's Center of Raleigh,128 E. Hargett St., Suite 10, Raleigh, NC 27601. 919-829-3711.

NORTH DAKOTA

No listings.

OHIO

Adult Resource Center, The University of Akron, Buckingham Center for Continuing Education, Room 55, Akron, OH 44325-3102. 216-972-7448. Sandra B. Edwards, Director.

Career Initiatives Center, 1557 E. 27th St., Cleveland, OH 44114. 216-574-8998. Richard Hanscom, Director.

Cuyahoga County Public Library InfoPLACE Service, Career, Education & Community Information Service, 5225 Library Lane, Maple Heights, OH 44137-1291. 216-475-2225.

Hill & Hill Consulting, Inc., 393 Hawthorne Lane N.E., Warren, OH 44484. 216-856-4440. Barbara H. Hill, President.

J&K Associates, Inc., 607 Otterbein Ave., Dayton, OH 45406-4507. 513-274-3630. Pat Kenney, Ph.D., President.

New Career, 328 Race St., Dover, OH 44622. 216-364-5557. Marshall Karp, M.A., N.C.C., L.P.C., Owner.

Pyramid Career Services, Inc., 2400 Cleveland Ave., NW, Canton, OH 44709. 216-453-3767. Zandra Bloom, Director.

OKLAHOMA

Career Development Services, 5314 S. Yale, Suite 600, Tulsa, OK 74135. 918-495-1788. William D. Young, Ed.D.

OREGON

Career Development, PO Box 5099, Beaverton, OR 97006. 503-357-9233. Edward H. Hosley, Ph.D., Director.

Joseph A. **Dubay**, 425 NW 18th Avenue, Portland, OR 97209. 503-226-2656.

Marcia **Perkins-Reed & Associates**, 11830 SW Kerr Parkway, Suite 304, Lake Oswego, OR 97035. 503-245-2283.

Marion Bass **Stevens**, Ph.D., 2631 E. Congress Way, Medford, OR 97504. 503-773-3373.

Verk Consultants, Inc., 1441 Oak St., #7, P.O. Box 11277, Eugene, OR 97440. 503-687-9170. Larry H. Malmgren, M.S., C.R.C., President.

PENNSYLVANIA

Career by Design, 1011 Cathill Rd., Sellersville, PA 18960. 215-723-8413. Henry D. Landes, Career Consultant.

Career Development Center, Jewish Family & Children's Center, 5737 Darlington Road, Pittsburgh, PA 15217. 412-422-5627. Linda Ehrenreich, Director.

Career Management Consultants, Inc., 3207 N. Front St., Harrisburg, PA 17110. 717-233-2272. Louis F. Persico, Career Consultant.

Center for Adults in Transition, Bucks County Community College, Newtown, PA 18940. 215-968-8188.

Center for Career Services (CCS), 1845 Walnut Street, 7th floor, Philadelphia, PA 19103-4707. 215-854-1800. William A. Hyman, Director. Lucy Borosh, Aviva Gal, Tracey Tanenbaum, Career Counselors.

The **Creative Living Center**, 1388 Freeport Road, Pittsburgh, PA 15238. 412-963-8765. David R. Johnson, Director.

Options, Inc., 225 S. 15th St., Philadelphia, PA 19102. 215-735-2202. Marcia P. Kleiman, Director.

Priority Two, P.O. Box 343, Sewickley, PA 15143. 412-935-0252. *Six locations in the Pittsburgh area; call for addresses.* Pat Gottschalk, Administrative Assistant.

RHODE ISLAND

Career Designs, 120 Moore St., Providence, RI 02907. 401-521-2323. Terence Duniho, Career Consultant.

SOUTH CAROLINA

Career Counselor Services, Inc., 25 Woods Lake Road, Suite 324, Greenville, SC 29607. 803-370-9453. Al A. Hafer, Ed.D., N.C.C.C., N.C.C., L.P.C.

Greenville Technical College, Career Advancement Center, P.O. Box 5616, Greenville, SC 29606. 803-250-8281. F.M. Rogers, Director.

SOUTH DAKOTA

Career Concepts Planning Center, Inc., 1602 Mountain View Rd., Suite 102, Rapid City, SD 57702. 605-342-5177, toll free: 1-800-456-0832. Melvin M. Tuggle, Jr., President.

Sioux Falls College, The Center for Women, 1501 South Prairie, Glidden Hall, Sioux Falls, SD 57105. 605-331-6697.

TENNESSEE

Career Resources, 2323 Hillsboro Rd., Suite 508, Nashville, TN 37212. 615-297-0404. Jane C. Hardy, Principal/Career Counselor.

Mid-South Career Development Center, 2315 Fisher Place, Knoxville, TN 37920. 615-573-1340. W. Scott Root, President/Counselor.

S.O.S. (Secretarial Office Services), 314 N. White St., Athens, TN 37303. 615-745-4513. Adelia Wyner, Consultant.

TEXAS

Career Action Associates, 12655 N. Central Expressway, Suite 821, Dallas, TX 75243. 214-392-7337. Joyce Shoop, L.P.C. Office also at 1325 8th Avenue, Ft. Worth, TX 76112. 817-926-9941. Rebecca Hayes, L.P.C.

Career Management Resources, 222 W. Las Colinas, Suite #2114, Irving, TX 75039; 214-556-0786. Mary Holdcroft, M.Ed., L.P.C., N.C.C.

Richard S. Citrin, Ph.D., Psychologist, Iatreia Institute, 1152 Country Club Ln., Ft. Worth, TX 76112. 817-654-9600.

Counseling Services of Houston, 1964 W. Gray, Suite 204, Houston, TX 77019. 713-521-9391. Rosemary C. Vienot, M.S., Licensed Professional Counselor, Director.

Employment/Career Information Resource Center, Corpus Christi Public Library, 805 Comanche, Corpus Christi, TX 78401. 512-880-7004. Lynda F. Whitton-Henley, Career Information Specialist.

Maydelle Fason, Employment Consultant, 1607 Poquonock Road, Austin, TX 78703. 512-474-1185.

New Directions Counseling Center, 8140 North Mopac, Bldg. II, Suite 230, Austin, TX 78759. 512-343-9496. Jeanne Quereau, M.A., Licensed Professional Counselor.

New Life Institute, 1203 Lavaca, Austin, TX 78701-1831. 512-469-9447. Bob Breihan, Director.

San Antonio Psychological Services, 6800 Park Ten Blvd., Suite 208 North, San Antonio, TX 78213. 210-737-2039.

Mary Stedham, Counseling/Consulting Services, 2434 S. 10th, Abilene, TX 79605. 915-672-4044.

VGS, Inc. (Vocational Guidance Service), 2600 S.W. Freeway, Suite 800, Houston, TX 77098. 713-535-7104. Beverley K. Finn, Director.

UTAH

University of Utah, Center for Adult Development, 1195 Annex Bldg., Salt Lake City, UT 84112. 801-581-3228.

VERMONT

No listings.

VIRGINIA

Tanya Bodzin, NCCC, Career Consultant, 9215 Santayana Drive, Fairfax, VA 22031. 703-273-6040.

Change & Growth Consulting, 1334 G Street, Woodbridge, VA 22191. 703-494-8271. Also: 2136-A Gallows Road, Dunn Loring (Tyson's Corner area), VA 22027. 703-569-2029. Barbara S. Woods, M.Ed., NCC, LPC, Counselor.

Educational Opportunity Center, 7010-M Auburn Ave., Norfolk, VA 23513. 804-855-7468. Agatha A. Peterson, Director.

Golden Handshakes, Church of the Epiphany, 11000 Smoketree Dr., Richmond, VA 23236. 804-794-0222. Jim Dunn, Chairperson; also at Winfree Memorial Baptist Church, 13617 Midlothian Turnpike, Midlothian, VA 23113. 804-794-5031. Phil Tibbs, Volunteer Coordinator.

Hollins College, Women's Center, P.O. Box 9628, Roanoke, VA 24020. 703-362-6269. Tina Rolen, Career Counselor.

Life Management Services, Inc., 301 Gregson Drive, Cary NC 27511. Hal and Marilyn Shook, President and Vice President.

Mary Baldwin College, Rosemarie Sena Center for Career and Life Planning, Kable House, Staunton, VA 24401. 703-887-7221.

Office for Women, The Government Center, 12000 Government Center Parkway, Suite 318, Fairfax, VA 22035. 703-324-5730. Betty McManus, Director.

Psychological Consultants, Inc., 6724 Patterson Ave., Richmond, VA 23226. 804-288-4125.

Virginia Commonwealth University, University Career Center, 907 Floyd Ave., Room 2007, Richmond, VA 23284-2007. 804-367-1645.

The Women's Center, 133 Park St., NE, Vienna, VA 22180. 703-281-2657. Conda Blackmon.

Working From The Heart, 1309 Merchant Lane, McLean, VA 22101. Jacqueline McMakin and Susan Gardiner, Co-Directors.

WASHINGTON

Career Management Institute, 8404 27th St. West, Tacoma, WA 98466. 206-565-8818. Ruthann Reim, M.A., N.C.C., President.

Diane Churchill, Box 30128, Spokane, WA 99223. 509-458-0961.

The Individual Development Center, Inc. (I.D. Center), 1020 E. John, Seattle, WA 98102. 206-329-0600. Mary Lou Hunt, N.C.C., M.A., President.

People Management Group International, 924 First Street, Suite A, Snohomish, WA 98290. 206-563-0105. Arthur F. Miller, Jr., Chairman.

University of Washington Extension, GH-21, Career Development Services, 5025 25th Ave. NE, Suite 205, Seattle, WA 98195. 206-543-3900.

Centerpoint Institute for Life and Career Renewal, Career Consultants, 624 Skinner Bldg., 1326 Fifth Ave., Seattle, WA 98101. 206-622-8070. Carol Vecchio, Career Counselor. *A multifaceted center, with various workshops, lectures, retreats, as well as individual counseling.*

WEST VIRGINIA

No listings.

WISCONSIN

Making Alternative Plans, Career Development Center, Alverno College, 3401 S. 39th St., P.O. Box 343922, Milwaukee, WI 53234-3922. 414-382-6010.

David **Swanson**, Career Seminars and Workshops, 7235 West Wells Street, Wauwatosa, WI 53213-3607. 414-774-4755, 414-259-0265.

WYOMING

Lifetime Career Consultants, P.O. Box 912, Jackson, WY 83001. 307-733-6544. Barbara Gray. Also P.O. Box 1867, Jackson, WY 83001. 307-733-4471. Caryn Haman.

National Education Service Center, P.O. Box 1279, Riverton, WY 82501-1279. 307-856-0170.

University of Wyoming, Career Planning and Placement Center, PO Box 3195/Knight Hall 228, Laramie, WY 82071-3195. 307-766-2398.

U.S.A. -- NATIONWIDE

Forty Plus Clubs. A nationwide network of voluntary, autonomous nonprofit clubs, manned by its unemployed members, paying no salaries, supported by initiation fees and monthly dues. At this writing, there are clubs in the following cities (listed alphabetically by States): *California:* Laguna Hills, Los Angeles, Oakland, San Diego, San Jose; *Colorado:* Colorado Springs, Fort Collins, Lakewood; *District of Columbia:* Washington; *Hawaii:* Honolulu; *Illinois:* Chicago; *Minnesota:* St. Paul; *New York:* New York, Buffalo; *Ohio:* Columbus; *Pennsylvania:* Philadelphia; *Texas:* Houston, Dallas; *Utah:* Murray, Ogden, Provo; *Washington:* Bellevue; and in *Canada:* Toronto. If you live in or near any of these cities, you can check the white pages of your Phone Book for their address and phone number; also you can call Forty Plus of New York, 15 Park Row, New York, NY 10038, 212-233-6086 to get current information about any of the nationwide locations -- to see if the club is still there, or if there is a new club nearer where you live -- and what their current address and phone number are.

CANADA

(These are listed by Provinces, from East Coast to West Coast, rather than in alphabetical order)

Sue **Landry**, Enhancing Your Horizons Consulting, 25 Birchwood Terr., Dartmouth, Nova Scotia B3A 3W2. 902-464-9110.

Robin T. **Hazell & Associates**, 60 St. Clair Ave. E., Seventh Floor, Toronto, Ontario M4T 1N5. 416-961-3700.

YMCA Career Planning & Development, 15 Breadalbane St., Toronto, Canada M4Y 2V5. 416-324-4121.

KPMG Peat Marwick Stevenson & Kellogg, 2300 Yonge Street, Toronto, Ontario, M4P 1G2. 416-483-4313. Contact Tom LePoidevin (offices in major cities across Canada). ·

Changes by Choice, 190 Burndale Ave., North York, Ontario M2N 1T2. 416-590-9939. Patti Davie.

Susan **Steinberg**, M.Ed., 74 Denlow Blvd., Don Mills, Ontario M3B 1P9. 416-449-6936.

Des Roches, Wallace, Bond Inc., 360 Albert St., Suite 1701, Ottawa, Ontario K1R 7X7. 613-238-7636. Kenneth Des Roches.

Job-Finding Club, 516-294 Portage Ave., Winnipeg, Manitoba R3C 0B9. 204-947-1948.

Susan **Curtis**, M.Ed., 4513 West 13th Ave., Vancouver, British Columbia V6R 2V5. 604-228-9618.

Alice **Caldwell**, P.B. #19009, 4th Avenue Postal Outlet, Vancouver, British Columbia V6K 4R8. 604-737-7842.

See next page for Overseas listing.

OVERSEAS

(Listed by country and city, in bold type.)

Switzerland

Cabinet Daniel Porot, 1, rue Verdaine, CH-1204, **Geneve, Switzerland**, phone 41 22 311 04 38. Daniel Porot, Founder. *Daniel is co-lecturer with me each summer at our international workshop.*

Kessler-Laufbahnberatung, Alpenblickstr. 33, CH-8645, **Jona b. Rapperswil, Switzerland**, phone 055 27 46 48. Peter Kessler, Counselor.

England

Castle Consultants International, Thames House, 140 Battersea Park Road, **London England**, SW1V RBB, phone 071 622 7011. Walt Hopkins, Founder and Director. *By the time you see this, Castle Consultants will have moved; call information at your phone company to find new phone listing (and address).*

The Chaney Partnership, Hillier House, 509 Upper Richmond Rd. West, **London, England** SW14 7EE, phone 081 878 3227. Isabel Chaney, B.A.

Brazil

Adigo Consultores, Av. Doria 164, **Sao Paulo SP, 04635-070 Brazil**, 55 11 530 0330. Alberto M.Barros, Director.

Australia

Centre for WorkLife Counselling, P.O. Box 407, **Spit Junction, (Sydney area) Australia** 2088. phone 61 969-4548. Paul Stevens, Director. Paul is the dean of career counseling in Australia.

Judith Bailey, Designing Your Life, 10 Nepean Pl., **Macquarie Australia**, ACT 2614, phone 61 06 253 2231.

Robert J. Bisdee & Associates, 22 Allenby Ave., Malvern E., **Victoria, Australia** 3145, phone 61 03 885 4716. Dr. Bob Bisdee, Director.

Imogen Wareing & Associates Pty Ltd, 105 Mowbray Road, **Willoughby NSW 2068, Australia**, 61 02 967 2300. Imogen Wareing, Director.

New Zealand

KPMG Peat Marwick Career Centre, 135 Victoria St., **Wellington, New Zealand**, 64 04 802 1227. Felicity McLennan.

Readers often contact us to ask which of these overseas counselors are familiar with my approach to job-hunting and career-changing. The answer is: all of the overseas counselors listed above have attended my two-week workshop, and therefore know my approach well.

Judy Feierstein, M.A., 46/2 Derech Bet Lechem, **Jerusalem 93504, Israel**, phone (02) 71 06 73.

Lori Mendel, 14/3 Zui Bruk, **Tel Aviv 63423, Israel,** phone (03) 29 28 30.

Addendum to Appendix A

IF YOU ARE A CAREER COUNSELOR, OR WANT TO BE ONE

If you liked the *language* (subject matter) of this book *a lot* you may of course be thinking about the possibility of becoming a career counselor yourself.

The field broadly called 'career development,' as I said earlier, breaks down into two lesser fields: **choosing what to do** (career assessment/ vocational counseling); and **discovering how to find it** (career-change/ creative job-hunting). Since the focus of *Parachute* is on career-change and alternative forms of job-hunting, I have only listed resources dealing with that side of career counseling, **not** the much broader field of career development -- whose materials would fill an encyclopedia.

Books:

Bolles, Richard Nelson, *What Color Is Your Parachute?: A Practical Manual for Job-Hunters and Career-Changers* (current edition; the newest edition appears at the end of October each year). Ten Speed Press, Box 7123, Berkeley, CA 94707.

Bolles, Richard Nelson, *The Three Boxes of Life: An Introduction to Life/ work Planning*. 1981. *(Same publisher as above.)*

Azrin, Nathan H., and Besalel, Victoria A., *Job Club Counselor's Manual: A Behavioral Approach to Vocational Counseling*. 1988. Pro-Ed, 8700 Shoal Creek Blvd., Austin, TX 78757. 512-451-3246. For any counselor interested in working with job-hunters more than one at a time, this work is *mandatory* reading. Nathan invented the job club idea, and when followed *faithfully* it has a very high success rate (around 86%). Problem is: every technique described in Nathan's book was designed to eliminate some difficulty or obstacle to your client's job-hunt, and each time you try to take shortcuts with his program and cut out *this* technique or *that* (as counselors are *very* wont to do), you *re-introduce* into your client's job-hunt the problem that the technique was designed to eliminate. Therefore, if you're going to use this manual, use it *faithfully.*

The Guide To Basic Skills Jobs: 2nd ed., *Vols. I and II*. RPM Press, Inc., P.O. Box 31483. Tucson, AZ 85751. 602-886-1990. 1993. *$69.95, with a money- back guarantee.* A catalog of viable jobs for individuals with only basic work skills and/or limited education and/or limited general aptitudes -- such as persons with physical impairments, limited English proficiency, migrant workers, welfare recipients, persons with mental illness, etc. The database is *broken out* from the D.O.T., but a concise, easy-to-use classification system is added. This volume identifies over 5,000 major occupations which re- quire no more than an eighth-grade level of education, and no more than one year of specific vocational preparation. Based upon research originally done by occupational analysts at North Carolina State University, and U.S.E.S. *Immensely useful book* if you counsel any of the above populations.

Porot, Daniel, *Comment Trouver Une Situation.* Les Editions d'Organisations, 5, rue Rousselet, F-75007 Paris. 1985. If you read French, this is Daniel's approach to the job-hunt. Since he is *the* expert in Europe, it is *of course* well worth reading.

Lathrop, Richard, *The Job Market.* The National Center for Job-Market Studies, Box 3651, Washington, DC 20007. *What would happen if we decreased the length of the job-hunt in America,* and other iconoclastic ideas which are also eminently sensible.

Parker, Yana, *Resume Pro: The Professional's Guide.* Ten Speed Press, P.O. Box 7123, Berkeley, CA 94707. 1993. This book/kit attempts to teach professionals (human resource staff, educators, career counselors, and others) how to go about the writing of resumes. *Extremely* thorough and helpful for those-who-*like*-resumes-despite-all-I've-said-in-chapter-3.

See the bibliography in Appendix B, for additional books, especially books related to the particular client populations that you desire to counsel. Also, see the catalogs on page 406.

Periodicals or Newsletters:

Career Planning & Adult Development Newsletter, published monthly by the Career Planning and Adult Development Network, 4965 Sierra Rd., San Jose, CA 95132. Free to Network members (Membership costs $49 in U.S., $64 for overseas). A single issue for non-members is $4.50. Richard L. Knowdell, Editor.

Career Opportunities News, published six times a year by Garrett Park Press, Box 190, Garrett Park, MD 20896. Useful news for counselors (and job-hunters) about employment fields, fellowships, new books, etc. $30/yr ($25 prepaid). Robert Calvert, Jr., Editor.

ReCareering Newsletter: An Idea and Resource Guide to Second Career and Relocation Planning, published ten times a year by Publications Plus, Inc., 801 Skokie Blvd., Suite 221, Northbrook, IL 60062-4027. $55/yr. Sharon B. Schuster, Editor.

Human Resource Development News, published three times a year (February, May, and November) by Career Counselor Services, Suite 324, 25 Woods Lake Rd., Greenville, SC 29607. $12.50/yr (if paid by check). Al A. Hafer, Editor.

The Damn Good Resume Pro Newsletter, A National Newsletter for professionals who write resumes, this has become a kind of non-electronic *bulletin-board* where members of this particular profession can meet and exchange ideas. Published quarterly. P.O. Box 3289, Berkeley, CA 94703. Yana Parker, Editor. She has also published other materials for resume professionals, which are listed elsewhere in this book (see *Author Index*).

Counselor Educator and Grad Student Networker, for those interested in research, syllabi, and programs related to the training of counselors. A Service of the NCDA/ACES Counselor Educator and Graduate Student Career Development Network. Order from Rich Feller, ED 222, Colorado State University, Ft. Collins, CO 80523. Fax: 303-491-1317. Phone: 303-491-6879.

The Journal of Employment Counseling, a professional journal concerned with research, theory, and new and improved job counseling techniques and tools. It does not deal so much with the job-hunt, as with counseling; and the counseling is pretty much along the traditional job-hunting lines. This is the official publication of the National Employment Counseling Association, a division of the American Counseling Association (ACA),[4] 5999 Stevenson Ave., Alexandria, VA 22304. $20/yr.

> *All the above periodicals or newsletters have a subscription fee, as noted. To be sure the newsletter meets your particular needs or interests, I recommend you ask for a sample issue, prior to putting down your money on a subscription.*

Computer Software, Film, Audiotape, Videotape:

For those who wish to explore the *non-print arena,* there are directories, which you can order, such as:

650 Career Videos: Ratings Reviews and Descriptions. 1994. Rich Feller, Clearinghouse on Video Usage, Colorado State University, School of Occupational and Educational Studies, Fort Collins, CO 80523. 303-491-6879.

In addition to directories, there are catalogs. Below is a *sampling* (only) of some free catalogs, which you can write and ask for -- no matter where you are, in the world. Some of these catalogs feature not only software, but also film, videotape, audiotape, and assessment instruments -- *plus books, and workbooks, of course.* Others list only books. I have tried to indicate the range of the catalog, in the listing.

Catalogs of Job-Hunting Materials:

Career Development Resources Catalog. Career Research & Testing, 2005 Hamilton Ave., San Jose, CA 95125. Lists books, reference books, journals, workbooks, assessment instruments, audiotapes, videos, computer software, and workshops. Has the computerized D.O.T.

Career Planning and Job Search Catalog. JIST Works, Inc., 720 North Park Avenue, Indianapolis, IN 46202.

Catalog. Careers, Inc., 1211 10th St., SW, P.O. Box 135, Largo, FL 34649-0135.

---

4. Previously known as the American Association for Counseling and Development (AACD), and -- before that -- as the American Personnel and Guidance Association (APGA).

Catalog. Reed Reference Publishing, 121 Chanlon Road, New Providence, NJ 07974. R.R. Bowker and other publishers' reference books, plus CD-ROMs, computer software, and online services.

Catalog. Wintergreen/Orchard House, P.O. Box 15899, New Orleans, LA 70175-5899. Lists many JIST materials, hence is duplicatory of the first catalog, above. But also lists other's materials: CD-ROMs, games, maps, videotapes, workbooks, and books. Has the computerized D.O.T.

Catalog of job-quest books. Planning/Communications, 7215 Oak Ave., River Forest, IL 60305.

The Crisp Catalog. Crisp Publications, Inc., 1200 Hamilton Court, Menlo Park, CA 94025-9600. One section on career books. They are famous for their "50-Minute Books."

Gale's Guide to Job Hunting Resources. Gale Research, Inc., 835 Penobscott Bldg. Detroit, MI 48226-4094. Primarily reference books.

Garrett Park Press Catalog. Garrett Park Press, Box 190, Garrett Park, MD 20896. Books, workbooks, wall-charts.

Jobs & Careers for the 1990s: 2761 Resources to Plan Your Future. From Impact Publications, 9104-N Manassas Drive, Manassas Park, VA 22111. Books.

Job & Career Library. Consultants Bookstore, Templeton Road, Fitzwilliam, NH 03447. Books.

Masterco Career Catalog. Masterco, P.O. Box 7382, Ann Arbor, MI 48107. Books.

PAR Catalog of Professional Testing Resources. Contains 37 pages of career assessment and planning resources. Assessment instruments, books, tapes, journals. PAR: Psychological Assessment Resources, Inc., P.O. Box 998, Odessa, FL 33556. John Holland's official publisher.

Peterson's Guides, P.O. Box 2123, Princeton, NJ 08543. Books, reference books.

Employee Development Catalog. Pfeiffer & Company, 8517 Production Avenue, San Diego, CA 92121-2280. Books, workbooks, video.

Sunburst Videos for Grades K–12 & Up. Sunburst Communications, P.O. Box 40, Pleasantville, NY 10570-0040.

Ten Speed Press Catalog, Ten Speed Press, Box 7123, Berkeley, CA 94707. Books. They often have a listing of just their career-related books. (As I write, it is called *The 1994 Career-Planning, Business Know-How and Skills for Personal Growth List*).

VGM *Career Books 1994.* NTC Publishing Group, 4255 West Touhy Ave., Lincolnwood, IL 60646-1975. 1-708-679-5500. Books, CD-ROMs, plus an interesting series of books on careers in various fields: physical therapy, masonry, homecare services, desktop publishing, robotics, tool and die, veterinary medicine, etc.

The Whole Work Catalog: Career Resources. The New Careers Center, Inc., P.O. Box 339-AJ, Boulder, CO 80306. Books and videos from over 175 different sources.

Writer's Digest Catalog. Writer's Digest Books, 1507 Dana Ave., Cincinnati, OH 45207. Books related to specific careers, such as writing, the arts, etc.

Additional Software Programs
(not in the catalogs above)

Most of these are for the IBM computer family; rarely, the Macintosh. A listing here is for supplemental information only, and does not constitute a recommendation or endorsement on my part:

Jackson, Tom, *The Perfect Resume Computer Kit.* Permax Systems Inc., P.O. Box 6455, Madison, WI 53716-0455. Assists in preparing resumes, based on Tom's very popular book. Enables the user to prepare customized, target resumes. There is both a Personal Version and a Counselor's Version. For IBM computers and compatibles.

Parker, Yana, *Ready to Go Resumes (Self Teaching Resume Templates).* Damn Good Resume Service, P.O. Box 3289, Berkeley, CA 94703. 1991. This is a computer disk, and manual, for both Macintosh and IBM computers and compatibles. It is based on her very popular book.

Visual Resume™. Heapsort Software, P.O. Box 324, Holly, MI 48442-0324. 1994. Gives the user who is interested in preparing a chronological resume, the ability to produce such a resume in a very unusual visual layout format (an $8\frac{1}{2} \times 11$" page, lying on its side, with a time bar at the bottom); also does cover letters, and labels. $19.95 when ordered directly from the publisher (Michigan residents add 6% sales tax). For IBM computers and compatibles.

Easy Working Resume Kit™. Spinnaker Software Corporation, 201 Broadway, Cambridge, MA 02139. 1992. Written only for IBM computers and compatibles. The merits of this software aside, the program has an *excellent* manual, including a long, helpful, and realistic section called *"Beyond Resumes,"*™ -- obviously written by someone who knows what she is talking about, and who is wise and witty to boot. This company also publishes *PFS: Resume and Job Search Pro,* for IBM computers and compatibles. A *Windows* version is available.

Career Navigator. Drake Beam Morin, Inc., 100 Park Ave., New York, NY 10017. Computer-based training and guidance during one's job-search. For IBM computers and compatibles.

'Meeting Places' for Career Counselors:

If your computer has a modem, and you are experienced at going *online,* then you will want to know about the computer bulletin board that exists especially for those interested in the field of job search, careers, and the world of work. It is called *Self Directed Job Search Techniques and Job Placement Issues: JOBPLACE.* It is not a place to list job-openings, but rather a place for professionals to *meet,* and chat about the latest research, studies, and experience with job search. It exists on Bitnet or Internet, and is a LISTSERV managed list. *(If you haven't the slightest idea what I just said, find some friend of yours who is a wiz at 'going online' and let them initiate you into the mysteries of modem-travel.)* Subscriptions are free. For details, contact Drema Howard, Ph.D., Associate Director, University of Kentucky Career Center, 201 Mathews Bldg., Lexington KY 40506. Fax: 606-258-1085.

If you are interested in course syllabi from courses in career development, career counseling and/or career planning, there is a clearinghouse for such materials, maintained by Dr. Stan Cramer, Dept. of Counseling & Educational Psychology, Faculty of Educational Studies, 409 Christopher Baldy Hall, SUNY Buffalo, Amherst, NY 14260.

Career Assessment Instruments:

This, of course, is a wide world. There are a *million* assessment instruments out there: the Strong Interest Inventory, the Holland SDS, the Myers-Briggs, and a host of others -- plus some quasi-instruments, such as my own *Quick Job-Hunting (and Career-Changing) Map: How to Create A Picture of Your Ideal Job or Next Career.*

If you want to know about instruments available to you, see: Kopes, Jerome T., and Mastice, Marjorie Moran, eds., *A Counselor's Guide to Career Assessment Instruments.* 1988 ed. Published by the American Counseling Association, 5999 Stevenson Ave., Alexandria, VA 22304.

Counselor Training:

By Others: There are countless training opportunities for career counselors in the U.S. and abroad. *Career Planning & Adult Development Newsletter,* mentioned earlier (published monthly by the Career Planning and Adult Development Network, 4965 Sierra Rd., San Jose, CA 95132) maintains a *very good* calendar of these events, and anyone interested in further training would be well advised to be receiving this *Newsletter.*

By Me: Whenever the subject of training comes up, I am asked (endlessly) whether or not *I* do any teaching. We receive hundreds of letters and phone calls each year asking this. Since I would like to cut down on the mail and phone calls, and also save *you* some trouble, I will give you the desired information, right here.

I do not do any training or speaking, except in August of each year, when I teach nonstop for fourteen days along with my esteemed colleague from Europe, Daniel Porot, whose insights you have seen frequently in the main body of this book. We call it:

Two Weeks of
LIFE/Work Planning
at the Inn of the Seventh Mountain

This is not, as its name would suggest, held in the Orient. The Inn of the Seventh Mountain is a beautiful and popular resort on the outskirts of **Bend, Oregon**, which -- as everyone knows -- is in the center of the United States (Honolulu is 3,000 miles to the West, New York City is 3,000 miles to the East).

The workshop is always in August, always the first Friday through the third Friday. Contrary to earlier announcements, there will be a workshop in 1995; the dates are August 4–18. In 1996, the dates are August 2–16. Since two weeks is a long time, and people who attend usually do so in lieu of their regular summer vacation, we have deliberately put this workshop at a first-class vacation resort, which past participants have delighted in --

as they can 'have their cake and eat it, too.' The Inn has two swimming pools, waterslide, hot baths/saunas, hiking trails, tennis, whitewater rafting, horseback riding, moped rental, bicycle rental, roller-skating, ski-lifts to the top of Mount Bachelor, and other vacation amenities, outdoor eating -- with *wonderful* food -- all in a lovely pine-forest setting near the foot of a large mountain topped with snow even in the summertime. To enjoy all these amenities, you should plan to come early and/or stay late.

The total training at this workshop exceeds 100 hours, and is limited to the first 60 people who apply, each year. In age participants have ranged from 17 to 74, have embraced all ethnic groups, and have come from all parts of the world. In 1994, for example, participants came from The Netherlands, Germany, Switzerland, England, Japan, Venezuela, Canada, New Zealand, and Australia -- as well as the U.S. *(obviously)*. Year after year people say that this was close to the most enjoyable fifteen days of their entire life. *Be sure to bring your playful self.*

Our methodology at this workshop is to have you master the principles of life/work planning by rigorously applying them to *your own life* during the two weeks, rather than discussing the problems of clients or their case histories, etc., as is often the fashion these days. Because of this methodology, **the workshop is useful to anyone, and each year over half the people who attend are not career counselors** -- but job-hunters of all ages, career-changers, homemakers, union organizers, CEOs, teachers, people facing a move, people facing retirement, the recently divorced, college students, clergy, and so forth.

The tuition for this intensive training is $2,000 and there are neither discounts for early registration, nor scholarships available, inasmuch as the workshop is a fundraiser for our work throughout the world, during the rest of the year. This tuition includes all materials and sessions.

The cost of the room and board at the Inn, with all its facilities, is **additional**, and begins at $110 a day *for your room (shared with roommate), breakfast, lunch, dinner, and two refreshment breaks each day.* The cost may be more, depending on the accommodations desired.

The workshop is filled first come, first served, and is immensely popular. In 1994, it filled up nine months ahead of time -- though there are usually some last-minute cancellations. For a brochure and registration blank, write to:

Norma Wong, Workshop Registrar
What Color Is Your Parachute?
P.O. Box 379
Walnut Creek, CA 94597

Phone No.: 1-510-935-1865 (10 a.m.–12 noon,
Monday thru Friday, Pacific Coast Time).
Fax No.: 1-510-932-4864 (twenty-four hours a day).

The Inn of the Seventh Mountain
Bend, Oregon

My son, be admonished:
of making many books there is no end;
and much study is a weariness of the flesh.

Ecclesiastes

Appendix B
Bibliography:

Books and Notes for Job-Hunters and Career-Changers

A SAMPLER
OF INFORMATION SOURCES
for You, as Job-Hunter and Career-Changer,
To Use

Here is a list of *some* of the library books which -- from the experience of career-changers and job-hunters before you -- will likely prove useful *at one time or another* during the research phase (Chapters 11 and 12) of your career-change or job-hunt. You may find them at your local public library (of course), but don't forget other libraries that may be near you, such as a business library or a local university, college, or community college library.

Some of these books, of course, are inexpensive enough for you to purchase, if you want to -- from your local bookstore (particularly those dealing with job leads). But the rest are hideously expensive, so thank God for your local library.

Which book to consult? Why, the one that may help you with the particular questions you're trying to find answers to, regarding the *targets* of your career choice, or job-hunt, at any given moment. You *must* know what those questions are. For, the surest way to make certain your trip to the library is a total waste of time, is to be *hazy* about what you're trying to find out.

So, please, before you go to the library, each time, write out on a piece of paper, for your own use, "This is the information I am trying to find out *today:*_____ ." Be specific. Be clear.

For help on a question no one seems to know the answer to, try the National Referral Center at the Library of Congress, 202-287-5670. Also, you can call the Federal Information Center of the General Services Administration at 202-755-8660 to find the names of experts in any field.

Now, let's look at books in your local library that may help you with whatever questions you have about the *targets* of your job-hunt.

The directories which immediately follow are categorized by the *primary* arena of their information, namely:

1. Outlook
2. Fields (Occupations or Industries)
3. Companies
4. Individuals (as Contacts or Employers)
5. Vacancies or Job Leads

Each may, however, have information that spills over into the other categories.

Your local library should have many if not most of these resources. Ask your local librarian for help. If there is no librarian available, or at least no *helpful* librarian, there are *(mercifully)* indexes/indices to all these directories:

- Klein's *Guide to American Directories;* and
- *Directories in Print, 1994,* 10th ed. Gale Research, Inc., 835 Penobscott Bldg., Detroit, MI 48226-4094, which contains over 15,000 current listings of directories, indexed by title or key word or subject (over 3,500 subject headings).

See also:

Encyclopedia of Business Information Sources, 10th ed. Gale Research, Inc., 835 Penobscott Bldg., Detroit, MI 48226-4094. Identifies electronic, print and live resources dealing with 1,500 business subjects. Their companion volume is entitled *Business Organizations, Agencies and Publications Directory,* 6th ed., listing over 24,000 entries, such as federal government advisory organizations, newsletters, research services, etc.

Directory of Special Libraries and Information Centers 1994, 18th ed. Gale Research, Inc., 835 Penobscott Bldg., Detroit, MI 48226-4094. Lists 22,000 research facilities, on various subjects, maintained by libraries, research libraries, businesses, nonprofit organizations, governmental agencies, etc. Detailed subject index, using over 3,500 key words.

1. Outlook

Occupational Outlook Handbook. Department of Labor, NTC Publishing Group, 225 W. Touhy Ave., Lincolnwood, IL 60646.

Occupational Outlook Handbook for College Graduates. Superintendent of Documents, U.S. Government.

Petras, Kathryn & Ross, *Jobs '94: By Career, By Industry, By Region.* 1993. Fireside, Rockefeller Center, 1230 Avenue of the Americas, New York, NY 10020. Indicates the outlook, industry by industry. Also lists the leading U.S. companies, associations, directories, and periodicals in each field.

2. Fields
Occupations or Industries

Dictionary of Holland Occupational Codes.

Dictionary of Occupational Titles.

Encyclopedia of Associations 1994. Vol. 1, National Organizations of the U.S.; Vol. 2, Geographic and Executive Indexes; Vol. 3, New Associations and Projects. Gale Research, Inc., 835 Penobscott Bldg., Detroit, MI 48226-4094. Lists 25,000 organizations, associations, clubs and other nonprofit membership groups that are in the business of giving out information. There is a companion series of books: *Regional, State and Local Organizations 1994,* a five volume set, which lists over 50,000 similar organizations on a regional, state, or local level. There is another companion volume, also: *International Organizations 1993.* This lists 4,000 international organizations, concerned with various subjects. There was still another companion volume, *Association Periodicals,* 1st ed., 1987, which listed 12,000 newsletters, periodicals and journals put out by national associations in particular. It is still available, but no longer updated.

National Trade and Professional Associations of the United States. 29th ed., 1994. Columbia Books, Inc., Publishers, 1212 New York Avenue, N.W., Suite 330, Washington, DC 20005.

Newsletters in Print. 7th ed. 1994. Gale Research, Inc., 835 Penobscott Bldg., Detroit, MI 48226-4094. Detailed entry on 10,000 newsletters in various subject fields, or categories. It includes newsletters that are available only online, through a computer and modem.

Standard and Poor's Industry Surveys. Good basic introduction, history, and overview of any industry you may be interested in.

Standard Industrial Classification Manual. 1991. Reprint of material originally published by the U.S. Government Printing Office. Available from: Gordon Press, P.O. Box 459, Bowling Green Station, New York, NY 10003. Gives the Standard Industrial Classification code number for any field or industry -- which is the number used by most business references in their indices.

The 1994 Information Please® Business Almanac & Desk Reference, Seth Godin, Editor. 1993. Houghton Mifflin Company, 215 Park Ave. So., New York, NY 10003. All kinds of information about industries, with addresses and contacts plus any other business question you might be curious about (computers, etc.).

U.S. Industrial Outlook 1993. Reprinted from material published by the U.S. Department of Commerce. Available from JIST Works, 720 N. Park Ave., Indianapolis, IN 46202. Covers 350 manufacturing and service industries. Gives the trends and outlooks for each industry that you may be interested in. Updated annually.

And, for specific industries or fields:

Communications: *Telecommunications Directory, 1994–1995.* 6th ed. Gale Research, Inc., 835 Penobscott Bldg., Detroit, MI 48226-4094. Lists over 2,000 national and international firms dealing with communications systems, teleconferencing, videotext, electronic mail, fax services, etc.

Computers: *Information Industry Directory 1994.* 15th ed. Gale Research, Inc., 835 Penobscott Bldg., Detroit, MI 48226-4094. Lists 30,000 computer-based information systems and services, here and abroad. Their companion volume, *Computers and Computing Information Resources Directory,* 1st ed. Gale Research, Inc., 835 Penobscott Bldg., Detroit, MI 48226-4094, lists trade shows, conventions, users' groups, associations, consultants, etc., worldwide.

Government: *United States Government Manual.* U.S. Government Printing Office, Stop SSMR, Washington, DC 20402.

Hobbies: *National Recreational Sporting and Hobby Organizations of the U.S.* Columbia Books, Inc., 777 14th St. NW, Washington, DC 20005.

Physical Sciences, Engineering, Biological Sciences: *Directory of Information Resources in the United States.* Washington, DC, Library of Congress.

Research: *Research Center Directory 1994.* 19th ed. Gale Research, Inc., 835 Penobscott Bldg., Detroit, MI 48226-4094. Also: *Research Services Directory,* 6th ed. The two volumes together cover some 13,000 services, facilities, and companies that do research into various subjects, such as feasibility studies, private and public policy, social studies and studies of various cultures, etc.

Statistics: *Statistics Sources 1994.* 18th ed. Gale Research, Inc., 835 Penobscott Bldg., Detroit, MI 48226-4094. Tells you where to find statistics on more than 20,000 specific topics. Key live sources are also featured.

Teaching & Training: *Training and Development Organizations Directory,* 5th ed. Gale Research, Inc., 835 Penobscott Bldg., Detroit, MI 48226-4094. For those of you interested in teaching or training, it lists over 2,500 firms and their areas of interest and expertise.

3. Companies
Large Companies

Company/college/association/agency/foundation *Annual Reports.* Get these directly from the personnel department or publicity person at the company, etc., or from the Chamber or your local library.

Corporate and Industry Research Reports. Published by R.R. Bowker/Martindale-Hubbell, 121 Chanlon Rd., New Providence, NJ 07974. Can be very helpful.

Corporate Technology Directory. 1993. Lists companies by the products they make or the technologies they use. Corporate Technology Information Services, Inc., 12 Alfred St., Suite 200, Woburn, MA 01801-9998.

Directory of American Research and Technology: Organizations Active in Product Development for Business. 1994. R.R. Bowker, 121 Chanlon Rd., New Providence, NJ 07974.

Directory of Corporate Affiliations. National Register Publishing Co., Inc.

Dun & Bradstreet's Million Dollar Directory. Very helpful.

Dun & Bradstreet's Million Dollar Directory–Top 50,000 Companies. Very helpful. An abridged version of Dun's *Million Dollar Directory Series.*

Dun & Bradstreet's Reference Book of Corporate Managements.

F & S Indexes (recent articles on firms).

F & S Index of Corporations and Industries. Lists "published articles" by industry and by company name. Updated weekly.

Fitch Corporation Manuals.

Fortune Magazine's 500; they also publish interesting articles during the rest of the year, on major corporations, such as *"America's Most Admired Corporations."* Visit your local library, and browse back issues.

Hoover's Handbook of American Business 1994, ed. by Gary Hoover, Alta Campbell, and Patrick J. Spain. 1993. Publishers: The Reference Press, 6448 Highway 290E., Suite E-104, Austin, TX 78723. 800-486-8666. Profiles of over 500 major U.S. companies. A special section on the companies that have created the most jobs in the last 10 years and those that have eliminated the most jobs.

Hoover's Handbook of World Business 1993, ed. by Alan Chai, Alta Campbell, and Patrick J. Spain. 1993. Profiles of nearly 200 major European, Asian, Latin American, and Canadian companies who employ thousands of Americans both in the U.S. and abroad.

How To Read A Financial Report: Wringing Cash Flow and Other Vital Signs Out of the Numbers. 3rd ed. by John A. Tracy, CPA. John Wiley & Sons, Business Law/General Books Division, 605 Third Avenue, New York, NY 10158-0012. Also Chichester, Brisbane, Toronto and Singapore.

Job Seeker's Guide to Private and Public Companies. Gale Research Inc., 835 Penobscott Bldg,. Detroit, MI 48226-4094. 15,000 companies described in four regional volumes. They also publish a number of career directories for various careers, such as radio & television, healthcare, advertising, newspapers, travel & hospitality, public relations, magazines, etc.

Macmillan's Directory of Leading Private Companies.

Moody's Industrial Manual (and other Moody manuals).

National Business Telephone Directory used to be published by Gale Research, Inc., 835 Penobscott Bldg., Detroit, MI 48226-4094. In one single alphabetical listing, contains phone numbers, address and city for over 350,000 business and industrial establishments that have more than 20 employees. Particularly useful when you know the name of an organization, but not what city or state it is located in. Since this is technically out of print, see if your library has a back copy.

National Directory of Addresses and Telephone Numbers. 1993. Omigraphics, Gale Research, Inc., 835 Penobscott Bldg., Detroit, MI 48226-4094.

Periodicals: some worth perusing in your public library, in addition to *Fortune,* mentioned above, are *Business Week, Dun's Review, Forbes,* and the *Wall Street Journal.*

Registers of manufacturers for your state or area (e.g., *California Manufacturers Register*).

Standard and Poor's Corporation Records.

Standard and Poor's Industrial Index.

The Adams Jobs Almanac 1994, by the Editors of Bob Adams, Inc. 1994. Bob Adams, Inc., 260 Center St., Holbrook, MA 02343. Gives a sampling of the major companies in thirty-one industries, together with the kinds of positions they are usually looking for -- when they're looking. Has a state-by-state index of the major employers, plus an introductory session on career outlooks and job-hunting. This same publisher has a *JobBank Series* which you can find in your local bookstore. Currently there are *JobBank* books for: Atlanta, Boston, the Carolinas, Chicago, Dallas–Fort Worth, Denver, Detroit, Florida, Houston, Los Angeles, Minneapolis, New York, Ohio, Philadelphia, Phoenix, St. Louis, San Francisco, Seattle, Tennessee, and Washington DC.

Thomas' Register. Thomas Publishing Co. There are, in fact, 27 volumes in the Thomas register. All the manufacturers there are of 52,000 products and services, plus catalogs, contacts, and phone numbers.

Walker's Manual of Western Corporations. 1992. Walker Western Research Co., 1452 Tilia Ave., San Mateo, CA 94402.

Ward's Business Directory, 3 vols. (Vol. 1, Largest U.S. Companies; Vol. 2, Major U.S. Private Companies; Vol. 3, Major International Companies). Gale Research, Inc., 835 Penobscott Bldg., Detroit, MI 48226-4094. Updated yearly. Despite the titles, helpful in identifying smaller companies, as well as large.

Small Companies

Hoover's Handbook of Emerging Companies 1993-1994, ed. by Patrick J. Spain, Alta Campbell, and Alan Chai. Lists and profiles of 250 smaller, emerging companies with high growth rates. A sampler for those seeking employment at smaller companies.

Chamber of Commerce data on an organization or field that interests you (visit the Chamber in the appropriate city or town).

Many public libraries have very efficient database search capabilities, through their computers, and can dig up, copy and mail to you copies of reports on local companies (for a modest cost). For example, one Pennsylvania job-hunter got the Cleveland (Ohio) Library to send him copies of annual reports on a Cleveland-based company. So, when you get to the point where you're researching organizations, if there's an organization or company that particularly interests you, you might want to try contacting the nearest large public library to their home base, and see what that library can turn up for you.

Better Business Bureau report on a particular organization that you may be interested in (call the BBB in the city where the organization is located). These reports sometimes only tell you if there are outstanding, unresolved complaints against a company; but that is a useful thing to know -- if there are such.

4. Individuals
(As Contacts or Potential Employers)

Starer, Daniel, *Who Knows What: The Essential Business Resource Book.* 1992. A Henry Holt Reference Book, Henry Holt and Company, Inc., 115 West 18th St., New York, NY 10011. Lists industries, associations, periodicals, companies, and individuals in more than 500 subject areas.

Consultants and Consulting Organizations Directory 1993. 14th ed. Gale Research, Inc., 835 Penobscott Bldg., Detroit, MI 48226-4094. Lists over 15,000 firms, individuals and organizations engaged in consulting work. Consultants are usually experts in their particular field, and hence may be useful to you in your information search about that job or career-change that you are contemplating.

Dun's Consultants Directory.

Contacts Influential: Commerce and Industry Directory. Businesses in particular market area listed by name, type of business, key personnel, etc. Contacts Influential, Market Research and Development Services, 321 Bush St., Suite 203, San Francisco, CA 94104, if your library doesn't have it.

Standard and Poor's Register of Corporations, Directors and Executives. Key executives in 32,000 leading companies, plus 75,000 directors.

Who's Who in Finance and Industry, and all the other Who's Who books. Useful once you have the name of someone-who-has-the-power-to-hire, and you want to know more about them.

American Society for Training and Development Directory: Who's Who in Training and Development, 1640 King St., Box 1443, Alexandria, VA 22313-2043.

Investor, Banker, Broker Almanac.

American Men and Women of Science.

5. Vacancies
or Job Leads

Professional's Private Sector Job Finder, 1994–1995, by Daniel Lauber. 1994. Planning/Communications, 7215 Oak Ave., River Forest, IL 60305. Lists over 2,500 associations, directories, journals, trade magazines, newsletters, computerized job-listings, online services, job-matching services, salary surveys, etc. -- *categorized* very helpfully by fields, industries and occupations -- where contacts may be found, or job-leads advertised. Includes international job sources. Very thorough.

Non-Profits' Job Finder, 1994–1995, by Daniel Lauber. 1994. Planning/ Communications, 7215 Oak Ave., River Forest, IL 60305. Lists over 1,350 associations, directories, journals, trade magazines, newsletters, computerized job-listings, online services, job-matching services, foundations, grants, and salary surveys, etc. -- dealing with education and all of the non-profit sector -- where contacts may be found, or job-leads advertised. Very thorough.

LeCompte, Michelle, ed., *JOB HUNTER'S SOURCEBOOK: Where to find employment leads and other job search resources.* 1992. Gale Research, Inc., 835 Penobscott Bldg., Detroit, MI 48226-4094. A similar exceptional resource, as it tells you how to find sources of information and job-leads for a whole variety of occupations (155, in all). Somebody did their homework well. See if there is an updated version, by the time you read this.

Caveat: the sources listed in these books *may be* as bereft of job leads as anyone else, especially during 'hard times.' But once you know what field you want to be in, get your hand on the *latest version* of these books in your local bookstore or by mail, and see what sources they list, that might know of jobs. If the source you want is hideously expensive, see if your local library has it.

JOB-HUNTING BOOKS
FROM OTHER LEADERS IN THE FIELD

No one book can speak to every reader. While Parachute *has helped millions of people, the truth is that some people are not able to use it. But they may be able to use another book. If you are one of these, I have listed below the primary texts from the other leaders in this field of career planning and job-hunting. You may find that* Parachute *doesn't speak to you, but that one of these other authors does.*

It may also be that while Parachute *is helping you, you feel you need additional inspiration, or you feel you have special needs because of your situation or handicap (your age, sex, background, etc.) where you need or want more light shed. That section begins on page 424.*

Finally, if no *book seems helpful to you in your job-search or career-change dilemma, all is not lost. Consider strongly the possibility of signing up with some reputable career counselor (see Appendix A), who can give you the kind of guidance that no book can.*

Wegmann, Robert, and Chapman, Robert, *The Right Place at the Right Time: Finding a Job in the 1990s.* 1987, revised and updated, 1990. Ten Speed Press, Box 7123, Berkeley, CA 94707. Highly highly recommended. The late Bob Wegmann knew more about what was going on in the world of work than anyone else in the country. Here are his insights for us to still profit by. There is another book by these two authors, along with Miriam Johnson: *Work in the New Economy: Careers and Job Seeking into the 21st Century.* 1989. Updated. JIST Works, 720 North Park Ave., Indianapolis, Indiana 46202. Highly recommended, of course. Bob Wegmann's insights in another form.

Sher, Barbara, *Wishcraft: How to Get What You Really Want.* 1983. Ballantine Books, 201 E. 50th St., New York, NY 10022. A very helpful book; our readers love it. Barbara is a great workshop leader, and if you have a chance to hear her, take it! She is witty, helpful and smart. She also has a newer book out, with Barbara Smith: *I Could Do Anything If I Only Knew What It Was: How to Discover What You Really Want and How to Get It.* 1994. Delacorte Press, Bantam Doubleday Dell Publishing Group, Inc., 1540 Broadway, New York, NY 10036. Obviously, fans of her first book will want to read this also.

Jackson, Tom, *Guerrilla Tactics in the New Job Market* (2nd ed.). 1991. Bantam Books, 1540 Broadway, New York, NY 10036. A very popular and useful book, now revised for the '90s. Tom has some great ideas and insights found in no other author's work.

Jackson, Tom, *Not Just Another Job: How to Invent a Career That Works for You–Now and in the Future.* 1992. Times Books, a division of Random House, Inc., 201 E. 50th St., New York, NY 10022.

Figler, Howard E., *The Complete Job-Search Handbook: All the Skills You Need to Get Any Job and Have a Good Time Doing It.* 1988, Revised and Expanded Edition. Henry Holt & Co., Inc., 115 W. 18th St., New York, NY 10011. Identifies the twenty skills the job-hunter needs in order to pull off a job hunt *successfully.* A very unusual approach to the subject of skills, as well as to the subject of the job-hunt.

Miller, Arthur F., and Mattson, Ralph T., *The Truth About You: Discover What You Should Be Doing with Your Life.* 1977, 1989. Ten Speed Press, Box 7123, Berkeley CA 94707. I like this book a lot. I know of no other book that sets out to do what my friend Arthur has done here: look for *overall patterns* in your choice of jobs -- within the overarching context of *faith.* The process is still an art, not a science, and some readers will be frustrated by that. But the rest of you should find it suggestive and thought-provoking.

Haldane, Bernard, *Career Satisfaction and Success: How to Know and Manage Your Strengths.* 1988. Published by Wellness Behavior, 2821 Second Ave., #1002, Seattle, WA 98121. A rumor has been going around, for years, that (1) I was once a client of *the agency* that bears Bernard's name, and that (2) I recommend that agency. Neither has ever been true, believe me. Bernard *himself* is something else again. He is the oldest figure in this field -- he is in his eighties -- and through his writings, was the original fountainhead of ideas in this field, and thus still well worth reading.

Krannich, Ronald L., *Change Your Job, Change Your Life! High Impact Strategies For Finding Great Jobs in the 90s.* 1994. This is an updated version of Ron's earlier title, *Careering and Re-Careering For the 90s.* Very thorough. Ron is a prolific writer; he is the author of over thirty books in this field.

Yate, Martin, *Knock 'em Dead: The Ultimate Job Seeker's Handbook,* rev. ed. 1994. Bob Adams, Inc., 260 Center St., Holbrook, MA 02343. Omnipresent in U.S. bookstores, currently, this book should be easy to find. Very popular.

Campbell, David P. *If You Don't Know Where You're Going, You'll Probably End Up Somewhere Else.* 1990. Tabor Publishing, 200 E. Bethany Dr., Allen, TX 75002. A little book, useful for people to whom the whole idea of career planning is brand new.

Stevens, Paul, *Stop Postponing the Rest of Your Life.* 1993. Ten Speed Press, P.O. Box 7123, Berkeley, CA 94707. A classic text from our friends in Australia, now revised and updated.

OTHER RESOURCES BY RICHARD BOLLES

Bolles, Richard N., *The Three Boxes of Life, and How To Get Out of Them.* 1978. 480 pages. Ten Speed Press, Box 7123, Berkeley, CA 94707. $14.95. 350,000 copies in print.

With a co-author:

Crystal, John C., and Bolles, Richard N., *Where Do I Go From Here With My Life?* 1974. 272 pages. Ten Speed Press, Box 7123, Berkeley, CA 94707. $11.95. 150,000 copies in print.

Bolles, Richard N., *How to Create A Picture of Your Ideal Job or Next Career, Advanced Version* (revised) *of the Quick Job-Hunting (and Career-Changing) Map.* 1991. Ten Speed Press, Box 7123, Berkeley, CA 94707. An 8½ × 11 inch 48–page workbook, which expands upon Chapters 9, 10, and 11 in this book; in color. $5.95.

Bolles, Richard N., *The Quick Job-Hunting Map for Beginners.* 1990. Ten Speed Press, Box 7123, Berkeley, CA 94707. A workbook version of the Map for high school students just entering the labor force, and those other job-hunters who may prefer a simpler alternative to the Map above. $1.25.

Bolles, Richard N., "The Anatomy of a Job." 1991. A 24 × 36 inch poster, designed as a worksheet to be used with *How to Create A Picture* (above). It lists the families of skills on one side, and has a flower-diagram on the other, that can be filled in. Ten Speed Press, Box 7123, Berkeley, CA 94707. $4.95.

Bolles, Richard N., *How to Find Your Mission in Life.* 1991. Ten Speed Press, Box 7123, Berkeley, CA 94707. A gift-book edition of the Epilogue in this book. $5.95.

Bolles, Richard N., *Job-Hunting Tips For The So-Called Handicapped or People Who Have Disabilities. A Supplement to What Color Is Your Parachute?* 1991. Ten Speed Press, Box 7123, Berkeley, CA 94707. 61 pages $4.95.

OTHER VERSIONS OF PARACHUTE

Italian: Bolles, Richard Nelson, *Ce l'hai il paracadute? Guida pratica per chi cerca o vuole cambiare lavoro.* Translated and adapted by Giuseppe Mojana; preface by Fabrizio Luzzatto-Giuliani. 1992. Sperling & Kupfer, Via Borgonuovo, 24, 20121 Milano, Italy.

Polish: Bolles, Richard Nelson, *Spadochron: Praktyczny podrecznik dla planujacych kariere, szukajacych pracy i zmieniajacych zawod.* Translated by Pawel Ziolkowski. 1993. Fundacja Inicjatyw Spoleczno-Ekonomiczynch, 00-054 Warszawa, Jasna 22.

Spanish: Bolles, Richard N., *¿De Qué Color Es Su Paracaidas?* 1983. Editorial Diana, S.A., Roberto Gayol 1219, Mexico, D.F.

French: Bolles, Richard N., *Chercheurs d'emploi, n'oubliez pas votre parachute.* Translated by Daniel Porot. Sylvie Messinger, éditrice, 31 rue de l'Abbé-Grégoire, Paris 6e, France. 1983. Also: Bolles, Richard N., *Chercheurs d'emploi, n'oubliez pas votre parachute.* Translated by Daniel Porot. Guy Saint-Jean Editeur Inc. 674 Place Publique, Laval, Quebec H7X 1G1, Canada. 1983.

Dutch: Bolles, Richard N., *Werk zoeken-een vak apart, Een professionele aanpak voor het vinden van een (nieuwe) baan.* Translated by F.J.M. Claessens. 1983. Uitgeverij Intermediair, Amsterdam/Brussels.

Japanese: Bolles, Richard N., *'87 What Color Is Your Parachute?* (In Japanese) 1986. A newer translation is in the works. Japan UNI Agency, Inc., Ten Speed Press and Writers House, Inc., NY.

German: A German translation used to exist, but it is now out of print. A newer translation is in the works.

OTHER COUNTRIES' CAREER BOOKS

French: Porot, Daniel, *Votre entretien d'embauche: 107 conseils pour le Reussir.* Premiere edition. 1990. Les Editions d'organisation, 26, avenue Emile-Zola, F - 75015 Paris. Tel: 45-78-61-81. Highly, highly recommended, for those who read French.

Danish: Lausten, Torben, *Kan vingerne bære? Håndbog i JOBJAGT og karriereudvikling.* 1989. Udgivet af Forlaget Thorsgaard ApS, Frederikssund, Denmark.

Japanese: Brockman, Terra, *The Job Hunter's Guide to Japan.* 1990. Kodansha International/USA Ltd., 114 Fifth Ave., New York, NY 10011.

Advice
and a Sampler
of U.S. Resources

Most of you will find that the main body of *Parachute* tells you all you need to know, in order to successfully conduct your job-hunt. However, *if* you are in one of the groups listed below, and you want additional guidance or information, I have made further comments, and listed some U.S. resources, most of which can be mail-ordered from any part of the world (hence, I have given the publisher's address, in each case).

If you consider yourself a member of some group, not listed above, that *some* employers are prejudiced against *(for example, gays and lesbians)*, then the reason *that group* is not listed here is that generally speaking, the advice in Chapter 13, and especially pages 335–337, is what you most need to know.

If you do not find, below, what you are looking for, there are three kinds of places where you can look further.

(1) Your **local bookstores** -- go to more than one, browse, and see what they have. Disadvantage: you have to buy the book, if you want it. Advantage: They've got the latest, most up-to-date edition *(usually -- though not always)*. Furthermore, they can order for you almost any book *that is still in print* -- and you'll know *that,* by whether or not it is listed in a reference book most bookstores have, called *Books In Print.* Ask.

(2) Your local **public libraries**, or nearby community college library. If they have a friendly reference librarian, by all means ask to see him or her.

They can be worth their weight in gold to you. Tell them your problem or interest, and see what they can dig up. Disadvantage: a library may not have the latest edition of a book (see what edition of *Parachute* they're carrying, for example). Advantage: you can borrow a book for free, and furthermore, the reference librarian often knows of hidden treasures, buried in articles and clippings, which could be the answer to your prayers.

(3) **Mail order.** There are a number of mail order places which specialize in career books. Their catalogs are listed in the Addendum, at the end of Appendix A, beginning on page 406. Disadvantage: you have to wait to get the book (but if you phone, you can order them by Federal Express, so sometimes it's *next day*). Advantage: often, you can order it from anywhere in the world, and their listings of career books, tapes, videos and software, are far more extensive than you will find in the average bookstore, or library.

Job-Hunting Notes and U.S. Resources

1. ELEMENTARY OR HIGH SCHOOL STUDENTS, AND SUMMER JOBS

If you are a high school student looking for work, you already know that you face especial difficulties during your job-hunt. You *can* overcome these difficulties. But you do need to be aware of what they are.

In the U.S., employers currently are turning down, on average, 5 out of every 6 young people who apply for a job, and some companies report that fewer than 1 in 10 applicants meet *their* skills-needs. What's the problem? In a 1991 Harris Poll,[1] 78% of employers said graduates *do not have enough discipline in their work habits.* (That means graduates: failed to show up regularly, balked at doing tasks they considered 'beneath them,' failed to accomplish assigned tasks, arguing that as long as they just kept busy they were doing enough, and failed to go 'the extra mile.') Furthermore, in the area of skills, 90% of all employers felt that high school graduates "do not know how to solve complex problems."

As for simpler skills, such as **reading**, **writing**, **math**, *or typing* (as, on a computer keyboard), many graduates lack these as well. Evidence? Well, consider some U.S. Statistics: in 1945, the written vocabulary of a 6 to 14-year-old American child was 25,000 words. Today it is only 10,000. The average young adult in the U.S. is reading at only a 2.6 level of English proficiency, while current jobs require a proficiency, on the average, of 3.0 *(going up to 3.6 by the year 2000, experts say).*

---

1. Reported in the *San Francisco Chronicle* 9/30/91.

If you are still in high school, **get those skills** -- in reading, writing, math, and typing -- while you are there. If you are *out* of high school, but lack these skills, consider seriously going to night school at your local high school or community college, to make up for lost time.

In spite of the difficulties reported above, any high school student who is willing to diligently follow the job-hunting strategies in this book, particularly Chapters 9, 10, 11, as well as 3 and 4, should be able to put themselves well ahead of the pack. The rules are: *Know your skills. Know what you want to do. Talk to people who have done it. Find out how they did it. Do the homework, on yourself and the companies, thoroughly. Seek out the person who actually has the power to hire; use contacts to get in to see him or her. Show them how you can help them with their problems.* Cut no corners, take no shortcuts.

Below are some books that you or your parents and counselors may find additionally helpful (I have concluded the listing below with some resources proper for elementary school, since many parents are becoming concerned about career development for their children, even while the latter are still in elementary school, and some teachers and counselors want to at least broach the subject of *What do you want to do, when you grow up?* during those years):

Farr, J. Michael, and Pavlicko, Marie, *The JIST Job Search Course: A Young Person's Guide to Getting & Keeping a Good Job.* 1990. Job Information & Seeking Training (JIST) Works, Inc., 720 North Park Ave., Indianapolis, IN 46202-3431. Phone: 317-264-3720; Fax: 317-2645-3709. For high school juniors and seniors.

The Guide To Basic Skills Jobs: 2nd ed., *Vols. 1 and II.* 1993. RPM Press, Inc., P.O. Box 31483. Tucson, AZ 85751. 602-886-1990. A catalog of viable jobs for individuals with only basic work skills and/or limited education and/or limited general aptitudes -- such as persons with physical impairments, limited English proficiency, migrant workers, welfare recipients, persons with mental illness, etc. The database is *broken out* from the D.O.T., but a concise, easy-to-use classification system is added. These volumes identify over 5,000 major occupations which require no more than an eighth-grade level of education, and no more than one year of specific vocational preparation. Based upon research originally done by occupational analysts at North Carolina State University, and U.S.E.S. *Immensely useful book* if you counsel any of the above populations.

Kimeldorf, Martin, *Write Into A Job: Resumes and More.* 1990. Meridian Education Corporation, 236 E. Front St., Bloomington, IL 61701. Written particularly for entry-level or high school job-seekers. Teaches them how best to describe their marketable skills, in resumes or in other forms.

Kennedy, Joyce Lain, and Laramore, Dr. Darryl, *Joyce Lain Kennedy's Career Book.* 2nd ed., 1992. VGM Career Books, NTC Publishing Group, 4255 W. Touhy Ave., Lincolnwood, IL 60646-1975. Joyce is probably the most popular and knowledgeable syndicated columnist on the subject of careers, while Darryl has written other books on youth and jobs. Updated for the'90s.

Barkley, Nella, *How to Help Your Child Land The Right Job (without being a pain in the neck)*. 1993. Workman Publishing Company, Inc., 708 Broadway, New York, NY 10003. Nella worked with John Crystal for a number of years before he died, and now heads his Center.

Henderson, Douglass, *Get Ready: Job-Hunters Kit* (for high school students). This package includes: *Get Ready, Teachers Manual; Get Ready, Students Manual;* and cassette. 1980. Done in 'rap' style, with music. Very popular. Get Ready, Inc., a subsidiary of Educational Motivation, Inc., Box 18865, Philadelphia, PA 19119.

Mosenfelder, Donn, *Vocabulary for the World of Work*. 1985. Educational Design, Inc., 47 W. 13th St., New York, NY 10014. The 300 words that people entering the workforce most need to know.

Parramore, Barbara M., and Hopke, William E., *Early Occupational Awareness Program for Kindergarten and Grades One and Two*. 1994. Garrett Park Press, P.O. Box 190, Garrett Park, MD 20896.

Kimeldorf, Martin, *Job Search Education*. 1985. Educational Design, Inc., 47 W. 13th St., New York, NY 10011. Worksheets for the young job-hunter. Educational Design puts out a number of different books for elementary and high school students, in addition to the ones listed here, and they have a catalog of such materials, which you can ask for.

Chaney, Marti, and Thayer, Vicki, *Childhood Dreams Career Answers*. 1991. LifeWorks Press, P.O. Box 19476, Portland, OR 97280-0476.

As for **summer jobs in the U.S. or elsewhere**, here are the best-known directories for high school or college students. Most of them are annually updated, and the year of their revision often appears in their title:

Beusterien, Pat, ed., *Summer Employment Directory of the United States*. Issued in annual revisions. The year of the revision appears in the title of the book. Peterson's Guides, P.O. Box 2123, Princeton, NJ 08543.

Hatchwell, Emily, ed., *Directory of Summer Jobs in Britain*. Peterson's Guides, P.O. Box 2123, Princeton, NJ 08543. Issued in annual revisions.

Woodworth, David, ed., *Directory of Overseas Summer Jobs*. Issued in annual revisions. Peterson's Guides, P.O. Box 2123, Princeton, NJ 08543.

2. COLLEGE STUDENTS

If you are a college graduate or student looking for work, you already know that you face especial difficulties during your job-hunt. You *can* overcome these difficulties. But you do need to be aware of what they are.

The major problem is the false belief that there is a job that goes with the degree. *After all, don't corporate recruiters just come on campus during your senior year, and clamor for you to come work for them?* Well, no, they don't. In the U.S., for example, only one in three graduates had jobs waiting for them at graduation time in 1991. At some colleges or universities, that figure was only one in ten.[2] All other college graduates have to hunt -- hard -- after they are out. The situation is likely to improve *some* during the rest of the 1990s, but in most cases it is *you* who is going to have to take

2. *USA Today*, 5/1/92.

charge of your job-hunt. You can no longer rely on corporate recruiters coming to campus (if you ever could). The race for the best jobs belongs not to the strong, but to those who take initiative, are persistent, and know how to conduct their job-hunt themselves.

That leads us to the second problem, which is that job-hunting isn't taught in most colleges, even though it has today become a necessary survival skill. So, you'll have to pick it up on your own -- as you already know, or you wouldn't be looking at this book.

The rules are easy to learn, since they are the same for you as they are for everyone: *Know your skills. Know what you want to do. Talk to people who have done it. Find out how they did it. Do the homework, on yourself and the companies, thoroughly. Seek out the person who actually has the power to hire; use contacts to get in to see him or her. Show them how you can help them with their problems.*

Memorize Chapters 8, 9, 10, 11, 12, 13, and 14 in this book, as well as Chapters 3 and 4, please. And *do* the exercises therein. Cut no corners, take no shortcuts.

Remember that one out of seven students, in some sections of the country, get their job at the place where they interned.[3] So, internships might be an important part of your planning during the four years.

For those who do get a job, here were the average starting salaries in a recent year (1992):

For Those with a Bachelor's Degree:	$27,037
For Those with a Master's Degree:	$33,660
For Those with an MBA:	$36,175
For Those with a Ph.D.:	$38,068

If you want further reading, here it is:

Shingleton, Jack, *Which Niche? Answers to the most common questions about careers and job hunting.* 1989, 1969. Bob Adams, Inc., 260 Center St., Holbrook, MA 02343. A little book, marvelous for its brevity, and its humor. It has many cartoons, by the well-known and gifted San Francisco cartoonist, Phil Frank.

Phifer, Paul, *College Majors and Careers: A Resource Guide for Effective Life Planning.* Rev. ed. 1993. Garrett Park Press, Box 190, Garrett Park, MD 20896.

Phifer, Paul, *Career Planning Q's & A's: A Handbook for Students, Parents, and Professionals.* 1990. Garrett Park Press, Box 190, Garrett Park, MD 20896.

Figler, Howard, *Liberal Education and Careers Today.* 1989. Garrett Park Press, Box 190, Garrett Park, MD 20896. Good stuff, as is everything from Howard's pen.

Books on summer jobs are listed at the end of Section 1, above.

---

3. *San Francisco Chronicle,* 5/27/92.

3. IMMIGRANTS TO THE U.S.

Immigrants represent 8% of the U.S. workforce.[4] Between 1980 and 1989 some 8.6 million people immigrated to the U.S. legally, from overseas -- the highest since 1910–1919. In this decade, by the year 2,000, 10 million more are expected.

Among those groups growing the fastest are: Vietnamese, now 614,547 strong in the U.S. (as of the 1990 census), having grown 134.8% from 1980 to 1990; Asian Indian, 815,447, grew 125.6% in the same period; Korean, 798,849, grew 125.3; Chinese, 1,645,472, grew 104.1%; Filipino, 140,577, grew 81.6%; Mexican, 13,495,938, grew 54.4%; Puerto Rican, 2,727,754, grew 35.4%; and Cuban, 1,043,932, grew 30%.[5]

If you are newly arrived in this country, and are looking for work, you already know that you face especial difficulties during your job-hunt. You *can* overcome these difficulties. But you do need to be aware of what they are. And, how to overcome them.

Most of what you need to know, on both counts, can be learned in two ways. First of all, by talking to other immigrants, who have been here longer than you have, and have already 'learned the ropes.' And secondly, by reading this book you are holding in your hands, especially Chapters 3 and 4.

You will discover the chief job-hunting handicaps you need to overcome are your level of education, and your fluency (or lack of fluency) in English.

The rules are the same for you as they are for everyone else: *Know your skills. Know what you want to do. Talk to people who have done it. Find out how they did it. Do the homework, on yourself and the companies, thoroughly. Seek out the person who actually has the power to hire; use contacts to get in to see him or her. Show them how you can help them with their problems.* Pay particular attention to Chapters 9, 10, and 11. Also study Chapters 3, 4, 12, 13, and 14. Cut no corners, take no shortcuts.

If you want further reading, there is:

Friedenberg, Joan E., Ph.D., and Bradley, Curtis H., Ph.D., *Finding a Job in the United States.* 1988, 1986. NTC Publishing Group, 4255 W. Touhy Ave., Lincolnwood, IL 60646-1975. A guide for immigrants, refugees, limited-English-proficient job-seekers, foreign-born professionals -- anyone who is seeking work in the United States. It contains job information based on the successful experience of job-seekers, plus advice from the U.S. Department of Labor. Includes information about American job customs and laws related to immigration, as well as a systematic plan for job-hunting.

---

4. Monthly Labor Review, Dec. 1992, *"How do immigrants fare in the U.S. labor market?"*
5. Census Bureau figures, as reported in the New York Times, 9/6/92.

4. WOMEN

Approximately 74% of all women aged 20 to 44 years of age -- that totals over 57 million women -- are in the workforce, currently employed or looking for work.

When women first started coming into the world of work in droves, which was in the early 1970s, there was a widespread feeling that they needed special job-hunting techniques -- and that they needed career counselors who catered particularly to women job-hunters. Consequently, books for women job-hunters came out in those days by the bushel basket, and counselors catering just to women *thrived.* That day has passed, and now it is widely recognized that the advice for women who go job-hunting is the same as it is for men: *Know your skills. Know what you want to do. Talk to people who have done it. Find out how they did it. Do the homework, on yourself and the companies, thoroughly. Seek out the person who actually has the power to hire; use contacts to get in to see him or her. Show them how you can help them with their problems. Cut no corners, take no shortcuts.*

Since this realization dawned, there has been a great decline in the number of *women's* job-hunting books -- though a few do still appear each year. In spite of this trend, it is foolish to claim that there are no unique problems to women who are job-hunting. There are. You *can* overcome these problems, but you need to be aware of what they are.

Some problems reside within the myths that still dance in the heads of *some* employers, particularly *male* employers. Some *still* believe, for example, that if they hire a woman, she will be out sick more than a man. (As my mother always used to say when she couldn't believe the ideas some people had: *Honestly, what is the world coming to?*)

Well, anyway, if you are a woman going job-hunting, it will be useful to have some statistics at your fingertips. In this instance, the statistics in the U.S., at least (from the National Center for Health Statistics), are: women average 5.5 lost work days per year while men miss 4.3 days. In other words, women take only one more sick day *per year* than men do. Next?

There are problems that women face *as* they get the job, or *after* they get the job. Salary is a major one. Single women are notoriously underpaid, whether with children or without. The number of single parents in America currently -- most of them women -- is 10.1 million; of these, 2.1 million live in households headed by someone else -- most often, their parents.[6] The reason they do this is overwhelmingly because they can't afford to live on their own. Said one, "I'd have to earn twice my present salary in order to be able to live on my own." Married women don't fare much better, salarywise. True, in roughly one out of every five marriages, the wife is out-earning her mate; but then there are the other four. On average, working wives earned $13,250 in a recent year[7] compared to working husbands who averaged $29,150 that same year.

Part of the inequity is due to the fact that 50% of all working wives only work part-time. Wives working full-time averaged $18,930 in a recent year[8]

---

6. Reported in the *San Francisco Chronicle,* 4/28/92.

7. 1987, the last year for which statistics were available as we went to press.

8. 1987, again.

which is better than the $13,250 cited above -- but still far below husbands' average salary of $29,150. In general men get paid more than women of equal experience and training, for the same positions -- 20% more, on average.

There are ways of dealing with this. It begins with your choice of vocation. If most other people with the same job title as yours are men, you are more likely to be paid fairly. If you're in a new field, you are more likely to be paid fairly. If your job title is unusual, you are more likely to be paid fairly -- and even have room to negotiate just as good a salary as a man would get.

You *can* increase the salary offered you, *if* you know something about salary negotiation, before you go in for the job interview. Be *sure* and study Chapter 14, in this book.

Related to salary is the problem of child-care. In a relatively recent year, 1987, it was found, about one-third of the nation's 18.2 working mothers at that time had to pay for child-care -- and this cost them between $2,000 and $6,000 annually; the average was $2,305. For the working poor, child-care costs represented one-fifth of their income. Needless to say, these costs reduce the *net* amount of their already-low paycheck, considerably. In 1992, the lowest paid child-care workers earned $5.08 per hour, while the highest paid earned $8.19 per hour.[9] Some 60% of major corporations and roughly 10% of smaller businesses are 'family friendly,' offering *direct* or *indirect* assistance for child-care needs. But only .1% or approximately 5,600 firms in the U.S. offer formal programs.[10]

Another problem is that of sexual harassment or abuse in the workplace. While harassment in this crazy topsy-turvy world can sometimes be inflicted by women managers on the men or women they work with, or by males on males, the vast majority of harassment is done by males to females; and the harassment ranges from infinitely subtle to infinitely gross. The crux of the problem lies in *some* men's egos, insecurity, insensitivity, and in their assumption that women basically think like they do. They do not.

One evidence for a wide difference in the way the two sexes think, is the fact that 75% of men in the workplace find sexual advances from the opposite sex *flattering*, while 75% of women in the workplace find them *offensive*.[11]

Again, a similar proportion of men naively see nothing wrong with offering to spend extra **time**, inside or outside of work, helping women clients or women workers whom they happen to like; whereas a like proportion of women increasingly now tend to see this behavior as wrong.

9. From the Child Care Employee Project, of Oakland, California, as reported in *The New York Times*, 4/18/93, page F-25.
10. *Working Woman* Magazine, June 1993 issue. If you want help in getting some company to consider a child-care program, Child Care Action Campaign, 330 7th Ave., New York, NY 10001 has a description of 29 companies' programs (ranging from 6 to 230 employees), that you can ask for, called *Not Too Small To Care,* and the Families and Work Institute, same address, has *The Corporate Reference Guide to Work-Family Programs,* outlining 76 programs run by major corporations.
11. According to a survey done in the U.S., in 1992.

Naive men think this offer of their time to be *'open-hearted,'* while many women *(though not all)* -- because they have had prior experience with such offers from *devious* men, who intended it as a prelude to seduction -- hold such behavior to be always *'unprofessional,'* and *'inappropriate,'* at the least, or *'the beginning of sexual aggression,'* at the most.

Clearly, men and women need to educate each other.

When women are asked why they silently put up with harassment, subtle or gross, their universal reply is: "Because I need the job."

The idea of not putting up with it, but instead filing a sexual harassment suit, winning it, thus getting rid of your nemesis, and then being able to continue working in that same organization, is a wonderful vision. But do count the cost. Jobs are not just a series of tasks. They are people environments. Much depends on your having *good* rapport with the rest of the staff. Absent that rapport -- if you are shunned by your co-workers or superiors, in the aftermath of winning your sexual harassment suit -- your *wonderful* job can turn into *'the job from hell'* very quickly.

Moreover, future male employers are often reluctant to hire you if you are (unfairly) viewed as 'a trouble-maker,' based on your having filed this harassment suit; I have had to counsel three women to whom this has happened. Of course, if you limit your future job-hunting to firms run by women, this may not be a factor; on the contrary, they may regard you as a heroine. However, the accent is on the word *may.*

My advice is simple: if you think that filing a harassment suit is not going to fundamentally harm your rapport with the people you have to work with (let us say *everyone* dislikes the person who is your nemesis), and you are not worried about what it will do to your future employability, then seek out some good advice (I mean, from a lawyer), and if it is agreed that a suit is a good idea, by all means go ahead with it.

On the other hand, if you think that filing such a suit *is* going to irreparably damage the people environment for you at that job, and in the future, and you therefore decide not to file it, *don't* just decide to stay at that place and continue to take the abuse. Don't 'knuckle under.' Don't let anyone -- even your best friend, partner or spouse -- tell you *"Well, hey, if it's a good job and you like everything else about it, just put up with the sexual innuendos."* A good job, with sexual harassment present, is now by definition a bad job.

What keeps people in bad jobs *(most often)* is lack of confidence in their ability to go find another job, of equal merit. So, take command of your life. Sharpen up your job-hunting skills, *now.* Devour this book. Do all the exercises. When you're confident about your ability to go find another job, go find it. *Then* quit this one. You *don't* need to lose your self-esteem for a paycheck.

It's obvious the workplace is still a pretty chauvinist place, despite some limited improvement over the years. This is reflected not merely in sexual harassment, but also in another problem: that of the invisible *'glass ceiling.'* This now well-known phrase refers to the difficulty women have, in getting promoted beyond a certain point. At lower levels, women are doing better than they used to. They now represent 41% of all managers in the U.S.,

40% of all managers in Canada, and 40% of all managers in Australia.[12] But when you get to higher levels, it's a different story. *Oops! The glass ceiling!* In U.S. organizations in general, women hold fewer than 11% of high-ranking jobs, and less than 3% of top-level jobs.[13] This explains why so many women are gravitating instead to small organizations, or forming their own companies.

The number of women-owned businesses totaled 6.5 million in 1992.[14] They provide jobs for 10% of all U.S. workers, or close to 12 million people. This is more than the total employees of the 500 largest corporations in America -- 11.7 million. 40% of women-owned businesses have been in business twelve years or longer. If the idea of following in their footsteps interests you, be *sure* and study Chapter 6. Women who are thinking of starting their own business can get counseling over the phone, from the American Women's Economic Development Corporation (AWED), Monday through Friday, between 9 a.m. and 5 p.m. Eastern time, at a cost of $10 for up to ten minutes. The hotline offers an expert in the area in which the caller needs help. Longer counseling, up to one and a half hours, is also offered, at a cost of $35. If calling from New York City, Alaska, or Hawaii, call 212-688-1900. If calling from any other area, call 1-800-222-AWED. Both services may be charged to major credit cards.

Due partly to the obstacles cited above, partly to the hard times we are in, partly to many mothers' desire to be with their children while they may, partly to women concluding they want more time to smell the flowers, some women are dropping out of the workplace and taking on the role of homemaker. In 1990, the percentage of women in the work-force did not increase over the previous year, for the first time since 1948. In fact, it dropped. So, if you're contemplating dropping out of the workforce, for any of the above reasons, don't feel lonely, as though you were going against the trend. You've got lots of company. Even though this means you will not be going job-hunting, I would still advise you to do Chapters 9 and 10, in order to be clear about how you want to use your energies and skills, in the home and community.

If you're moving in the other direction, from the house to the marketplace, there are some *very* helpful resources you may want to get your hands on. The first listing is for either male or female homemakers:

Berg, Astrid, *Finding the Work You Love: A Woman's Career Guide.* 1994. Resource Publications, Inc., 160 E. Virginia St., #290, San Jose, CA 95112-5876.

Nivens, Beatryce, *Careers for Women without College Degrees.* McGraw-Hill Book Company, 11 West 19th St., New York, NY 10011. 1988. Has some useful information about the skills required for some typical occupations

---

12. Reported in *USA Today*, 2/5/93, as the result of a survey by The International Labor Organization.
13. *Ibid.*
14. Reported in *The (Bend, Oregon) Bulletin*, 4/19/93, p. A5, quoting *Working Woman* magazine. For further statistics, see: *Women Owned Businesses: The New Economic Force*, the 1992 Data Report of the National Foundation for Women Business Owners, available from them at 1377 K St., N.W., Suite 637, Washington, D.C. 20005.

that a woman might be considering. She has also written: *How To Change Careers.* 1990. The Putnam Publishing Group, 390 Murray Hill Pkwy., Dept. B, East Rutherford, NJ 07073.

If you are interested in sales positions, you will want to know about the National Association for Professional Saleswomen, P.O. Box 2606, Novato, CA 94948. They have chapters across the country, and they publish a newsletter, called *Successful Saleswoman.*

If it's daycare that concerns you, there are directories beginning to come out now, such as:

The New York Daycare Directory (Includes northern New Jersey and southwestern Connecticut). Bob Adams, Inc., 260 Center St., Holbrook, MA 02343.

The Boston Daycare Directory. Bob Adams, Inc., 260 Center St., Holbrook, MA 02343.

5. MINORITIES (BLACK, HISPANIC, NATIVE AMERICANS, OR ASIAN)

Minorities comprise the coming workforce of the year 2000. Already, one out of every three *new* workers in the U.S. is either Black, Hispanic, or Asian, according to the Bureau of Labor Statistics. One out of every five workers, new or experienced, was from one of these minorities in 1986 and one out of every four workers will be, by the year 2000.

In spite of this, if you are a member of one of the minorities, you already know that you face especial difficulties in looking for a job. You *can* overcome these difficulties. But you need to be aware of what they are.

The principal one is the mental view that others have of the world. I call this *tribalism,* and it is the root of so many troubles throughout the world: in the Persian Gulf region, the Middle East, Yugoslavia, Russia, Africa, and -- *of course* -- here. So long as whites remain dominant among employers, here, *tribalism* and its bastard offspring, *prejudice,* will be something you have to take into account.

Everyone is familiar with the consequences that this tribalism has had for **blacks**: while the number of affluent black households (a yearly income of $50,000 or more) doubled between 1982 and 1987, nonetheless 33% of the nation's 30.2 million blacks still live in poverty; black unemployment in 1988 averaged 11.7%, versus 5.5% for the nation; the median 1987 income of black families was only 56% of that of white families.

Other minorities run into the same tribalism. Minorities hold fewer than 1% of senior management jobs in this country.[15] So, if you're a member of a minority, that's what you're up against. Now, what can you do about it -- what will help you compete more successfully in the job-market? Answer: *Know your skills. Know what you want to do. Talk to people who have done it. Find out how they did it. Do the homework, on yourself and the companies, thoroughly. Seek out the person who actually has the power to hire; use contacts to get in to see him or her. Show them how you can help them with their problems.* Pay particular attention to Chapters 3, 4, 9, 10, and 11. Also study Chapters 12,

15. Reported in *USA Today,* 4/24/92.

13, and 14, *as though your life depended on it*. Cut no corners, take no shortcuts.

When it comes time to look for sources of information, or contacts, the following may be of help, in your local library, or direct from the publisher:

Kastre, Michael F., and Kastre, Nydia Rodriguez, and Edwards, Alfred G., *The Minority Career Guide*. 1993. Peterson's, P.O. Box 2123, Princeton, NJ 08543.

Johnson, Willis L., ed., *Directory of Special Programs for Minority Group Members: Career Information Services, Employment Skills Banks, Financial Aid Sources*, 5th ed. 1990. Garrett Park Press, Box 190, Garrett Park, MD 20896.

Minority Organizations: A National Directory. 4th ed. 1992. Garrett Park Press, Box 190, Garrett Park, MD 20896. An annotated directory of 9,700 Black, Hispanic, Native American, and Asian American organizations.

The Black Resource Guide. 10th ed., 1992. Black Resource Guide, Inc., 501 Oneida Pl., NW, Washington, DC 20011. A comprehensive list of over 3,000 black resources or organizations in the U.S.

6. EXECUTIVES, THE BUSINESS WORLD AND CORPORATE JOBS

If you are an executive looking for work, you already know that you face especial difficulties during your job-hunt. You *can* overcome these difficulties. But you do need to be aware of what they are. And, how to overcome them.

The first is, there are a lot of other executives out there, job-hunting at the same time you are. This most recent recession hit white-collar workers *hard*. In other words, you've got a lot of stiff competition. That's why the average job search period for executives was 6.8 months recently.[16]

Secondly, the length of your job-search will likely be related to your age, and the amount of salary that you are seeking. One large outplacement firm kept records and discovered that if an executive was 25–34 years of age, the average length of their job-hunt was about 20 weeks, but if over 55 years in age, it took almost 30 weeks. They further discovered that for those seeking an annual salary of $40,000 to $75,000, the average length of their job-hunt was about 25 weeks, while for those seeking more than $100,000, the average length of their job-hunt was almost 30 weeks.[17] That's what you're up against.

However, these statistics reflect not only a difficult job-market, but *more importantly* the method of job-hunting that executives traditionally depend upon. Chapter 3, in this book, describes executives' traditional method of job-hunting, mostly because they don't know any better. Avoid that method, like the plague.

Your salvation depends on the same creative job-hunting methods as anyone else: *Know your skills. Know what you want to do. Talk to people who*

16. According to Drake Beam Morin Inc., for the year 1990.
17. Reported in the *National Business Employment Weekly*, in the 8/27/89 edition. Statistics were for the year 1989.

*have done it. Find out how they did it. Do the homework, on yourself and the
companies, thoroughly. Seek out the person who actually has the power to hire; use
contacts to get in to see him or her. Show them how you can help them with their
problems.* Pay particular attention to Chapters 3, 4, 9, 10, and 11, *as though
your life depended on it.* Also study Chapters 12, 13, and 14. Cut no corners,
take no shortcuts.

If you aren't yet an executive, but think you would like to be one, know
what you are walking into. According to a 1990 survey by Accountemps, it
ain't all glamor: the average business executive reports that he or she
spends on average 60 hours a year *on hold* on the phone, and 128 hours a
year reading or writing unnecessary memos, and 288 hours a year attending unnecessary meetings. To get a more precise fix on the kind of executive that you'd like to be, in the kind of company that you'd like to work
for, go talk to executives who are already there, and ask them what their
week is like.

For would-be executives, and experienced executives alike, there are
the following additional helps:

Drucker, Peter, *Management: Tasks, Responsibilities, Practices.* 1993. Harper-
Business, 10 E. 53rd St., New York, NY 10022. A classic. Should be absolutely required reading for anyone contemplating entering, changing to,
or becoming a professional within any organization in the business world.

Burton, Mary Lindley, and Wedemeyer, Richard A., *In Transition: From
the Harvard Business School Club of New York's Career Management Seminar.*
HarperBusiness, 10 E. 53rd St., New York, NY 10022. 1991.

7. GOVERNMENT JOBS
(FEDERAL, STATE & LOCAL)

In the U.S., government was the one area where hiring increased
overall, during the the toughest times -- though of course there have been
cutbacks in some places, growth in others.

If you want to work for the Federal government, you will have to learn
how to fill out an SF-171 form, in many if not most cases. There are guides
to help you do this:

Smith, Russ, *The Right SF-171 Writer.* 1994. Impact Publications, 4580
Sunshine Court, Woodbridge, VA 22192.

DataTech's *Quick & Easy 171s.* A software program (for MS-DOS or
Windows, only) that produces the SF-171 for Federal job-seekers. Ap-
proved by the U.S. Office of Personnel Management. Personal *(single user)*
version: $49.95. Order from Impact Publications, 4580 Sunshine Court,
Woodbridge, VA 22192.

The novice government job-hunter assumes that civil service exams
introduce a mechanical impartiality to hiring decisions; not so. If, during
your informational interviewing (see Chapter 11 here in *Parachute*) you
encounter a federal manager who likes you, and wants to hire you, you
can bet your bottom dollar they will do everything they can to guide you
through the examination maze -- since any manager worth their salt has
long since learned how to creatively use the government's standard oper-

ating procedures to their own best advantage. This applies to local and state government positions, as well as federal. For further reading or help:

Krannich, Ronald L., and Krannich, Caryl Rae, *Find a Federal Job Fast!* 2nd ed. 1992. Impact Publications, 4580 Sunshine Court, Woodbridge, VA 22192. They have other federal job-hunting aids, as you will discover when they send you their catalog.

Government Job Finder, 1994–1995, by Daniel Lauber. 1994. Planning/ Communications, 7215 Oak Ave., River Forest, IL 60305. Lists over 1,600 associations, directories, journals, trade magazines, newsletters, computer- ized job-listings, online services, job-matching services, salary surveys, etc. -- dealing with local, state, or federal government work in the U.S. and abroad -- where contacts may be found, or job-leads advertised. Very thorough.

8. 'RECOVERING PEOPLE' (FROM ALCOHOLISM, DRUGS, OTHER CHEMICAL DEPENDENCIES, CO-DEPENDENCIES), AND OTHER '12-STEP PROGRAM PEOPLE'

You know what I'm going to say: if you are 'in recovery' and looking for work, you may face especial difficulties during the hiring interviews. You *can* overcome these difficulties. But you do need to be aware of what they are. And, how to overcome them.

Any prejudice about your history can be overcome if you: *Know your skills. Know what you want to do. Talk to people who have done it. Find out how they did it. Do the homework, on yourself and the companies, thoroughly. Seek out the person who actually has the power to hire; use contacts to get in to see him or her. Show them how you can help them with their problems.* Pay particular attention to Chapters 3, 4, 9, 10, and 11, *as though your life depended on it.* Also study Chapters 12, 13, and 14. Cut no corners, take no shortcuts.

If you want additional help, there are the following resources:

Tanenbaum, Nat, and Eric A., *The Career Seekers: A Program for Career Recovery.* 1988. This book is for people who are actively practicing any 12- step program, or are in counseling for co-dependency; but its principles apply to all who see themselves as 'recovering people.' Very useful supple- ment to *Parachute.* Order from Nat Tanenbaum, 21 Timberlane Circle, Pisgah Forest, NC 28768. 704-884-2995.

Whitfield, Charles L., M.D., *A Gift to Myself.* 1990. Health Communica- tions, Inc., 3201 SW 15th St., Deerfield Beach, FL 33442. Deals with root emotional issues often blocking job-hunters in recovery.

9. EX-MILITARY

If you are an ex-military person who has decided to look for work outside the military, in the general workplace, you already know that you will have some problems convincing the world you know *anything* except how to wage war. You *can* convince them, but it will take work.

Your major problem is that you speak a different language from those out there in the world. You have been living in a sub-culture within our general culture, and this sub-culture is in many respects like the general job-market, *except* that it has its own unique vocabulary. It is *crucial* that you sit down and inventory the skills you have been using during your time in the military (Chapters 9, 10, and 11 in this book are *mandatory* for you to *do*). Take especial care to take your skills and fields of knowledge out of the military *jargon*, and translate them into language that is understood in the general marketplace.

There are two aids to help you do this: (1) Each service's personnel manual has a section where military jobs and tasks are cross-coded to the civilian *Dictionary of Occupational Titles.* (2) There is also a two-volume Military Occupation Training Data series, available from Defense Manpower Data Center, 1600 Wilson Blvd., Suite 400, Arlington VA 22209, which does the same thing.

If you are or were an officer, you should know that the Retired Officers Association (TROA), 201 N. Washington Street, Alexandria, VA 22314-2529, 703-838-8117, has an Officer Placement Service which maintains a comprehensive job-search library, a computerized placement service, and resume critiques for their members. It is, however, open only to officers who become members of TROA.

Officer or not, your salvation depends on the same creative job-hunting -- and career-changing -- methods as anyone else: *Know your skills. Know what you want to do. Talk to people who have done it. Find out how they did it. Do the homework, on yourself and the companies, thoroughly. Seek out the person who actually has the power to hire; use contacts to get in to see him or her. Show them how you can help them with their problems.* Pay particular attention to Chapters 3, 4, 9, 10, and 11, *as though your life depended on it.* Also study Chapters 12, 13, and 14. Cut no corners, take no shortcuts.

An additional book:

Schlachter, Gail Ann, and Weber, R. David, *Financial Aid for Veterans, Military Personnel, and Their Dependents 1990–1991.* 1990. Reference Service Press, 1100 Industrial Road, Suite 9, San Carlos, CA 94070. Outlines over 1,000 programs open to veterans and their dependents. See if there is an updated version, by the time you read this.

10. CLERGY AND RELIGIOUS

If you are an ordained person who has decided to look for work outside the church, in the general workplace, you already know that you will have some problems convincing the world you know *anything* except theology. As a matter of fact, you *can* convince them, but it will take work.

Your major problem is that you speak a different language from those out there in the world. Like the military (above), you have been living in a sub-culture within our general culture, which describes your skills and work-experience in its own unique vocabulary. It is *crucial* that you sit down and inventory the skills you have been using during your time in the clergy (Chapters 9, 10, and 11 in this book are *mandatory* for you to *do*), and that you take especial care to *translate* your skills and fields of knowledge out of the clerical *jargon* and into language that is understood in the general marketplace.

The rules for *your* job-hunt, or career-change, are the same as they are for everyone: *Know your skills. Know what you want to do. Talk to people who have done it. Find out how they did it. Do the homework, on yourself and the companies, thoroughly. Seek out the person who actually has the power to hire; use contacts to get in to see him or her. Show them how you can help them with their problems.* Pay particular attention to Chapters 3, 4, 9, 10, and 11, *as though your life depended on it.* Also study Chapters 12, 13, and 14. Cut no corners, take no shortcuts.

In case you want further reading, or counseling, the books and counselors who look at job-hunting and career-changing particularly from a religious point of view are to be found at the end of The Epilogue, on page 464.

11. EX-OFFENDERS

If you are an ex-offender, and are looking for work, *of course* you are going to face especial difficulties during the hiring interviews, because of your history. You *can* deal with this problem, if you remember this above all: all employers divide into two groups: those who will be bothered by your incarceration, and those who won't be. Your job is to find the second group of employers, and just thank the first very politely for their time.

With the second, your case will be helped immeasurably if you: *Know your skills. Know what you want to do. Talk to people who have done it. Find out how they did it. Do the homework, on yourself and the companies, thoroughly. Seek out the person who actually has the power to hire; use contacts to get in to see him or her. Show them how you can help them with their problems.* Cut no corners, take no shortcuts.

If you want to start working on this while you are still in prison, devour *this* book. Pay particular attention to Chapters 3, 4, 9, 10, and 11, *as though your life depended on it.* Do all the pertinent exercises therein. Also study Chapters 12, 13, and 14. Cut no corners, take no shortcuts.

If you decide you want to work on a college degree program while you are in prison, it can be done. See the Appendix entitled, "Advice for People in Prison," in John Bear's *College Degrees by Mail: 100 Good Schools that Offer Bachelor's, Master's, Doctorates and Law Degrees by Home Study.* 1991. Ten Speed Press, Box 7123, Berkeley, CA 94707.

Once you're out, and you are job-hunting, Federal/State Employment Offices can often be of particular assistance to ex-offenders. All offices can provide for bonding of ex-offenders, if needed to obtain employment. They also have information on tax breaks for employers who hire ex-offenders. The larger offices even have Ex-Offender Specialists.

The Fortune Society, 39 W. 19th St. (between 5th & 6th Avenues), New York, NY 10011. 212-206-7070. JoAnne Page, Executive Director. This Society works primarily with people who can come to their office, but they can also direct ex-offenders to the *Prisoners' Assistance Directory,* developed by the ACLU; the *Directory of Programs Serving Families of Adult Offenders,* published by the U.S. Department of Justice; *Post-Release Assistance Programs for Prisoners,* published by McFarland & Co., Inc.; and the *Guide to Community Services,* a publication of the Community Resource Network -- all of which will list resources for the area of the country in which you wish to find employment. The Society publishes the *Fortune News,* which is sent to you if you send them a contribution.

If all else fails, contact your local Chamber of Commerce or United Way, to see if they can tell you which community service organizations work with ex-offenders in your town or city.

For further reading: *A Survival Sourcebook . . . A Living Skills Guide* from Cega Services, Box 81826, Lincoln, NE 68501. (Ask them for the current price of this sourcebook: 402-464-0602.)

12. PEOPLE WITH DISABILITIES OR HANDICAPS

If you have a physical, mental, emotional, or other disability, and are looking for work, *of course* you are going to face especial difficulties during the hiring interviews, because of your disability. You *can* deal with this problem, if you remember this above all: all employers divide into two groups: those who will be bothered by your disability, and those who won't be. Your job is to find the second group of employers, and just thank the first very politely for their time, plus secure any referrals they may be able to suggest.

With the second, your case will be helped immeasurably if you: *Know your skills. Know what you want to do. Talk to people who have done it. Find out how they did it. Do the homework, on yourself and the companies, thoroughly. Seek out the person who actually has the power to hire; use contacts to get in to see him or her. Show them how you can help them with their problems.* Cut no corners, take no shortcuts.

Now, as to books and other resources for further help:

Bolles, Richard N., *Job-Hunting Tips For The So-Called Handicapped or People Who Have Disabilities. A Supplement to What Color Is Your Parachute.* 1991. Order from Ten Speed Press, Box 7123, Berkeley, CA 94707. 61 pages. $4.95.[18]

Azrin, Nathan H., and Besalel, Victoria A., *Job Club Counselor's Manual: A Behavioral Approach to Vocational Counseling.* Pro-Ed, 8700 Shoal Creek Blvd., Austin, TX 78758. 512-451-3246. 1980. This is a detailed description of a particular method of job-hunting, called "the job club," which Nathan invented back in 1970, in order to find a more structured way in which to help persons with disabilities, as they went about their job-hunt. This manual explains in great detail how to set up such a club. Furthermore, chapter 14 in Azrin's book has a section on "Evaluation of the Job Club with Job-Handicapped Persons," which reports the success of this method with those who are disabled: 95% of those people with disabilities who were in the Job Club found jobs within 6 months, compared to 28% in a non-job-club control group. The job club's participants got salaries which were 22% higher than those in the control group who found jobs. Nathan

---

18. If you wish to save this money, you can consult your local library to see if it has a copy of the booklet, *or* a copy of the 1990 or 1991 editions of *Parachute,* since this stuff first appeared as an Appendix in the back of those editions.

has written another manual for those disabled job-hunters who cannot find a job club near them, spelling out how to follow the job club techniques all by yourself. That book is: Azrin, Nathan H., and Besalel, Victoria A., *Finding A Job*. Ten Speed Press, P.O. Box 7123, Berkeley, CA 94707. 1982.

If you want information about what resources exist to help you in your job-hunt, there is the Clearinghouse on Disability Information, U.S. Department of Education, Rm. 3132, Switzer Bldg., Washington, DC 20202-2524. 202-732-1241. It publishes an INFOPAC on Employment of Individuals with Disabilities, which you may ask for, that lists all kinds of groups, agencies, and programs throughout the country that exist to assist people with disabilities in finding employment or training for employment. They also publish a list of Selected Federal Publications Relating to Disability.

They also distribute Summary of Existing Legislation Affecting Persons with Disabilities, that summarizes in some detail all the federal laws that protect you, serve you, or offer you help. The Clearinghouse has a simpler version of the above publication, called the Pocket Guide to Federal Help for Individuals with Disabilities, which you can buy from the Superintendent of Documents, U.S. Government Printing Office, Washington, DC 20402.

For employers concerned about employing people with disabilities, there is: the *Enhanced Edition of the EEOC's Technical Assistance Manual for Compliance with the Americans with Disabilities Act,* available from Rehab Publications, P.O. Box 22606, San Francisco CA 94122.

For those desiring some information about the 300 or so independent living centers or programs in this country, there is the *Directory of Independent Living Programs,* published by Research and Training Center on Independent Living, 3400 Bissonnet, Suite 101, Houston, TX 77005. Contact Laurel Richards, 713-666-6244.

Kimeldorf, Martin, and Edwards, Jean, *Numbers That Spell Success: Transitions to Work and Leisure Roles for Mildly Handicapped Youth.* Ednick Communications, Box 3612, Portland, OR 97208. 1988.

For persons who are "print handicapped" or for other reasons can't read books or journals:

The National Library Service for the Blind and Physically Handicapped, Library of Congress, 1291 Taylor St. NW, Washington, DC 20542, has put many books on career planning and job-hunting (such as *Parachute*) on tape, which they will send, with special playback equipment, to your home and back, free, if you are able to prove a "print handicap."

Recording for the Blind, Inc., 20 Roszel Rd., Princeton, NJ 08540, likewise has translated job-hunting books for the print handicapped and visually impaired.

Also every state has library services of recorded books, usually lodged in the state library or the state agency for the blind. Any counselor, social worker, or blind person in your state should know where this is.

If there's something you're looking for, and you just can't find it locally, try the Library of Congress in Washington, DC.

13. PEOPLE FACING RETIREMENT
OR ALREADY RETIRED

Now, a word or two about **retirement** in the U.S.: if you work in a company with 20 or more employees, they cannot since 1986 force you to retire just because you reach a specified age, though they can force you to retire for unsatisfactory performance of your job at any age. Does this mean there are a lot more 'older workers' now than there used to be? No, strangely enough, it does not. In 1950, 46% of men over 65 were still in the labor force; and now that percentage is less than 17%. Most men and women now leave the workforce before they turn 63. In fact, one-third of all career jobs now end by age 55.[19]

What happens **after** retirement? The percentages, according to a relatively recent study,[20] are that half of the elderly who are out of the workforce are satisfied with their situation, one-quarter are simply *unable* to work (presumably because of health), and one-quarter are very unhappy with the fact that they aren't working.

The numbers underlying those percentages are these:[21] 21.5 million Americans are between ages 50 and 64, of whom 13.3 million are working, and 8.2 million are not. Of the latter, 4.7 million don't want to work, 1.6 million are unable to, and almost 2 million would like to be back at work. In fact, one out of three retired **men** does return to the labor force, usually within two years.[22]

If you are retired, and would like to return to work, *of course* you are going to face especial difficulties during the hiring interviews, because of your age. You *can* deal with this problem, if you remember this above all: all employers divide into two groups: those who will be bothered by your age, and those who won't be. Your job is to find the second group of employers, and just thank the first very politely for their time.

With the second, your case will be helped immeasurably if you: *Know your skills. Know what you want to do. Talk to people who have done it. Find out how they did it. Do the homework, on yourself and the companies, thoroughly. Seek out the person who actually has the power to hire; use contacts to get in to see him or her. Show them how you can help them with their problems.* Cut no corners, take no shortcuts.

As you probably already know, in the U.S. your desire to work will be complicated by Social Security requirements, which amount basically to a disincentive to work: in order to continue to receive full benefits, *as of 1993 the rules were:* you must not earn more than $7,680 a year if you are under 65. You will lose $1 in benefits for every $2 that you earn above that limit. If you are 65 to 69, you must not earn more than $10,560. You will lose $1 in benefits for every $3 that you earn above that limit. After you reach 70, however, there is no limit. Check with your local Social Security office to find out if the limits have been raised, by the time you read this.

19. *Monthly Labor Review,* July 1992, "Trends in retirement age by sex, 1950–2005."
20. Reported in *The New York Times,* 4/22/90.
21. Reported in *National Business Employment Weekly,* 2/18/90.
22. Reported in *American Demographics,* 12/90. Statistics for women in retirement are not yet available.

If you want to work primarily (or solely) to supplement your retirement income, the foregoing is a serious disincentive, indeed. On the other hand, if you want to work for the pure joy of working, the economic disincentive will probably not faze you. You can always volunteer your time (see Chapter 5), without cost to the place where you serve. Now, to further reading.

If you're trying to plan what your retirement will be like, even if you don't work, there is:

Chapman, Elwood N., *Comfort Zones: Planning Your Future.* 3rd ed. 1993. Crisp Publications, Inc., 1200 Hamilton Court, Los Altos, CA 94025-9600, or Career Research & Testing, 2005 Hamilton Ave., Suite 250, San Jose, CA 95125-9872. A very popular and practical guide for retirement planning.

How to Plan Your Successful Retirement, 1988. AARP Book Publication, American Association for Retired Persons, 601 E Street NW, Washington, DC 20049.

If you want some guidance about possible places to retire to, in the U.S., there are these three resources:

Richard Boyer and David Savageau, *Places Rated Almanac: Your Guide to Finding the Best Places to Live in North America,* rev. ed. 1993. Prentice-Hall, 15 Columbus Circle, New York, NY 10023. A marvelous book. Immensely helpful for anyone weighing where to move next. All 343 metropolitan areas are ranked and compared for living costs, job outlook, crime, health, transportation, education, the arts, recreation, and climate. Has numerous helpful diagrams, charts and maps, showing (for example) earthquake risk areas, tornado and hurricane risk areas, the snowiest areas, the stormiest areas, the driest areas, and so on. Highly recommended. A knockout of a book.

Savageau, David, *Retirement Places Rated.* 3rd ed. 1990. Prentice Hall Press, 15 Columbus Circle, New York, NY 10023. 151 top retirement areas ranked and compared for costs of living, housing, climate, personal safety, services, work opportunities, and leisure living. Highly recommended. Tremendously useful. He updates it periodically.

Best-Rated Retirement Cities & Towns, 1988. Consumer Guide Publications International, Ltd., 7373 N. Cicero Ave., Lincolnwood, IL 60646. A review of 100 of the most attractive retirement locations across America.

If you want to know what retired people do, by way of work, after retirement, the classic on this subject is:

Bird, Caroline, *Second Careers: New Ways to Work After 50.* 1992. Little, Brown and Company, Time Warner Bldg., 1271 Avenue of the Americas, New York, NY 10020. The subject of this book is not what 'seniors' *ought* to do after age 50, but what in fact they *do* do . . . and why. This book is her 'report to the nation' of her analysis of some 36,000 questionnaires sent in by readers of *Modern Maturity* magazine. Highly recommended.

Introduction

As I started writing this section on "Religion and Job-Hunting," I toyed at first with the idea of following what might be described as an "all-paths approach" to religion. But, after much thought, I decided not to try that. This, because I have read many other writers who tried, and I felt the approach failed miserably. An "all-paths" approach to religion ends up being a "no-paths" approach, even as a woman or man who tries to please everyone ends up pleasing no one. It is the old story of the "universal" vs. the "particular."

Those of us who do career counseling could predict, ahead of time, that trying to stay universal is not likely to be helpful, in writing about religion. We know well from our own field that truly helpful career counseling depends upon defining the **particularity** or uniqueness of each person we try to help. No employer wants to know only what you have in common with everyone else. He or she wants to know what makes you unique and individual. As I have argued throughout this book, the identification and inventory of your uniqueness or *particularity* is crucial if you are ever to find meaningful work.

This particularity invades and carries over to *everything* a person does; it is not suddenly "jettisonable" when he or she turns to religion. Therefore, when I or anyone else writes about religion I believe we **must** write out of our own particularity -- which *starts,* in my case, with the fact that I write, and think, and breathe as a Christian. So, this article speaks from my own personal Christian perspective. I want you to be forewarned.

I have always been acutely aware, however, that this is a pluralistic society in which we live, and that I owe a great deal of sensitivity to the readers of my books who may have convictions very different from my own. I rub up against these different convictions, daily. By accident and not design it has turned out that the people who work or have worked here in my office with me, over the years, have been predominantly Jewish, along with some non-religious and a smattering of Christians. Furthermore, **Parachute's** more than 4 million readers have included Christians of every variety and persuasion, Jews, members of the Baha'i faith, Hindus, Buddhists, adherents of Islam, and believers in 'new age' religions, as well as (of course) secularists, humanists, agnostics, atheists, and many others. Consequently, I have tried to be very courteous toward the feelings of all my readers who come from other persuasions or convictions than my own, *while at the same time* counting on them to translate my Christian thought forms into their own thought forms -- since this ability to thus translate is the indispensable *sine qua non* of anyone who aspires to communicate helpfully with others.

In the Judeo-Christian tradition from which I come, one of the indignant Biblical questions is, "Has God forgotten to be gracious?" The answer was a clear No. I think it is important *for all of us* also to seek the same goal. I have therefore labored to make this section gracious as well as helpful.

R. N. B.

The Epilogue

Religion
and
Job-Hunting:

How to Find Your Mission in Life

How I Came To Write This

Some time ago, a woman asked me how you go about finding out what your Mission in life is. She assumed I would know what she was talking about, because of a diagram which appears a number of times in one of my other books, The Three Boxes of Life:

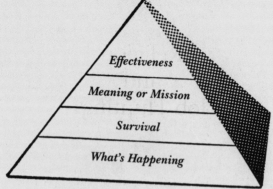

The Issues of the Job-Hunt

As this diagram asserts, the question of one's Mission in life arises naturally as a part of many people's job-hunt.

She told me that what she was looking for was not some careful, dispassionate, philosophical answer, where every statement is hedged about with cautions and caveats -- "It may be . . ." or "It seems to me . . ." Nor did she want to know why I thought what I did, or how I learned it, or what Scriptures support it. "I want you to just speak with passion and conviction," she said, "out of what you most truly feel and believe. For it is some vision that I want. I am hungry for a vision of what I can be. So, just speak to me of what you most truly feel and believe about our mission in life. I will know how to translate your vision into my own thought forms for my own life, when I reflect afterwards upon what you have said. But I want you to talk about this now with passion and conviction -- please."

And so, I did. And I will now tell you what I said to her.

The Motive for Finding
A Sense of Mission in Life

We begin with the fact that, according to fifty years of opinion polls conducted by the Gallup Organization, 94% of us believe in God, 90% of us pray, 88% of us believe God loves us, and 33% of us report we have had a life-changing religious experience (*The People's Religion: American Faith in the 90s. Macmillan & Co. 1989*).

It is hardly surprising therefore, that so many of us are searching these days for some sense of mission. Career counselors are often afraid to give help or guidance here, for fear they will be perceived as trying to talk people into religious belief. It is a groundless fear. Clearly, the overwhelming majority of U.S. job-hunters and career-changers already have their religious beliefs well in place.

But, we want some guidance and help in this area, because we want to *marry* our religious **beliefs** with our **work**, rather than leaving the two -- our religion and our work -- compartmentalized, as two areas of our life which never talk to each other. We *want* them to talk to each other and uplift each other.

This marriage takes the particular form of a search for a Sense of Mission because of our conviction that God has made each of us unique, even as our fingerprints attest. We feel that we are not just another grain of sand lying on the beach called humanity, unnumbered and lost in the 5 billion mass, but that God caused us to be born and put here for some unique reason: so that we might contribute to Life here on earth something no one else can contribute in quite the same way. At its very minimum, then, when we search for a sense of Mission we are searching for reassurance that the world is at least a little bit richer for our being here; and a little bit poorer after our going.

Every keen observer of human nature will know what I mean when I say that those who have found some sense of Mission have a very special joy, "which no one can take from them." It is wonderful to feel that beyond eating, sleeping, working, having pleasure and *it may be* marrying, having children, and growing older, you were set here on Earth for some special purpose, *and* that you can gain some idea of what that purpose is.

So, how does one go about this search?

I would emphasize, at the outset, two cautions. First of all, though I will explain the steps that seem to me to be involved in finding one's Mission -- based on the learnings I have accumulated over some sixty years, I want to caution you that these steps are not the only Way -- by any means. Many people have discovered their Mission by taking other paths. And you may, too. But hopefully what I have to say may shed some light upon whatever path you take.

My second caution is simply this: you would be wise not to try to approach this problem of "your Mission in life" as primarily an **intellectual** puzzle -- for the mind, and the mind alone, to solve. To paraphrase Kahlil Gibran, *Faith* is an oasis in the heart that is not reached merely by the journey of the mind. It is your will and your heart that must be involved in the search as well as your mind. To put it quite simply, it takes the total person to learn one's total Mission.

It also takes the total disciplines of the ages -- not only modern knowledge but also ancient thought, including the wisdom of religion, faith, and the spiritual matters. For, to put it quite bluntly, the question of Mission inevitably leads us to God.

The Main Obstacle in Finding Your Mission in Life: Job-Hunting Compartmentalized from Our Religion or Faith

Mission challenges us to see our job-hunt in relationship to our faith in God, because *Mission* is a religious concept, from beginning to end. It is defined by Webster's as "a continuing task or responsibility that one is destined or fitted to do or specially called upon to undertake," and historically has had two major synonyms: *Calling* and *Vocation*. These, of course, are the same word in two different languages, English and Latin. Regardless of which word is used, it is obvious upon reflection, that a Vocation or Calling implies *Someone who calls*, and that a destiny implies *Someone who determined the destination for us*. Thus, unless one opts for a military or governmental view of the matter, the concept of Mission with relationship to our whole life lands us inevitably in the lap of God, before we have even begun.

There is always the temptation to try to speak of this subject of *Mission* in a secular fashion, without reference to God, as though it might be simply "a purpose you choose for your own life, by identifying your enthusiasms, and then using the clues you find from that exercise to get some purpose you can choose for your life." The language of this temptation is ironic because the substitute word used for "Mission" -- *Enthusiasm* -- is derived from the Greek, *'en theos,'* and literally means "God in us."

It is no accident that so many of the leaders in the job-hunting field over the years -- the late John Crystal, Arthur Miller, Ralph Mattson, Tom and Ellie Jackson, Bernard Haldane, Arthur and Marie Kirn, and myself -- have been people of faith. If you would figure out your Mission in life, you must also be willing to think about God in connection with your job-hunt.

The Secret of Finding Your Mission in Life: Taking It in Stages

The puzzle of figuring out what your Mission in life is, will likely take some time. It is not a *problem* to be solved in a day and a night. It is a *learning process* which has steps to it, much like the process by which we all learned to eat. As a baby we did not tackle adult food right off. As we all recall, there were three stages: first there had to be the mother's milk or bottle, then strained baby foods, and finally -- after teeth and time -- the stuff that grown-ups chew. Three stages -- and the two earlier stages were not to be disparaged. It was all Eating, just different forms of Eating -- appropriate to our development at the time. But each stage had to be mastered, in turn, before the next could be approached.

The Three Stages of Mission:
What We Need to Learn

By coincidence, there are usually three stages also to learning what your Mission in life is, and the two earlier stages are likewise not to be disparaged. It is all "Mission" -- just different forms of Mission, appropriate to your development at the time. But each stage has to be mastered, in turn, before the next can be approached. And so, you may say either of two things: You may say that you have *Three Missions in Life.* Or you may say that you have *One Mission in Life, with three parts to it.* But there is a sense in which you must discover what those three parts are, each in turn, before you can fully answer the question, "What is my Mission in life?" Of course, there is another sense in which you never master any of these stages, but are always growing in understanding and mastery of them, throughout your whole life here on Earth.

As it has been impressed on me by observing many people over the years (admittedly through *Christian spectacles*), it appears that the three parts to your Mission here on Earth can be defined generally as follows:

(1) *Your first Mission here on Earth* is one which you share with the rest of the human race, but it is no less your individual Mission for the fact that it is shared: and it is, **to seek to stand hour by hour in the conscious presence of God, the One from whom your Mission is derived.** *The Missioner before the Mission,* is the rule. In religious language, your Mission here is: *to know God, and enjoy Him forever, and to see His hand in all His works.*

(2) Secondly, once you have begun doing that in an earnest way, *your second Mission here on Earth* is also one which you share with the rest of the human race, but it is no less your individual mission for the fact that it is shared: and that is, **to do what you can, moment by moment, day by day, step by step, to make this world a better place, following the leading and guidance of God's Spirit within you and around you.**

(3) Thirdly, once you have begun doing that in a serious way, *your third Mission here on Earth* is one which is uniquely yours, and that is:

a) **to exercise that Talent which you particularly came to Earth to use -- your greatest gift, which you most delight to use,**

b) **in the place(s) or setting(s) which God has caused to appeal to you the most,**

c) **and for those purposes which God most needs to have done in the world.**

When fleshed out, and spelled out, I think you will find that there you have the definition of your Mission in life. Or, to put it another way, these are the three Missions which you have in life.

The Two Rhythms of the Dance of Mission:
Unlearning, Learning,
Unlearning, Learning

The distinctive characteristic of these three stages is that in each we are forced to *let go* of some fundamental assumptions which the world has *falsely* taught us, about the nature of our Mission. In other words, throughout this quest and at each stage we find ourselves engaged not merely in a process of *Learning*. We are also engaged in a process of *Un*learning. Thus, we can restate the above three Learnings, in terms of what we also need to *un*learn at each stage:

• We need in the first Stage to *un*learn the idea that our Mission is primarily to keep busy *doing* something (here on Earth), and learn instead that our Mission is first of all to keep busy being something (here on Earth). In Christian language (and others as well), we might say that we were sent here to learn how *to be* sons of God, and daughters of God, before anything else. *"Our Father, who art in heaven . . ."*

• In the second stage, "Being" issues into "Doing." At this stage, we need to *un*learn the idea that everything about our Mission must be *unique* to us, and learn instead that some parts of our Mission here on Earth are *shared* by all human beings: e.g., we were all sent here to bring more gratitude, more kindness, more forgiveness, and more love, into the world. We share this Mission because the task is too large to be accomplished by just one individual.

• We need in the third stage to *un*learn the idea that that part of our Mission which is truly unique, and most truly ours, is something Our Creator just *orders* us to do, without any agreement from our spirit, mind, and heart. (On the other hand, neither is it something that each of us chooses and then merely asks God to bless.) We need to learn that God so honors our free will, that He has ordained our unique Mission be something which we have some part in choosing.

• In this third stage we need also to *un*learn the idea that our unique Mission must consist of some achievement which all the world will see, -- and learn instead that as the stone does not always know what ripples it has caused in the pond whose surface it impacts, so neither we nor those who watch our life will always know *what we have achieved* by our life and by our Mission. *It may be* that by the grace of God we helped bring about a profound change for the better in the lives of other souls around us, but it also may be that this takes place beyond our sight, or after we have gone on. And we may never know what we have accomplished, until we see Him face-to-face after this life is past.

• Most finally, we need to *un*learn the idea that what we have accomplished is our doing, and ours alone. It is God's Spirit breathing in us and through us which helps us to do whatever we do, and so the singular first person pronoun is never appropriate, but only the plural. Not "*I* accomplished this" but "*We* accomplished this, God and I, working together . . ."

That should give you a general overview. But I would like to add some random comments on my part about each of these three Missions of ours here on Earth.

Some Random Comments About Your First Mission in Life

Your first Mission here on Earth is one which you share with the rest of the human race, but it is no less your individual Mission for the fact that it is shared: and that is, **to seek to stand hour by hour in the conscious presence of God, the One from whom your Mission is derived.** The Missioner before the Mission, is the rule. In religious language, your Mission is: to know God, and enjoy Him for ever, and to see His hand in all His works.

Comment 1: How We Might Think of God

Each of us has to go about this primary Mission according to the tenets of his or her own particular religion. But I will speak what I know out of the context of my own particular faith, and you may perhaps translate and apply it to yours. I will speak as a Christian, who believes (passionately) that Christ is the Way and the Truth and the Life. But I also believe, with St. Peter, "that God shows no partiality, but in every nation any one who fears him and does what is right is acceptable to him." (Acts 10:34-35)

Now, Jesus claimed many unique things about Himself and His Mission; but He also spoke of Himself as the great prototype for us all. He called himself "the Son of Man," and He said, "I assure you that the man who believes in me will do the same things that I have done, yes, and he will do even greater things than these . . ." (John 14:12)

Emboldened by His identification of us with His life and His Mission, we might want to remember how He spoke about His Life here on Earth. He put it in this context: **"I came from the Father and have come into the world; again, I am leaving the world and going to the Father."** (John 16:28)

If there is a sense in which this is, in even the faintest way, true also of our lives (and I shall say in a moment in what sense I think it is true), then instead of calling our great Creator "God" or "Father" right off, we might begin our approach to the subject of religion by referring to the One Who gave us our Mission and sent us to this planet not as "God" or "Father" but -- *just to help our thinking* -- as: **"The One From Whom We Came and The One To Whom We Shall Return,"** when this life is done.

If our life here on Earth be at all like Christ's, then this is a true way to think about the One who gave us our Mission. We are not some kind of eternal, pre-existent *being*. We are **creatures**, who once did not exist, and then came into Being, and continue to have our Being, only at the will of our great Creator. But as creatures we are both body and soul; and although we know our body was created in our mother's womb, our soul's origin is a great mystery. Where it came from, at what moment the Lord created it, is something we cannot know. It is not unreasonable to suppose, however, that the great God created our *soul* before it entered our body, and in that sense we did indeed stand before God before we were born; and He is indeed **"The One From Whom We Came and The One To Whom We Shall Return."**

Therefore, before we go searching for "what work was I sent here to do?" we need to establish or in a truer sense *reestablish* -- contact with this **"One From Whom We Came and The One To Whom We Shall Return."** Without this reaching out of the creature to the great Creator, without this reaching out of *the creature with a Mission* to *the One Who Gave Us That Mission*, the question **what** *is my Mission in life?* is void and null. The *what* is rooted in the *Who*; absent the Personal, one cannot meaningfully discuss The Thing. It is like the adult who cries, "I want to get married," without giving any consideration to *who* it is they want to marry.

Comment 2: How We Might Think of Religion or Faith

In light of this larger view of our creatureliness, we can see that *religion* or *faith* is not a question of whether or not we choose to (*as it is so commonly put*) "have a relationship with God." Looking at our life in a larger context than just our life here on Earth, it becomes apparent that some sort of relationship with God is a given for us, about which we have absolutely no choice. God and we **were and are** related, during the time of our soul's existence before our birth and in the time of our soul's continued existence after our death. The only choice we have is what to do about **The Time In Between,** i.e., what we want the nature of our relationship with God to be during our time here on Earth and how that will affect the *nature* of the relationship, then, after death.

One of the corollaries of all this is that by the very act of being born into a human body, it is an inevitable that we undergo a kind of *amnesia* -- an amnesia which typically embraces not only our nine months in the womb, our baby years, and almost one third of each day (sleeping), but more importantly any memory of our origin or our destiny. We wander on Earth as an amnesia victim. To seek after Faith, therefore, is to seek to climb back out of that amnesia. Religion or faith is **the hard reclaiming of knowledge we once knew as a certainty.**

Comment 3: The First Obstacle to Executing This Mission

This first Mission of ours here on Earth is not the easiest of Missions, simply because it is the first. Indeed, in many ways, it is the most difficult. All can see that our life here on Earth is a very physical life. We eat, we drink, we sleep, we long to be held, and to hold. We inherit a physical body, with very physical appetites, we walk on the physical earth, and we acquire physical possessions. It is the most alluring of temptations, *in our amnesia*, to come up with just a *Physical* interpretation of this life: to think that the Universe is merely interested in the survival of species. Given this interpretation, the story of our individual life could be simply told: we are born, grow up, procreate, and die.

But we are ever recalled to do what we came here to do: that without rejecting the joy of the Physicalness of this life, such as the love of the blue sky and the green grass, we are to reach out beyond all this to **recall** and recover a *Spiritual* interpretation of our life. *Beyond* the physical and *within* the physicalness of this life, to detect a Spirit and a Person from beyond this Earth who is with us and in us -- the very real and loving and awesome Presence of the great Creator from whom we came -- and the One to whom we once again shall go.

Comment 4: The Second Obstacle to Executing This Mission

It is one of the conditions of our earthly amnesia and our creatureliness that, sadly enough, some very *human* and very *rebellious* part of us *likes* the idea of living in a world where we can be our own god -- and therefore loves the purely Physical interpretation of life, and finds it *anguish* to relinquish it. Traditional Christian vocabulary calls this **"sin"** and has a lot to say about the difficulty it poses for this first part of our Mission. All who live a thoughtful life know that it is true: our greatest enemy in carrying out this first Mission of ours is indeed *our own* heart and our own rebellion.

Comment 5: Further Thoughts About What Makes Us Special and Unique

As I said earlier, many of us come to this issue of our Mission in life, because we want to feel that we are unique. And what we mean by that, is that we hope to discover some "specialness" intrinsic to us, which is our birthright, and which no one can take from us. What we, however, discover from a thorough exploration of this topic, is that we are indeed special -- but only because God thinks us so. Our specialness and uniqueness reside in Him, and His love, rather than in anything intrinsic to our own *being*. The proper appreciation of this distinction causes our feet to carry us in the end not to the City called Pride, but to the Temple called Gratitude.

What is religion? Religion is the service of God out of grateful love for what God has done for us. The Christian religion, more particularly, is the service of God out of grateful love for what God has done for us in Christ.

Phillips Brooks, author of
O Little Town of Bethlehem

Comment 6: The Unconscious Doing of
The Work We Came To Do

You may have *already* wrestled with this first part of your Mission here
on Earth. You may not have called it that. You may have called it simply
"learning to believe in God." But if you ask what your Mission is in life,
this one was and is the precondition of all else that you came here to do.
Absent this Mission, and it is folly to talk about the rest. So, if you have
been seeking faith, or seeking to strengthen your faith, you have -- willy
nilly -- already been about *the doing of the Mission you were given.* Born into
This Time In Between, you have found His hand again, and reclasped it.
You are therefore ready to go on with His Spirit to tackle together what
you came here to do -- the other parts of your Mission.

Some Random Comments About
Your Second Mission in Life

Your second Mission here on Earth is also one which you share with
the rest of the human race, but it is no less your individual mission for the
fact that it is shared: and that is, **to do what you can moment by moment,
day by day, step by step, to make this world a better place -- following
the leading and guidance of God's Spirit within you and around you.**

Comment 1: The Uncomfortableness of
One Step at a Time

Imagine yourself out walking in your neighborhood one night, and
suddenly you find yourself surrounded by such a dense fog, that you have
lost your bearings and cannot find your way. Suddenly, a friend appears
out of the fog, and asks you to put your hand in theirs, and they will lead
you home. And you, not being able to tell where you are going, trustingly
follow them, even though you can only see one step at a time. Eventually
you arrive safely home, filled with gratitude. But as you reflect upon the
experience the next day, you realize how unsettling it was to have to keep
walking when you could see only one step at a time, even though you had
guidance in which you knew you could trust.

Now I have asked you to imagine all of this, because this is the essence
of the second Mission to which *you* are called -- and *I* am called -- in this
life. It is all very different than we had imagined. When the question,

"What is your Mission in life?" is first broached, and we have put our hand in God's, as it were, we imagine that we will be taken up to *some mountain-top,* from which we can see far into the distance. And that we will hear a voice in our ear, saying, "Look, look, see that distant city? That is the goal of your Mission; that is where everything is leading, every step of your way."

But instead of the mountaintop, we find ourself in *the valley* -- wandering often in a fog. And the voice in our ear says something quite different from what we thought we would hear. It says, **"Your Mission is to take one step at a time, even when you don't yet see where it all is leading, or what the Grand Plan is, or what your overall Mission in life is. Trust Me; I will lead you."**

Comment 2: The Nature of This Step-by-Step Mission

As I said, in every situation you find yourself, you have been sent here to do whatever you can -- moment by moment -- that will bring more gratitude, more kindness, more forgiveness, more honesty, and more love into this world.

There are dozens of such moments every day. Moments when you stand -- as it were -- at a spiritual crossroads, with two ways lying before you. Such moments are typically called **"moments of decision."** It does not matter what the frame or content of each particular decision is. It all devolves, in the end, into just two roads before you, *every time.* **The one** will lead to *less* gratitude, *less* kindness, *less* forgiveness, *less* honesty, or *less* love in the world. **The other** will lead to *more* gratitude, *more* kindness, *more* forgiveness, *more* honesty, or *more* love in the world. Your Mission, each moment, is to seek to choose the latter spiritual road, rather than the former, *every time.*

Comment 3: Some Examples of This Step-by-Step Mission

I will give a few examples, so that the nature of this part of your Mission may be unmistakably clear.

You are out on the freeway, in your car. Someone has gotten into the wrong lane, to the right of *your* lane, and needs to move over into the lane you are in. You *see* their need to cut in, ahead of you. **Decision time.** In your mind's eye you see two spiritual roads lying before you: the one leading to less kindness in the world (you speed up, to shut this driver out, and don't let them move over), the other leading to more kindness in the world (you let the driver cut in). **Since you know this is part of your Mission, part of the reason why you came to Earth, your calling is clear. You know which road to take, which decision to make.**

You are hard at work at your desk, when suddenly an interruption comes. The phone rings, or someone is at the door. They need something from you, a question of some of your time and attention. **Decision time.**

In your mind's eye you see two spiritual roads lying before you: the one leading to less love in the world (you tell them you're just too busy to be bothered), the other leading to more love in the world (you put aside your work, decide that God may have sent this person to you, and say, "Yes, what can I do to help you?"). **Since you know this is part of your Mission, part of the reason why you came to Earth, your calling is clear. You know which road to take, which decision to make.**

Your mate does something that hurts your feelings. **Decision time.** In your mind's eye you see two spiritual roads lying before you: the one leading to less forgiveness in the world (you institute an icy silence between the two of you, and think of how you can punish them or otherwise get

even), the other leading to more forgiveness in the world (you go over and take them in your arms, speak the truth about your hurt feelings, and assure them of your love). **Since you know this is part of your Mission, part of the reason why you came to Earth, your calling is clear. You know which road to take, which decision to make.**

You have not behaved at your most noble, recently. And now you are face-to-face with someone who asks you a question about what happened. **Decision time.** In your mind's eye you see two spiritual roads lying before you: the one leading to less honesty in the world (you lie about what happened, or what you were feeling, because you fear losing their respect or their love), the other leading to more honesty in the world (you tell the truth, together with how you feel about it, in retrospect). **Since you know this is part of your Mission, part of the reason why you came to Earth, your calling is clear. You know which road to take, which decision to make.**

Comment 4: The Spectacle Which Makes the Angels Laugh

It is necessary to explain this part of our Mission in some detail, because so many times you will see people wringing their hands, and saying, *"I want to know what my Mission in life is,"* all the while they are cutting people off on the highway, refusing to give time to people, punishing their mate for having hurt their feelings, and lying about what they did. And it will seem to you that the angels must laugh to see this spectacle. *For these people wringing their hands,* their Mission was right there, on the freeway, in the interruption, in the hurt, and at the confrontation.

Comment 5: The Valley vs. The Mountaintop

At some point in your life your Mission may involve some grand *mountaintop experience,* where you say to yourself, "This, this, is why I came into the world. I know it. I know it." *But until then,* your Mission is here in *the valley,* and the fog, and the little callings moment by moment, day by day. More to the point, it is likely you cannot ever get to your mountaintop Mission unless you have first exercised your stewardship faithfully in the valley.

It is an ancient principle, to which Jesus alluded often, that if you don't use the information the Universe has already given you, you cannot expect it will give you any more. If you aren't being faithful in small things, how can you expect to be given charge over larger things? (Luke 16:10,11,12; 19:11-24) If you aren't trying to bring more gratitude, kindness, forgiveness, honesty, and love into the world each day, you can hardly expect that you will be entrusted with the Mission to help bring peace into the world or anything else large and important. If we do not live out our day-by-day Mission in the valley, we cannot expect we are yet ready for a larger *mountaintop* Mission.

Comment 6: The Importance of Not Thinking of This Mission As 'Just A Training Camp'

The valley is not just a kind of "training camp." There is in your imagination even now an invisible *spiritual* mountaintop to which you may go, if you wish to see where all this is leading. And what will you see there, in the imagination of your heart, but the goal toward which all this is pointed: **that Earth might be more like heaven. That human's life might be more like God's.** That is the large achievement toward which all our day by day Missions *in the valley* are moving. This is a *large* order, but it is accomplished by faithful attention to the doing of our great Creator's **will** in little things as well as in large. It is much like the building of the pyramids in Egypt, which was accomplished by the dragging of a lot of individual pieces of stone by a lot of individual men.

The valley, the fog, the going step-by-step, is no mere training camp. The goal is real, however large. **"Thy Kingdom come, Thy will be done, on Earth, as it is in heaven."**

Some Random Comments About Your Third Mission in Life

Your third Mission here on Earth is one which is uniquely yours, and that is:

a) **to exercise that Talent which you particularly came to Earth to use -- your greatest gift which you most delight to use**

b) **in those place(s) or setting(s) which God has caused to appeal to you the most,**

c) **and for those purposes which God most needs to have done in the world.**

Comment 1: Our Mission Is Already Written, "in Our Members"

It is customary in trying to identify this part of our Mission, to advise that we should ask God, in prayer, to speak to us -- and **tell us** plainly what our Mission is. We look for a voice in the air, a thought in our head, a dream in the night, a sign in the events of the day, to reveal this thing which is otherwise *(it is said)* completely hidden. Sometimes, from just such answered prayer, people do indeed discover what their Mission is, beyond all doubt and uncertainty.

But having to wait for the voice of God to reveal what our Mission is, is not the truest picture of our situation. St. Paul, in Romans, speaks of a law "written in our members," -- and this phrase has a telling application to the question of **how** God reveals to each of us our unique Mission in life. Read again the definition of our third Mission (above) and you will see: the clear implication of the definition is that God has **already** revealed His will to us concerning our vocation and Mission, by causing it to be **"written in our members."** We are to begin deciphering our unique Mission by studying our talents and skills, and more particularly which ones (or One) we most rejoice to use.

God actually has written His will *twice* in our members: *first in the talents* which He lodged there, and secondly *in His guidance of our heart*, as to which talent gives us the greatest pleasure from its exercise (**it is usually the one which, when we use it, causes us to lose all sense of time**).

Even as the anthropologist can examine ancient inscriptions, and divine from them the daily life of a long lost people, so we by examining **our talents** and **our heart** can *more often than we dream* divine the Will of the Living God. For true it is, our Mission is not something He **will** reveal; it is something He **has already** revealed. It is not to be found written in the sky; it is to be found written in our members.

Comment 2: Career Counseling:
We Need You

Arguably, our first two Missions in life could be learned from religion
alone -- without any reference whatsoever to career counseling, the subject of this book. Why then should career counseling claim that this question about our Mission in life is its proper concern, *in any way?*

It is when we come to this third Mission, which hinges so crucially on
the question of our Talents, skills, and gifts, that we see the answer. If
you've read the body of this book, before turning to this Epilogue, you
know without my even saying it, how much the identification of Talents,
gifts, or skills is the province of career counseling. Its expertise, indeed its
raison d'etre, lies precisely in the identification, classification, and (forgive
me) "prioritization" of Talents, skills, and gifts. To put the matter quite
simply, career counseling knows how to do this better than any other discipline -- **including** traditional religion. This is not a defect of religion,
but the fulfillment of something Jesus promised: "When the Spirit of
truth comes, He will guide you into all truth." (John 16:12) Career counseling is part (we may hope) of that promised late-coming truth. It can
therefore be of inestimable help to the pilgrim who is trying to figure out
what their greatest, and most enjoyable, talent is, as a step toward identifying their unique Mission in life.

If career counseling needs religion as its helpmate in the first two stages
of identifying our Mission in life, religion repays the compliment by clearly needing career counseling as **its** helpmate here in the third stage.

And this place where you are in your life right now -- facing the job-
hunt and all its anxiety -- is the perfect time to seek the union within your
own mind and heart of both career counseling (as in the pages of this
book) and your faith in God.

Comment 3: How Our Mission Got Chosen:
A Scenario for the Romantic

It is a mystery which we cannot fathom, in this life at least, as to why
one of us has this talent, and the other one has that; why God chose to
give one gift -- and Mission -- to one person, and a different gift -- and
Mission -- to another. Since we do not know, and in some degree cannot
know, we are certainly left free to speculate, and imagine.

We may imagine that before we came to Earth, our souls, *our Breath,
our Light*, stood before the great Creator and volunteered for this Mission.
And God and we, together, chose what that Mission would be and what
particular gifts would be needed, which He then agreed to give us, after
our birth. Thus, our Mission was not a command given peremptorily by
an unloving Creator to a reluctant slave without a vote, but was a task
jointly designed by us both, in which as fast as the great Creator said, **"I
wish"** our hearts responded, **"Oh, yes."** As mentioned in an earlier Comment, it may be helpful to think of the condition of our becoming human
as that we became amnesiac about any consciousness our soul had before
birth -- and therefore amnesiac about the nature or manner in which our
Mission was designed.

Our searching for our Mission now is therefore a searching to recover the memory of something we ourselves had a part in designing.

I am admittedly a hopeless romantic, so of course I like this picture. If you also are a hopeless romantic, you may like it too. There's also the chance that it just may be true. We will not know until we see Him face-to-face.

Comment 4: Mission As Intersection

There are all different kinds of voices calling you to all different kinds of work, and the problem is to find out which is the voice of God rather than that of society, say, or the superego, or self-interest. By and large a good rule for finding out is this: the kind of work God usually calls you to is the kind of work (a) that you need most to do and (b) the world most needs to have done. If you really get a kick out of your work, you've presumably met requirement (a), but if your work is writing TV deodorant commercials, the chances are you've missed requirement (b). On the other hand, if your work is being a doctor in a leper colony, you have probably met (b), but if most of the time you're bored and depressed by it, the chances are you haven't only bypassed (a) but probably aren't helping your patients much either. Neither the hair shirt nor the soft birth will do. **The place God calls you to is the place where your deep gladness and the world's deep hunger meet.**

Frederick Buechner
Wishful Thinking -- A Theological ABC

Excerpted from *Wishful Thinking -- A Theological ABC* by Frederick Buechner. Copyright © 1973 by Frederick Buechner. Reprinted with permission of HarperCollins, Inc.

Comment 5: Examples of Mission As Intersection

Your unique and individual mission will most likely turn out to be a mission of Love, acted out in one or all of three arenas: either in the Kingdom of the Mind, whose goal is to bring more Truth into the world; or in the Kingdom of the Heart, whose goal is to bring more beauty into the world; or in the Kingdom of the Will, whose goal is to bring more Perfection into the world, through Service.

Here are some examples:

"My mission is, out of the rich reservoir of love which God seems to have given me, to nurture and show love to others -- most particularly to those who are suffering from incurable diseases."

"My mission is to draw maps for people to show them how to get to God."

"My mission is to create the purest foods I can, to help people's bodies not get in the way of their spiritual growth."

"My mission is to make the finest harps I can so that people can hear the voice of God in the wind."

"My mission is to make people laugh, so that the travail of this earthly life doesn't seem quite so hard to them."

"My mission is to help people know the truth, in love, about what is happening out in the world, so that there will be more honesty in the world."

"My mission is to weep with those who weep, so that in my arms they may feel themselves in the arms of that Eternal Love which sent me and which created them."

"My mission is to create beautiful gardens, so that in the lilies of the field people may behold the Beauty of God and be reminded of the Beauty of Holiness."

Comment 6: Life As Long As Your Mission Requires

Knowing that you came to Earth for a reason, and knowing what that Mission is, throws an entirely different light upon your life from now on. You are, generally speaking, delivered from any further fear about how long you have to live. You may settle it in your heart that you are here until God chooses to think that you have accomplished your Mission, or until God has a greater Mission for you in another Realm. You need to be a good steward of what He has given you, while you are here; but you do not need to be an anxious steward or stewardess.

You need to attend to your health, *but you do not need to constantly worry about it.* You need to meditate on your death, *but you do not need to be constantly preoccupied with it.* To paraphrase the glorious words of G. K. Chesterton: **"We now have a strong desire for living combined with a strange carelessness about dying. We desire life like water and yet are ready to drink death like wine."** We know that we are here to do what we came to do, and we need not worry about anything else.

Final Comment: A Job-Hunt Done Well

If you approach your job-hunt as an opportunity to work on this issue as well as the issue of how you will keep body and soul together, then hopefully your job-hunt will end with your being able to say: "Life has deep meaning to me, now. I have discovered more than my ideal job; I have found my Mission, and the reason why I am here on Earth."

For Further Reading

Most, though not all, of the following resources are written from a Judaic-Christian viewpoint, but they should be suggestive and helpful for people of any faith, as you mentally translate these texts into your own thought-forms and concepts of your faith:

Mattson, Ralph, and Miller, Arthur, *Finding a Job You Can Love.* Thomas Nelson Publishers, Nelson Place at Elm Hill Pike, Nashville, TN 37214. 1982. The most useful, I think, of all the books in this section.

Lewis, Roy, *Choosing Your Career, Finding Your Vocation: A Step by Step Guide for Adults and Counselors.* Integration Books, Paulist Press, 997 Macarthur Blvd., Mahwah, NJ 07430. 1990. Particularly helpful for mid-life issues.

Blanchard, Tim, *A Practical Guide to Finding and Using Your Spiritual Gifts.* Tyndale House Publishers, Inc., Wheaton, Illinois.

Moran, Pamela J., *The Christian Job Hunter.* Servant Publications, 840 Airport Blvd., Box 8617, Ann Arbor, MI 48107. 1984.

Edwards, Lloyd, *Discerning Your Spiritual Gifts.* Cowley Publications, 980 Memorial Drive, Cambridge, MA 02138. 1988.

Moore, Christopher Chamberlin, *What I Really Want To Do . . . : How to Discover The Right Job.* CBP Press, Box 179, St. Louis, MO 63166. 1989.

Roskind, Robert, *In The Spirit of Business: Applying the Principles of A Course in Miracles to Business.* Celestial Arts, P.O. Box 7123, Berkeley, CA 94707. 1992.

A Center for the Practice of Zen Buddhist Meditation, *That Which You Are Seeking Is Causing You to Seek.* Available from the Center, P.O. Box 91, Mountain View, CA 94042. 1990. A *great* title, and a very interesting book, written -- of course -- from the Buddhist point of view, with one of the contributors being a woman who was dying (and has since died) from cancer.

Staub, Dick; Trautman, Jeff; and Cutshall, Mark, eds., *Intercristo's CAREER KIT: A Christian's Guide to Career Building.* Intercristo, 19303 Fremont Ave. N., Seattle WA 98133. 1985. Booklets (6) and cassette tapes (3) enclosed in binder.

Wehrheim, Carol and Cole-Turner, Ronald S., *Vocation and Calling. Introduction/Hearing God's Call/Sharing Gifts: An Intergenerational Study Guide.* United Church Press, 475 Riverside Dr., 10th fl., New York, NY 10115. 1985.

Rinker, Richard N., and Eisentrout, Virginia, *Called to Be Gifted and Giving: An Adult Resource for Vocation and Calling.* United Church Press, 475 Riverside Dr., 10th fl., New York, NY 10115. 1985.

For Counseling

All counselors in these centers are sincere; many are also very skilled. If you run into a clerical counselor who is sincere but inept, you will probably discover that the ineptness consists in an inadequate understanding of the distinction between career **assessment** -- roughly comparable to taking a snapshot of people as they are in one frozen moment of time -- vs. career **development** -- which is roughly comparable to teaching people how to take their own motion pictures of themselves, from here on out.

Having issued this caution, however, I will go on to add that at some of these centers, listed below, are some simply *excellent* counselors who fully understand this distinction, and are well trained in that empowering of the client, which is what career *development* is all about.

We begin with counseling centers founded primarily to help **clergy** (though in most cases not restricted just to them). No profession has developed, or had developed for it, so many resources to aid in career assessment as has this profession.

THE OFFICIAL INTERDENOMINATIONAL
CAREER DEVELOPMENT CENTERS

The Career and Personal
Counseling Service
St. Andrew's Presbyterian College
Laurinburg, NC 28352
919-276-3162
Also at: 4108 Park Rd., Suite 200
Charlotte, NC 28209
704-523-7751
Elbert R. Patton, Director

The Career and Personal
Counseling Center
Eckerd College
St. Petersburg, FL 33733
813-864-8356, Ext. 356
John R. Sims, Director

The Center for Ministry
8393 Capwell Dr., Suite 220
Oakland, CA 94621-2123
510-635-4246
Robert L. Charpentier, Director

Lancaster Career
Development Center
561 College Ave.
Lancaster, PA 17603
717-397-7451
L. Guy Mehl, Director

North Central Career
Development Center
3000 Fifth St. NW
New Brighton, MN 55112
612-636-5120
John Davis, Director

Northeast Career Center
407 Nassau Street
Princeton, NJ 08540
609-924-9408
Roy Lewis, Director

Career Development Center
of the Southeast
531 Kirk Rd.
Decatur, GA 30030
404-371-0336
Robert M. Urie, Director

Midwest Career
Development Service
1840 Westchester Blvd.
Westchester, IL 60154
708-343-6268
Also at: 2501 North Star Rd.
Columbus, OH 43221
614-486-0469
Also at: 754 N. 31st St.
Kansas City, KS 66110
Ronald Brushwyler, Director

Southwest Career
Development Center
Box 5923
Arlington, TX 76011
817-640-5181
William M. Gould, Jr.,
Director-Counselor

Center for Career
Development and Ministry
70 Chase St.
Newton Center, MA 02159
617-969-7750
Stephen Ott, Director.

Clergy wishing to stay within the parish ministry, but wanting help with the search, will want to know about:

Mead, Loren B., and Miller, Arthur F., and Ayers, Russell C., and Bolles, Richard N., *Your Next Pastorate: Starting the Search.* Order #AL122 from The Alban Institute, Inc., 4125 Nebraska Ave., N.W., Washington, DC 20016.

And now, on to centers which are open to anyone, and do career counseling from a spiritual point of view:

ALSO DOING CAREER COUNSELING FROM A RELIGIOUS POINT OF VIEW

(These are listed by general geographical location, from West Coast to East Coast, North to South)

People Management Group International, P.O. Box 33608, **Seattle, WA** 98133. 206-443-1107. Arthur F. Miller, Jr., Chairman. Dick Staub, President.

Bernard Haldane, 2821 2nd Ave., Suite 1002, **Seattle, WA** 98121. 206-448-0881. A pioneer in the clergy career management and assessment field, Bernard teaches *(totally independently of the agency which bears his name)* seminars and training of volunteers (particularly in churches) to do job-search counseling.

Lifework Design, 448 S. Marengo Ave., **Pasadena, CA** 91101. 818-577-2705. Kevin Brennfleck, M.A., and Kay Marie Brennfleck, M.A., Directors.

Olson Counseling Services, 8720 Frederick, Suite 105, **Omaha, NE** 68124. 402-390-2342. Gail A. Olson, P.A.C.

Ministry of Counseling and Enrichment, 1333 N. 2nd St., **Abilene, TX** 79601. 915-675-8131. Mary Stedham, Director.

New Life Institute, Box 1666, **Austin, TX** 78767. 512-469-9447. Bob Breihan, Director.

Institute of Worklife Ministry, 2650 Fountainview Drive, Suite 444, **Houston, TX** 77057. 713-266-2456. Diana C. Dale, Director.

Life Stewardship Associates, 6918 Glen Creek Dr., SE, **Dutton, MI** 49316. 616-698-3125. Ken Soper, M.Div., M.A., Director.

CareerConcepts, 1451 Elm Hill Pike, Suite 314, **Nashville, TN** 37210. 615-367-5000. Robert H. McKown.

Mid-South Career Development Center, 2315 Fisher Place, **Knoxville, TN** 37920. 615-573-1340. W. Scott Root, Director.

Career and Personal Counseling Center, 1904 Mt. Vernon St., **Waynesboro, VA** 22980. 703-943-9997. Lillian Pennell, Director.

Center for Growth & Change, Inc., 6991 Peachtree Ind. Blvd., Suite 310, **Norcross, GA** 30092. 404-441-9580. James P. Hicks, Ph.D., L.P.C., Director.

Career Pathways, 601 Broad St., **Gainesville, GA** 30501. 800-722-1976. Lee Ellis, Director. Offers career-guidance from a Christian point of view, through the mails -- based on questionnaires and various instruments or inventories which they send you.

Judith Gerberg Associates, 250 West 57th St., **New York, NY** 10107. 212-315-2322. Judith Gerberg.

Index

Every page of the book, including footnotes and appendices, is indexed except that book titles are included only if they appear in the main text.

Counseling occupations, 274
Country, moving to the, 141–42, 143, 147–49
Courtesy, 347
Creative approach
to career change, 164–65, 179–80
to job-hunting, 57, 58
"Creative minority, the," 178
Criminal justice job ads, 39
Criminals, resources for ex-offenders, 439–40
Crystal, John, 178, 259, 262, 448
Cultivating new contacts, 316–17
Curriculum vitae. *See* resumes

D

D.O.T. (Dictionary of Occupational Titles), 162, 163, 167, 170–71, 184, 280, 438
Data
See also Fields; Knowledge
diagram of skills, 194–95
form of information preferred, 235–36
hierarchy of skills, 184
informational interviewing, 269–99
Daycare, 431
Deception, 293
Degrees
career change and, 163–64
of career counselors, 387
Delphi, 46
Depression, 78–107
activity during unemployment, 96–104
avoiding or banishing, 83–104
emotional aspects, 86–88
as gift-bearing messenger, 105–07
lack of money as cause, 79
meaning of, 81–82
medical approach to, 81
mental aspects, 88–92
multiple goals during unemployment, 96–104
physical aspects, 83–85
sleep loss and, 83–84
spiritual aspects, 92–96
unemployment as cause, 80
Describing skills, 208–13, 218
Destiny. *See* Mission in life
Diagrams and charts
See also Lists
A – B = C, 130
anatomy of ideal job, 172
budget (personal), 368–69

career change, creative process of, 165
career change, types of, 160, 161
career counselor search, 385
career or occupational families (World of Work), 272–79
career targets, 286–87
favorite subjects, 226
fears behind employers' questions, 354–56
flower diagram of interests, 234, 239, 242, 245, 247, 250, 251
flower diagram of skills, 210–12
Memory Net, 198–99
paths through job-land, 174–75
PIE Method, 260–61
prioritizing grids, 205–07
RIASEC theory, 168
skill priorities, 183
skills hierarchy, 184
skills keys, 190–95
skills learned during a career, 182
stories revealing skills, 188
subjects of interest, 226
Three Boxes of Life, 446
when to negotiate salary, 366
Dictionaries. *See* Books; Directories; Resources
Dictionary of Holland Occupational Codes, 170–71
Dictionary of Occupational Titles, 162, 163, 167, 170–71, 184, 280, 438
Diet and depression, 85
Dieting and depression, 97–98
Dietitians, 274
Directly applying in person, 58, 59–60, 306–07, 312–13
Directories
See also Books; Resources
executive search firms, 35
occupational titles, 162, 163, 167, 170–71, 280
online job-postings, 47, 49
online services, 48
overseas employment, 145, 146
placement offices, 62
places to live, 140, 141
target organizations, 290
want ads not in newspapers, 38–39
Disabilities, 69, 335–37, 440–41
Disabled humor, 100
Downsizing, 16, 17, 20
Dream vocation, 254–55
Dual careers, 112

Relationship with God, 452
Relatives
　See also Contacts; Friends
　job-leads from, 58, 60–61
　as support group candidates, 71–72
Religion. *See* Mission in life; Spirituality
Relocating, 138–51
　choosing a place, 139–41
　to the country, 141–42, 143
　finding jobs from afar, 147–49
　if you can't go in person, 149
　for job opportunities, 139–40
　joy of, 150–51
　for the location itself, 140–41
　overseas, 143–47
　reasons for, 138
Repairers, 277–78
Rescue, 22–23
Researching
　See also Books; Directories; Re-
　　sources
　career counselors, 382–91
　salaries, 370–75
　target careers, 292–95
Resource Person, presenting yourself
　as, 344–46
Resources, 424–43
　See also Books; Directories
　for career counselors, 404–10
　for clergy and religious profession-
　　als, 438–39
　for college students, 427–28
　for ex-military people, 437–38
　for ex-offenders, 439–40
　for executives, the business world
　　and corporate jobs, 435–36
　for government jobs, 436–37
　for immigrants to the U.S., 429
　for minorities, 434–35
　for Mission in life, 462
　for people with disabilities or
　　handicaps, 440–41
　for "recovering people," 437
　for retirement, 442–43
　for summer jobs for elementary and
　　high-school students, 425–27
　for women, 430–34
Restructuring, 16, 17
Resumes
　approaching large organizations,
　　308–12
　books on, 322–23
　computer programs for, 408
　defined, 28
　effectiveness of, 27, 28–29

example, 310, 311
form for, 309–11
online, 46
with thank-you notes, 350
want ad responses, 36
Retirement resources, 442–43
Retraining for career change, 162–64,
　285
RIASEC theory (Holland Code), 168–71
Rules
　for dealing with abandonment, 95
　for dealing with anger, 87–88
　for dealing with meaninglessness, 91
　for dealing with sleep problems, 84
　on hiring and firing, 18–19
　for new ways of working, 132
Rural relocation, 141–42, 143, 147–49

S

Salary, 359–77
　See also Fees; Money
　determining negotiability, 370
　determining the range, 363, 374–75
　determining your needs, 367–69
　examples of research, 372–73
　favorite rewards, 244–45
　five keys to negotiation, 364–75
　getting it in writing, 376–77
　getting the highest possible, 376–77
　inequities for women, 430–31
　job-hunt time and, 435
　level and, 244
　as major criterion of employers,
　　364–65
　mentioning a figure, 366–67
　as part of jobs, 158
　poverty and reduced earnings, 360
　range, 363, 374–75
　reason for negotiation, 14
　researching, 370–75
　statistics, 363
　summary, 377
　timing of negotiation, 343, 344,
　　364–66
　want ad requests, 42
Sales occupations, 276
Samplers. *See* Lists
School
　campus recruiters, 307–08
　career counselor training, 409–10
　degrees, 163–64, 387
　going back to, 102, 162–64, 166, 285
　knowledge acquired outside of, 224
　placement offices, 58, 62–63

Author Index

Other Resources

Additional materials by Richard N. Bolles to help you with your job-hunt:

HOW TO CREATE A PICTURE OF YOUR IDEAL JOB OR NEXT CAREER

This workbook (8½ by 11 inches) is designed to lead the reader through a series of detailed exercises, expanding upon Chapters 9 and 10 in *Parachute*. $5.95

THE ANATOMY OF A JOB

This 24 by 36 inch poster serves as a worksheet to supplement the workbook above *(How to Create A Picture . . .)*. The 'Skills Keys' are on one side, and the 'Flower' is on the other side. $4.95

HOW TO FIND YOUR MISSION IN LIFE

This is a gift book version of the current Epilogue in *Parachute*. Judging by the mail Dick Bolles receives, this is a favorite of readers who want their work to fulfill a purpose and bring more than simply money to their lives. $5.95

THE MISSION POSTER

This colorful 24 by 36 inch poster summarizes the main ideas in the booklet above *(How to Find Your Mission in Life)*. $4.95

JOB-HUNTING TIPS FOR THE SO-CALLED "HANDICAPPED" OR PEOPLE WHO HAVE DISABILITIES

Originally published as an appendix in *Parachute*, this popular material is now only available as a separate booklet. In this work, Dick Bolles uses his unique perspective on job-hunting and career-change to address the experiences of the disabled in doing these tasks. $4.95

For Order Form see next page.

To: Ten Speed Press
P.O. Box 7123
Berkeley, CA 94707

I would like to order:

_____ copies of **HOW TO CREATE A PICTURE OF YOUR IDEAL JOB OR NEXT CAREER** @ $5.95 each.   _____

_____ copies of the poster **THE ANATOMY OF A JOB** @ $4.95 each.   _____

_____ copies of **HOW TO FIND YOUR MISSION IN LIFE** @ $5.95 each.   _____

_____ copies of **THE MISSION POSTER** @ $4.95 each.   _____

_____ copies of **JOB-HUNTING TIPS FOR THE SO-CALLED "HANDICAPPED" OR PEOPLE WHO HAVE DISABILITIES** @ $4.95 each.   _____

Subtotal $ _____

Postage is $2.50 for the first item ordered and 50¢ for each additional item.

Postage $ _____

Total $ _____

Check or money order only, please, made out to Ten Speed Press.

Send to: (please print)

Name_____

Organization _____

Mailing Address_____

City, State, Zip_____

Update for 1996

TO: PARACHUTE
      P.O. Box 379
      Walnut Creek, CA 94597

I think that the information in the '95 edition needs to be
changed, in your next revision, regarding (or, the following
resource should be added):

_____

_____

_____

_____

_____

I cannot find the following resource, listed on page _____ :

_____

_____

_____

_____

_____

Name _____

Address _____

Please make a copy.

Submit this so as to reach us by February 1, 1995. Thank you.